MW00444524

Prentice Hall Advanced Reference Series

Computer Science

TEXT
COMPRESSION

Timothy C. Bell
University of Canterbury

John G. Cleary
University of Calgary

Ian H. Witten
University of Calgary

PRENTICE HALL, Englewood Cliffs, New Jersey 07632

Library of Congress Cataloging-in-Publication Data

BELL, TIMOTHY C., (Date)
  Text compression / Timothy C. Bell, John G. Cleary, Ian H. Witten.
    p.   cm. — (Prentice Hall advanced reference series)
  Includes bibliographical references (p. 303)
  ISBN   0–13–911991–4
  1. Text processing (Computer science)   I. Cleary, John G.
  II. Witten, I. H. (Ian H.)   III. Title.   IV. Series.
  QA76.9. T48B45   1990
  005—dc20   89–23206
                    CIP

Editorial/production supervision
  and interior design: *Carol L. Atkins*
Cover design: *Karen A. Stephens*
Manufacturing buyer: *Ray Sintel*

Prentice Hall Advanced Reference Series

 © 1990 by Prentice-Hall, Inc.
A Division of Simon & Schuster
Englewood Cliffs, New Jersey 07632

The publisher offers discounts on this book when ordered
in bulk quantities. For more information, write:
    Special Sales/College Marketing
    Prentice-Hall, Inc.
    College Technical and Reference Division
    Englewood Cliffs, NJ 07632

Printed in the United States of America
10 9 8 7 6 5 4 3 2

ISBN   0-13-911991-4

Prentice-Hall International (UK) Limited, *London*
Prentice-Hall of Australia Pty. Limited, *Sydney*
Prentice-Hall Canada Inc., *Toronto*
Prentice-Hall Hispanoamericana, S.A., *Mexico*
Prentice-Hall of India Private Limited, *New Delhi*
Prentice-Hall of Japan, Inc., *Tokyo*
Simon & Schuster Asia Pte. Ltd., *Singapore*
Editora Prentice-Hall do Brasil, Ltda., *Rio de Janeiro*

CONTENTS

PREFACE

Compression means making things smaller by applying pressure. Text compression is not about physically squashing text, but about finding ways to represent it in fewer bits or bytes. It is necessary that the coded form can be decompressed to reconstitute the original text (otherwise, compression is trivial!), and it is usually important that the original is recreated exactly, not approximately. This differentiates text compression from many other kinds of data reduction, such as voice or picture coding, where some degradation of quality may be tolerable if a more compact representation is thereby achieved.

Even though technology has made enormous strides in computer storage capacity, interest in text compression has never been greater—cynics might want to relate this to Parkinson's law. People often wonder if compression will continue its popularity as personal computers and workstations acquire disk storage of many megabytes, perhaps gigabytes. Evidence so far indicates that users are always interested in achieving a two- or threefold increase in capacity at no cost. To draw a rather extreme analogy, no matter how much you earned, you would probably hesitate to turn up your nose at the chance of tripling your salary!

Compression also enables full use to be made of limited transmission bandwidth. Despite impressive advances in wideband communication technology (satellites, microwaves, fiber optics), many of us communicate daily with computers over telephone channels. Long-haul networks also often transmit over the lowly telephone network. Text compression can triple effective bandwidth, reducing communication costs and end-user frustration. But what of the future? Will telephone companies lay voice/data lines right to the subscriber's doorstep and eliminate the need for compression in user–computer communication? Will cable provide domestic consumers with wideband interactive communication? Maybe, but the future seems a long time coming. And like the salary increase, threefold speed-ups might still be hard to resist.

This book introduces the subject of text compression, laying particular stress on *adaptive* methods—those that adjust dynamically to the characteristics of a message as it is transmitted. Of course, many of the techniques described are also able to compress nontextual data, even speech and pictures. However, we are concerned exclusively with *exact* compression methods, and these are often inappropriate for signals that are fundamentally analog in nature. Restricting attention specifically to text not only addresses a very important and widespread compression problem, but also frees us from having to consider how to incorporate constraints appropriate to different domains and allows us to concentrate on specific techniques for constructing models *adaptively*.

Text compression provides an unparalleled practical example of information theory in action. Indeed, the compressibility of English was thoroughly investigated by Shannon about the time of the birth of information theory. Since then, it has become a fascinating playground for anyone interested in methods of adaptation and prediction. Two of us (JGC and IHW) became involved with compression in the early 1980s precisely because we were seeking ways to assess methods of adaptation, or "learning," objectively. The trouble with any adaptive system is that on any particular task it may learn, its performance will inevitably be inferior to that of a special-purpose machine designed specifically for that task. Of course, the advantage of adaptation is flexibility, but that is very hard to quantify. Text compression offers an ideal test bed for adaptive methods, for it is easy to set up realistic scenarios in which adaptive schemes outperform fixed ones (almost any real-life text compression situation will do). Then you can stop worrying about the benefits of adaptive vis-à-vis fixed models, and get on with the work of designing suitable algorithms for adaptation.

Inevitably this book is rather theoretical in places—after all, compression is information theory at work—and this may put off the practically minded reader. We hope it doesn't, for the principal messages can be plainly understood without mathematical crutches. We have tried to confine the heavier and more detailed analyses to appendices that follow some of the chapters. But there is some substantial theoretical work toward the end of Chapter 2, in much of Chapter 3, at the end of Chapter 7, and at the beginning of Chapter 9. These parts can be safely skipped by the reader who wants to get on with the main arguments, although they make important contributions to those who seek deeper understanding. To make life easier for those who choose to skim, there is a glossary, including a summary of notation, at the end of the book to serve as a reference for the meaning of technical terms. To make life easier for those who are eager to apply compression to a particular problem at hand, a note for the practitioner at the end of Chapter 1 indicates where the most significant practical methods are described.

STRUCTURE OF THE BOOK

The book opens with an example of text compression from the eighteenth century (friends have warned that this is an unsuitable beginning for a book describing the frontiers of technology; we disagree). Chapter 1 explains the motivation for text compression and describes a variety of ad hoc methods that have been used. It is necessary to get these out of the way because while almost everyone has some ideas for a pet scheme for compressing text, techniques tailored to take advantage of specific regularities are—or should be—a thing of the past. Except where economy of time and memory consumption is more important than compression, these ad hoc methods have been superseded by more principled methods of adaptive compression.

In the second chapter we introduce fundamental concepts from information theory and discrete modeling theory. The fact that information content or "entropy" has more to do with what might have been said rather than what has been said (or stored, or transmitted) raises the question of how to specify what might have been. The answer is via probabilistic models: context models, state models, grammar models. Each model's entropy can be calculated, and so can the probability of a particular message with respect to that model. Two appendices show that the entropy is a lower bound for the average compression that can be achieved, and give examples of how exact message probabilities can be calculated from models in some simple cases.

In Chapter 3 we discuss the whole idea of adaptation. Adaptive models change as a message is processed so that they are better suited to that message. Statistics collected on the fly are used to encode future characters. These statistics are inevitably based on a rather small sample, but are closely tailored to the particular message being coded. This creates a tension between approximate but adaptive models and accurate but fixed ones. It is clear that an adaptive model cannot always be better than a static one, for you might just be very lucky with the latter and transmit only messages that match it closely. However, it transpires that in a wide range of circumstances, adaptive models can only be *slightly* worse than any static one. Conversely, a static model may be *arbitrarily* worse than an adaptive one. To prove these ideas requires some theory, but their import can be understood without working through in detail. Two appendices contain some auxiliary mathematics needed for the main results.

In Chapter 4 we address the characteristics of natural language. We present analyses of a large sample of English text, bringing out those features that can be exploited for compression; and include both letter- and word-frequency statistics. Theoretical models of language are also examined. For example, a common model of word frequency is the Zipf distribution, which is often held to account for the fact that common words are, by and large, shorter than rare ones through a principle of "least effort." However, Chapter 4 establishes that Zipf's law is very easily achieved by simple random processes, and does not need to be explained by recourse to such a principle. We also present the methodology and results of experiments that have been performed to determine the true entropy of natural languages.

We may as well admit that we had a great deal of difficulty deciding where to site Chapter 4. Were it not for the fact that it makes considerable use of entropy, it would fit nicely immediately after Chapter 1. That concept is introduced in Chapter 2, but it seemed a shame to disturb the flow from the consideration of models there to the study of adaptation in Chapter 3. So natural language ended up being deferred until Chapter 4, but you are invited to read this material earlier if you so desire.

Practical algorithms for coding using the probabilities supplied by a model are covered in Chapter 5. A well-known method is Huffman's algorithm, but the more recent arithmetic coding technique is superior in almost all respects and is the main topic of this chapter. It represents information at least as compactly—sometimes considerably more so. Its performance is optimal without the need for blocking of input data. It encourages a clear separation between the model for representing data and the encoding of information with respect to that model. It accommodates adaptive models easily. It is computationally efficient. Yet many authors and practitioners seem unaware of the technique; indeed, there is a widespread misapprehension that Huffman coding cannot be improved upon. We also present efficient implementations of arithmetic coding in the special cases of large alphabets and binary alphabets. An appendix gives a working program that implements arithmetic encoding and decoding, while another proves a small technical result required in the chapter.

The foundations have now been laid to describe models that can be used in practice, and this is done in the following chapters. In Chapter 6 we describe how to combine a number of different context-based models into a single one with good compression performance. The basic idea is that small models converge quickly and therefore perform well early on, while larger ones give better results when more text has been seen. A general framework for blending such models is introduced, and then several different practical methods are described. The resulting systems give better text compression than any others presently known, albeit at the expense of speed and memory usage. The chapter concludes with a discussion of implementation techniques and their time, space, and compression trade-offs.

It is worthwhile evaluating state modeling techniques as well as context-based ones, for state models seem to promise economies in both storage space and time required to trace through the model. In Chapter 7 we look at state-based methods and conclude that they turn out to be less useful than one might expect. One specific technique that constructs a state model incrementally is described in detail. However, on closer analysis it is found to be equivalent to a context-based predictive modeler. It is, nevertheless, an eminently practical method for text compression.

A different approach from the statistical method of modeling and coding is dictionary coding. In Chapter 8 we describe a variety of dictionary methods, from ad hoc codes to the popular and more principled Ziv–Lempel approach. By and large, these techniques are simple, fast, and give good compression. The idea is to accumulate a dictionary of phrases and replace phrases in the text by indexes to the dictionary. The Ziv–Lempel approach is particularly attractive because it is adaptive; that is, the dictionary is constructed as coding proceeds so that it never needs to be transmitted explicitly.

At last, the wealth of techniques that have been described are compared in Chapter 9. A proof is developed that dictionary coders can be simulated by statistical coders, and we conclude that future research aimed at optimizing compression performance should concentrate on statistical methods—although dictionary schemes certainly prove less resource-hungry. As it happens, this conclusion is corroborated by the outcome of a large-scale compression competition held in Australia early in 1988, on which this chapter contains a brief report. We also give results of a large number of our own experiments in which a variety of actual texts were compressed. These show the relative merits of various algorithms in different practical circumstances.

We finish in Chapter 10 by branching out into the untidy world of broader applications of the text compression techniques that have been studied. These applications utilize the models developed for text compression in diverse ways. One speeds up text entry by predicting what will come next. Another tracks the behavior of someone using an electronic calculator, helping them to perform repetitive operations. A third assists with command input to an interactive computer system. We also show how arithmetic coding can be used to add redundancy to messages for the purpose of error control, and assess the potential of adaptive modeling as a method of encryption. Finally, we review the application of adaptive methods to (exact) picture compression.

Apart from those at the end of Chapters 2, 3, and 5, there are two appendices to the book itself which include some additional technical information. Appendix A describes a host of methods for coding integers as a sequence of bits. These codes are used by several text compression schemes, especially dictionary coding methods. Appendix B introduces a collection of texts that we have used to evaluate the performance of compression schemes. This corpus contains several different types of files which are likely subjects for compression.

ACKNOWLEDGMENTS

As in any enterprise of this size there are a lot of people to thank, and it is a great pleasure to have this opportunity to record our gratitude. First, our mentors—John Andreae, Brian Gaines, and John Penny—who stimulated our interest in these topics and patiently guided our development and understanding. Next, colleagues and students who have worked with us on aspects of adaptive prediction, modeling, and allied topics: John Darragh, Jeff Gottfred, Saul Greenberg, Bruce MacDonald, Merav Michaeli, Ian Olthof, and Una O'Reilly. Special thanks go to Radford Neal for furthering our understanding of arithmetic coding and writing the program in Appendix 5A; he coauthored the paper from which Chapter 5 was adapted and contributed a great deal to that work. We owe an immense debt to Alistair Moffat, who developed and implemented several of the methods we describe—the efficient algorithm for coding with large alphabets presented in Chapter 5, that for the trie-based statistical encoder of Chapter 6, and the MTF scheme used in Chapter 9—and coauthored the paper from which Section 7-4 was culled; he also kindly read through the entire book and made a host of useful suggestions. Ed Fiala and Dan Greene kindly gave us permission to publish their LZFG algorithm and ran numerous experiments on their implementation to see how well it did with our test files; they also read Chapters 8 and 9 carefully and came up with several improvements. Richard Brent gave us details of the LZH compression method; Peter Tischer provided the LZT implementation; and Joe Orost supplied the LZC program (UNIX *compress*). Harold Thimbleby and Brent Krawchuk made many valuable editorial suggestions. We enjoyed, and benefited from, helpful discussions with numerous others at various times: in particular, Gordon Cormack, Nigel Horspool, Glen Langdon, Bruce McKenzie, Krzysztof Pawlikowski, and Ross Williams. A draft of the book was field tested by Warwick Heath, David Jaggar, Stephen Neil, and Robert Sinton in a graduate course on text compression at the University of Canterbury, New Zealand.

The test file "book1" was provided by the Oxford Text Archive, Oxford University Computing Centre. Figure 1-1 is reproduced by kind permission from *The old telegraphs* by Geoffrey Wilson, published in 1976 by Philimore & Company Ltd, Shopwyke Hall, Chichester, West Sussex, England. Figure 8-4 contains an extract from *The hitch-hiker's guide to the galaxy* by Douglas Adams, published by Pan Books Ltd., London. Tamara Lee did a wonderful job of patiently and tirelessly redrawing the 100-odd remaining figures.

Generous support for this research has been provided by the Natural Sciences and Engineering Research Council of Canada. We have enjoyed using the excellent facilities of the Computer Science Department at Calgary. We are especially grateful to a VAX-11/780 and various Macintoshes for tirelessly printing and reprinting innumerable drafts, and for compressing thousands of texts (we used over a month of CPU time in producing results for this book).

Finally, and above all, our heartfelt thanks go to Dorothy, Judith, and Pam for putting up with everything; and to Anna, James, Laura, Michael—who was born in the middle of it all—Nikki and Scott for tirelessly, and delightfully, distracting us from our work.

Timothy C. Bell
John G. Cleary
Ian H. Witten

WHY COMPRESS TEXT?

Toward the end of the eighteenth century the British Admiralty needed a fast means of sending messages between London and the naval stations on the coast. A system was devised using a series of cabins, typically about 5 miles apart, on hilltops between London and the ports. Each cabin had six large shutters on its roof (Figure 1-1), which could be seen from adjacent cabins. A message was transmitted along the line by setting up a pattern on a set of shutters in London. This was relayed by operators at each cabin until it reached the port. These *shutter telegraphs* were capable of transmitting messages over many miles in just a few minutes.

Different arrangements of shutters represented the letters of the alphabet and the numerals. Each of the six shutters could be opened or closed, which allowed 64 combinations, more than enough to code the requisite characters. The redundant combinations were employed to represent common words and phrases such as "and," "the," "Portsmouth," "West," and even "Sentence of court-martial to be put into execution." This *codebook* approach enabled messages to be transmitted considerably faster than could be achieved with a character-by-character approach. This codebook shutter telegraph system is an early example of text compression; that is, the use of short codes for common messages and longer codes for uncommon messages, resulting in a reduction in the average length of a message.

There were two main drawbacks to the codebook scheme. One was that the operators at the terminating stations had to be able to use a codebook, and this skill

1

Figure 1-1   A shutter telegraph cabin.

commanded a higher wage. The second was that although few errors occurred, the effect of an error was considerably greater when a codebook was used than for a character-by-character transmission. Consider the effect of the erroneous receipt of the code for "Sentence of court-martial to be put into execution"!

The advantages and disadvantages of using a codebook in this situation illustrate some of the main issues surrounding the use of text compression: the trade-off of faster transmission (or less storage space) against greater effort for processing, and the problem of errors. A secondary advantage of the scheme was that a person observing a relay station would have considerable difficulty interpreting a coded message, so that some security was achieved for the information being transmitted.

In the 1820s, Louis Braille devised a system, still in common use today, which enables the blind to "read" by touch. In the Braille system (Figure 1-2), text is represented on a thick sheet of paper by raised dots. The dots are located in cells with six positions, each position being either flat or raised. Each cell usually represents a letter of the alphabet. Unfortunately, Braille books are very large because each cell uses the area of about 10 printed letters, and heavy paper is necessary to emboss the dots. It is not surprising that Braille uses compression to reduce the size of these books. As with the shutter telegraphs, there are 64 possible combinations of dots in a cell. Not all of these are needed to represent the alphabet and numerals, and the spare codes can be used to represent common words and groups of letters.

The Braille system has been revised several times since it was invented, and several grades have now been defined, each applying a different amount of compression and therefore a different trade-off between ease of reading and the size of books. Two grades are commonly used. Grade 1 Braille is uncompressed; each cell corresponds to

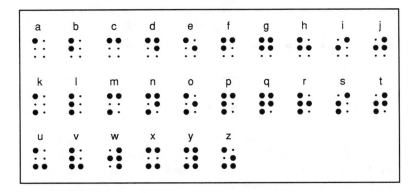

Figure 1-2   The letters of the alphabet in Braille.

one character. Grade 2 Braille uses 189 "contractions" and "abbreviated words." The examples in Figure 1-3 show that a variety of devices are used. Some of the spare cells represent words ("and," "for," "of," etc.) and pairs of letters ("ch", "gh", "sh", etc.). Others are used to "escape" to a new set of meanings for the following cell; for example, the "dot 5" symbol followed by "e," "f," or "m" represents the words "ever," "father," or "mother," respectively. Finally, some words are contracted to a few letters, such as "about" (ab), "above" (abv), and "according" (ac). Figure 1-4 illustrates the use of Grade 2 Braille, where 21 characters are coded in 9 cells. A 20% saving in space over Grade 1 Braille is more typical for English text. This saving is at the expense of more effort for the writer and reader, but since Grade 2 Braille is widely used, the trade-off is apparently considered worthwhile.

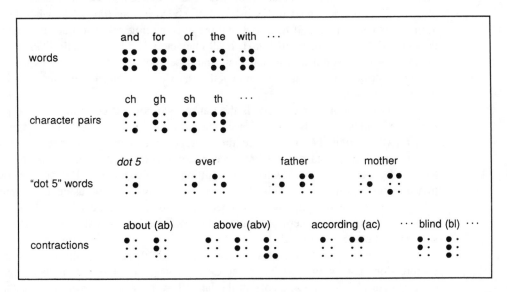

Figure 1-3   Grade 2 Braille.

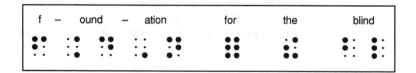

Figure 1-4   A grade 2 Braille coding.

Economizing on space is not the only reason for using the "compressed form" of Braille. For most people, the slowest part of reading Braille is recognizing the cells. If the text is compressed there will be fewer cells to recognize, so the rate of reading increases—provided that readers can interpret cells faster than they can recognize them. There are two main types of error that can occur when reading Braille: The reader may misread a cell, or if a page is damaged, some cells may be incorrect. The effect of errors on Grade 2 Braille can be a lot more severe than for Grade 1, since larger portions of the text are affected by each error.

It seems that text compression comes naturally to people designing a code for communication. When Samuel Morse was contemplating codes for an electromagnetic telegraph in 1832, he initially considered schemes where only the 10 numerals could be transmitted. He would then use a codebook for words, names, dates, and sentences. By 1835 he had abandoned this idea in favor of the celebrated Morse code, which uses dots and dashes to represent letters, numerals, and punctuation, as shown in Figure 1-5.

In Morse code a dash is three times as long as a dot, and each dot or dash is separated by a space the same length as a dot. The space between characters is allocated three of these time units, and the interword space has seven units. Morse code is designed so that common characters are coded in fewer units than rare ones. For example, the most common letter in English, "e", is coded in four time units, while the character "z" is coded in 14. It turns out that the average time taken to transmit a character is typically 8.5 units for English text. If all characters had been equally likely to occur, the average time to transmit a character would be about 11 units, so by exploiting the uneven distribution of character probabilities, Morse reduced the time required to transmit messages.

A weakness of Morse's code is the transmission of text containing a high proportion of numerals, such as a set of accounts. The average time required to transmit a numeral (0 to 9) is 17 units, twice the average time required to encode characters. Under normal circumstances numerals occur rarely, and we are happy to use more time to encode them. However, when transmitting mainly numerical data, the rate of transmission becomes low. This illustrates the disadvantage of using a compression scheme where the designer had preconceptions about the type of data that will be transmitted, and this concern predisposes us toward schemes that adapt themselves to suit the data being transmitted.

The century or two that have elapsed since these early illustrations of text compression have witnessed an extraordinary change in information handling. The development of information theory in the late 1940s provided a great boost to the field of communication, for it enabled the information content of a message to be quantified

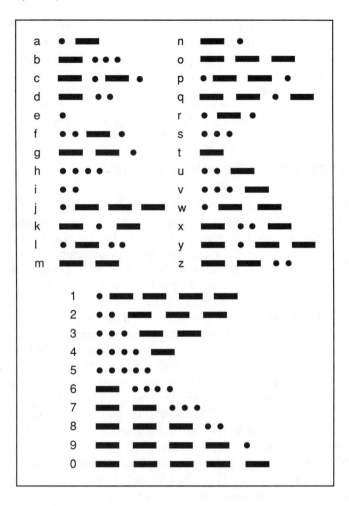

Figure 1-5   Morse code.

and measured. The invention of the microprocessor at the beginning of the 1970s made it economically feasible to implement compression systems that save communication channel capacity. The development of cheap, large-scale, random-access storage in the 1980s completed the technological prerequisites for sophisticated data compression methods. However, the real revolution has been in the theory and practice of adaptive algorithms for exact data compression, which have undergone a dramatic transformation over the last 15 years.

Despite the changes that have occurred, we need text compression to economize on transmission bandwidth just as the British Admiralty did in 1790, to improve the human–machine interface just as Braille did in 1820, and to reduce communication time just as Morse did in 1838. And our capacity to achieve it has improved enormously. Modern techniques can often reduce files to a third of the space that they would normally occupy, and this saving means millions of dollars of real money to organizations operating computers and digital communications networks.

In the remainder of this chapter we discuss the relationship between compression and prediction, partition the compression problem into the two components of modeling and coding, consider the advantages and disadvantages of the use of compression, look at the use of compression in practice, and deal with some *ad hoc* schemes for compressing text. A section at the end gives a sneak preview of the "best" methods.

1.1 COMPRESSION, PREDICTION, AND MODELING

Data compression is inextricably bound up with *prediction*.[1] In the extreme case, if you can predict infallibly what is going to come next, you can achieve perfect compression by dispensing with transmission altogether! Even if you can only predict approximately what is coming next, you can get by with transmitting just enough information to disambiguate the prediction. It is not entirely obvious how to do so—that is what this book is about. But you can glimpse the relationship between compression and prediction even in the simple compression situations that were described above.

The designers of the shutter telegraph for the Admiralty embedded in their system the prediction that words and phrases such as "and," "the," "Portsmouth," "West," and "Sentence of court-martial to be put into execution" would occur more frequently in messages than words like "arguably," "Seattle," "Witten," and "To boldly go where no man has gone before." To the extent that this prediction is correct, their system achieves good compression. If the assumption turns out to be incorrect, it will still be possible to transmit messages—for all words can be spelled out in terms of the 26 letters—but transmission will be inefficient because many of the assigned codes will never be used. Similarly, Morse predicted that letters like "e" and "t" would be more common than "z", not just in all the English that had been written up to 1832, but also in all the novel English sentences that would be constructed and transmitted using his coding scheme over the next 150 years. This prediction turned out to be largely correct, although for commercial applications his implicit assumption that numerals would be rare was not.

Calling these simple statistical regularities "predictions" may seem specious, even trivial. And of course the predictions employed by modern compression methods are considerably more involved, taking the current context into account to make predictions as accurate as possible. To see the role of prediction in data compression most clearly, it is worth digressing to take a brief glance at methods of compressing fundamentally analog signals such as speech.

1.1.1 Inexact Compression

It goes without saying that text compression ought to be *exact*—the reconstructed message should be identical to the original. Exact compression is also called *noiseless* (because it does not introduce any noise into the signal) or *reversible* (because the

[1]A glossary of terms specific to text compression is provided at the end of the book.

compression can be reversed to recover the original input exactly). Strangely, perhaps, much work on data compression has been concerned with inexact techniques.

If what is to be compressed is a speech signal, or a picture, or telemetry data, then exact methods are unnecessary; indeed, they may be undesirable. Since such signals are fundamentally analog in nature, the digital representation itself is an approximation. The act of creating it introduces noise because the digital signal cannot be identical to the original analog signal. Of course, engineers strive to ensure that the quantization noise is imperceptible. To do this, they must sample the signal sufficiently often to capture the high-frequency information and to ensure that each sample is represented digitally with sufficient precision. For example, in speech communication it is common to take 8000 samples per second and digitize each with 8-bit accuracy. This leads to a data rate of 64,000 bits per second (bits/s), which is sufficient for "telephone-quality" speech but not for music or birdsong.

When such information is compressed, approximate reproduction is good enough provided that the noise introduced is below an acceptable threshold. Indeed, it would be senseless to try to transmit the low-level noise faithfully through a communication channel. For example, the lowest-order bit of each 8-bit speech sample may flicker randomly when the signal level wavers around each digitization threshold. This randomness will prevent regularities being identified that could be exploited for compression. By their very nature, noisy signals cannot be compressed and are therefore expensive to transmit.

A common method of inexact compression is *linear prediction*, which is used to compress speech and other analog information. Here the value of the input is sampled at regular intervals, and both the encoder and decoder attempt to predict what the next sample will be, based on the trend of recent samples (see Figure 1-6). Assuming that the prediction is reasonably accurate, the correct value for the new sample will be close to the predicted value, and the encoder need only send a small number to tell the decoder what the difference, or *error*, is. Compression is achieved if this error can be represented in fewer bits than would be needed to represent the sample values directly.

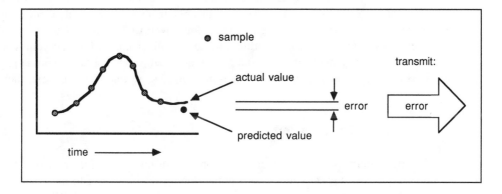

Figure 1-6   Linear prediction.

This illustrates a situation in which prediction is used very explicitly as a basis for compression. At its simplest, each previous sample could be treated as a prediction of the next, so that what is transmitted is the difference between successive samples. The system predicts no change in the sample value, and any change that does occur is a prediction error and must be transmitted explicitly. This is often called *differential coding*. Alternatively, two previous samples could be used and the prediction extrapolated on a constant-difference basis. This is predicting a uniform rate of change in the samples. Any "acceleration" will produce errors that must be transmitted explicitly.

For speech coding it is not uncommon to use as many as 10 previous samples, weighted and summed to produce a prediction. The linear weighted sum gives the technique its name of "linear" prediction. It is reasonable that different previous samples should be weighted differently, for recent samples may well have more influence on the prediction than those in the more distant past. Determining the weights to use is difficult, however, because the optimum values vary for different segments of the speech. What is done is to adapt the weights based on the signal itself, giving *adaptive* linear prediction. Adaptive techniques are also invaluable for text compression and play a major role in our story. But we are getting ahead of ourselves.

Transmitting the error in these ways is exact, although little compression is achieved since although the error is usually much smaller than the signal (and therefore occupies less bits), occasionally it is quite large. For example, in differential coding, a sharp change in the signal will cause a difference that might be as large as the signal itself. If prediction is based on several previous samples, predictions will in general be more accurate, but there will still be occasions where they are way out. Prediction is a risky business—it is hard to *guarantee* good results! (The racetrack and stock market are the places for those who can guarantee their predictions.)

Unfortunately, when allocating a fixed number of bits for the prediction error, it is necessary to accommodate the greatest value that will be encountered. Consequently, we can expect little or no compression. In actuality, people would limit the error signal to a much smaller range than the original signal occupies, to reduce the data rate as much as possible. When error peaks occur that are too large to be transmitted, the maximum possible error value is sent several times in a row, so that the receiver eventually catches up with the original signal. The system can only handle a limited dynamic range, and when it is exceeded, a distortion called "slope overload" occurs. This is just like the overload you get when your children turn the amplifier up too high on your stereo system, when components of the stereo are being asked to operate faster than is physically possible. For speech compression, such inaccuracies are tolerable. For text, they would be disastrous!

1.1.2 Exact Compression

Analog techniques such as linear prediction are not much help for predicting text, since text is not continuous. You cannot say that the letter "j" is close to the letter "k" in the sense that you can say that a sample value of 0.915 is close to 0.917. Anyway, it is unlikely that you would want to know *approximately* what the next letter is! When compressing text we need to use *exact compression*. When Braille and Morse designed their codes, they took this for granted, and throughout this book we will do the same.

Formally, a sequence of symbols x_1, x_2, ..., x_N is encoded "exactly" (or "noiselessly") into another sequence y_1, y_2, ..., y_M when the original sequence x can be uniquely determined from y. If the x_i and y_i are drawn from the same alphabet (say, the binary alphabet $\{0, 1\}$), then y is a compressed form of x when $M < N$.

Just as inexact compression can be performed by attempting to predict what will come along next, so can exact compression. Figure 1-7 shows a *source* of text and a *predictor*. The predictor attempts to *model* the source, and if he is successful in getting the same model as the source, he can confidently tell what will come next. Of course, it would be naive to think that we can predict text with complete accuracy. In fact, it would be an insult to humanity to suggest that people might be *that* predictable! For

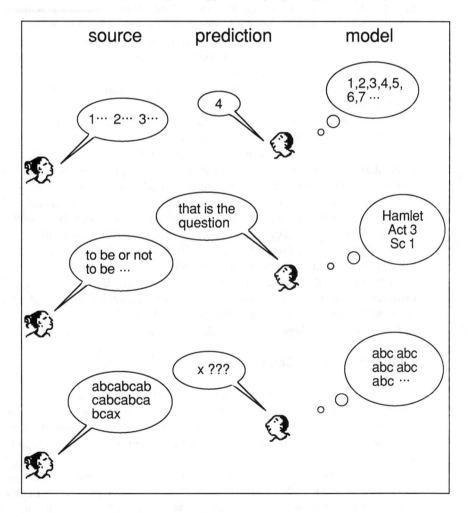

Figure 1-7   Predicting text.

example, in the third part of Figure 1-7, the predictor thinks that the model has been discovered, only to find that the letter "x" appears unexpectedly.

The situation is analogous to that of linear prediction. There we made predictions, but always catered to the fact that prediction errors would occur by transmitting these error corrections explicitly. Our hope was that the errors would generally be small and occupy fewer bits than the original samples. This hope is borne out in practice if one is prepared to tolerate the occasional overload condition. What corresponds to this process for discrete signals, such as the letters of text?

Instead of just guessing what the next character is, a predictive model for exact compression assigns a *probability* to every possible outcome. For example, after the sequence "abcabcabcabca" we might estimate a probability of 9/10 for the letter "b" and 1/250 for each of the other 25 letters of the alphabet. (Justifying such estimates might be difficult, but let's leave that for later.) Once each letter has a probability, likely letters can be represented by short codes, and unlikely ones by long codes, just as in Morse code. If our model is any good, most of the probabilities for letters that actually occur next will be large, so we will normally be sending short codes (such as Morse's codes for "e" or "a"). Hence compression will be achieved. The task of assigning optimal sequences of bits, based on probabilities, is called *coding*. This is an important problem and is examined carefully in Chapter 5.

So for exact compression, "predicting the next character" really means "estimating a probability distribution for the next character," and this is done in a model for the text. The more the model resembles the source of the text, the better the messages can be compressed. Since the source of most text is ultimately a person, we ideally want to model that person's thought processes to predict what they will come up with next. Of course, this is not possible, so in practice we resort to approximate models. Despite the fact that the models are approximate, they can still be used for exact compression—we are not relying on accuracy of the model for accuracy of the transmission. Even if the model is grossly wrong, predicting garbage with high probability and the characters that actually occur with very low probability, the message will still be recovered exactly. What happens is that the text will not be compressed very much, and might even be expanded. It would be as if Morse got the letter frequencies wrong and allocated long codes to "e" and "a" and short ones to "z" and "q". People could still communicate without error using Morse code; it would just be less efficient.

1.1.3 Modeling and Coding

As Figure 1-7 illustrates, all predictions are based on a model of the input. The task of finding a suitable model for text is an extremely important problem in compression, and much of this book is devoted to techniques for modeling. Once predictions are available, they are processed by an encoder that turns them into binary digits to be transmitted.

This idea of separating the compression process into these two parts—an encoder and a separate modeler that feeds information to it—is one of the major advances in the theory of data compression over the last decade. The prediction, in the form of a probability distribution over all messages, is supplied by a model. The encoder is given this prediction, along with the actual message that occurs. It then constructs a compressed representation of the actual message with respect to the probability distribution. (In practice, messages are generally coded one character at a time, rather than all at once.) This is entirely analogous to the way that differential coding of digitized speech constructs a compressed representation of the next sample value by subtracting the predicted value from it. But here is the crucial difference. In the probabilistic case the encoder is *universal*—it does not need to know where the predictions come from and so can work with many different models. Contrast this with the differential coding case, where the coder has the unenviable task of deciding how many bits to allocate to the difference (which depends on the accuracy of prediction, the frequency and magnitude of peak errors, the tolerable level of overload, and so on).

This separation helps us to rationalize the great diversity of different data compression schemes that have been proposed. It provides a touchstone that allows the motley crew of ad hoc schemes to be reduced to a few different types of modeler that can be combined with a few different types of encoder. It highlights similarities between coding schemes which superficially seem to be quite different. It provides a clear basis for selecting a data compression technique that is appropriate to a new compression problem.

Quite apart from these pragmatic reasons, the separation is valuable from a conceptual point of view because modeling and coding are very different sorts of activity. The problem of constructing an encoder has been completely solved, in a way that is as close to "optimal" as practically to make no difference (we will define what this means later). The only residual issues are matters of efficient implementation, which will always depend on the technology available. Not so the problem of constructing models for different kinds of data (or even different kinds of text). This is more of an artistic endeavor which is not soluble in the same definitive way as constructing an encoder.

Some compression schemes do not appear to use the modeling/coding paradigm. This is because the modeling and coding tasks can be intertwined. In Chapter 9 we will see how to extract probabilistic models from such schemes, and discover what sort of prediction they are using to achieve compression.

Perhaps one of the reasons that data compression has not traditionally been divided into modeling and coding is that we do not separate them ourselves when thinking about the world. For example, if you were asked to predict what would happen if you were to step in front of a speeding bus or what letter will follow "...q", you might answer "I would most likely be killed or end up in hospital" or "The most likely letter is u unless it is the last letter of Iraq." Obviously, we have in our heads quite sophisticated models of the physics of speeding objects and of letter frequencies in English. However, the models are not expressed in a way that is very useful for data compression.

Computers are much better than people at doing bookkeeping. (There are many other things that people are good at, but computers are not!) In particular, computers can keep track of how often various things have happened and might be able to answer the questions above by "There is a 50% probability that you will be killed, 45% probability that you will be very sick, and 5% probability that you will get off without a scratch" or "u with 98% probability, punctuation with 2% probability, and nothing else is possible." Given a well-defined model like this that can come up with probabilities for every eventuality, a universal encoder can be used to do the rest of the data compression process.

1.1.4 Static and Adaptive Modeling

Figure 1-8 shows how modeling is used in practice. The encoder and decoder both have the same model. The former generates codes using the model, and the decoder interprets the codes correctly with reference to the same model. It is important for good performance that the model be kept appropriate for the text, but at the same time the decoder must always be using the same one as the encoder. If the model is never changed, transmission may become inefficient because the model was not designed for the text. (Recall the problem that Morse code has when handling numeric data.) On the other hand, if a new model is transmitted frequently, any benefits of compression will be negated. There are three ways that the encoder and decoder can maintain the same model: *static, semiadaptive,* and *adaptive modeling.*

In *static* modeling the encoder and decoder agree on a fixed model, regardless of the text to be encoded. This is the method used for shutter telegraphs. The operators at each end of the telegraph were given identical codebooks. If the operators were reliable, all messages would be correctly encoded and decoded.

Suppose that the Navy's telegraph system had been opened to the general public. There would then have been a wide variety of topics being transmitted through the telegraph system, and the codebooks used would not have been very helpful. For example, there would have been less demand for messages like "Sentence of court-martial to be put into execution." The supervisor of the telegraph would probably have a new codebook prepared containing more general common words, and issue a copy to each operator. To get a copy of the codebook to the distant operator, he could have it sent through the telegraph.

If the supervisor wanted the codebooks to be even better suited to the messages being sent, he could require the operators to use a *semiadaptive* scheme like this: Before the operator sends a message, he reads it, writes down the most frequently used words,

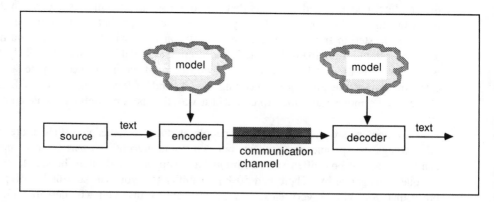

Figure 1-8   Using a model for compression.

and uses them to make up a codebook specifically for that message. He then transmits the codebook, followed by the coded message. The receiving operator writes down the codebook, and then uses it to decode the message. A disadvantage of this semiadaptive scheme is that sending a codebook for each message could take a substantial amount of time. Also, the sending operator must see the entire message before it can be transmitted (i.e., two passes are required for encoding).

Both of these disadvantages of the semiadaptive scheme can be overcome rather elegantly by using the following *adaptive* scheme. The sending operator begins transmitting a message letter by letter, which the receiving operator can decode. Both operators write down each word as it is transmitted. By agreement, when a word has been transmitted or received twice in the same text, both operators add it to the codebook, allocating it the next spare code. From there on that word can be transmitted using the new code. Before long the codebooks will contain codes specifically tailored for the topic and language of the message. Of course, the system assumes that the operators are completely reliable and consistent.

The illustration shows how remarkable adaptive modeling is. Both operators have identical codebooks well suited to the message, yet *the codes were never explicitly transmitted*. In general, a compression scheme is said to use adaptive coding if the code used for a particular character (or phrase) is based on the text already transmitted.

The adaptive shutter telegraph system might not work very well in practice because the operators could not guarantee to be infallible in the construction of the codebook. However, this is not such a problem with computers, as the encoder and decoder can be made consistent by using an exact duplicate of the encoder's codebook construction program in the decoder. A theoretical comparison of static and adaptive modeling in Chapter 3 will show that little, if any, compression is sacrificed by using adaptive modeling, and that a lot can be lost if nonadaptive modeling is used inappropriately.

1.2 THE IMPORTANCE OF TEXT COMPRESSION

The mushrooming amount of text stored on and transmitted between computers has increased the need for text compression despite continuing improvements in storage and transmission technology. A single compact disk (CD) can store 600 million characters, which is more than enough for a comprehensive encyclopedia. But even the huge amount of storage offered by a CD is insufficient for some purposes, and publishers are looking to text compression to avoid multivolume publications.

The amount of compression that can be obtained using current techniques is usually a trade-off against speed and the amount of memory required. Fast ad hoc schemes typically reduce English text to around 70% of its original size, while more theoretically sound approaches can improve this compression ratio to about 40%. Some of the slower schemes use larger amounts of memory to achieve compression ratios as favorable as 25%. Some experiments discussed in Chapter 4 indicate that the best ratio that will be achieved in the future will never be less than around 12%. Clearly, there is considerable potential for savings to be made by the use of compression. We will now consider some of the issues involved in deciding if these economies are worthwhile.

Saving storage space is a common reason for the use of compression. The compression techniques in Braille can reduce the size of books by 20%, or decrease the number of volumes needed to store one printed book. For computers, compression can increase the amount of information stored on a disk, allowing more text to be stored before a new disk must be purchased. By compressing data on magnetic tapes, not only are fewer tapes needed, but fewer shelves are used to store the tapes and less time is taken to read them. The principal difficulty of storing text in a compressed form occurs if the text must be accessed randomly. Usually, it is practical to start reading a compressed file only at its beginning.

Sometimes searching can be accelerated by compressing the search key rather than decompressing the text being searched. Consider a Braille reader searching for the word "according." If the text is Grade 1 Braille (uncompressed), there would be nine cells to check for a match. If the text is Grade 2, there would be only two cells to match. And not only are fewer comparisons required, but there is less data to search.

The compression of transmitted data has a double benefit. First, the cost of transmission is reduced. For example, the relay operators on shutter telegraphs had fewer codes to relay across the country, so they worked shorter hours. Second, the effective speed of transmission increases because the same amount of information is transmitted in a smaller amount of time. This is illustrated by the Braille code, where text may be read faster if it is compressed. For the enormous amount of data transmitted between computers, the transmission rate is usually limited by the bandwidth of the communication channel, and increasing the bandwidth is often very difficult, if not impossible. It follows that there are many situations where transmission could be accelerated by the application of compression—from international communications (which results in a saving in cost) to a disk controller (where a compressed file is read faster than its uncompressed counterpart). Bandwidth on radio links is becoming particularly hard to obtain, and compression has the potential to provide more efficient transmission on a channel that cannot otherwise be improved.

For all these economies, someone has to do the compression and decompression. This might be accomplished by a dedicated microprocessor, specialized hardware, or by the computer on which the data are stored. If a dedicated device is used, the only cost is the initial outlay. If the existing computer is used, there is the ongoing cost of processing time, as well as the initial cost of buying or implementing a scheme. Nevertheless, using an existing computer will often be worthwhile. The processing time used to compress data will often be paid off by reduced communications charges, or it may even be that the time invested is repaid later because the data are processed in a compressed form. If the compression is not urgent, it could be performed when the processor is idle, either in the background during the day, or overnight.

A common complaint against compression is the sensitivity of compressed data to errors. We believe it would be very disappointing if compressed data were *not* sensitive to errors—for that would indicate further redundancy in the information, a missed opportunity for additional compression. The redundancy in text is not an efficient way to combat noise, partly because it is not designed for the kind of noise that typically occurs on communication lines and storage media, and partly because it cannot easily be used by a machine to detect errors automatically. For example, if noise hits the telephone line that connects my terminal to the computer as I type, I may not notice the few garbage characters that appear. The redundancy of English is not exploited by my computer to correct errors; nor is it easy to see how it could be. And suppose I do notice the errors. While this benefit is certainly attributable to using a redundant communication channel, the price exacted is dear. A noise-combating protocol could be designed to cope with such errors with much more reliability and much less redundancy than that of English.

The redundancy of natural language evolved for human, not machine, use, and strategies need to be reengineered for artificial transmission. The modern paradigm for transmission is depicted in Figure 1-9. First, natural redundancy is removed from the message by compression. Then redundancy is added—redundancy that has been carefully designed to combat the kind of noise suffered by the particular communication channel employed. This approach provides an efficient, economical way to achieve the maximum transmission rate for a given level of error performance, and the rate will usually be significantly greater than it would be for raw text.

A side effect of using compression is that some encryption is achieved because the lack of redundancy in a compressed file removes the opportunity to use statistical regularities to break a code. Adaptive schemes generally change their coding after each character transmitted, so in this situation the codebreaker's task is compounded.

A detail to consider when a text is compressed and archived is to ensure that it can be decompressed if it is needed at a later date. In Section 9-5 we discuss some techniques that help to prevent the situation where a file becomes unreadable because the appropriate decompression program has been lost.

1.2.1 Compression in the Workplace

The following examples illustrate how savings can be achieved in practice by the application of compression.

Word processing.   MacWrite is one of several word processors available for the Apple Macintosh computer. The disk drives on early versions of the computer would only accept 400-kilobyte (Kbyte) disks, and most of this space could easily be

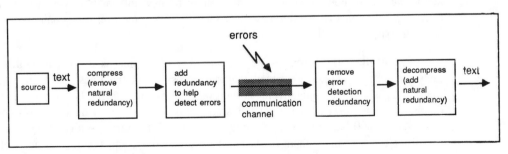

Figure 1-9   Error detection for compression.

consumed by the operating system and word processor. Unless another disk drive was purchased, only a small amount of space was left for storing text files. This situation prompted the authors of MacWrite to invent a simple compression scheme. Instead of using 8 bits to code each character, either 4 or 12 bits are used, depending on how common the character is. On average about 6.4 bits are used for each character, so an overall saving is made. This represents a 25% increase in the amount of text that can be stored in that small space left on the disk.

Modem enhancement.   Because of the low bandwidth of telephone lines, it is very difficult to build modems that can communicate at more than 9600 bit/s. A way to increase the effective rate of data transfer is to pass data through a compression device before transmission. One device designed for this purpose is Racal-Vadic's *Scotsman III* data compressor, which can transparently compress and decompress data for a variety of blocking protocols. The manufacturer claims that this machine can reduce data to half of its original size. This means that a 19.2-Kbit/s data stream can be reduced to 9600-bit/s, transmitted over a standard telephone via a 9600-bit/s modem, and reconstructed back to 19.2 Kbit/s at the other end; yet the use of compression is completely transparent to the communicating devices. By adding an optional multiplexor, the Scotsman III can simulate two full-duplex 9600-bit/s lines, or four half-duplex 9600-bit/s lines, over a single 9600-bit/s line. This reduces the number of leased lines and modems required for communications, representing a considerable saving over a period of time. A cyclic redundancy check (CRC) is applied to each block to detect errors, and because compressed messages are short, more blocks are sent error-free, and retransmission costs are reduced. The capital outlay for such compressors may well be worthwhile if communication costs are halved.

Another system that uses compression to improve the speed of a modem is PCTERM. It is designed to handle the sporadic traffic encountered between an interactive terminal and a host computer. Compression is performed by software on the host and in the terminal (the terminal is actually an emulator running on a personal computer). The compression algorithm is slow to encode but decodes very economically, and this balance matches the power of the computers performing each task. The use of compression makes a 1200-bit/s line appear to be working at 9600-bit/s. The apparent transmission speed will fluctuate with the amount of compression, but this is not a problem because poor compression is usually caused by new information, which takes time to read, while text that has already been seen (e.g., a screen refresh) compresses well and is transmitted rapidly.

Facsimile machines.   Facsimile (fax or telecopier) is a popular method for transmitting hard copies of printed material across telephone lines. Each page to be transmitted is digitized into several million black-and-white pixels. If one bit is used to represent each pixel, each page generates hundreds of kilobytes of data, and to transmit this over a 4800-bit/s phone line would take over 7 minutes. With this system you could not transmit more than 70 pages in an 8-hour day, and taking into account the phone charges, a courier would often give better service at a lower cost!

Invariably, there is a lot of redundancy in a digitized page, and consequently, substantial compression can be achieved. Two standard codes for compressing facsimile documents have been adopted. One allows a typical document to be transmitted in about 60 seconds, while the other is mainly for double-resolution digitizations, and can transmit a document in about 75 seconds. The use of compression has increased the throughput of the Fax machine by a factor of 7, and reduced the per page cost of transmission by the same factor, making this a feasible communication medium for many businesses.

A variety of compression methods were proposed for the facsimile standard, but in the end a simple nonadaptive approach was chosen. Eight test documents were used to fine-tune the two schemes, and it turns out that the amount of compression achieved is fairly insensitive to the nature of the document. One advantage of this particular nonadaptive code is that it performs satisfactorily in the absence of error correction. A page is scanned and transmitted line by line, with the end of each line well marked, so the effect of an error is usually confined to the line in which it occurs. Often it is possible to detect that an error has occurred by counting the number of pixels in a line generated by the decoder. If a serious error is detected, the decoding machine can take steps to conceal the offending line.

Netnews.   Many UNIX systems are linked by an informal network called "UUCP." Each day several megabytes of news are exchanged worldwide over this network. Each site on the "net" receives news, and may pass it on to other sites. In this fashion the news usually manages to propagate over the entire network. Sites are typically connected by a 1200- or 2400-bit/s telephone link. News articles are accumulated at a site, periodically "batched" into files of about 50 Kbytes, and sent to connected sites. Each batch takes about 10 minutes to transmit, so they are small enough that if an error occurs, a batch can be retransmitted without too much time wasted.

A batch of news can be compressed to about half of its original size, so the use of compression provides the usual benefits: the news travels faster, and the telephone charges are reduced. These savings are significant but must be weighed against the extra time the processor spends performing the compression. An experiment to check this has produced a surprising result. The system used for the experiment was a Vax 750 with a 1200-bit/s modem. To send two 50-Kbyte batches of uncompressed news, the communications program used about 40 seconds of processor time. Compressing the news from 100 Kbytes to 50 Kbytes took about 13 seconds, and because there was half as much data to send, the communications program used only 24 seconds of processor time. The total amount of processor time used to compress and send the news was 37 seconds, which is *less* than the 40 seconds needed to send the news uncompressed! If the same batch of news was to be sent to several sites the saving would be even more significant. So, for this site at least, compressing the news pays off on all fronts—transmission speed, telephone charges, *and* processor time.

File archiving.   The program ARC creates and maintains archives of files for personal computers. Before a file is stored in an archive it is analyzed to find how well each of four available compression schemes will reduce its size, and then it is compressed using the best method. The four alternatives are (1) to apply no compression, which guarantees that files will not require more storage space than previously; (2) a form of run-length coding, which is described in Section 1-3; (3) Huffman coding, described in Section 5-1; and (4) Ziv–Lempel coding (the LZC variation, to be precise) of Section 8-3. Of course, at least two bits must be prepended to the archived file to identify which form of compression has been used, so in the worst case a file will be expanded by this small amount. The ARC program is very popular for distributing files on electronic bulletin boards, since several files associated with one program can be packaged together and compressed for efficient transmission and storage.

1.3 AD HOC COMPRESSION METHODS

It is very easy to dream up methods of compression that exploit some of the natural redundancy in text. In the past, practitioners often had favorite tricks which they used for compressing particular kinds of data. However, techniques tailored to take advantage of idiosyncratic repetitions and regularities are—or should be—a thing of the past. Adaptive models discover for themselves the regularities that are present, and do so more reliably than people. They are not influenced by prejudice or preconception, or rather, their preconceptions are dictated precisely and predictably by the kind of text used to prime them.

In this section we describe a few examples of ad hoc, nonadaptive, schemes for text compression. They are not recommended for general use, but are included as a foil to accentuate, by contrast, the elegance and parsimony of adaptive coding techniques. Some of the schemes (e.g., run-length coding) have analogs in general compression paradigms (first-order Markov models) and performed a valuable historical role in the development of text compression.

Here, as elsewhere in this book, we assume that text is normally stored in 8-bit bytes as ASCII (American Standard Code for Information Interchange) codes, with only 7 of the bits being significant. As shown in Table 1-1, the ASCII alphabet includes upper- and lowercase letters, numerals, special symbols, and a sprinkling of extra control codes. These last have standard interpretations such as "ht" (horizontal tab, which assists in formatting tables by moving the print position along to standard places), "bel" (rings the bell on the terminal), and "etx" (end of transmission). In tables and examples throughout this book we denote the space character by "•" when we need to make it visible explicitly. For transmission, 7-bit ASCII is often augmented to 8 bits by the addition of a parity bit at the leftmost end. For reliable media it is usually stored in 8-bit bytes, with the addition of zero as the most significant bit.

The set of all distinct characters used in a text is often referred to as an alphabet. We will denote the size of an alphabet by q, and this may have various values in different situations. The conventional English alphabet contains 26 characters, but the space character is essential for displaying text, so a minimal alphabet must contain 27 characters (Figure 1-10a). For general applications the alphabet would include upper- and lowercase letters, numerals, punctuation, and special symbols. Figure 1-10b shows

TABLE 1-1   ASCII CODES

0000000	nul	0000001	soh	0000010	stx	0000011	etx
0000100	eot	0000101	enq	0000110	ack	0000111	bel
0001000	bs	0001001	ht	0001010	nl	0001011	vt
0001100	np	0001101	cr	0001110	so	0001111	si
0010000	dle	0010001	dc1	0010010	dc2	0010011	dc3
0010100	dc4	0010101	nak	0010110	syn	0010111	etb
0011000	can	0011001	em	0011010	sub	0011011	esc
0011100	fs	0011101	gs	0011110	rs	0011111	us
0100000	•	0100001	!	0100010	"	0100011	#
0100100	$	0100101	%	0100110	&	0100111	'
0101000	(	0101001	)	0101010	*	0101011	+
0101100	,	0101101	-	0101110	.	0101111	/
0110000	0	0110001	1	0110010	2	0110011	3
0110100	4	0110101	5	0110110	6	0110111	7
0111000	8	0111001	9	0111010	:	0111011	;
0111100	<	0111101	=	0111110	>	0111111	?
1000000	@	1000001	A	1000010	B	1000011	C
1000100	D	1000101	E	1000110	F	1000111	G
1001000	H	1001001	I	1001010	J	1001011	K
1001100	L	1001101	M	1001110	N	1001111	O
1010000	P	1010001	Q	1010010	R	1010011	S
1010100	T	1010101	U	1010110	V	1010111	W
1011000	X	1011001	Y	1011010	Z	1011011	[
1011100	\	1011101	]	1011110	^	1011111	_
1100000	'	1100001	a	1100010	b	1100011	c
1100100	d	1100101	e	1100110	f	1100111	g
1101000	h	1101001	i	1101010	j	1101011	k
1101100	l	1101101	m	1101110	n	1101111	o
1110000	p	1110001	q	1110010	r	1110011	s
1110100	t	1110101	u	1110110	v	1110111	w
1111000	x	1111001	y	1111010	z	1111011	{
1111100	l	1111101	}	1111110	~	1111111	del

such an alphabet containing 94 characters (this is the alphabet of the Brown corpus, a body of some 6 million characters of text that is analyzed in Chapter 4). The ASCII code can represent an alphabet of 128 characters, although 33 of these are special

```
•abcdefghijk
lmnopqrstuvw
xyz
```

(a)

```
•!"#$%&'()*+,-./0123456789:;<>?@ABCDEFG
HIJKLMNOPQRSTUVWXYZ[\]^_`abcdefghijklmn
opqrstuvwxyz{|}~
```

(b)

Figure 1-10   Two alphabets:
(a) 27 characters; (b) 94 characters.

control codes. Even larger alphabets may be required in practice. For example, the alphabet of the present book includes characters such as "•", "—", "Σ", and "μ", as well as those in Figure 1-10b.

1.3.1 Irreversible Compression

One good way of reducing text is to throw part of it away. Since the exact input cannot then be recovered from the compressed version, such techniques are described as *irreversible*. (Irreversible compression is sometimes called "compaction.") The most effective irreversible compression is to throw away the information entirely!

Many characters stored in computer files are not essential to meaning. An extreme case is the white space that used to be required to pad out lines to fixed-length records. In the bad old days when punched cards dominated the human–machine interface, many systems allocated space in 80-byte units and all lines were 80 characters long. The use of variable-length records was a significant, although unsung, advance in computer usage which provided effective and welcome data "compression." Another form of irreversible compression is abbreviation, which is a process where redundant characters are removed from a word. An abbreviation method is considered successful if most words remain distinct after being abbreviated. In this sense, abbreviation is a form of hashing.

More pertinent to contemporary systems is the fact that the position of line boundaries may be disregarded in running text. So, also, may the size of any white space present. Multiple spaces, line boundaries, and "tab" characters may all be replaced by single spaces. Much punctuation is inessential to the meaning of the text, and in some applications may be omitted entirely. The distinction between upper- and lowercase characters is usually not important.

If all characters that are not letters—digits, punctuation, and special symbols— are removed so that just letters remain, there are only 27 possible characters (including space). These can be represented in five bits rather than the usual eight. Coupled with white-space compaction, this could easily reduce text to 50% of its original size— irreversibly. Figure 1-11 illustrates these and other ad hoc compression techniques on a small example of text.

1.3.2 Run-Length Encoding

A simple idea for compressing text reversibly, so that the original can be recovered exactly, is to replace sequences of repeated space characters with a count of the number of spaces. There must, of course, be some way of telling that the count is to be interpreted as such and not as a character itself. One might reserve one special character code as a flag indicating that the next byte is a space count; then as many as 256 space characters could be compacted into two bytes. The same trick could be done for other characters that often come together, such as underlines.

This is a special case of *run-length encoding*, where sequences of consecutive identical characters are replaced by the length of the run. This idea is particularly useful when the alphabet is small. For example, with black-and-white pictures the alphabet contains just two characters, 1 (for black) and 0 (for white). Such pictures can usefully be stored as a sequence of 1-byte integers that represent run lengths. The first integer

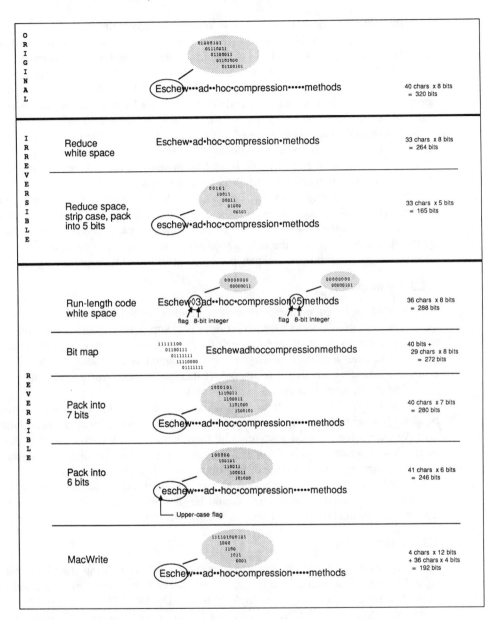

Figure 1-11   Examples of ad hoc compression methods.

gives the number of black pixels with which the first scan line begins (it could be zero), and subsequent integers record the lengths of white and black runs alternately. A run of more than 255 pixels cannot be represented as a single byte. Instead, the first 255 could be recorded, then a zero-length run of the opposite color inserted, followed by the rest of the original run.

This bit-wise run-length coding is not particularly suitable for ASCII text, but methods have been proposed to reassign the character codes so that it would be effective. The codes "0000000" and "1111111" could be assigned to the two most common characters ("•" and "e"), codes such as "0111111" and "0011111" are assigned to the next most common characters, and so on. This approach is not as sensible as it might appear because each new character code can be translated to a definite number of bits that will be generated in the output of the run-length coding, so the entire system is simply assigning a variable number of bits to each character—the more likely the character, the fewer bits it is coded in. Although the ranking of code lengths may be correct, the assignment of such code lengths should be more systematic; here it is at the mercy of how the permutations of 7-bit numbers happen to work out.

Run-length coding works when symbols do not occur independently but are influenced by their predecessors. Given that a symbol has occurred, that symbol is more likely than others to occur next. If this is not the case, coding runs (rather than symbols) will not compress the information. The same effect can be achieved in a more general way by the coding techniques presented in subsequent chapters.

1.3.3 Bit Mapping

Replacing multiple space characters with flag and count bytes is worthwhile only when more than two spaces occur together. It does not work when spaces exhibit no unusual tendency to cluster together, even though they may be particularly common characters. One way to take advantage of an uneven distribution is to associate a bit with each character, indicating whether it is a space. If it is, no further information is needed. If it is not, the character code must be included too.

It is usually inconvenient to store these bits alongside the characters themselves, because they upset byte alignment and this makes it more difficult to manipulate the text. An alternative is to use a separate bit map, with a bit for each character. Each bit indicates whether or not it is a space. This gives the positions of all spaces, so that only nonspace characters need be stored. Of course, what is really happening is that a space is assigned a 1-bit code, and other characters have their codes increased by 1 bit. It is reasonable that the code for a space should be shorter than the codes for other characters, but this particular choice of lengths is rather arbitrary.

1.3.4 Packing

Characters are often packed together to save space. Instead of being stored one per byte, eight 7-bit ASCII characters can be packed into seven bytes. Some older computers had words that were not an integral multiple of 8 bits. The DEC PDP-10 packed five ASCII characters into each 36-bit word, with one bit left over. The older CYBER machines used a 6-bit character code so that each 60-bit word held 10 characters. The restriction to 64 characters (6 bits) caused some problems, for by the time 26 uppercase letters, 10 digits, and a few spacing and punctuation characters are included, there is no room left for lowercase letters. Consequently, one character was designated as a shift into lowercase mode. Every lowercase character was preceded by this and so occupied 12 bits. However, in those days people rarely used mixed-case text (e.g., card readers were uppercase only).

The text storage scheme of MacWrite mentioned earlier is related to this approach. The 15 commonest characters, "•etnroaisdlhcfp", are each represented in 4 bits. The final 4-bit code is reserved as an escape to indicate that the next byte is to be interpreted as a normal 8-bit ASCII character. Thus the 15 most common characters are coded in 4 bits, and all others in 12 bits. For some texts, such as text completely in uppercase, this scheme will expand, not compress. To prevent this, each paragraph is coded only if its size is reduced. An extra bit is associated with each paragraph to signal whether or not it has been compressed. This scheme typically compresses text to 80% of its original size.

1.3.5 Differential Coding

When compressing a sequence of records in a file, or a sorted list of keys, it is often worthwhile coding the difference between successive items rather than the items themselves. How the difference is calculated depends on the content of the records. A sequence of dates might be coded as the number of days between adjacent dates; a line from a bit-map picture could be represented by the set of pixels that differ from the previous line; a record in a file need only store the fields that are different from those in the previous record.

Front compression is a special case of differential coding, suitable for lexically sorted lists such as an alphabetical dictionary of words. It is based on the observation that most words share the same initial letters as their predecessor. The repeated letters are simply replaced with a number representing the size of this common prefix. Figure 1-12 shows part of a dictionary and its front compression coding.

1.3.6 Special Data Types

Special kinds of data call for special treatment. Binary-coded decimal (BCD) is a way of representing integers with each digit stored in 4 bits; a byte can then represent 100 numbers. Integers stored in ASCII, of course, consume 8 bits per digit and a byte can only represent a single digit. The most economical way to store integers is in pure binary notation, since then each byte can represent 256 numbers.

Dates within a year can be expressed as a day number between 1 and 365 (or 366), a convention based on the Julian calendar introduced by Caesar in 46 B.C. This consumes 2 bytes instead of the 12 required for a character representation such as "21 September." Notations such as 09-21 provide an intermediate compromise.

```
a            a
aback        1back
abacus       4us
abalone      3lone
abandon      3ndon
abase        3se
abash        4h
abate        3te
```

Figure 1-12   Part of a dictionary and its front compression coding.

A common convention for date and time is *yymmddhhmmss*, where *yy* is the last two digits of the year, the first *mm* the month number, *dd* the day number in the month, *hh* the hour number (24-hour system), the second *mm* the minute number, and *ss* the seconds. This represents times to the second between 1900 and 2000 in 12 characters. More human-readable is the 24-character string "Mon Sep 21 12:34:56 1987." More economical is a 4-byte integer in seconds since the turn of the century, a coding that is good for over 130 years.

A tailor-made representation for a particular kind of data clearly has greater potential to achieve compression than any general-purpose method. However, a growing trend in information processing is to keep representations human-readable as far as possible. It will often be more attractive to compress a file containing a lot of dates using a general-purpose adaptive compression algorithm than to create a tailor-made packed format and the necessary programs to convert to and from that representation.

1.3.7 Move to Front (MTF) Coding

This adaptive scheme is designed for compressing language that can be broken up into words. It works on the principle that the appearance of a word in the input makes that word more likely to occur in the near future. The mechanism that exploits this is analogous to a stack of books; when a book is required, it is removed from the stack and is returned to the top after use. This way, books used frequently will be near the top and therefore easier to locate.

An MTF coder simulates the bookstack with a dynamic list of words. As the input is processed, each word is looked up in the list and if it happens to occur as the *i*th entry, is coded by the number *i*. Then it is moved to the front of the list so that if it occurs soon after, it will be coded by a number smaller than *i*. The number is coded so that the smaller its value, the shorter its code, so more likely words are represented more compactly. One suitable method of obtaining variable code lengths is to code position number *i* as the binary representation of *i* prefixed by $\lfloor \log i \rfloor$ zeros. For example, the codes for 1, 2, 3, and 4 are 1, 010, 011, and 00100, respectively. Other variable-length codes for the integers have been proposed and are described in Appendix A at the end of the book.

Initially, the list is empty, and provision is made to transmit a new word for the list by sending the code for the first unused position in the list as a flag, followed by the new word. Figure 1-13 gives an example of MTF coding. Because coding is adaptive, both the encoder and decoder must maintain identical lists.

1.4 THE SUBJECT OF TEXT COMPRESSION

Until 15 years ago the subject of text compression was principally a large collection of ad hoc schemes similar to those just described, plus the theoretically sound (but practically unattractive) technique of Huffman coding. It is only recently that the subject has become mature through the development of significant theory which has led to practical and general algorithms. We will present the theory on which current techniques are based, and for the practitioner, the resulting efficient algorithms are also given, with the details necessary to implement them.

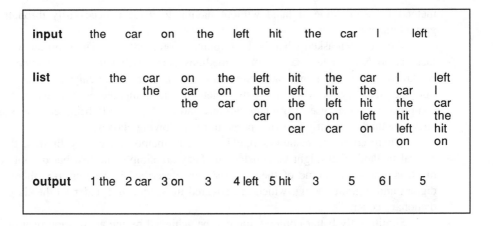

input	the	car	on	the	left	hit	the	car	I	left

list		the	car	on	the	left	hit	the	car	I	left
		the	car	on	the	left	hit	the	car	I
			the	car	on	the	left	hit	the	hit	car
				car	on	the	left	on	left	hit	the
					car	on	car	car	on	left	hit
										on	on

Figure 1-13   MTF (bookstack) coding.

There are two general methods of performing compression: *statistical* and *dictionary* coding. In statistical coding each symbol is assigned a code based on the probability that it will occur. Highly probable symbols get short codes, and vice versa, as in Morse code. In dictionary coding groups of consecutive characters, or "phrases," are replaced by a code. The phrase represented by the code can be found by looking it up in a "dictionary." It is only recently that it has been shown that most practical dictionary coding schemes can be outperformed by a related statistical coding scheme. It is because of this result that we believe that statistical coding is the approach that will continue to yield the best compression in the future.

It is convenient that statistical coding can be approached as two separate tasks—modeling and coding. Modeling assigns probabilities to symbols, and coding translates these probabilities to a sequence of bits. Adaptive modeling, where the compressor adapts itself to suit the particular text being compressed, is a particularly elegant and efficient technique that is almost universally superior to nonadaptive methods, and this will be one of our main themes. The largest part of this book is devoted to modeling (Chapters 2, 3, 4, 6, and 7), since it is the model that dictates the amount of compression that will be achieved. The other part of the statistical approach is the coder. The problem of constructing an optimal coder was solved completely with the discovery of arithmetic coding (Chapter 5). Dictionary coding schemes are covered in Chapter 8, the methods introduced are compared in Chapter 9, and other problems that can be solved by the techniques developed in the book are investigated in Chapter 10.

1.5 A NOTE FOR THE PRACTITIONER

The approach of this book is to lay a sound theoretical foundation, which is then used as the basis for a variety of practical compression methods. The purpose of this theory is to justify the design of the methods, but it need not be studied in order to implement them, so here we offer a guide for the practitioner who wishes to choose a suitable method for a situation at hand without having to wade unnecessarily through background material.

We are often asked what the best compression method is. The short answer is that there is no *best* method; a wealth of methods exist, each with its own strengths and weaknesses. The question is addressed fully in Chapter 9, particularly in the introduction and Section 9-3, where the better methods are compared empirically in terms of compression, speed, use of primary storage, and the type of file being compressed. The "best" methods currently known emerge in the following classes.

Where computer resources (CPU time and memory) are very limited, there are several methods that might be considered. They are simple and fast but do not achieve much compression. Some of these codes were described in Section 1-3; there is also digram and *n*-gram coding, which are covered in Section 8-2 under the heading "static dictionary coders."

Significantly better compression can be achieved by the application of a moderate amount of computing resources. The Ziv–Lempel (LZ) coders dominate this class. The LZFG method generally gives the best compression, with a moderate use of resources for both encoding and decoding. For a different balance, the LZB method uses more time and/or memory for encoding, but is particularly economical for decoding. Both LZ methods are described in Section 8-3, along with several other variations. The description of LZFG is built on those of LZ78 and LZJ, while LZB is described as a variation of LZ77 and LZSS. Suitable data structures for faster LZB encoding are given in Section 8-4.

The greatest compression is almost always achieved by finite-context models driving an arithmetic coder. The empirical comparison reveals that the PPMC finite-context model gives excellent compression for a variety of files, although it is somewhat slower than the Ziv–Lempel coders, and works best when memory is plentiful. PPMC is described in Section 6-3 (based on techniques introduced in Sections 6-1 and 6-2). It generates probabilities that are intended to be coded via arithmetic coding; the function of arithmetic coding is covered in the introduction to Chapter 5, and a full implementation of it is given in Appendix 5A.

NOTES

A detailed history of the shutter telegraphs has been written by Wilson (1976). More information about computer speech and speech compression is available in Witten (1982b). The use of compression for compact disks is discussed in Lambert and Ropiequet (1986).

The MacWrite compression algorithm is described by Young (1985). PCTERM is presented in Auslander et al. (1985). The CCITT Facsimile standard is discussed by Hunter and Robinson (1980). The experiments on compressing netnews were performed by Jerry Aguirre of Olivetti. Netnews uses LZC, which is described in Section 8-3. The description of the ARC file archiving program is for version 5, for the IBM PC. ARC is available from System Enhancement Associates, 21 New Street, Wayne, NJ 07470. A similar archiver called PKARC is available from PKWARE, Inc., 7032 Ardara Avenue, Glendale, WI 53209.

Work on automatically abbreviating words is presented by Bourne and Ford (1961). The idea of reassigning character codes so that they are suitable for run-length coding was proposed by Lynch (1973). Differencing compression techniques are described by Gottlieb et al. (1975). Front compression is also mentioned by Robinson and Singer (1981). More specialized techniques for compressing lists of words have been designed for applications such as spelling checkers and database searching. An efficient (but irreversible) method for reducing the storage requirements of a spelling checker dictionary is given by Nix (1981). A method for saving main memory at the expense of disk storage for a list of database keys is described by Fraenkel and Mor (1983).

The MTF scheme was independently invented by Ryabko (1980), Horspool and Cormack (1983), Bentley et al. (1986) and Elias (1987). Each evaluates several variations on the basic idea. Bentley et al. give an elaborate data structure to maintain the list efficiently and give a detailed analysis of its speed performance, while Elias analyses the compression performance. The practical implementation and performance of MTF is discussed by Moffat (1987).

```
45h[0j45thwGw45hqU9d
poejrg[4wky]p435q)b&
[0wejg[04jy42yj3*k!d
p0w4j5g[235-k6t0=w~n
[0ewjg04jy04jy4j;qmy
omh][krty-jk46-[p"qb
p[jw435y      h[ps0%x
[psdhkj  8w3  5y9mwq
germhj-53k=  64k?ti
[ewjhj4wth   30o#r0b
e[wmb[p  65,.u;g4{@
65[];.9      0.o~x6
germhj-53k=ukj64:3xf
[ewjhj4wth56430o*wm<
e[wmb[preh65,.u;aYlD
+[3fgm56rt0-"-23jsg!
[;jyt%ERghj(0;';Hd4=
1U5terEDghp=][>?kyeW
```

INFORMATION
AND MODELS

In Chapter 1 we examined some ad hoc coding schemes that were intended to take advantage of regularities in text as perceived by their designers. But could the codes be improved? Should run-length coding use 4- or 8-bit integers? How many bits should MacWrite use to encode common characters? What is the optimal choice of codes? To answer these questions, we must turn to the field of information theory.

One of the fundamental ideas in information theory is that of *entropy*, which is a measure of the amount of order or redundancy in a message. Entropy is a number that is small when there is a lot of order and large when there is a lot of disorder. It is intimately related to data compression because the length of a message after it is encoded should ideally be equal to its entropy. However, entropy is a slippery measure, because it can only be evaluated relative to an estimate of the probabilities of different messages. Different estimates are provided by different *models*. There are a number of ways of constructing models, some of which will be described. Our everyday experience makes it reasonable that the entropy for a piece of text should be relative. For example, a Chinese reader looking at a piece of English text will see less order and regularity than a native English reader will, and vice versa.

Now, the entropy tells us exactly how long to make the encoded version of each *message*, but in practice it is very desirable to be able to construct the encoded message incrementally and transmit it incrementally. That is, as each character of the message is read a small part of the encoded message is constructed and immediately transmitted. It is possible to do this in a way that exactly simulates coding the message as a whole, but that is computationally very demanding. Accordingly, approximate models are constructed using the notion of *conditioning classes*. Combined with the probabilistic encoders of Chapter 5, these allow efficient incremental encoding.

2.1 MEASURING INFORMATION

Everyone knows how to measure information stored in a computer system. It comes in bits, bytes, kilobytes, megabytes, or gigabytes; only a certain amount will fit on your floppy disk; and you ignore warnings such as "disk space nearly full" or "memory overflow" at your peril. Information transmitted on communication links is quantified similarly; low-cost modems transmit data on telephone lines at 1200 bits/s; high-speed local area networks work at 10 Mbits/s. Aren't these commonplace notions all there is to measuring information?

No. The storage space occupied by a file is not a measure of the information itself, but only of the space required by a particular representation chosen for it. If it really did measure the file's intrinsic size, there would be no opportunity for data compression! We want our measure to be independent of representation details, for the whole idea of exact compression is to choose a representation that occupies less space but preserves all the information. Perhaps an alternative way of quantifying information might be in terms of semantic content. But this is fraught with contentious problems! How could we ever hope to agree on an objective metric for the semantic content of, say, a politician's speech or a book on text compression? Finding a way to quantify information is a tough nut to crack.

The solution is to accept that one cannot measure the information of a single message by itself. Information in its scientific, quantifiable, sense relates not to what you *do* say, but to what you *could* say. To select an "a" out of the set {a, b, c, ..., z} involves a choice that can be expressed as a certain amount of information—4.7 bits, to be precise. To select the word "a" out of the set {a, aardvark, aback, abacus, abaft, ..., zymotic, zymurgy} involves an entirely different amount of information—it is hard to quantify without a more precise specification of the set, but it is probably between 14 and 17 bits. To specify a graphic "a" out of all possible patterns that can be displayed on a 9×5 matrix of black-and-white pixels involves a binary choice for each pixel, or 45 bits of information.

According to this way of thinking, a large body of data may represent a small amount of information. To transmit or store, say, Tolkien's *Lord of the Rings* involves no information if it is known for certain beforehand that it is going to be transmitted or stored. To transmit either one of Tolstoy's *War and Peace* or Tolkien's *Lord of the Rings*, given that both are equally likely and nothing else is possible, requires just one bit of information.

Information is inextricably bound up with *choice*. The more choice, the more information is needed to specify the result of that choice.

2.1.1 Entropy

Suppose that there is a set of possible events with known probabilities $p_1, p_2, \ldots, p_n$ that sum to 1. The "entropy" of this set measures how much choice is involved, on average, in the selection of an event, or, equivalently, how uncertain we are of the outcome. In his pioneering work that marked the birth of information theory, Shannon postulated that the entropy $E(p_1, p_2, \ldots, p_n)$ should satisfy the following requirements:

- E is a continuous function of p_i.
- If each event is equally likely, E should be a steadily increasing function of n.
- If the choice is made in several successive stages, E should be the sum of the entropies of choices at each stage, weighted according to the probabilities of the stages.

The third condition appeals to an intuitive notion of what is meant by a multistage decision. As an example, one could create a two-stage procedure for deciding on one of the n possible events by choosing 1 or "the rest" with probabilities p_1 and $1-p_1$. If "the rest" were selected, it would be necessary to make a further choice of 2, 3, $\ldots$, or n, with probability distribution $p_2, p_3, \ldots, p_n$, appropriately renormalized. Call the entropies of these two choices $E_1 = E(p_1, 1-p_1)$ and $E_2 = E(p_2', p_3', \ldots, p_n')$, where the primes indicate renormalization. Then the condition simply states that $E = 1 \cdot E_1 + (1-p_1)E_2$. The weights 1 and $1-p_1$ are used because the first choice is made every time, while the second is made only with probability $1-p_1$.

As Shannon demonstrated, the only function that satisfies these requirements is

$$E(p_1, p_2, \ldots, p_n) = -k \sum_{i=1}^{n} p_i \log p_i, \tag{2-1a}$$

where the positive constant k governs the units in which entropy is measured. Normally, the units are "bits," where $k = 1$ and logs are taken with base 2:

$$E = -\sum_{i=1}^{n} p_i \log_2 p_i \text{ bits.} \tag{2-1b}$$

(Almost all logarithms in this book are base 2; we write "ln" on the rare occasions when natural logarithms are needed.) The minus sign merely reflects the desire for entropy to be a positive quantity, whereas being less than 1, probabilities always have negative logarithms.

The idea of the proof that Equation (2-1) fits the criteria for the entropy function is as follows. First, the operation of making a choice from $2n$ equally likely possibilities can be decomposed into making two choices, one with weight 1, from two equally likely alternatives, and another also with weight 1, from n equally likely possibilities. In other words,

$$E\left(\frac{1}{2n}, \frac{1}{2n}, \cdots, \frac{1}{2n}\right) = E\left(\frac{1}{2}, \frac{1}{2}\right) + E\left(\frac{1}{n}, \frac{1}{n}, \cdots, \frac{1}{n}\right).$$

Continuing in this way, the operation of making a choice from n equally likely possibilities, where n is a power of 2, is tantamount to making $\log n$ binary decisions:

$$E\left(\frac{1}{n}, \frac{1}{n}, \ \cdots \ , \frac{1}{n}\right) = E\left(\frac{1}{2}, \frac{1}{2}\right) \log n = -k \log \frac{1}{n}$$

where k is the information content of an equally weighted binary decision, $E(\frac{1}{2}, \frac{1}{2})$. Continuity arguments can be applied to extend this to the case of general n. Second, to analyze situations where the probabilities are not all equal, suppose that we have an n-way decision with $p_i = c_i/\Sigma c_j$, where the c_i are integers representing frequency counts. We know from the above that a choice from Σc_i equally likely possibilities involves an entropy of $k \log \Sigma c_i$. Such a choice can be broken down into a choice from n possibilities with probabilities $p_1, p_2, \ldots, p_n$, followed, once i is chosen, by a choice from c_i equally weighted possibilities. Consequently,

$$k \log \sum c_i = E(p_1, p_2, \ldots, p_n) + k \sum p_i \log c_i,$$

so

$$E(p_1, p_2, \ldots, p_n) = -k \left(\sum p_i \log c_i - \log \sum c_i\right)$$

$$= -k \left(\sum p_i \log c_i - \sum p_i \log \sum c_i\right)$$

$$= -k \sum p_i \log \frac{c_i}{\sum c_i}$$

$$= -k \sum p_i \log p_i,$$

which is Equation (2-1a).

2.1.2 Compression

Entropy is a measure of quantity of information. However, as defined above it applies only to a probability distribution, that is, a set of choices with probabilities summing to 1. We are often more interested in quantifying the information content of a particular choice, than in knowing the average over all possible choices. If the probability of a choice is p_i, its information content or entropy is defined as the negative logarithm of its probability, or

$$E_i = -\log p_i \text{ bits.}$$

This means that more likely messages, having greater probabilities, contain less "information." In other words, the more surprising the message, the more information it contains. For example, in our world the message "I walked to work today" will usually convey considerably less information than the message "I teleported to work today." In fact, a message that is certain to occur conveys no information (or surprise) at all, while an impossible message would contain an infinite amount.

Our definition of the information content of an individual event relates nicely to the definition of the entropy of a decision between events in Equation (2-1). Given an n-way decision between events whose individual probabilities and entropies are p_1, p_2, ... and E_1, E_2, ..., respectively, the average entropy of the individual decisions is

$$E = \sum_i p_i E_i.$$

Plugging in the formula above for the individual entropies E_i leads to

$$E = -\sum_i p_i \log p_i \text{ bits,}$$

which is the same as the overall entropy of the decision given by Equation (2-1). Thus we can say that the overall entropy is the average of the entropy of the individual decisions involved.

Before attempting text compression, we must first characterize the set of possible messages that might be transmitted. Often the messages being considered will be long and the probability of any particular message very low. Consequently, the entropy of that choice, being the negative logarithm of its probability, will be large. For example, consider a message of 1000 random "a"s and "b"s where both characters have a probability of 1/2 of occurring at each position in the message. The probability of a particular message is 2^{-1000}—a very small number indeed! What is the entropy of such a message according to the formula given above? The negative logarithm of the probability, using base 2, is 1000 bits. Of course, this is exactly what we would expect to be the information content of this particular message.

Having identified the set of potential messages, the idea of performing compression is to come up with a set of codes, one for each possible message. Each code is a unique string of symbols (usually bits), and a particular one of these strings will select one particular message from among all possibilities. There is no requirement to take entropies into account when generating codes. For example, you could take a particular message—even a very unlikely one—and decide to allocate it a very short code. In the extreme case, you might decide to code it as just one bit. This will have the effect of shortening the code for one very unlikely message, but it will be necessary to lengthen the codes for all other messages by about one bit in order that each message can be distinguished uniquely by its code alone.

While entropy need not be taken into account when assigning codes, it is nevertheless advisable to do so. Shannon's fundamental result, called the "noiseless source coding theorem," shows that the average number of binary symbols per source symbol can be made to approach the source entropy but no less. We will see in Chapter 5 how the technique of arithmetic coding provides a concrete demonstration of the positive part of the theorem by actually showing how to construct optimal codes. The proof of the negative part, that no code can do better (on average) than the entropy, is not difficult but is rather tedious and is given in Appendix 2A. It is worth emphasizing that it is only true *on average*—you can sometimes be lucky and beat the odds, but you cannot do so consistently. The entropy figure can be achieved by assigning a code that gives each message a representation that occupies $-\log p$ bits, p being its probability.

Such a choice makes the average value of the code lengths equal to $-\Sigma p_i \log p_i$, the same as the entropy of the ensemble of messages, and hence minimizes the average code length. So our rather abstract consideration of entropy in the preceding section has given us a very precise rule for how good we can expect compression to be.

2.2 MODELS

It is all very well to say that information is about what might have been said, stored, or transmitted, but it does raise the question of how to specify what might have been. The "..." is hardly ambiguous in the alphabet example {a, b, c, ..., z}, assuming that we are agreed on how to write English, and that it *is* English; and somewhat less so in the dictionary example {a, aardvark, aback, abacus, abaft, ..., zymotic, zymurgy}; but would be positively enigmatic were we to try to specify the set containing all English writing, from alphabets to *Lord of the Rings*—and beyond.

To specify might-have-beens more precisely, the notion of a "model" is needed. Then we can speak of the amount of information contained in a given message *with reference to the model*. At this point we take our leave of examples such as "all English writing," or even "Tolkien's writing," for there are no easy models of these sets. In fact, one main theme of this book is that successful text compression is tantamount to making models that capture the salient features of such sets. Such models will often be very large.

The fundamental role of a model is to supply probabilities for the messages. Usually, we do not calculate the probabilities in one go. Instead, the probability of the message is built up incrementally, starting at the beginning of the message and working through it symbol by symbol. As in our analysis of entropy above, we make our choice in many small bites rather than making one large choice. The probability of the message is computed by taking the probability of the first symbol and multiplying it by the probability of the second symbol, and so on. Multiplying the probabilities corresponds to adding the code lengths, or concatenating the codes.

2.2.1 Finite-Context Models

For illustrative purposes, we can only present explicitly models of much more prosaic sets than "all Tolkien's writing"—sets like "all possible strings formed from the letters {a, b, c, ..., z, •}." Notice that this set, like those generated by many models that will be encountered, is infinite, but countable.

The simplest model for such a set is one that allocates a fixed probability for a letter irrespective of its position in the message. In Chapter 4 we discuss ways of estimating such probabilities for natural language. One estimate for the probabilities of "t","h","e", and "•", made by analyzing a sample of English text, is 0.076, 0.042, 0.102, and 0.177, respectively. The probability of the entire message "the•" is then calculated as

$$0.076 \times 0.042 \times 0.102 \times 0.177 = 5.76 \times 10^{-5}.$$

From this probability we can calculate the optimum coding of the message "the•" to be 14.1 bits ($= -\log_2 5.76 \times 10^{-5}$) for this particular model. However, better models will produce better results.

A more sophisticated way of computing the probabilities of the symbols is to recognize that the probability of a symbol will differ depending on the character that precedes it. For example, the probability of a "u" following a "q" in the sample was 0.991, compared with 0.024 if the preceding character is ignored. Similarly, the probability of an "h" occurring is 0.307 if the last character was a "t", compared with 0.042 if the last character is not known. Using this information about preceding characters gives the following probability for "the•" :

$$0.076 \times 0.307 \times 0.479 \times 0.345 = 3.86 \times 10^{-3} = 2^{-8.02},$$

so "the•" can be coded in 8.02 bits using this more sophisticated model. In this example we do not know what character precedes "t", so its probability is estimated independently of the preceding character.

This type of model can be generalized to those where o preceding characters are used to determine the probability of the next character. This is referred to as an *order-o fixed-context model*. The first model we used above was an order-0 model, and the second an order-1 model. Models of up to order 11 have been used in some of the experiments reported later in the book. The model where every symbol is given an equal probability is sometimes referred to as an order –1 model, as it is even more primitive than the order-0 model. It is not very useful on its own, but does have some value when generalizing more complex techniques for computing probabilities.

It is tempting to think that very high order models should be used to obtain the best compression—after all, the order-1 model in the example above compressed the message "the•" to almost half the size of the order-0 model, and this trend should continue as the order increases. This is true to some extent. As an extreme example, consider an order-10,000 model. If 10,000 characters (a couple of pages of text) are provided, this context will be almost unique among all literature, and the next character could be predicted with great confidence. However, we can also see the problems that high-order models can create: We need to be able to estimate probabilities for any context, and the number of possible contexts increases exponentially with the order of the model. Thus large samples of text are needed to make the estimates, and large amounts of memory are needed to store them. Also, we have ignored the coding of the first 10,000 characters of the message!

2.2.2 Finite-state models

Not every type of dependency between symbols is best represented by a finite-context model. One natural example is the sequence of bases along a string of DNA. There are four possible bases (A, C, G, or T) at each base position. They occur in triplets, where each of the 64 possible combinations codes one of the 21 possible protein subunits or some signal such as "start" or "stop." The probability of one of the bases occurring is strongly influenced by its position within the triplet—first, second, or third. But the only way to find out the position is to count back to the start of the DNA sequence and decide at which position the cycle started. Knowing the previous base or even a number of previous bases does not help much in finding out what the current triplet alignment is. One way to solve this would be for the coder to carry along with it a count of the current position within a triplet and increment it each time a symbol is encountered.

A general kind of scheme that covers this type of model as well as the simpler fixed-context models is a *finite-state probabilistic model*. These are often called "Markov models" after the mathematician A. A. Markov (1856–1922), although we prefer the term "finite-state" because "Markov model" is sometimes used loosely to refer to finite-*context* models. Finite-state models are based on finite-state machines (FSMs). They have a set of states S_i, and a set of transition probabilities p_{ij} that give the probability that when the model is in state S_i it will next go to state S_j. Moreover, each transition is labeled with a character, and no two transitions out of a state have the same label. Thus any given message defines a path through the model that follows the sequence of characters in the message, and this path (if it exists) is unique. Also, a probability for any message can be computed by multiplying the probabilities out of each state.

Finite-state models are able to implement finite-context models. For example, an order-0 model of single-case English text has a single state with 27 transitions leading out of it and back to it: 26 for the letters and 1 for space. An order-1 model has 27 states (one for each character) with 27 transitions leading out from each. An order n model has 27^n states with 27 transitions leading out of each. Figures 2-1a and 2-1b

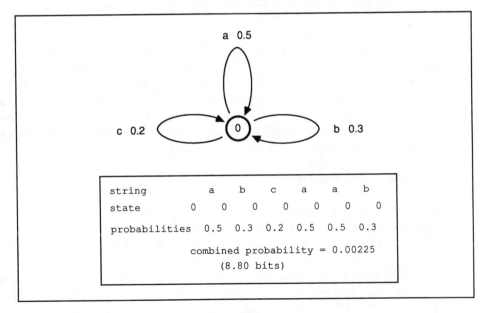

(a)

Figure 2-1   State diagrams for examples of finite-state models: (a) order 0.

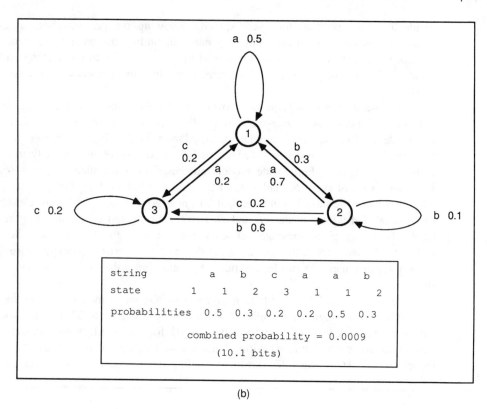

string   a   b   c   a   a   b

state   1   1   2   3   1   1   2

probabilities   0.5 0.3 0.2 0.2 0.5 0.3

combined probability = 0.0009

(10.1 bits)

(b)

Figure 2-1(cont)   State diagrams for examples of finite-state models: (b) order 1.

show order-0 and order-1 models for reduced alphabets using the letters {a,b,c}, together with a message and its probability. The transitions are represented by arrows and the states by circles. The simplest model for our DNA example has three states, one for each position within a triplet, and four transitions leading out from each state. Figure 2-2 shows a diagrammatic representation of such a model.

2.2.3 Grammar Models

Even the more sophisticated finite-state model is unable to capture some situations properly. Imagine a very simplified computer language (a little reminiscent of LISP) where the only symbols allowed are {a, (,),•}. All messages have balanced parentheses and are terminated with a "•", which can only occur at the end of a message. In some situations, partway through a message there may be symbols that cannot occur. For example, if parentheses are already balanced, another ")" cannot occur. Similarly, if parentheses are unbalanced, "•" cannot occur. The problem is that it is impossible to spot these situations just by looking at a finite number of preceding symbols. Figure 2-3a shows a finite-state model that partially captures the language. Unfortunately, it is limited to a finite nesting depth for parentheses of two, so a message such as "(((a)))" is

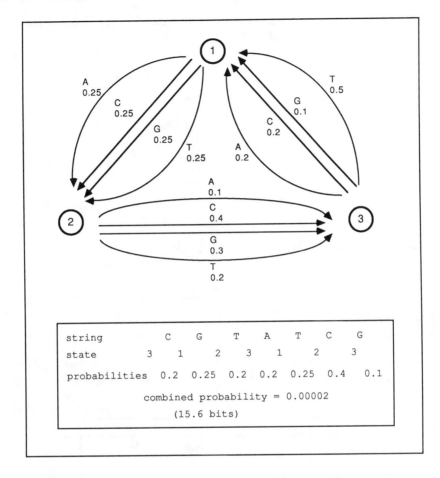

Figure 2-2   Finite-state model for DNA.

forbidden. In general $n+2$ states are necessary if depth n bracketing is to be handled correctly. So messages with arbitrary nesting of parentheses cannot be captured by any finite-state model.

A different type of model, which can accommodate all nesting depths, is a grammar with probabilities associated with each production. Figure 2-3b shows such a grammar. The message to be modeled is parsed according to the grammar and its probability computed by multiplying together the probability of each production used. This type of model has proved very successful when compressing text in a formal language, such as Pascal programs. However, it is of little value for natural language texts. It may also be noted that the very general formulation of the grammar prevents it from capturing certain effects that the finite-state model can deal with. For example, if the probability of an "a" varies with the depth of bracketing, the finite-state model can represent this down to its limit of nesting. In contrast, the grammar treats all nesting depths equally and is unable to vary the probabilities with depth unless new productions are

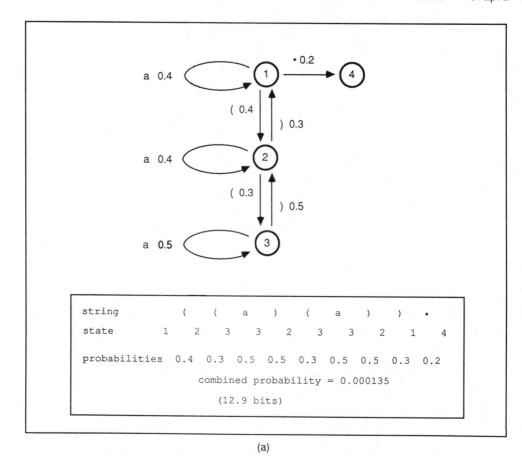

(a)

Figure 2-3   Models for "parenthesis language:" (a) Finite-state model.

introduced. Natural languages tend to have very limited nesting of grammatical constructs, so the more general formulation of a grammar is overkill.

A more pragmatic reason for preferring finite-state models to grammar models is that it is very difficult to find a grammar for natural language. Constructing one by hand would be tedious and unreliable, so ideally a grammar should be induced mechanically from samples of text. However, this is not feasible because induction of grammars requires exposure to examples that are *not* in the language being learned in order to decide what the boundaries of the language are. Some sort of heuristic approach could be used, but finite-state models are popular because they are easy to use, and appear to be sufficiently powerful to model natural language adequately.

2.2.4 Ergodic Models

The property of "ergodicity" is often mentioned in connection with probabilistic models. This means that as any sequence produced in accordance with the model grows

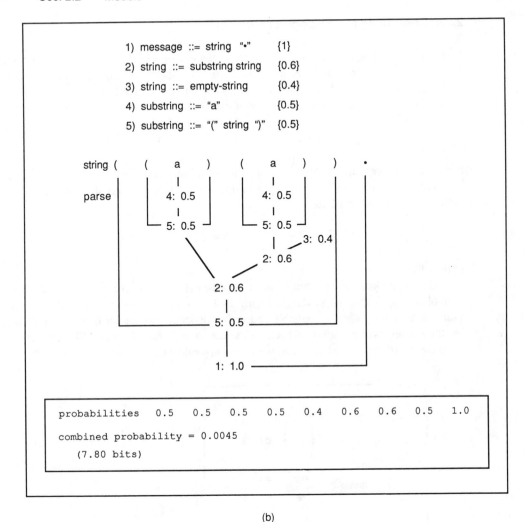

1) message ::= string "•"   {1}

2) string ::= substring string   {0.6}

3) string ::= empty-string   {0.4}

4) substring ::= "a"   {0.5}

5) substring ::= "(" string ")" {0.5}

string ((a   )   (a   )   )   •

parse | 4: 0.5   4: 0.5

         5: 0.5   5: 0.5

                                      3: 0.4

                              2: 0.6

               2: 0.6

               5: 0.5

               1: 1.0

probabilities   0.5   0.5   0.5   0.5   0.4   0.6   0.6   0.5   1.0

combined probability = 0.0045

   (7.80 bits)

(b)

Figure 2-3(cont)   Models for "parenthesis language:" (b) Probabilistic grammar.

longer and longer, it becomes entirely representative of the entire model. To get an intuitive feeling for the concept, consider a nonergodic system—a box holding dynamite. Some decisions conceal forever the consequences of choosing alternatives. The action of lighting a match, for example, will take the system into a state from which recovery of the original state is impossible! Consequently, a sequence that contains this action early will not become representative of the original system no matter how long it grows, because parts of the system are permanently inaccessible. In contrast, the models of Figure 2-1 are ergodic, because they contain no dead ends—from each state, every other can be reached. All state models normally used in connection with natural language are ergodic.

2.2.5 Computing the Entropy of a Model

Now we can at last consider the information content of actual messages. Suppose that we choose a 63-symbol message at random from the source of Figure 2-4a. There are six choices for each symbol, so 6^{63} messages are possible. Each has the same probability, namely 6^{-63}. The entropy of this set of messages is

$$-\sum_{i=1}^{6^{63}} 6^{-63} \log 6^{-63} = -\log 6^{-63} = 63 \log 6 = 162.9 \text{ bits.}$$

It would have been simpler to note that generating such a message involves 63 separate, independent, decisions. Every symbol of the message has six possibilities, each with probability 6^{-1}, so contributes

$$-\sum_{i=1}^{6} 6^{-1} \log 6^{-1} = \log 6 = 2.585 \text{ bits/symbol}$$

to the total.

The same kind of reasoning can be used to calculate the entropy of the set of 63-symbol messages that the model of Figure 2-4b generates. The set is exactly the same as in the previous case (all possible sequences of length 63 drawn from the alphabet), but the entropy will be different because the message probabilities are different. Again, since the decisions are independent, we need only calculate the entropy of each,

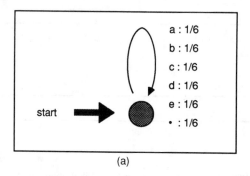

(a)

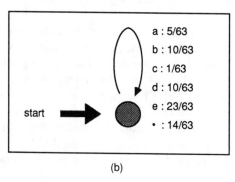

(b)

Figure 2-4   Models for an artificial six-symbol language: (a) equiprobable; (b) order 0.

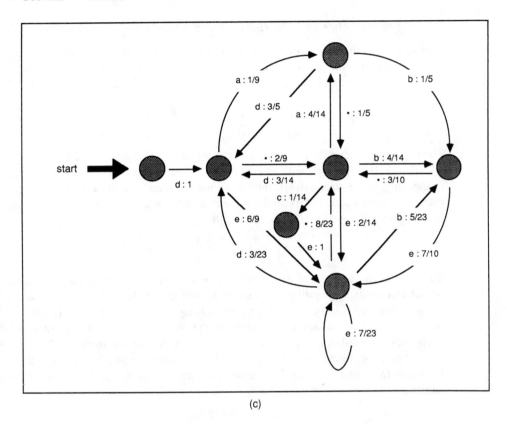

(c)

Figure 2-4(cont)   Models for an artificial six-symbol language: (c) order 1.

$$-\frac{5}{63}\log\frac{5}{63}-\frac{10}{63}\log\frac{10}{63}-\frac{1}{63}\log\frac{1}{63}-\frac{10}{63}\log\frac{10}{63}-\frac{23}{63}\log\frac{23}{63}-\frac{14}{63}\log\frac{14}{63}$$

$$=\frac{-(5\log 5+10\log 10+1\log 1+10\log 10+23\log 23+14\log 14-63\log 63\ )}{63}$$

$$= 2.241 \text{ bits/symbol,}$$

and multiply the result by 63 to get an entropy of 141.2 bits for a 63-symbol message from this source.

Usually, what we want to measure is not the entropy of the source itself, but the entropy of a particular message from the source. For example, from the model of Figure 2-4b a message comprising 63 consecutive "c"s is fairly unlikely, while one comprising 63 "e"s is much more likely. The probability of the former is $(1/63)^{63} = 2^{-376.6}$, while that of the latter is $(23/63)^{63} = 2^{-91.6}$. Recall that the entropy of a particular message i with respect to a source is defined as the log of its probability with respect to that source:

$$E_i = -\log p_i.$$

dab•ee•a•bebe•deed•deb•adee•adee•ee•deb•bebe•bebe•adee•bed•ceed

with respect to the source of Figure 2-4b. This is a very special string because it was used to construct the model—the probabilities in the model are exactly those in the string. Since it contains 5 "a"s, 10 "b"s, 1 "c", 10 "d"s, 23 "e"s, and 14 "•"s, its probability is

$$\left(\frac{5}{63}\right)^5 \cdot \left(\frac{10}{63}\right)^{10} \cdot \left(\frac{1}{63}\right)^1 \cdot \left(\frac{10}{63}\right)^{10} \cdot \left(\frac{23}{63}\right)^{23} \cdot \left(\frac{14}{63}\right)^{14}.$$

The log of this is exactly the entropy of the source—141.2 bits, or 2.241 bits/symbol.

To evaluate entropy with respect to the model of Figure 2-4c is considerably more challenging, since successive symbols are not independent. It is easy to compute the entropy of each state. For example, the one at the top has three arrows emanating from it, with probabilities 3/5, 1/5, 1/5; so its entropy is

$$-\frac{3}{5} \log \frac{3}{5} - \frac{1}{5} \log \frac{1}{5} - \frac{1}{5} \log \frac{1}{5} = 1.37 \text{ bits.}$$

To calculate the entropy of the model as a whole we need to find the state-occupancy probabilities—the probability, for each state, that the model will be in that state at any point. These obviously depend on the starting state, but for ergodic models they eventually tend to values independent of the start state. Call the asymptotic state-occupancy probabilities $s_1, s_2, ..., s_k$, where the states are numbered 1, 2, ..., k. Each state i has a transition probability t_{ij} to each other state j, where $t_{ij} = 0$ when there is no transition from i to j. Then the vector S of state-occupancy probabilities satisfies the equation

$$S = T'S;$$

in other words, S is an eigenvector of the transpose T' of the transition matrix T. Once the asymptotic state-occupancy probabilities are determined using standard matrix methods, the entropy of the model as a whole is the sum of the entropies of individual states weighted by their probabilities.

More often we just want to find the entropy of a particular message. This involves simply tracing it through the model and summing the entropies of the transitions encountered on the way. Unfortunately, the examples of 63 "c"s and 63 "e"s cannot be generated by the model of Figure 2-4c, so their entropy with respect to it is undefined (one might say that it is infinite, since their probability is zero). The entropy of the message above "dab•ee ..."—which was used to generate the probabilities in the model—is 101.3 bits (1.61 bits/symbol).

So far there has been no mention of how messages are terminated. We talked of the entropy of messages with a certain length, but there was no indication of how the model might be stopped when that length was reached. In many communication systems the length of messages is transmitted separately from their text. Then, as far as compression is concerned, it can just be assumed that each message has a certain, known, length and the termination problem can be ignored when calculating entropy. However, this does raise the question of how the lengths are transmitted and whether compression is concerned, it can just be assumed that each message has a certain, known, length and the termination problem can be ignored when calculating entropy. However, this does raise the question of how the lengths are transmitted and whether they could be compressed in any way.

It is more common to reserve a special symbol EOM (end of message), which is not used in the body of messages, to signal their end. Then most states of models will have a transition labeled with EOM. Some models, for example that of Figure 2-3a, may only permit messages to end in certain states, in which case only those will have EOM transitions.

Recall that models like those that have been described are suitable for supplying probabilities to a universal encoder, such as a Huffman or arithmetic coder. An arithmetic coder can code messages in the number of bits indicated by the entropy of the model being used, that is, in the minimum size possible for the model chosen. Huffman coding will achieve this only under special conditions. The attraction of this modeling/coding approach is that the task of compression is split into two phases that can be attacked independently. This is exactly what we intend to do, and we will continue with the theory of modeling on the assumption that text can be compressed to the size dictated by the entropy of the model used. Coding techniques are considered in Chapter 5.

2.2.6 Conditioning Classes

We have seen informally how to compute the entropy of messages with respect to models, but to construct actual encoders we need to introduce these ideas in a more formal and rigorous way. A good point to start is with the probabilities of the complete messages. Given these message probabilities, the theory of entropy dictates that each message should be assigned a compressed length of $-\log p$, where p is the probability of the message. Unfortunately, coding an entire message at once is not very practical. It requires that all of it be seen before the probability and the resultant code are computed, and such global probabilities are difficult to calculate. This has been done for a few very simple systems, under the title of *enumerative coding*, but the computational demands are high in anything other than these simple cases. A couple of examples of this are given in Appendix 2B.

The first step toward making it possible to perform the probability calculation is to break it into a series of steps, just as was done earlier when finding the correct form for the entropy equation and when calculating message entropies. First we need to arm ourselves with a little notation (all notation is summarized in the Glossary at the end of the book). Messages, or strings of symbols, are written as $\mathbf{x}$ or $\mathbf{y}$. To refer to some substring within the message, say symbols 2 to 12 of $\mathbf{x}$, we write $\mathbf{x}[2..12]$. A single symbol, say the twelfth symbol of $\mathbf{x}$, is written $\mathbf{x}[12]$. A probability is written using the letter "p" or some variant, say "p'", so the probability of the message $\mathbf{x}$ is written $p(\mathbf{x})$. The unique message which contains no symbols is written as Λ. It is easy to write down the name of this message, but it becomes enigmatic when we try to write it down itself!

One further notation is needed before we can proceed, and that is the probability that a string **y** is the prefix of any message. This is written p'(**y**), and can be computed by summing the probabilities of all strings of which **y** is a prefix. So, for example, p'(Λ) = 1, since Λ is a prefix of all possible messages and the sum of the probabilities of all possible messages is 1.

Thus armed, let us decompose the probability of the message **x** into parts as follows:

$$p(\mathbf{x}[1..n]) = \frac{p'(\mathbf{x}[1])}{p'(\Lambda)} \frac{p'(\mathbf{x}[1..2])}{p'(\mathbf{x}[1])} \frac{p'(\mathbf{x}[1..3])}{p'(\mathbf{x}[1..2])} \cdots \frac{p'(\mathbf{x}[1..n])}{p'(\mathbf{x}[1..n-1])} \frac{p(\mathbf{x}[1..n])}{p'(\mathbf{x}[1..n])}. \quad (2\text{-}2)$$

This is trivially correct as the successive terms cancel leaving only p(**x**[1..n]) and p'(Λ), which is equal to 1. The terms of interest here are the ratios

$$\frac{p'(\mathbf{x}[1..i+1])}{p'(\mathbf{x}[1..i])}.$$

These ratios are themselves probabilities. In fact, they are the probabilities that the symbol **x**[i+1] will follow the string **x**[1..i], and are more commonly written as *conditional probabilities*:

$$p(\mathbf{x}[i+1]\,|\,\mathbf{x}[1..i]) \equiv \frac{p'(\mathbf{x}[1..i+1])}{p'(\mathbf{x}[1..i])}. \quad (2\text{-}3)$$

Earlier, when reasoning about what the entropy function should be, the entropy of a particular probability was constructed by making a series of choices. Here again, the probability of the entire message is reduced to a sequence of choices, one for each symbol in the message.

One detail of Equation (2-2) that needs to be discussed is the rather curious final ratio p(**x**[1..n])/p'(**x**[1..n]). This is the probability that a string will be a message, divided by the probability that it will be the start of some message. If we assume that we can always tell unambiguously from the message itself when it has ended, this ratio will either be 1 (the last symbol of the message is **x**[n]) or 0 (the message is not yet complete at **x**[n]). In the literature this assumption is called the *unique prefix* property; that is, no message can be a prefix of another message. The most common way of ensuring that it holds is to use the special end of message (EOM) symbol, which only appears as the last symbol of a complete message. Another way is to have fixed-length messages, so that the ratio is always 1 for some particular value of n. A third way is to transmit the length of the message prior to the message itself. A fourth is to have all messages infinitely long, that is, to assume continuous transmission.

Equation (2-2) does not help at all unless the conditional probabilities are easier to calculate than the overall probability of the message. This is usually accomplished by approximating these conditional probabilities. The result is that the overall messages are not always compressed optimally, but it is much easier to do the calculations. Appendix 2B gives some examples of calculating exact message probabilities for some simple situations, and shows how difficult this can be.

A very general way of approximating the probability calculations is to ignore part of the message seen so far when computing conditional probabilities. For example, if p''(s | t u) is the conditional probability that s will follow the pair of symbols t and u (in that order) anywhere in a message, we might make the following approximation:

$$p(\mathbf{x}[i+1] \mid \mathbf{x}[1..i]) \approx p''(\mathbf{x}[i+1] \mid \mathbf{x}[i-1..i]).$$

This reduces the context required for the prediction of $\mathbf{x}[i+1]$ from the entire preceding message to the preceding two symbols only. A general way to make such approximations is to assign each possible context string to some *conditioning class*. In our example above there would be one conditioning class for each possible pair of symbols. The most general form of the approximation to exact message probabilities is then

$$p(\mathbf{x}[i+1]\mid\mathbf{x}[1..i]) \approx p''(\mathbf{x}[i+1]\mid U(\mathbf{x}[1..i])),$$

where $U(\mathbf{x}[1..i])$ is the conditioning class of the string $\mathbf{x}[1..i]$. In principle, any computable function can be used to calculate the conditioning classes. In practice, only a few possibilities are useful. The one used almost exclusively throughout this book is some finite number of symbols at the end of the string, as in the example above, where the last two symbols of the string were used.

Looking back to the example models presented informally at the beginning of this chapter, we can identify the conditioning classes and the function U used. In all finite-state models the conditioning class is given by the current state. To find the conditioning class of a particular string, you start at the beginning of the string with an initial state and step through each state in order. Of course, we are normally interested in incremental execution, and the current state is maintained as a variable and changed to the next state as each symbol is processed and coded. Finite-context models are a special case where the conditioning class can be determined from a few characters at the end of the current string. The only small problem here is the necessity to deal with the very start of the message when insufficient symbols have been seen to determine the current context. For example, with an order-4 model, at least four symbols must have been seen before the conditioning class is determined. Most messages are much longer than the order of the model, so some ad hoc solution is used, either assuming that the message is primed with some sequence of default characters or using an order-0 model at the start of the message.

For the parenthesis language with an indefinite amount of nesting, the conditioning class is the current production. For this to be well defined it must be possible to parse every prefix string unambiguously. For example, the grammar of Figure 2-3b unambiguously parses the "aaa" in "(aaa)" as a substring "a" followed by the string "aa", not as the string "aa" followed by the substring "a". So the prefix "(a" must be followed immediately by a string, and its conditioning class is the production "string." Methods have been found to ensure that a grammar is unambiguous and to identify the conditioning class in more complex grammars.

In summary, the process of encoding a message can be reduced to an incremental operation. Incremental conditional probabilities are calculated using some conditioning classes, and these are fed to an incremental universal encoder. The encoder then transmits an encoded bit stream to the receiver. The receiver decodes the message using the same conditioning classes and conditional probabilities as the encoder, finally emitting the reconstituted message. Figure 2-5 depicts this process. One point of interest is that the decoder must know the current conditioning class before decoding the next symbol. However, we have been very careful to let the conditioning class depend only on the preceding symbols which the decoder has already determined, so all is well.

The foundations have now been laid to examine the two components of the statistical approach to text compression: modeling and coding. Modeling deals with the construction of the type of models that we have analyzed in this chapter, and coding enables us to use the probabilities in a model to code a message. In Figure 2-5, the transmitter and receiver have identical modelers with identical input and output, but the encoding and decoding functions are inverses of each other.

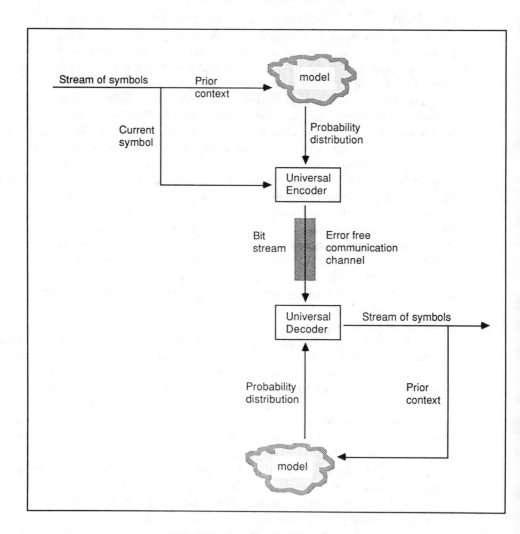

Figure 2-5   Incremental encoding of messages.

NOTES

The best introduction to information theory and the idea of entropy is still Shannon and Weaver (1949), which contains the original classic monograph by Shannon (1948) with a useful, less technical, introduction by Weaver. The use of grammars—principally for compressing Pascal programs—has been explored by Cameron (1986) and Katajainen et al. (1986). Cameron also shows how to ensure that the grammar is unambiguous and how to identify the conditioning classes. Angluin and Smith (1983) give a survey of techniques for inducing grammars from language samples. Conditioning classes are introduced by Rissanen and Langdon (1981). Exact probabilities were used for enumerative coding by Cover (1973), from which the examples of Appendix 2B are taken.

APPENDIX 2A   NOISELESS SOURCE CODING THEOREM

In Chapter 5 we will see how to code messages so that the average code length approaches the entropy. A sneaking suspicion may remain that we can do better; but it can be proved that this is not possible. This result was first established by Shannon (1948), in his "noiseless source coding theorem." The following inductive proof is different from Shannon's. Informally, the proof divides a set of codes into two classes according to whether the first bit is a "0" or a "1". By the inductive hypothesis both of these subsets (with the first bit removed) can be assumed to perform no better than the entropy. The inductive step shows that the combination of the two sets is also no better than the entropy.

Consider a set of messages with probabilities $p_i = c_i/C$, where C and the c_i are strictly positive integers representing frequency counts, and $C = \sum c_i$. The proof is by induction on C with the hypothesis that for any set of counts c_i the average code length, call it A_C, is bounded by the entropy:

$$A_C \geq -\sum \frac{c_i}{C} \log \frac{c_i}{C} = -\sum p_i \log p_i.$$

This is trivially true whenever there is just one message with $c_1 = C$. In particular it is true for all sets of counts when $C = 1$.

We assume that the hypothesis is true for some C, and then prove it for $C+1$. Given a set of codes for these new messages, they can be split into two classes depending on the value of the first bit of their respective codes: those where the first bit is 0 and those where the first bit is 1. The sums of the counts of the messages in these two classes will be two numbers:

$$C_0 = \sum_0 c_i \quad \text{and} \quad C_1 = \sum_1 c_i,$$

where $\sum_b$ indicates summation over codes where the first bit is b. By definition, $C_0 + C_1 = C+1$. Also, it is clearly not optimal to have either of C_0 or C_1 equal 0 (this amounts to adding a single wasted bit to the beginning of all messages). So we can bound the counts by $1 \leq C_0, C_1 \leq C$.

The average code length of all the messages is given by the weighted average of the code lengths for the two classes plus 1 (the initial bit). Assuming optimal codes for the two classes and using the induction hypothesis yields

$$A_{C+1} \geq 1 - \frac{C_0}{C+1} \sum_0 \frac{c_i}{C_0} \log \frac{c_i}{C_0} - \frac{C_1}{C+1} \sum_1 \frac{c_i}{C_1} \log \frac{c_i}{C_1}$$

$$= 1 - \sum_0 \frac{c_i}{C+1} \log \frac{c_i}{C_0} - \sum_1 \frac{c_i}{C+1} \log \frac{c_i}{C_1}$$

$$= 1 - \sum_0 \frac{c_i}{C+1} \log c_i - \sum_1 \frac{c_i}{C+1} \log c_i - \frac{C_0}{C+1} \log \frac{1}{C_0} - \frac{C_1}{C+1} \log \frac{1}{C_1}$$

$$= - \sum \frac{c_i}{C+1} \log \frac{c_i}{C+1} + 1 + \log \frac{1}{C+1} - \frac{C_0}{C+1} \log \frac{1}{C_0} - \frac{C_1}{C+1} \log \frac{1}{C_1}.$$

The first term is the entropy for the new class of messages, so to prove the bound it is sufficient to show that

$$0 \leq 1 + \log \frac{1}{C+1} - \frac{C_0}{C+1} \log \frac{1}{C_0} - \frac{C_1}{C+1} \log \frac{1}{C_1}$$

$$= 1 + \frac{C_0}{C+1} \log \frac{C_0}{C+1} + \frac{C_1}{C+1} \log \frac{C_1}{C+1}.$$

Letting $f = C_0/(C+1)$, so that $C_1/(C+1) = 1 - f$, this is equivalent to the inequality

$$0 \leq 1 + f \log f + (1-f) \log (1-f), \qquad 0 < f < 1.$$

By taking the derivative of this function, it can be shown that it has a single minimum in the range when $f = 1/2$. At this point the function evaluates to 0, thus proving the inequality.

APPENDIX 2B   EXAMPLES OF CALCULATING EXACT MESSAGE PROBABILITIES

In this appendix we give some examples of exact encoding probabilities taken from work on enumerative coding. The material in this appendix is used later only in Chapter 3, where adaptive and nonadaptive models are formally compared. The less mathematically inclined reader may wish to skip it.

In enumerative encoding the model is a finite set of messages that are assumed to be equiprobable. Define the function $N(\mathbf{y})$ to be the number of times $\mathbf{y}$ appears as a prefix in some message. The total number of messages is given by $N(\Lambda)$. Given this function, the probability that a string will be a prefix is given by $p'(\mathbf{y}) = N(\mathbf{y})/N(\Lambda)$. Using equation (2-3) and canceling the terms $N(\Lambda)$, the conditional probabilities can be written as

$$p(\mathbf{x}[i+1] \mid \mathbf{x}[1..i]) = \frac{N(\mathbf{x}[1..i+1])}{N(\mathbf{x}[1..i])}. \tag{2-4}$$

Example 1: Order-0 Weighted Model

Let the set of messages be strings taken from the alphabet $\{0,1\}$ with some specified number of "0"s and "1"s in the string. Let the number of "0"s be n^0 and the number of "1"s be n^1. The length of the messages will be $n = n^0 + n^1$. Define the function $c^0(\mathbf{y})$ to be the number of "0"s in the string $\mathbf{y}$ and $c^1(\mathbf{y})$ to be the number of "1"s. Given some message $\mathbf{x}$, the number of different ways the string $\mathbf{x}[1..i]$ can be a prefix is the number of ways of arranging the remaining "0"s and "1"s, giving the binomial expression

$$N(\mathbf{x}[1..i]) = \frac{(n-i)!}{c^0(\mathbf{x}[i+1..n])!\ c^1(\mathbf{x}[i+1..n])!}.$$

Using (2-4), canceling, and rearranging gives the conditional probabilities

$$p(w \mid \mathbf{x}[1..i]) = \frac{c^w(\mathbf{x}[i+1..n])}{n-i}. \tag{2-5}$$

That is, the probability that w will be the next symbol is the ratio of the number of times w will occur in the rest of the string divided by the total number of characters left in the string.

Example 2: Order-1 Weighted Model

Consider those messages $\mathbf{x}$ that have fixed values for the four counts $c^{00}(\mathbf{x})$, $c^{01}(\mathbf{x})$, $c^{10}(\mathbf{x})$, and $c^{11}(\mathbf{x})$, where, for example, $c^{00}(\mathbf{x})$ is the number of times the subsequence 00 occurs in $\mathbf{x}$. The set of possible messages comprises all strings $\mathbf{x}$ that satisfy the given set of counts.

When computing $N(\mathbf{x}[1..i])$ there will be two cases, depending on whether $\mathbf{x}[i]$ is 0 or 1. In each case the expression will depend on counts taken over the completion of the string: for example, $c^{00}(\mathbf{x}[i+1..n])$, which will be abbreviated by c^{00}. Consider first the case when $\mathbf{x}[i] = 0$. We must compute a combinatorial formula for the number of strings that can follow it. This can be done in two parts, as the arrangement of "0"s and "1"s are largely independent of one another. Consider a simple example where the rest of the string has three "0"s and four "1"s. Considering the distribution of "0"s only, the string can be viewed as an alternation of "0"s immediately following "1"s (written below as "a"s) and "0"s which immediately follow other "0"s (written as "b"s). Then the string can be rewritten as

$\mathbf{x}[i]$							$\mathbf{x}[n]$
0	1	1	0	0	1	1	0
			a	b			a

So the total number of ways of rearranging the "0"s is the number of ways of rearranging 2 "a"s and one "b" ($3!/(2!\ 1!)$). Similarly, the "1"s can be rewritten as

$$
\begin{array}{c|ccccccc}
\mathbf{x}[i] & & & & & & & \mathbf{x}[n] \\
0 & 1 & 1 & 0 & 0 & 1 & 1 & 0 \\
 & a & b & & & a & b &
\end{array}
$$

In this case the rewritten string must start with an "a" (a "0"-to-"1" transition), as the symbol preceding the string is a "0". So the number of ways of rearranging the "1"s is the number of ways of rearranging one "a" and two "b"s, not two "a"s as a naive analysis might suggest.

In the general case the total number of "0"s is given by the sum $c^{10} + c^{00}$ and the total number of "1"s is given by the sum $c^{11} + c^{01}$. Reasoning as above, the total number of strings following $\mathbf{x}[1..i]$ is given by

$$
N(\mathbf{x}[1..i-1]\,0) = \frac{(c^{10}+c^{00})!}{c^{10}!\,c^{00}!} \frac{(c^{11}+c^{01}-1)!}{c^{11}!\,(c^{01}-1)!}
$$

and

$$
N(\mathbf{x}[1..i-1]\,1) = \frac{(c^{10}+c^{00}-1)!}{(c^{10}-1)!\,c^{00}!} \frac{(c^{11}+c^{01})!}{c^{11}!\,c^{01}!}.
$$

Using Equation (2-4), it is not difficult to show that the conditional probabilities $p(w \mid \mathbf{x}[1..i])$ depend only on w and $\mathbf{x}[i]$. There are two cases, one where the next symbol is equal to $\mathbf{x}[i]$ and the other where it is not ($\mathbf{x}[i] = \overline{w}$). This allows the probabilities to be expressed compactly for the general case where $i \geq 1$ as

$$
p(w \mid \cdots w) = \frac{c^{ww}}{c^{ww} + c^{\overline{w}w}}, \tag{2-6a}
$$

$$
p(\overline{w} \mid \cdots w) = \begin{cases} \dfrac{c^{ww}}{c^{ww} + c^{\overline{w}w}}, & c^{ww} > 0 \\[2mm] 1, & c^{ww} = 0, \end{cases} \tag{2-6b}
$$

where $w = 0$ or 1 and $\overline{w} = 1$ or 0, respectively. In the special case for the first symbol of the sequence, $N(\Lambda) = N(0) + N(1)$, and taken with (2-4), this gives

$$
p(w \mid \Lambda) = \frac{c^{w\overline{w}}(c^{ww} + c^{\overline{w}w})}{c^{w\overline{w}}(c^{ww} + c^{\overline{w}w}) + c^{\overline{w}\overline{w}}(c^{\overline{w}\,\overline{w}} + c^{w\overline{w}})}. \tag{2-6c}
$$

The complexity of these expressions compared with those of Example 1 portends a rapid increase in complexity when higher-order models are used. Note also that these formulas do not satisfy the naive interpretation that the probability of w is the number of times w follows the symbol $\mathbf{x}[i]$ in the rest of the message, divided by the number of times $\mathbf{x}[i]$ occurs in the rest of the message. Such an interpretation holds only for the very simple order-0 model discussed above. The exact probabilities are an improvement on the simpler interpretation because they exploit knowledge about the data more fully. However, the exact approach is computationally demanding, and it is more practical to approximate probabilities.

Table 2-1 gives an example of the computation of exact and approximate conditional probabilities. The first example uses the model of all messages containing three

"0"s and four "1"s. The exact enumerative probabilities are taken from Equation (2-5), and for the order-0 finite-state model the frequency of "0"s and "1"s is used. The exact probabilities generate only 5.13 bits, compared with 6.90 bits for the approximate ones. The second part uses the order-1 weighted model; that is, the model is the set of all strings where the sequence 00 occurs once, 01 twice, 10 once, and 11 twice. There are 12 such possible messages. The conditional probabilities for the exact enumeration are taken from Equation (2-6). The order-1 finite-state model has two states, one for each possible preceding symbol. For example, the probabilities are obtained by counting the number of times a "1" follows a "0". For the initial character, the order-0 frequency of "0"s and "1"s was used. Note that these approximate probabilities differ significantly from the exact values and result in a compressed message of 6.73 bits as opposed to 3.58.

TABLE 2-1 EXAMPLE OF ENUMERATIVE PROBABILITIES AND FINITE-CONTEXT MODEL APPROXIMATIONS

	$i =$	1	2	3	4	5	6	7	Message probability	Bits
	$x[i] =$	**0**	**1**	**1**	**0**	**0**	**1**	**1**		
Order-0 enumeration [Eq. (2-5)]		$\frac{3}{7}$	$\frac{2}{3}$	$\frac{3}{5}$	$\frac{1}{2}$	$\frac{1}{3}$	1	1	$\frac{1}{35}$	5.13
Order-0 Markov model		$\frac{3}{7}$	$\frac{4}{7}$	$\frac{4}{7}$	$\frac{3}{7}$	$\frac{3}{7}$	$\frac{4}{7}$	$\frac{4}{7}$	$\frac{6912}{823543}$	6.90
Order-1 enumeration [Eq. (2-6)]		$\frac{1}{2}$	$\frac{1}{2}$	$\frac{2}{3}$	$\frac{1}{2}$	1	1	1	$\frac{1}{12}$	3.58
Order-1 Markov model		$\frac{3}{7}$	$\frac{2}{3}$	$\frac{2}{3}$	$\frac{1}{3}$	$\frac{1}{3}$	$\frac{2}{3}$	$\frac{2}{3}$	$\frac{16}{1701}$	6.73

ADAPTIVE
MODELS

An adaptive model is one that changes or adapts as a message is encoded so that it better suits that message. In Chapter 1 the idea of adaptation was introduced by having the Admiralty's encoders keep a book of commonly used words and assign a single code to each word when it was transmitted for the second time. It is slightly magical that such a scheme can work and that the sender and receiver both have the same idea of what the current model is. However, the strategy can be carried off successfully by having the sender adapt the model only after a symbol has just been encoded and the receiver only after it has just been decoded.

For example, here is one way that an adaptive order-0 model might be implemented for an input alphabet containing 27 characters. An array of 27 counts is maintained by both encoder and decoder, with each count initially set to one. From these counts each character is assigned an estimated probability of 1/27. Both encoder and decoder can independently construct identical codes from these estimates, since they are using identical models. The encoder uses these codes to transmit the first character, and then adds one to the count for that character, changing its estimated probability to 2/28. Meanwhile, the decoder determines the character from the code received, outputs it, and adds one to its count so that its estimated probability is 2/28 in the decoder's model also. Coding continues in this manner, with the estimated probabilities adapting to the type of text being compressed, yet the encoding and decoding models remain identical with no transmission overhead. In practice, more sophisticated models containing many conditioning classes are used, but these can still be updated adaptively in the same, implicit, way.

In terms of the more formal development of probabilistic models there are two things that can be adapted: the probabilities associated with a particular conditioning class and the set of conditioning classes themselves. These are sometimes referred to as the *statistics unit* (or *parameters)* and *structure*, respectively. Data compression techniques use simple structures, and updating these structures presents little difficulty. On the other hand, updating the parameters (probabilities) looks at first sight to be trivial, whereas in fact it presents two knotty problems.

The most obvious way of estimating the probability of symbols in a conditioning class is to count the number of times each symbol has occurred in that class. For example, if a conditioning class has occurred 10 times and an "a" 5 times in that class, the probability of an "a" is estimated as 0.5. A very natural way to do this in an adaptive model is to count the number of occurrences over the text encoded so far. Each time a conditioning class occurs, its total count is incremented, as well as the count for the symbol that occurred—which must be one of the symbols in the context of that conditioning class. Unfortunately, this simple and obvious technique is wrong. It does not allow for symbols that have never occurred, which should by rights be assigned a zero probability. A symbol with probability 0 will be assigned a code of length $-\log 0$, which is infinite! A suitable fix would seem to be to assign some small probability to each unseen symbol and adjust the other probabilities accordingly. Unfortunately, there is no one way of computing what this small probability should be. This is called the *zero-frequency problem* and is considered in some detail a little later.

A related problem is that of collecting accurate statistics for each of the conditioning classes. There are two opposing tendencies here: First, the counts involved in estimating probabilities should be as large as possible so that statistical errors are minimized; second, there should be many different conditioning classes so that the probabilities will accurately reflect the current context. Consider, for example, an order-5 finite context model of text. It could have $27^5 \approx 14 \times 10^6$ conditioning classes. Until at least 14 million characters have been seen there will be contexts that have never occurred at all. This problem is referred to as the *best match problem*. Discussion of various solutions is deferred until the later chapters, which detail different adaptive models.

Despite these problems there are a great many advantages to adaptive models. In their simplest form they are started with no statistical information and one conditioning class. Thereafter the entire model is built up from this initial *tabula rasa*. This means that there is no need to spend time and effort to ensure that the sender and receiver have the same initial model, nor to ensure that they have an appropriate model for whatever text is to be encoded. This greatly simplifies the management of the compression scheme. A second advantage is that an adaptive model can deal well with a much larger class of texts than can a static model, which is defined before the text has even been seen. For example, we would expect an adaptive model to do equally well on different languages, such as English and French as well as Pascal and BASIC. A static model of English is not likely to do well on the other languages, no matter how carefully its probabilities have been estimated. The flexibility and robustness of adaptive models is particularly important in applications such as disk channels or adaptive modems, where it is very difficult to tell ahead of time what is likely to be transmitted.

These intuitive ideas are formalized later in a number of theorems which show that an adaptive model can perform only a little worse than the best possible static model (one whose statistics are derived from the text itself). The converse is not true—an adaptive model may perform much better than a static model if the text is different from what the static model is expecting. A corollary of these results is that an adaptive model can at worst cause a very small expansion of the original text, whereas a static model might cause a very large expansion if the text being compressed has just the wrong statistical properties. This robustness in the face of unexpected data is one of the most compelling arguments for using adaptive models.

As well as all these attractive properties, the bottom line is that the various adaptive techniques explained in this book achieve very good compression. The best published figures for compression of text of many kinds are all from adaptive algorithms. In this chapter we look first at the zero-frequency problem and then perform a theoretical comparison of adaptive and nonadaptive codes.

3.1 ZERO-FREQUENCY PROBLEM

The zero-frequency problem has its roots in a philosophical dispute going back at least as far as Kant and his *Critique of Pure Reason*. The practical import of the problem for us is that every time a symbol is encoded, all symbols which can possibly occur at that point must be predicted with a probability greater than zero. Even symbols that have never occurred before need to be assigned a small, but nonzero probability. The difficulty is that there appears to be no rational or best way to estimate what this small probability should be, and apparently reasonable assumptions about how to do it lead to paradoxes, as we see below.

The dilemma is seen in starkest form when we have no information at all about what will happen. An apparently reasonable principle is that each of a number of equally unknown alternatives should be allocated the same probability. This principle has been assumed in many guises by proponents of various theories of probability estimation. However, as early as 1878, C. S. Pierce pointed out that it leads to a paradox. To see this, let us accept the principle for the moment and perform a simple thought experiment.

We are given an urn which we are told contains 1000 balls of different colors, but have no information about the numbers of each color. A colleague will draw a ball from the urn and without showing it to us will tell us whether or not it is black. This experiment has two possible outcomes, and we have no knowledge about their probabilities. According to our principle, we should assign a probability of 1/2 to each outcome. Now consider a second experiment. Our colleague will now tell us whether each ball is black, white, or neither of those colors. The experiment now has three possible outcomes, which according to our principle should be given equal probabilities of 1/3. But this gives a contradiction, as our first estimate for the probability of a black ball is 1/2 and our second is 1/3.

Another example a little closer to the topic of text compression will emphasize this point. The modern English alphabet has 26 letters, so without any knowledge of actual English text each letter should be assigned the probability 1/26. However, before the introduction of printing by Gutenberg and the German printers, the English alphabet included another letter, "thorn," written "þ", which is rendered in modern type by the pair "th". Because þ did not occur in the German alphabet of the time, it slipped out of usage. So in this old English alphabet each letter and þ should be given the probability 1/27, whereas in the modern scheme the probability is 1/26 for the letters and 1/676 for "th". Thus the probability estimates depend on the arbitrary choice of the initial alphabet.

As we can see from the paradoxes noted above, the way that a problem is stated influences the estimates of the probabilities. Another way of saying this is that any assignment of probabilities is consistent with the laws of probability, and if we are to make an estimate, we must draw on some knowledge of the problem itself. For example, thermodynamics (which can be derived from statistical principles applied to large numbers of particles) makes the assumption that if you know nothing about a moving particle, each possible direction of travel is equally likely. This is unjustifiable using only the laws of probability, but is a good physical principle rooted strongly in our observation of how space behaves. It may also be that we can draw on a theoretical principle for assuming that symbols in an alphabet are equiprobable on the grounds that no reasonable alphabet will be constructed which includes letters that hardly ever occur (although one wonders what should be made of peculiar mathematical symbols such as ∂).

In experiments that we have done on coding many different types of messages, a number of alternative methods for estimating zero-frequency probabilities have been used. As might be expected, different techniques work better on some messages and not so well on others. It is possible to select robust methods that work reasonably well on most examples encountered in practice, but this is their only justification. There is no best way of estimating these probabilities.

The following two methods are suitable and will be used later in the comparison of adaptive and nonadaptive models. We assume that the probability of a symbol is estimated to be its relative frequency of occurrence in some sample; that is, the number of times it occurs in the sample is counted and divided by the size of the sample. Zero probabilities will arise for characters with a zero count. Adaptive code A adds 1 to the size of the sample, and divides this extra count evenly between characters that have not yet occurred. Adaptive code B adds 1 to the count of every character, so none can have a frequency of zero.

For example, consider the alphabet {a,b,c,d} and the sample "bccccbbb". The frequency counts for "a", "b", "c", and "d" are 0, 4, 5, and 0, respectively. Method A adds one to the size of the sample, estimating probabilities for "b" and "c" of 4/10 and 5/10, instead of 4/9 and 5/9. It then divides the remaining 1/10 evenly between the symbols "a" and "d", yielding estimated probabilities of 1/20, 4/10, 5/10, and 1/20. Method B adds one to all four counts to get 1, 5, 6, and 1, yielding estimated probabilities of 1/13, 5/13, 6/13, and 1/13, respectively.

3.2 COMPARISON OF ADAPTIVE AND NONADAPTIVE MODELS

There is a lingering doubt that raises itself about adaptive models—that the process of adaptation itself might cause loss of data compression. It is not possible to make a completely general statement such as "adaptive models will always be better than non-adaptive models," for the simple reason that one might be lucky with a static model and transmit only messages that are perfectly suited to it. However, there is a large range of circumstances where it can be proven that there is an adaptive model which will be only slightly worse than *any* static model. Conversely, it can be shown that a static model can be arbitrarily worse than adaptive models. Most is known about the case when the conditioning classes are held constant and only the conditional probabilities are varied. These results can then be used to relate static models to variable conditioning class models.

The first result we establish is that adaptive models can be only a little worse than the best nonadaptive models. To be more precise,

- Given a set of conditioning classes with K members, an alphabet with q symbols, and a message of length n, there are adaptive models that will take at most $Kq \log n$ bits more than the best possible nonadaptive model.

The difference of $Kq \log n$ is particularly significant because it is approximately the number of bits needed to represent a model of the message. This means that in semi-adaptive modeling, where the model must be sent with the message, approximately the same number of bits will be used as for a fully adaptive model.

A corollary to this result establishes that adaptive models are robust. That is, at worst an adaptive model can expand the original string only slightly:

- There is an adaptive model where the compressed string will be at most $(q+1)/2 \log n$ bits longer than the original string.

Conversely, it is possible to show that for any message there is a static model that can *arbitrarily* expand it, and by the corollary above it will be arbitrarily worse than a good adaptive code. Also, given a static model, there is a message where an adaptive code will do asymptotically better than the static model.

Another way of stating these results is that in the limit the difference in the per symbol entropy for the best static model and adaptive models will differ by a term of order $(\log n)/n$. This approaches zero in the limit of large n. In the case where the set of conditioning classes is being varied as well as the probability estimates, care is needed to ensure that adaptive models will converge in the limit.

The results are particularly strong, as very few assumptions are needed to prove them. Except for one asymptotic argument which assumes stationarity and ergodicity, no assumptions are made about the nature of the source generating a message. Similarly, at one point it is necessary to make the weak assumption that the conditioning function is a finite state machine; otherwise, any set of conditioning classes is allowed.

The remainder of this chapter is somewhat formal and the less mathematically inclined reader may want to skip it and be content with the informal discussion above.

3.2.1 Approximations to Enumerative Codes

To start our theoretical analysis, we return to the enumerative codes, of which we gave some examples in Appendix 2B. These are a touchstone, as they are optimal under the assumption that all allowed messages are equiprobable. Also, they are theoretically tractable and will allow us to connect conveniently with other, more realistic, codes. What we will do is consider some approximations to exact enumeration and then bound the difference between the performance of the exact enumeration and the approximations. The first algorithm to be examined is approximate enumeration. As well as being theoretically tractable, it can be implemented efficiently, unlike exact enumeration.

To start, we need a little more notation. Let the set $Z = \{0, 1 \ldots, K-1\}$ denote K conditioning classes. We will use the symbol z to represent one of these classes. The counting functions $c^0(\mathbf{x})$ and $c^1(\mathbf{x})$ played an important role in the analysis in Appendix 2B of an order-0 weighted model, as did $c^{00}(\mathbf{x})$, $c^{01}(\mathbf{x})$, $c^{10}(\mathbf{x})$, and $c^{11}(\mathbf{x})$ in the order-1 case. These can be generalized to $c^{zw}(\mathbf{x})$, which counts the number of times the symbol w follows a prefix with conditioning class z in the string $\mathbf{x}$. It will be useful to define $c^z(\mathbf{x})$ as the total number of times any symbol follows the conditioning class z in $\mathbf{x}$, that is,

$$c^z(\mathbf{x}) \equiv \sum_{w \in A} c^{zw}(\mathbf{x}).$$

Because no transition follows the last conditioning class in the message, this total may be 1 less than the number of times that z occurs in $\mathbf{x}$.

Now consider a generalized enumerative coding problem. Assume that both sender and receiver know the following about the string $\mathbf{x}$ which will be transmitted:

- Its alphabet, A.
- A conditioning function U that maps strings into conditioning classes; and its associated set of conditioning classes Z.
- The set of counts $c^{zw}(\mathbf{x})$, for all $z \in Z$, $w \in A$.
- The set of messages to be enumerated consists of all strings $\mathbf{x}$ over A that satisfy the given set of counts.
- All messages are equiprobable.

The earlier enumerative codes correspond to an ideal situation where the statistics for the message are known beforehand, so no static model can do better than they. In realistic situations it is most unlikely that a static model will be the correct one for a message, so static models can be expected to do considerably worse in practice. The following results show that the adaptive codes fare better: At worst they are only slightly inferior to the ideal enumerative code.

Recall from Appendix 2B that the enumeration function N can be used to compute exact conditional probabilities:

$$p(\mathbf{x}[i+1] \mid \mathbf{x}[1..i]) = \frac{N(\mathbf{x}[1..i+1])}{N(\mathbf{x}[1..i])}. \tag{3-1}$$

A subtle difference between the generalized problem and the examples of exact message probabilities given earlier (e.g., in Table 2-1) is that $U(\Lambda)$ is defined, that is, the first symbol of the string is predicted within the context of some conditioning class. As a result of this, the counts and the total number of possible strings will be slightly different from the earlier examples. For example, given the string $\mathbf{x} = 0110011$ and defining $U(\Lambda) = 0$, the counts based on the conditioning classes 0 and 1 will be $c^{00}(\mathbf{x}) = c^{01}(\mathbf{x}) = c^{11}(\mathbf{x}) = 2$, $c^{10}(\mathbf{x}) = 1$. In this example, $c^{01}(\mathbf{x}) = 2$ because 01 occurs twice in the string. $c^{00}(\mathbf{x})$ could be 1 since 00 only occurs once, except for the fact that defining $U(\Lambda) = 0$ gives the initial 0 a conditioning class of 0. To minimize the complexity of the notation in what follows, we will omit reference to the message $\mathbf{x}$ whenever reasonable. For example, the expression $c^{zw}(\mathbf{x}[i+1..n])$ will be written as $c^{zw}[i+1..n]$ and $c^{zw}(\mathbf{x})$ as c^{zw}.

Approximate Enumeration.   For a given string $\mathbf{x}$ and conditioning class z we can observe the order of occurrence of each of the c^z symbols that follow z. Conversely, if the ordering of symbols for each conditioning class is known, a unique $\mathbf{x}$ can be reconstructed. (Start with $z = U(\Lambda)$ and make $\mathbf{x}[1]$ the first symbol for z; then continue with $z = U(\mathbf{x}[1])$ and its first symbol; and so on until all of $\mathbf{x}[1..n]$ is built up.) The product of the number of possible orderings for each conditioning class gives an enumeration of all possible strings $\mathbf{x}$. An example below shows that this enumeration is only approximate, because some possible sets of orderings correspond to no valid message.

The number of ways of ordering the symbols that have been counted in the class z is calculated as follows. Each symbol w occurs c^{zw} times, and the number of places that these occurrences can be distributed among is equal to the total number of symbols that have been observed in the class, that is, c^z. The number of ways of doing this is given by the multinomial

$$\frac{c^z!}{\prod_{w \in A} c^{zw}!}.$$

The product over all conditioning classes gives the generalized approximate enumeration:

$$N^\sim[1..i] = \prod_{z \in Z} \frac{c^z[i+1..n]!}{\prod_{w \in A} c^{zw}[i+1..n]!}. \tag{3-2}$$

The superscript $^\sim$ is used to indicate that the enumeration is approximate. The corresponding conditional probabilities can be found from Equation (3-1) to be

$$p^{\sim}(w \mid \mathbf{x}[1..i]) = \frac{c^{zw}[i+1..n]}{c^{z}[i+1..n]}, \tag{3-3}$$

where $z = U(\mathbf{x}[1..i])$.

An example will now be used to show that this enumeration is not exact. Consider an order-1 model that has as parameters the four counts $c^{00}(\mathbf{x}) = c^{01}(\mathbf{x}) = c^{11}(\mathbf{x}) = 2$, $c^{10}(\mathbf{x}) = 1$, two conditioning classes 0 and 1, and $U(\Lambda) = 0$. The message of Table 3-1, 0110011, fits this model and has the ordering 0, 1, 0, 1 for conditioning class 0, and the ordering 1, 0, 1 for conditioning class 1. Alternatively, consider the ordering 0, 1, 1, 0 for conditioning class 0, and the ordering 0, 1, 1 for conditioning class 1. This generates the initial substring 010111, which cannot be completed because all transitions from 1 to 0 have been exhausted, yet a 00 transition remains. Thus an enumeration based on counting all possible orderings of transitions will always *over count* the number of possibilities. It can still be used for coding messages because all messages are included uniquely in the count. There will, however, be some loss of coding efficiency. Bounds on this loss are computed below.

Fixed-Frequency Model.   Fixed-frequency models are sometimes used in practical coding applications. They assume that the frequencies of symbols are constant and can thus be estimated from counts over the entire string. This notion of using fixed

TABLE 3-1   EXAMPLE OF ORDER-1 EXACT, APPROXIMATE, AND FIXED-FREQUENCY ENUMERATION

	$i =$	1	2	3	4	5	6	7		
	$\mathbf{x}[i] =$	**0**	**1**	**1**	**0**	**0**	**1**	**1**		
$c^{0}[i..n]$		4	3	2	2	2	1	0		
$c^{1}[i..n]$		3	3	3	2	1	1	1		
$c^{00}[i..n]$		2	1	1	1	1	0	0		
$c^{01}[i..n]$		2	2	1	1	1	1	0		
$c^{10}[i..n]$		1	1	1	1	0	0	0		
$c^{11}[i..n]$		2	2	2	1	1	1	1		
									Message probability	Bits
Exact [Eq. (2-6)]		$\frac{1}{2}$	$\frac{1}{2}$	$\frac{2}{3}$	$\frac{1}{2}$	1	1	1	$\frac{1}{12}$	3.58
Approximate [Eq. (3-3)]		$\frac{2}{4}$	$\frac{2}{3}$	$\frac{2}{3}$	$\frac{1}{2}$	$\frac{1}{2}$	1	1	$\frac{1}{18}$	4.17
Fixed frequency [Eq. (3-4)]		$\frac{2}{4}$	$\frac{2}{4}$	$\frac{2}{3}$	$\frac{1}{3}$	$\frac{2}{4}$	$\frac{2}{4}$	$\frac{2}{3}$	$\frac{1}{108}$	6.75

$U(\mathbf{x}[1..i]) = \mathbf{x}[i]$, $U(\Lambda) = 0$

frequencies can be generalized to any conditioning classes and gives the following formula for the conditional probabilities:

$$p^F(w \mid \mathbf{x}[1..i]) = \frac{c^{zw}}{c^z},$$ (3-4)

where $z = U(\mathbf{x}[1..i])$ and the superscript F is used to indicate fixed-frequency encoding. It can be seen to be an approximation to exact enumeration by computing an enumeration function N^F from these probabilities using (3-1):

$$N^F[1..i] = \prod_{z \in Z} \frac{(c^z)^{c^z[i+1..n]}}{\prod_{w \in A} (c^{zw})^{c^{zw}[i+1..n]}}.$$ (3-5)

Table 3-1 shows an example that includes exact enumeration, approximate enumeration, and a fixed-frequency model. The conditioning function for each of them has order 1, and it is also assumed that $U(\Lambda) = 0$. The table shows the counts of the tail of the message and the probabilities computed at each step, and the final code lengths. The example agrees with our theoretical result below that exact enumeration is always better than approximate enumeration, which is always better than fixed-frequency models. Although the same message is used, the results in Table 3-1 are slightly different from those in Table 2-1 because of the assumption that $U(\Lambda) = 0$. This is the same as assuming there is a 0 prefix to the left of the string, and means that only Equations (2-6a) and (2-6b) need be used for exact enumeration, without the special initial case of (2-6c).

Analytic Comparison.   To complete this section, bounds are derived on the relative efficiencies of the three codes introduced so far. We will show that exact enumeration is better than approximate enumeration, which is better than fixed-frequency enumeration. Bounds are also given on how much worse than exact enumeration the other two codes are. In the limit as the message becomes longer, these bounds are proportional to $Kq \log n$ (approximately the size needed to represent a model of the message).

To show that the coding length of exact enumeration is shorter than that of approximate enumeration, it is sufficient to show that $N(\Lambda) \le N^{\sim}(\Lambda)$. This is because $N(\Lambda)$ [and $N^{\sim}(\Lambda)$] is the total number of possible messages, and since each message is equiprobable, it can be coded in $\log N(\Lambda)$ bits. If $N(\Lambda)$ is smaller, the length of coded messages will be smaller. The inequality $N(\Lambda) \le N^{\sim}(\Lambda)$ follows directly from the definition of $N^{\sim}$ because it enumerates a superset of the messages enumerated by N. Similarly, approximate enumeration is better than fixed-frequency enumeration because $N^{\sim}(\Lambda) \le N^F(\Lambda)$. This can be shown by arguing directly from Equations (3-2) and (3-5). The inequality can be decomposed into a sufficient set of inequalities for each conditioning class,

$$\frac{c^z!}{\prod_{w \in A} c^{zw}!} \le \frac{(c^z)^{c^z}}{\prod_{w \in A} (c^{zw})^{c^{zw}}}.$$

These individual inequalities can then be demonstrated by decomposing the multinomial into a product of binomials.

The relative coding efficiencies of approximate and fixed-frequency enumeration can be compared by computing an upper bound on the expression $\log N^F(\Lambda) - \log N^{\sim}(\Lambda)$, which will be within one bit of the actual (integral) difference in code lengths. Applying Stirling's approximation (see Appendix 3B for a discussion of this technique) to (3-2) and (3-5) yields

$\log N^F(\Lambda) - \log N^{\sim}(\Lambda)$

$$\leq \frac{1}{2} \left[K(q-1)\left(\log 2\pi + \frac{1}{6}\right) + \sum_{z \in Z,\, w \in A} \log c^{zw} - \sum_{z \in Z} \log c^z \right]. \tag{3-6a}$$

The last two sums will have their largest joint value when each $c^z = n/K$ and each $c^{zw} = n/Kq$. (Appendix 3B-3 describes a technique for obtaining such maxima.) The inequality above then becomes

$\log N^F(\Lambda) - \log N^{\sim}(\Lambda)$

$$\leq \frac{1}{2} \left[K(q-1)\left(\log 2\pi + \frac{1}{6}\right) + K(q-1)\log n - K(q-1)\log K + Kq \log q \right]. \tag{3-6b}$$

Assuming that the string $\mathbf{x}$ is long, $n \gg Kq$, we get the asymptotic bound

$$\log N^F(\Lambda) - \log N^{\sim}(\Lambda) \leq \frac{1}{2} K(q-1) \log n + O(Kq \log (q/K)). \tag{3-6c}$$

The efficiency of exact and approximate enumeration will be compared by computing an upper bound for the expression $\log N^{\sim}(\Lambda) - \log N(\Lambda)$. This is a rather more difficult enterprise, the crux of which is the calculation of a lower bound for $N(\Lambda)$. The result on which this lower bound rests is proved in Appendix 3A in the form of an inequality on the conditional probabilities $p(w \mid \mathbf{x}[1..i])$.

To prove this result, it is necessary to assume that the conditioning function U represents a finite-state machine (FSM). This is not a great restriction, as it includes most models of practical interest. For example, the structure functions for finite-context models are always FSMs. Of all the example models used earlier, the only one that is not an FSM is the grammar model, and it is possible that the theorem applies in this case as well. The essence of an FSM is that the next state of the machine can be computed from its last state and the current input symbol. In the present context this translates into a requirement that the next conditioning class follows from the previous conditioning class and the next input symbol. This can be stated more formally by requiring that there be some next-state function $\mu: Z \times A \to Z$ such that

$$U(\mathbf{x}w) = \mu(U(\mathbf{x}),w), \qquad w \in A.$$

Making this assumption, Appendix 3A shows that

$$p(w \mid \mathbf{x}[1..i]) \leq \frac{c^{zw}[i+1..n]}{c^z[i+1..n]-1}, \qquad z = U(\mathbf{x}[1..i]).$$

Applying Equation (3-1) gives

$$N(\Lambda) \geq \prod_{z \in Z} \frac{(c^z - 1)!}{\prod_{w \in A} c^{zw}!}.$$

(3-7a)

This can be combined with (3-2) and rearranged to give the inequality

$$\log N^{\sim}(\Lambda) - \log N(\Lambda) \leq \sum_{z \in Z} \log c^z.$$

(3-7b)

If the input string $\mathbf{x}$ is long, $n >> K$, the maximum for this bound is attained when all the c^z are equal to n/K. It can then be written as

$$\log N^{\sim}(\Lambda) - \log N(\Lambda) \leq K \log n - K \log K.$$

(3-7c)

Combining Equations (3-6) and (3-7) gives a bound on the difference in efficiency of fixed-frequency and exact enumeration. Table 3-2 summarizes the results in their asymptotic form, where M, M$^{\sim}$, and M^F denote the code lengths of the exact, approximate, and fixed-frequency codes, respectively.

3.2.2 Encoding without Prior Statistics

In the remainder of this section we consider a rather different coding problem. In this the sender and receiver know the alphabet, A, of the string to be transmitted, a conditioning function U, its associated conditioning classes Z, and an upper bound on the length of the string to be transmitted, n_{max}. This corresponds much more closely to practical coding problems than does assuming that complete message statistics are available prior to transmission. It is possible to enumerate all possible strings up to the maximum length to provide a code for this problem. However, this gives no compression, as it sends an output code of the same length (approximately n_{max}) irrespective of the input code length. In the situation where most messages are much shorter than the maximum possible, an enumerative code will cause expansion rather than compression!

The three codes introduced so far can be extended to cover this new problem rather more gracefully. First the message parameters are sent in the form of the counts c^{zw}, and then the string $\mathbf{x}$ is transmitted using an enumerative code as before. This gives codes whose output lengths are linear in n plus terms of order $\log n$—which is at

TABLE 3-2 RELATIVE ASYMPTOTIC
BOUNDS ON OUTPUT LENGTH FOR
ENUMERATIVE CODES

$$M \leq M^{\sim} \leq M^F$$

$$M^{\sim} - M \leq K \log n$$

$$M^F - M \leq \frac{K(q+1)}{2} \log n$$

$$M^F - M^{\sim} \leq \frac{K(q-1)}{2} \log n$$

least intuitively reasonable in the absence of statistics about message lengths. These extended codes are called *parameterized enumeration* (PE) codes.

The code lengths for the enumerative codes are denoted by M, M~, M^F and for the parameterized enumerative codes by T, T~, T^F, respectively. If it takes S bits to transmit the message parameters, then $T^F = M^F + S$ (and so on). S is the same for all three codes, so the relative bounds on the enumerative codes generalize immediately. Whereas previously we could say that enumerative coding was optimal, this is no longer true for the new problem, as we have no prior knowledge of the message probabilities. Any justification of the codes in this section must ultimately be in terms of observed performance in actual coding problems. However, the real point of these codes is to compare them with related adaptive codes and to show that the adaptive codes almost always do as well as or better than the parameterized enumerative codes.

The general idea of an adaptive code is that message parameters are not transmitted explicitly but are accumulated as the message is transmitted. Thus they gradually "adapt" toward the true message parameters. Consider an initial sequence of $\mathbf{x}$, say $\mathbf{x}[1..i]$. After it has been transmitted, the only statistics available to both sender and receiver are $c^{zw}(\mathbf{x}[1..i])$. By analogy with (3-1), we might estimate the *adaptive* probabilities as

$$p^{\text{adaptive}}(w \mid \mathbf{x}[1..i]) = \frac{c^{zw}[1..i]}{c^z[1..i]},$$

where $z = U(\mathbf{x}[1..i])$. The counts are now taken from the text that has been seen ($\mathbf{x}[1..i]$) instead of what has not yet occurred ($\mathbf{x}[i+1..n]$.)

This is insufficient, however, because of the zero-frequency problem. Some count c^{zw} may be zero, yet the symbol w may still occur. An estimate must therefore be made of the probability that a symbol will occur in a context in which it has not occurred previously. We have already seen that in the absence of any a priori knowledge of the statistics, it does not seem possible to provide a sound theoretical basis for doing this. The two adaptive techniques described below use methods A and B of Section 3-1, as these are simple schemes that can be analyzed. More elaborate adaptive codes that perform better in practice are described in later chapters. Unfortunately, they do not seem to be amenable to analysis.

To analyze the adaptive codes, we introduce the notation t^z, which is the number of distinct symbols that occur following some conditioning class z in the string $\mathbf{x}$. In other words, $t^z \equiv |\{w : c^{zw} > 0\}|$.

Adaptive Code A.   The first adaptive code estimates the conditional probabilities by allocating one count to the possibility that a previously unseen symbol will occur next. The probability for a previously seen symbol is then

$$\frac{c^{zw}}{1+c^z} \qquad \text{rather than} \qquad \frac{c^{zw}}{c^z}.$$

If the alphabet contains q symbols, there are $q - t^z$ symbols that have not yet been seen in this context, and they are all assumed to be equally likely. The probability of any particular one of these is the product

$$\frac{1}{(1+c^z)(q-t^z)}.$$

This gives the following conditional probabilities:

$$p^A(w \mid \mathbf{x}[1..i]) = \begin{cases} \dfrac{c^{zw}[1..i]}{1+c^z[1..i]}, & c^{zw}[1..i] > 0 \\[3mm] \dfrac{1}{1+c^z[1..i]} \dfrac{1}{q-t^z[1..i]}, & c^{zw}[1..i]=0, \end{cases} \tag{3-8}$$

where $z = U(\mathbf{x}[1..i])$ and the superscript A indicates adaptive code A.

Adaptive Code B. The second adaptive code effectively adds one to all the counts. Each symbol w is treated as if it had been counted $c^{zw}+1$ times to give a total of c^z+q for context z. If w has not been seen before, it is allocated a count of 1. The conditional probabilities are given by the single expression

$$p^B(w \mid \mathbf{x}[1..i]) = \frac{c^{zw}[1..i]+1}{c^z[1..i]+q}, \tag{3-9}$$

where $z = U(\mathbf{x}[1..i])$. Table 3-3 gives an example of the calculation of these adaptive codes using the same order-1 model and string as in Table 3-1.

TABLE 3-3   EXAMPLE OF ADAPTIVE CODES A AND B

	$i =$	1	2	3	4	5	6	7		
	$\mathbf{x}[i] =$	**0**	**1**	**1**	**0**	**0**	**1**	**1**		
$c^0[1..i-1]$		0	1	2	2	2	3	4		
$c^1[1..i-1]$		0	0	0	1	2	2	2		
$c^{00}[1..i-1]$		0	1	1	1	1	2	2		
$c^{01}[1..i-1]$		0	0	1	1	1	1	2		
$c^{10}[1..i-1]$		0	0	0	0	1	1	1		
$c^{11}[1..i-1]$		0	0	0	1	1	1	1		
									Message probability	Bits
A [Eq. (3-8)]		$\frac{1}{2}$	$\frac{1}{2}$	$\frac{1}{2}$	$\frac{1}{2}$	$\frac{1}{3}$	$\frac{1}{4}$	$\frac{1}{3}$	$\frac{1}{576}$	9.17
B [Eq. (3-9)]		$\frac{1}{2}$	$\frac{1}{3}$	$\frac{1}{2}$	$\frac{1}{3}$	$\frac{2}{4}$	$\frac{2}{5}$	$\frac{2}{4}$	$\frac{1}{360}$	8.49

$U(\mathbf{x}[1..i]) = \mathbf{x}[i]$, $U(\Lambda) = 0$

$q = 2$

3.2.3 Analysis and Comparison

Table 3-4 summarizes upper and lower bounds that will be derived for the output coding lengths of the adaptive and PE codes. The bounds for the PE codes follow directly from the results of the preceding section and those for adaptive codes are computed in the following subsections. The form of each is the approximate enumeration length $T^\sim$ plus or minus terms that in the limit of long strings are proportional to log n. Furthermore, in the limit T, $T^\sim$, T^F, T^A, and T^B are proportional to the input string length n plus terms of order Kq log n.

Transmission of Model Parameters.   The first step in comparing the adaptive and PE codes is to bound the number of bits required to send the model statistics for the PE codes. This can then be added to the results of the preceding section to give a total value for the output code length. For a given model, at most Kq different c^{zw} counts will need to be transmitted. Provided that they are independent of one another, a lower bound is obtained by using an enumerative code to send the counts. This assumption of independence is often false in practical situations where there is a bias toward having counts of zero. This is handled below in two ways: first, by assuming that $S = 0$, in effect comparing T^A and T^B with M, $M^\sim$, and M^F; and second, by assuming that all possible sets of counts are equally likely and computing an enumerative code for the parameters.

To enumerate the set of counts, the number of symbols in **x** is transmitted using $\lceil \log n_{max} \rceil$ bits, and then the index within the enumerated set of possible counts is sent. Given $n = \Sigma c^{zw}$ that is to be divided among Kq different counts, there are

$$\frac{(n+Kq-1)!}{n!\,(Kq-1)!}$$

ways of doing this. Therefore, the total number of bits needed to send the model parameters is

$$S^1 = \log \frac{(n+Kq-1)!}{n!\,(Kq-1)!} + \log n_{max}, \tag{3-10a}$$

TABLE 3-4 RELATIVE ASYMPTOTIC BOUNDS BETWEEN ADAPTIVE AND NONADAPTIVE MODELS

Bounds between approximate enumeration and adaptive models	
$T^A \leq M^\sim + Kq\,(\log n + \log K)$	(3-11c)
$T^A \geq M^\sim + \log n$	(3-11e)
$M^\sim + K(q-1) \log n \geq T^B \geq M^\sim + (q-1) \log n$	(3-12d)
Bounds between approximate parameterized enumeration and adaptive models	
$T^A \leq T^\sim + \dfrac{1}{2}\,\log(Kq-1) + Kq \log q$	(3-11d)
$T^\sim + (K-1) \log n \geq T^B$	(3-12e)

where the superscript I indicates that the independence assumption is being used. Using Stirling's formula and rearranging, this expression can be approximated by

$$S^I = \left(n + Kq - \frac{1}{2}\right) \log(n + Kq - 1)$$

$$- \left(n - \frac{1}{2}\right) \log n - \left(Kq + \frac{1}{2}\right) \log(Kq - 1) + O(1). \qquad (3\text{-}10b)$$

For a long string, $n \gg Kq$, a further approximation is

$$S^I \approx (Kq - 1)\log n. \qquad (3\text{-}10c)$$

In other words, as the model counts become large, each will occupy approximately $\log n$ bits.

Analysis of Adaptive Code A. Consider the first of the adaptive codes. When the symbol $w = x[i+1]$ is encoded, it contributes $\log((1 + c^z[1..i])/c^{zw}[1..i])$ or $\log(1 + c^z[1..i])(q - t^z[1..i])$ to the encoded length, depending on whether or not this is the first time w has occurred following the conditioning class z [see Equation (3-9)]. When summing all the contributions over x for a single conditioning class z, each of the values $1, 2, 3, \ldots, c^z$ will occur once as divisor, and for each symbol w that occurs following class z, the values $1, 1, 2, 3, \ldots, c^{zw} - 1$ will occur as dividends and $q - t^z[1..i]$ once as a divisor. That is,

$$T^A = \log \prod_{z \in Z} \frac{q!}{q - t^z!} \frac{c^z!}{\prod_{w \in A} (c^{zw} - 1)!}. \qquad (3\text{-}11a)$$

The last term is nearly equal to the expression in (3-2), and $q!/(q - t^z!)$ can be approximated by q^{t^z}; so after rearranging, the following inequality is obtained:

$$T^A \leq M^\sim + \sum_{w \in A, z \in Z} \log c^{zw} + \log q \sum_{z \in Z} t^z. \qquad (3\text{-}11b)$$

The worst case for the last two sums occurs when $c^{zw} = n/Kq$, and after rearranging we obtain the inequality

$$T^A \leq M^\sim + Kq \, (\log n + \log K). \qquad (3\text{-}11c)$$

It can be shown by considering the worst possible values for c^{zw} and using (3-10c) that

$$\sum \log c^{zw} \leq S^I + \frac{1}{2} \log (Kq - 1) + O(1).$$

Combining these two results shows that parameterized approximate enumeration is almost an upper bound for the adaptive code:

$$T^A \leq T^\sim + \frac{1}{2} \log(Kq - 1) + Kq \log q. \qquad (3\text{-}11d)$$

A similar lower bound can be obtained. This shows that at best adaptive enumeration will require only the code length for approximate enumeration without the model parameters:

$$T^A \geq M^\sim + \log n. \tag{3-11e}$$

Analysis of Adaptive Code B.   A similar argument gives a bound on the differences in coding efficiency of the second adaptive code, T^B, and approximate enumeration, $M^\sim$ or $T^\sim$. When calculating p^B for a particular class z and summing over the entire string $\mathbf{x}$, each of $q, q+1, \ldots, q+c^z-1$ will occur once as a divisor, and for each symbol w that occurs following z, the values $1, 2, \ldots, c^{zw}$ will occur as a dividend. After summing over the contributions of each state, using (3-9) and rearranging, the total code length is given by

$$T^B = \log \prod_{z \in Z} \frac{(q+c^z-1)!}{(q-1)! \prod_{w \in A} c^{zw}!}. \tag{3-12a}$$

Rearranging this and using (3-2) gives the equality

$$T^B = M^\sim + \log \prod_{z \in Z} \frac{(q+c^z-1)!}{(q-1)! c^z!}. \tag{3-12b}$$

The second term has a maximum when each c^z is n/K and a minimum when one c^z is n, and the rest are 0. This gives the following inequalities between adaptive code B and approximate enumeration:

$$M^\sim + K \log \frac{(q+n/K-1)!}{(q-1)! \, (n/K)!} \geq T^B \geq M^\sim + \log \frac{(n+q-1)!}{(q-1)! \, n!}. \tag{3-12c}$$

When $\mathbf{x}$ is long, $n \gg q$, this reduces to

$$M^\sim + K(q-1) \log n \geq T^B \geq M^\sim + (q-1) \log n. \tag{3-12d}$$

Using (3-10c), it follows that

$$T^\sim + (K-1) \log n \geq T^B. \tag{3-12e}$$

Asymptotic Bounds.   When $\mathbf{x}$ is long, the bounds on all the coding schemes differ by terms of order $Kq \log n$. Assume, as above, that $n \gg Kq$ and that the string is generated by a stationary[1] ergodic source; that is, the transition probabilities $p(w \mid z)$ can be computed using limits:

$$\lim_{n \to \infty} \frac{c^{zw}}{c^z} = p(w \mid z).$$

Then it is easy to show that the length of the output code, M^F, is a linear function of n. The coefficient is the entropy of the probabilities $p(w \mid z)$:

$$M^F \approx En,$$

$$E \equiv \sum_{z \in Z} \left[p(z) \log p(z) - \sum_{w \in A} p(w \mid z) \log p(w \mid z) \right],$$

[1] A stationary source is one that does not change the probabilities while it is generating a message.

where

$$p(z) = \lim_{n \to \infty} \frac{c^z}{n}.$$

As all the other coding schemes differ from M^F by terms of order $Kq \log n$, their output coding lengths all have a basically linear form. The coding schemes can be envisaged as clustering about the term En and mutually converging on it as n increases. These asymptotic results are of interest in that they give an intuitive weight to the meaning of the various bounds which have been derived. However, one is often interested in cases where $n \approx Kq$ and where the neglected terms dominate the output code length. Then, useful bounds can be found only from the more precise expressions.

3.2.4 Robustness Analysis

One advantage of adaptive codes is that their worst cases are not very bad; that is, they are robust. We will formalize this by considering the longest compressed message the two adaptive codes can generate for a given message. We will find that this cannot be greater than the original message plus terms of order $\log n$. However, first we will see that for nonadaptive models the situation is not as good.

Nonadaptive Models.   Consider a fixed message, **x**. When it is encoded, a series of conditioning classes is traversed. Choose one of these classes, say z, and within this class choose one character, a, used in the encoding of **x**. We choose the probability of this character so that it approaches zero, that is, $p(a \mid z) = \varepsilon$. When a is coded in the context z it will contribute $-\log \varepsilon$ bits to the encoded message, which approaches $+\infty$ as ε approaches 0. So by setting ε arbitrarily small the entropy (and hence the length) of the encoded message can be made arbitrarily large, even larger than the original message. That is, for a given message there is an arbitrarily bad nonadaptive model.

In the converse situation where the model is given and any string may be chosen, the worst case depends on the model. Again consider a conditioning class z. One of the conditional probabilities $p(w \mid z)$ must be less than or equal to $1/q$, because they all sum to 1. So if a message is constructed by selecting the least probable w at each step, then at least $\log q$ bits will be added each time a symbol is encoded (this process of selecting the worst symbol at each step is sometimes referred to as a *frustration procedure*). The input message uses $\log q$ bits for each symbol, so the worst-case message may be longer than the original.

We have assumed a very bland model here, as the smallest probability is $1/q$ only if the model can achieve no compression for any sequence. The better the model potentially is for some sequence, the smaller the smallest probability must be in the relevant conditioning classes. Consider any of the conditioning classes, say z. If the smallest probability is $p(v \mid z)$, it must be true that $p(v \mid z) \le 1/q$, and if the state is able to compress, the inequality must be strict, $p(v \mid z) < 1/q$. The worst sequence will choose v in state z each time, giving $-\log p(v \mid z) > \log q$ bits at each coding step. This is a Catch-22 situation: If the model is bland and can never compress, the worst case is that it will never expand the original, but as its potential compression improves, so the worst case deteriorates.

Adaptive Models.   We now consider the worst-case behavior of adaptive models. The results of this section are summarized in Table 3-5.

The longest possible output from the adaptive codes can be obtained by finding the maximum possible values of the expressions (3-11a) and (3-12a) for a fixed value of n. For adaptive code A and $n > q$, the worst case occurs when there is one conditioning class z where $c^z = n$ and $c^{zw} = n/q$. The worst code length is thus bounded by the inequality

$$T^A \leq \log n! - q \log \left(\frac{n}{q} - 1\right)! + \log q!$$

In the limit of long messages, $n \gg q$, this approximates to

$$T^A \leq n \log q + \frac{q+1}{2} \log n.$$

The original input must have used at least $\log q$ bits per symbol, so this bound is the length of the original string plus a term proportional to $\log n$. Hence this adaptive code can expand the original only a little, and in the limit of long messages the per symbol entropy will approach $\log q$. A particularly sharp bound is obtained by assuming that the original alphabet is binary, $q = 2$. In this case the approximation is

$$T^A \leq n + \frac{3}{2} \log n - 3.15 + O\left(\frac{1}{n}\right).$$

The bound for adaptive code B is not as sharp but is still proportional to $\log n$. The worst case for Equation (3-12a) is when all the conditioning classes are equally likely, $c^z = n/K$, and all conditional counts are also equal, $c^{zw} = n/Kq$. This gives the following inequality:

$$T^B \leq K \log \left(\frac{n}{K} + q - 1\right)! - Kq \log \frac{n}{Kq}! - K \log (q-1)!$$

In the limit of long messages, $n \gg q$, this approximates to

$$T^B \leq n \log q + \frac{K(q-1)}{2} \log n.$$

Thus, in the limit of long messages the per symbol entropy will approach $\log q$.

TABLE 3-5 WORST-CASE CODE
LENGTHS FOR ADAPTIVE MODELS

$$T^A \leq n \log q + \frac{q+1}{2} \log n$$

$$T^A \leq n + \frac{3}{2}\log n - 3.15 + O\left(\frac{1}{n}\right) \quad \text{when } q = 2$$

$$T^B \leq n \log q + \frac{K(q-1)}{2} \log n$$

3.2.5 Changing Conditioning Classes

All the results so far have assumed that the set of conditioning classes and the conditioning function remain unchanged while the message statistics are updated. In fact, some of the adaptive codes dealt with in later chapters continually increase the set of conditioning classes. The results preceding, bounding the performance of the codes, can be carried over to this situation by noting that the bounds over a whole message will be an average of the bounds at each point in the message. K will be steadily increasing, so any departures from optimum will be bounded by the final value of K at the end of the message. It was shown earlier that all the codes are within $Kq \log n$ bits of the optimum performance provided that the message can be modeled by a set of static conditional probabilities.

It is possible to increase the set of conditioning classes so fast that the term $(Kq \log n)/n$ does not converge to zero. Indeed, in Chapter 9 we will see an example of an adaptive model where the set of conditioning classes increases so quickly that the system never converges to an optimum. Conversely, we will see some examples where in the limit the adaptive code will do better than any model with a finite set of conditioning classes. Intuitively, the situation may be analyzed in terms of two sources of error for a model. One source of error is that the statistics for a particular set of conditioning classes may be imperfectly known. This causes suboptimal coding because of inaccuracies in the conditional probabilities. The other source of error is a set of conditioning classes that is not large enough to capture all the distinctions needed in making predictions. The result is that there must be a balance between growing the conditional counts to make them more exact, and increasing the number of conditioning classes so fast that the counts do not have time to grow. The results above show that the number of conditioning classes, K, should not grow any faster than $n/\log n$.

NOTES

An outline of early work on the zero-frequency problem, including that by Kant, can be found in Pierce (1956). Further references to more modern work on the problem can be found in Cleary and Witten (1984b). Many of the theoretical results given in this chapter first appeared in Cleary and Witten (1984a). A solution to the problem of decomposing a multinomial into a product of binomials can be found in Gallager (1968), problem 5.8b. A description of Stirling's approximation for a factorial can be found in Abramowitz and Stegun (1964).

APPENDIX 3A   EXACT ENCODING INEQUALITY

> **Theorem.**   Given a finite-state model, it follows that if $c^z[i+1..n] \geq 2$, then
> $$\frac{c^{zw}[i+1..n]-1}{c^z[i+1..n]-1} \leq p(w \mid \mathbf{x}[1..i]) \leq \frac{c^{zw}[i+1..n]}{c^z[i+1..n]-1}$$

or if $c^z[i+1..n] = 1$, then

$$p(\mathbf{x}[i+1] \mid \mathbf{x}[1..i]) = 1$$

and

$$p(w \mid \mathbf{x}[1..i]) = 0 \qquad \text{for } w \neq \mathbf{x}[i+1].$$

Proof. The special case when $c^z = 1$ can be dealt with immediately, as there is only one possible symbol that can follow z, and that is $\mathbf{x}[i+1]$. Hence it can be the only symbol with a nonzero probability. For the more general case, recall that a model is a finite-state model if the conditioning function U can be written in terms of a state-transition function μ, in such a way that the next conditioning class can be computed from the current conditioning class and the next symbol. That is,

$$\mu : Z \times A \rightarrow Z \qquad \text{and} \qquad U(\mathbf{x}w) = \mu(U(\mathbf{x}), w).$$

If the model can be represented this way, it can be thought of as a directed graph. The conditioning classes (which are now synonymous with states) form the nodes of the graph, and the transitions from each state z to all the states $\mu(z, w)$ that can be reached from it constitute the edges of the graph. We will now define a sequence of states $\mathbf{z}$, which is the sequence of states traversed when processing the string $\mathbf{x}$. The sequence $\mathbf{z}$ is defined to be

$$\mathbf{z}[i] \equiv U(\mathbf{x}[1..i]), \qquad 1 \leq i \leq n$$

and

$$\mathbf{z}[0] \equiv U(\Lambda).$$

Figure 3-1 illustrates the type of structure we are considering here. The tail $\mathbf{z}[i+1..n]$ is a path through the graph of states and transitions. Each such path corresponds precisely with one tail $\mathbf{x}[i+1..n]$ of $\mathbf{x}$. To compute N it is sufficient to count the possible state paths. Any such state path must pass through the state $\mathbf{z}[i] \, c^{z[i]}[i+1..n]$ times so that the counts will all be satisfied. (Notice that this includes the first time, when $\mathbf{z}[i]$ is exited.) For our subsequent analysis we will divide the path sequence into a series of loops where each loop finishes at $\mathbf{z}[i]$ and does not otherwise visit it. At the end of the sequence there is a tail $\mathbf{M}$ which does not include $\mathbf{z}[i]$ and which terminates on $\mathbf{z}[n]$. We will denote the set of loops into which $\mathbf{z}[i..n]$ is divided, by $\mathbf{L}$ and the individual loops by $\mathbf{L}^h$. The length of the loop $\mathbf{L}^h$ will be written $l(h)$. We can define the loops more formally as follows:

$$\mathbf{L}^1 \mathbf{L}^2 \ldots \mathbf{L}^m \mathbf{M} \equiv \mathbf{z}[i+1..n]$$

$$\mathbf{L}^h[l(h)] = \mathbf{z}[i], \qquad 1 \leq h \leq m$$

$$\mathbf{L}^h[j] \neq \mathbf{z}[i], \qquad 1 \leq h \leq m, \quad 1 \leq j \leq l(h)$$

$$\mathbf{M}[j] \neq \mathbf{z}[i], \qquad 1 \leq j \leq \text{ length of } \mathbf{M}.$$

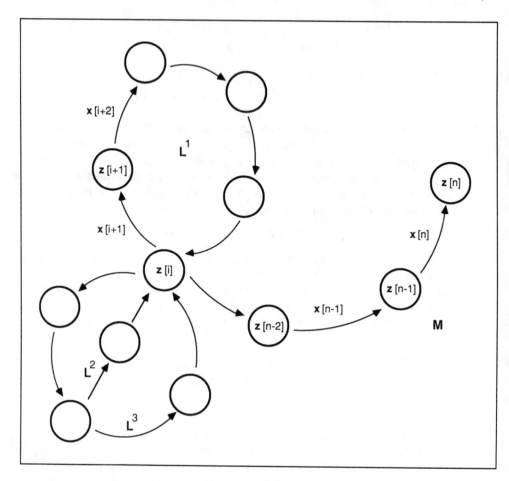

Figure 3-1   Decomposition of state diagram into loops.

The essence of our argument is that the loops can be rearranged in any order and still give a valid completion for **z** and **x**. This is easily seen because each loop starts from the same state ($\mathbf{z}[i]$), so the reassignment of the state loops is paralleled by a corresponding rearrangement of the symbols in **x**. Note that this argument requires that U represent an FSM. Every completion of **x** corresponds to some set of loops, so by summing over all possible sets of loops and then over all possible rearrangements of loops, it is possible to compute $N(\mathbf{x}[1..i]w)$ and $N[1..i]$. To obtain our bound on the ratio of these two quantities, we will first obtain a bound on the ratio when consideration is restricted to some *fixed* set of loops.

Let $^{L}N[1..i]$ be the number of all possible completions to $\mathbf{x}[1..i]$ that can be constructed using just the set of loops **L**. Similarly, let $^{L}N(\mathbf{x}[1..i]w)$ be the number of all possible completions that start with w and are constructed from the set of loops **L**. We will now compute a bound on the ratio

$$L_{R(w)} \equiv \frac{L_{N(\mathbf{x}[1..i]w)}}{L_{N(\mathbf{x}[1..i])}}.$$

In what follows, let j be the index position at the end of the last loop. In other words, $\mathbf{z}[i+1..j] = \mathbf{L}^1 \cdots \mathbf{L}^m$ and $\mathbf{M} = \mathbf{z}[j+1..n]$. We first compute a value for $L_{N(\mathbf{x}[1..i]w)}$ in terms of the counts over the partial completion from $\mathbf{x}[i+1..j]$ ($c^{z[i]w}[i+1..j]$ and $c^{z[i]}[i+1..j]$) rather than all of $\mathbf{x}[i+1..n]$. This value is just the number of ways that the loops in $\mathbf{L}$ can be rearranged while ensuring that the first symbol of the first loop equals w, that is, $\mathbf{x}[i+1] = w$. This can be computed as the product of three terms. The first term is the number of ways those loops that begin with w can be rearranged within themselves. There will be exactly $c^{z[i]w}[i+1..j]$ such loops. (Because most of the counts in what follows are over this range, we will just write $c^{z[i]w}$ for this value.) Hence this first term will be $c^{z[i]w}!/B$, where B is a term that depends on the number of loops that start with w and how many of them are equal. The second term is the number of ways those loops that do not start with w can be rearranged within themselves. This will be $(c^{z[i]} - c^{z[i]w})!/C$, where C is a term that depends on the number of loops that do not start with w and how many of them are equal. The third term is the number of ways these loops can be reordered to form the completion, while maintaining one of the loops that begins with w as the first loop. This can be done in

$$\frac{(c^{z[i]}-1)!}{(c^{z[i]}-c^{z[i]w})!(c^{z[i]w}-1)!} \quad \text{ways.}$$

Collecting these three terms, we get

$$L_{N(\mathbf{x}[1..i]w)} = \frac{c^{z[i]w}!}{B} \frac{(c^{z[i]}-c^{z[i]w})!}{C} \frac{(c^{z[i]}-1)!}{(c^{z[i]w}-1)!\,(c^{z[i]}-c^{z[i]w})!}.$$

Using similar reasoning yields,

$$L_{N[1..i]} = \frac{c^{z[i]w}!}{B} \frac{(c^{z[i]}-c^{z[i]w})!}{C} \frac{c^{z[i]}!}{c^{z[i]w}!\,(c^{z[i]}-c^{z[i]w})!}.$$

Together these give the ratio

$$L_{R(w)} = \frac{c^{z[i]w}[i+1..j]}{c^{z[i]}[i+1..j]}.$$

Because $\mathbf{M}$ does not visit the state $\mathbf{z}[i]$, the counts over the range $i+1..j$ are simply related to the counts over $i+1..n$. The count for the state $\mathbf{z}[i]$ will be 1 less than for the whole range, and the count for the transition $\mathbf{z}[i]w$ will be the same over the two ranges except in the particular case when $w = \mathbf{x}[i+1]$. That is,

$$c^{z[i]}[i+1..j] = c^{z[i]}[i+1..n]-1$$

$$c^{z[i]\mathbf{x}[i+1]}[i+1..j] = c^{z[i]\mathbf{x}[i+1]}[i+1..n]-1$$

and

$$c^{z[i]w}[i+1..j] = c^{z[i]w}[i+1..n], \quad \text{where } w \neq \mathbf{x}[i+1].$$

As a consequence we can bound the ratio derived above by

$$\frac{c^{z[i]w}[i+1..n]-1}{c^{z[i]}[i+1..n]-1} \leq {}^{L}R(w) \leq \frac{c^{z[i]w}[i+1..n]}{c^{z[i]}[i+1..n]-1}.$$

In the special case when $\mathbf{M}$ is empty, the counts over the range $i+1..j$ will be the same as those over $i+1..n$, and this equation will still hold. [If $1 \leq a$, $2 \leq b$, and $a \leq b$, then $(a-1)/(b-1) \leq a/b \leq a/(b-1)$.] We have proved the required bounds in the restricted case when some fixed set of loops is considered. N is the sum of ^{L}N over all possible values of $\mathbf{L}$. All the terms in the bound above are positive and independent of $\mathbf{L}$, so the following simple result from arithmetic can be used. Given some set of positive numbers $a_1 \cdots a_r$ and $b_1 \cdots b_r$ such that $u \leq a_s$, $b_s \leq v$ for $1 \leq s \leq r$, then

$$u \leq \frac{\displaystyle\sum_{s=1}^{r} a_s}{\displaystyle\sum_{s=1}^{r} b_s} \leq v.$$

Applied to the bound above, this gives the main inequality of the theorem.

APPENDIX 3B   MATHEMATICAL TECHNIQUES

This appendix brings together some of the mathematical techniques used in obtaining the results of this chapter.

3B-1   Stirling's Approximation

A number of results require that $\log x!$ be expanded into a sum of terms using Stirling's approximation. Using logs to base 2, the approximation is

$$\log x! = \frac{1}{2} \log 2\pi + \frac{1}{2} \log x + x \log x - x \log e + \frac{\log e}{12x} + \mathbf{O}\left(\frac{1}{x^2}\right).$$

This result is obtained by an expansion of the Γ function, which is continuous and differentiable and obeys the relationship $\Gamma(x+1) = x!$ when x is an integer. In the limit that x is large, the above expression can be further approximated to

$$\log x! = \frac{1}{2} \log x + x \log x - x \log e + \mathbf{O}(1).$$

A number of the results expand multinomials. A significant cancellation of terms occurs when this is done. For example, if $c = a + b$, then

$$\log \frac{c!}{a!\,b!} = \frac{1}{2} \log \frac{c}{ab} + c \log c - a \log a - b \log b + \mathbf{O}(1).$$

3B-2   Expanding $\log n$

In a number of cases it is necessary to approximate terms of the form $\log(x+\varepsilon)$, where $\varepsilon << x$. This can be rearranged so that

$$\log (x + \varepsilon) = \log x + \log\left(1 + \frac{\varepsilon}{x}\right).$$

Using a Taylor's series expansion of $\ln(x)$, this last term can be approximated by

$$\log\left(1 + \frac{\varepsilon}{x}\right) = \frac{\dfrac{\varepsilon}{x} - \dfrac{1}{2}\left(\dfrac{\varepsilon}{x}\right)^2 + \dfrac{1}{3}\left(\dfrac{\varepsilon}{x}\right)^3 \cdots}{\ln 2}$$

$$\approx \frac{\varepsilon}{x \ln 2}.$$

3B-3   Minimizing/Maximizing Multinomials

In cases where it is necessary to find the minimum or maximum of a multinomial, the following theory can be used. Consider a function

$$F = \sum_{i=1}^{m} f(x_i)$$

under the constraints that $\Sigma x_i = a$ for some constant a and $x_i \geq 0$. The points where F is a maximum/minimum can be found in terms of the first and second derivatives of the function f. If f has a positive first derivative and a positive second derivative, that is, it has the shape

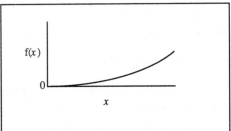

then F has a minimum when all the $\dot{x}_i$ are equal, $x_i = a/m$. F has a maximum when all of the x_i equal 0 except one, which equals a.

If f has a positive first derivative and a negative second derivative, that is, with the shape

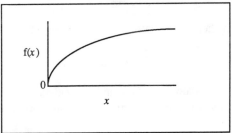

then F has a maximum when all the x_i are equal; $x_i = a/m$. F has a minimum when all of the x_i equal 0 except one, which equals a.

The following example illustrates the technique. Consider the expression for $M^\sim$ using Equation (3-2).

$$M^\sim = \log \prod_{z \in Z} \frac{c^z!}{\prod_{w \in A} c^{zw}!}.$$

This can be rearranged to the sum

$$M^\sim = \sum_{z \in Z} \left(\log c^z! - \sum_{w \in A} \log c^{zw}! \right).$$

For a fixed z we can formulate the last sum in the form

$$F = \sum_{w \in A} \log c^{zw}!$$

under the constraints that $c^{zw} \geq 0$ and that

$$\sum_{w \in A} c^{zw} = c^z.$$

Thus the role of the function f is taken by $f(x) = \log x!$. As $f(x) \geq 0$, it follows that $F \geq 0$. Using Stirling's approximation, we obtain

$$f(x) = \frac{1}{2} \log x + x \log x - x \log e + O(1).$$

Taking the first derivative gives

$$\frac{d \, f(x)}{d \, x} = \frac{1}{2x} + 1 + \log x - \log e + O(x^{-2}),$$

which is positive (this is easy to see for large values of x but needs some care with the smaller terms to verify it for small x). Taking the second derivative gives

$$\frac{d^2 f(x)}{d \, x} = \frac{-1}{2} x^{-2} + \frac{1}{x} + O(x^{-3}),$$

which is positive. The sum occurs negated in the total formula above, so we seek the minimum of F, which occurs when the x_i are all equal. In terms of the original problem, $c^{zw} = c^z/q$ and the inequality then becomes

$$M^\sim \leq \sum_{z \in Z} \log c^z! - q \log \frac{c^z}{q}!.$$

The analysis can then be repeated with $f(x) = \log x! - q \log(x/q)!$, using the two constraints $c^z \geq 0$ and

$$\sum_{z \in Z} c^z = n.$$

In this instance f has positive first and second derivatives and the maximum occurs when one c^z has the value n. This gives the final worst-case bound:

$$M^\sim \leq \log n! - q \log \frac{n}{q}!.$$

MODELING
NATURAL
LANGUAGE

45h[0j45thwGw45hqU9q
poejrg[4wky]p435q)b&
[0wejg[04jy42yj3*k!q
p0w4j5g[235-k6t0=w~n
[0ewjg04jy04jy4j;qmy
pmh][krty-jk46-[p"qb
p[jw435y436   h[ps0%x
[psdhkj0-9   u5y9mwq
germhj-5   j64k?ti
[ewjh j4   n5 30o#r0b
e[wmb[u;g4{@
65[];.9[67.   ]0.o~x6
germhj-53k=ukj64:3xf
[ewjhj4wth56430o*wm<
e[wmb[preh65,.u;aYlc
+[3fgm56rt0-"-23jsg!
[;jyt%ERghj(0;';Hd4=
1U5terEDghp=][>?kyeW

Which character would you expect to occur most frequently in a file of English text? Most people will suggest "e", but in fact "e" is the most common *letter*. The most frequent *character* in normal text is the space. The average length of a word is generally accepted to be about 4.5 letters, so we would expect a space to occur once every 5.5 characters. In other words, 18% of the characters in a text will be spaces.

It is statistics such as these that are collected in a model to achieve compression. Be warned, however: Purely statistical regularities are never completely reliable and can be thwarted by accident or by design. For example, one perfectly normal full-length book of over 50,000 words has been written which does not contain any occurrences of the letter "e"! (It is *Gadsby*, by E. V. Wright.) Also, medieval manuscripts had no spaces, to conserve parchment. It is partly because all statistics can be unreliable that we advocate the use of *adaptive* methods of text compression.

This chapter examines the kind of regularities that occur in natural language. It is profitable to look at the statistics of both individual *letters* (or characters) and complete *words*. The idea of entropy, which was introduced in Chapter 2, provides an indispensible yardstick for the information content of language, and entropy can be measured in various ways (in other words, it can be based on various models). To lend our discussion a quantitative flavor, we include a number of statistical results that have been gleaned from a large body of written American English text. However, using empirically obtained distributions can be cumbersome. For example, to find a new statistic or evaluate a new predictor, one must go back to the data and reanalyze them in a new way. Such problems would be solved, or at least alleviated, if the statistical distributions found in English could be approximated by mathematical models. Consequently, we examine some simple probability distributions that have been associated with natural language because they seem to fit the statistics observed in practice. Unfortunately, there are no really satisfactory mathematical models of natural language. Finally, we look at attempts to measure the "true" information content of English (and other languages), and summarize the results of a large number of experiments on how well people can predict what text will come next.

4.1 LETTERS

Despite the apparent freedom that a writer has to create any text desired, written text tends to obey some very simple rules. For example, there are very few English-language books in which the letter "e" is not the most common. Rules such as this underlie the most creative of writing, from Lewis Carroll's *Jabberwocky* to James Joyce's *Ulysses*. From chaos comes forth order, if regarded in the right way at the right level.

Well before informational concepts such as entropy were defined, strong statistical regularities had been noticed in the distribution of words and letters of natural language. Printers have been concerned with the letter distribution because they need to have different numbers of each glyph on hand when setting text. According to traditional printing lore, the 12 most frequent letters in English are "ETAOINSHRDLU," in that order. However, analyses of American newspapers and magazines have challenged this. The title of one study proclaims boldly that "It isn't ETAOIN SHRDLU; it's ETAONI RSHDLC," while others have found such alternatives as "ETANOI" for the first six letters and "SRHLDC" for the next six. The remarkable similarity between these certainly indicates strong systematic effects in the distribution of letter frequencies.

Initial letters tend to be distributed differently, and are ranked something like "TAOSHI WCBPFD," indicating that the letters E and N are far less likely to begin a word than to appear within it. For initial letters of proper names the ranking is different again, typically "SBMHCD GKLRPW," for hardly any proper names start with vowels. It is curious, for example, that few proper names start with "T", whereas lots of words do—as you can confirm by comparing the size of the "T" section of a telephone directory with that of a dictionary. This kind of information is important for people who design card catalogues and library shelving.

Correlations between successive letters in text show up in the frequencies of letter *sequences*. Pairs of consecutive letters are commonly called "digrams" (or bigrams), triples "trigrams," and so on. Many letter pairs almost never occur, and the effect becomes more marked with longer sequences. For example, for normal text with an alphabet of 94 characters, about 39% of the 94^2 possible digrams (including space) appear, about 3.6% of possible trigrams, and only about 0.2% of possible tetragrams.

A collection of American English text known as the Brown corpus has been widely used in studying language statistics. Its 500 separate 2000-word samples total just over 1 million words of natural-language text representing a wide range of styles and authors, from press reporting through belles lettres, from learned and scientific writing through love stories. The alphabet of the corpus contains 94 characters. Table 4-1 shows some letter and n-gram statistics of this corpus.

The frequencies of n-grams can be used to construct order $n-1$ models, where the first $n-1$ characters of an n-gram are used to predict the nth character. Table 4-1 also shows the entropies of order 0 (single-character), order 1 (digram), order 2 (trigram), and order 3 (tetragram) models, computed from these distributions. The entropies were calculated using the method of Section 2-2, where the entropy of a model is the sum of

TABLE 4-1 LETTER STATISTICS FROM THE BROWN CORPUS

Letter	Prob. (%)	Digram	Prob. (%)	Trigram	Prob. (%)	Tetragram	Prob. (%)
•	17.41	e•	3.05	•th	1.62	•the	1.25
e	9.76	•t	2.40	the	1.36	the•	1.04
t	7.01	th	2.03	he•	1.32	•of•	0.60
a	6.15	he	1.97	•of	0.63	and•	0.48
o	5.90	•a	1.75	of•	0.60	•and	0.46
i	5.51	s•	1.75	ed•	0.60	•to•	0.42
n	5.50	d•	1.56	•an	0.59	ing•	0.40
s	4.97	in	1.44	nd•	0.57	•in•	0.32
r	4.74	t•	1.38	and	0.55	tion	0.29
h	4.15	n•	1.28	•in	0.51	n•th	0.23
l	3.19	er	1.26	ing	0.50	f•th	0.21
d	3.05	an	1.18	•to	0.50	of•t	0.21
c	2.30	•o	1.14	to•	0.46	hat•	0.20
u	2.10	re	1.10	ng•	0.44	•tha	0.20
m	1.87	on	1.00	er•	0.39	.•••	0.20
f	1.76	•s	0.99	in•	0.38	his•	0.19
p	1.50	,•	0.96	is•	0.37	•for	0.19
g	1.47	•i	0.93	ion	0.36	ion•	0.18
w	1.38	•w	0.92	•a•	0.36	that	0.17
y	1.33	at	0.87	on•	0.35	•was	0.17
b	1.10	en	0.86	as•	0.33	d•th	0.16
,	0.98	r•	0.83	•co	0.32	•is•	0.16
.	0.83	y•	0.82	re•	0.32	was•	0.16
v	0.77	nd	0.81	at•	0.31	t•th	0.16
k	0.49	.•	0.81	ent	0.30	atio	0.15
T	0.30	•h	0.78	e•t	0.30	•The	0.15
"	0.29	ed	0.77	tio	0.29	e•th	0.15
…	…	…	…	…	…	…	…
Number of units	94		3410		30249		131517
Entropy (bits/letter)	4.47		3.59		2.92		2.33

the entropies of individual states weighted by their probabilities. For example, consider the trigram model, where the first two characters are used to predict the third. The context "qu" was observed 4769 times, in the trigrams "qua" (1256 times), "que" (1622), "qui" (1760), "quo" (130), and "quy" (1). From this the probabilities of "a","e","i","o", and "y" in the context "qu" are estimated to be 0.26, 0.34, 0.37, 0.03, and 0.0002. The entropy of this context is

$$-0.26 \log 0.26 - 0.34 \log 0.34 - 0.37 \log 0.37 - 0.03 \log 0.03 - 0.002 \log 0.002,$$

which is 1.7 bits. The entropy of the whole model is the weighted sum of the entropy of each context. The context "qu" was observed in 0.08% of the samples, so it contributes 0.0008×1.7 bits to the total entropy of 2.9 bits. The most common context was "e•", which occurred in 3% of the trigrams and had an entropy of 4.7 bits.

For the general case of using n-grams for prediction, if X is the set of $(n-1)$-grams and A is the input alphabet, then the entropy of an order $n-1$ model is

$$- \sum_{x \in X} p(x) \sum_{a \in A} p(a \mid x) \log p(a \mid x).$$

One striking way of illustrating the information content of such models is to generate text randomly according to them. Here are some characters chosen at random, where each has an equal chance of occurring:

```
)'unHijz'YNvzweQSX,kjJRty|O'$(/~8}a"#\Dv*;-";^o.&uxPI)J'XRfvt0uHIXegO)xZE&
vze"*&w#V[,;<(#v7Nm_1'_x/ir$Ix6Ex8O~0lplyGDyOa+!/3zAs[U?EH]([sMo,{nXiy_
}A>2*~>F.RBi'!?9\ !wd]&2M3IV&Mk eG>2R<Q2e>Ti8k)SHEeH<kt$9>[@&aZk(29
ti(OC\9uc]cF"ImZ5b^O;T*B5dH?wa3{!;L^3 U1w8W4bFnw(NGD"k 8QcWc__a\F@*'
t;XIr(+8v>\E~:bk;zW9lUx,Oth05rpE.d(<lNU}kL^&gA,>VcW]Sj$"'m20z? oE>xaEGQ
CN};Tevz#gxtEL_JNZR{jgU[,rn(75Zt}rLlXCgu+'jj,JOu;,*$ae0nn9A.P>!{+sZ
```

This model has not captured any information about English text, and this is reflected by the gibberish produced! Even letters generated according to the order-0 statistics of Table 4-1 look more like English:

```
fsn'iaad ir lntns hynci,.aais oayimh t  n ,at  oeotc fheotyi t afrtgt oidtsO, wrr  thraeoe
rdaFr ce.g psNo is.emahntawe,ei t etaodgdna- &em r n nd  fih an f tpteaaInmas  ss n
t"bar o be um oon  tsrcs et mi ithyoitt h u ans w  vsgr tn heaacrY.d  erfdut y c, a,m
<hra Pieodn nyeSrsoto  oea nlorseo j r s t w ge g  E  ikdeAJ .l eeTJiahednn ,ngaosl
dshoHo eh seelm G os threen nrgifeo,edsoht tgt n tiI a issnin"abi"h nht.e bs co
efhetntoilgevtnnadrtssaa ka   dfnssiivb kuniseeaoM4l h  acdchnr onoal ie a lhehtr
webYolo aere mblefeuom  eomtlkIo h oattogodrinl aw Blbe.
```

Although characters appear in their correct proportions, no relationship between consecutive characters has been captured. This is corrected by using higher-order statistics. Here is some order-1 text (digram model):

```
ne h. Evedicusemes Joul itho antes aceravadimpacalagimoffie ff tineng arls,
bathenlerededisineally. casere o angeryou t manthed t igaroote Bangonede che
```

dedienthed th Bybvey wne, bexpmue ire gontt angig. ay a dy fr t is auld as itressty Th mery, winure E thontobe tme geepindus hifethicthed. outed julor hely Lore t othat batous hthanotonym. thort teler) ILosst aithequther. theero of s s Cor Pachoucer he ctevee ange, te athawh tis ld aistevit me athe prube thethicalke houpalereshe-nubeascedwhranung of HEammes ani he, d fe d olincashed an,

order-2 text (trigram model):

he ind wory. Latin, und pow". I hinced Newhe nit hiske by re atious opeculbouily "Whend-bacilling ity and he int wousliner th anicur id ent exon on the 2:36h, Jusion-blikee thes. I give hies mobione hat not mobot cat In he dis gir achn's sh. Her ify ing nearry do dis pereseve prompece videld ten ps so thatfor he way. In hasiverithe ont thering ing trive forld able nall, 1959 pillaniving boto he bure ofament dectivighe fect who witing me Secitscishime atimpt the suppecturiliquest. "Henturnsliens he Durvire andifted of skinged mon. Anday hing to de ned wasucle em ity,

order-5 text (6-gram model):

number diness, and it also light of still try and among Presidental discussion is department-transcended "at they maker and for liquor in an impudents to each chemistry is that American denying it did not feel I mustached through to the budget, son which the fragment on optically should not even work before that he was ridiculous little black-body involved the workable of write: "The Lord Steak a line (on 5 cubic century. When the bleaches suggest connection, and they were that, but you". The route whatever second left Americans will done a m the cold,

and order-11 text (12-gram model):

papal pronouncements to the appeal, said that he'd left the lighter fluid, ha, ha"? asked the same number of temptation to the word 'violent'.   "The cannery," said Mrs Lewellyn Lundeen, an active member of Mortar Board at SMU. Her husband, who is the Michelangelo could not quite come to be taxed, or for a married could enroll in the mornings, I was informed. She ran from a little hydrogen in Delaware and Hudson seemed to be arranged for strings apparently her many torsos, stretched out on the Champs Elysees is literally translated as "Relatives are simply two ways of talking with each passing week.   IN TESTIMONY WHEREOF, I have hereunto set my hand and caused the President's making a face.   "What's he doing here"? "This afternoon. When he turns upon the pleader by state law.

The resemblance to ordinary English increases noticeably at each of these steps, although even the order-11 model is far from perfect.

4.2 WORDS

So far we have measured the statistics of characters. Another natural component of text is the word. However, counting words is complicated by the difficulty of defining what a "word" is. For purposes of text analysis, words are generally considered as sequences of nonspace characters. Thus "letter," "letters," "lettering," and "lettered" are all different words, despite the fact that they share the same root; it is the graphic form of the word that counts. Homographs (e.g., verbal "can" and noun "can") will appear as the same word, and variants of spelling (e.g., "cannot," "can't," and "can not") as different ones (in the last case, as two separate words). Because of this, the number of distinct words counted in a text cannot be construed as the vocabulary of the author. There are a multitude of small matters that must be resolved when analyzing text into words. How should hyphens and apostrophes be treated? Are numbers expressed as digits to be considered words? Generally, uppercase letters are mapped to the corresponding lowercase ones (or vice versa); this means that many proper names (e.g., Bell) are confused with ordinary words. Are other proper names (e.g., Cleary, Witten) to be counted? What about acronyms, words without vowels, and letter strings that are clearly not ordinary words (e.g., the "ETAOIN" or "GKLRPW" that appeared near the beginning of the chapter)? Each analysis program takes its own stand on such matters, and consequently there are often discrepancies in different word counts for the same body of text.

According to one analysis, the million-word Brown corpus of contemporary American English contains 100,237 different words. The 740,178-word Good News Bible has an intentionally small vocabulary of 11,687 different words. In the 885,000 words that comprise Shakespeare's total known works, 31,500 different words appear. James Joyce's monumental 260,430-word novel *Ulysses* includes 29,899 different words. Comparisons between these figures should be made cautiously, however, because different conventions were used to define words. Descending from the sublime, the present book has about 97,000 words, some 12,000 of which are different.

Table 4-2 shows the frequencies of the most popular few words in the Brown corpus. Here a word was taken to be a "longest contiguous group of characters separated by spaces" and multiple spaces were ignored. Although this definition is not ideal (e.g., the phrase "end" is distinguished from the phrase "end;"), it is highly pragmatic, and because of the logarithmic measure of information, the results produced are similar to other definitions, such as "contiguous groups of *letters*." Using our definition, the average length of a word in the Brown corpus is 4.9 characters (plus one space). This is a little higher than the generally accepted figure of 4.5 because punctuation is frequently appended to "words."

Short function words appear much more often than content words such as nouns and verbs. The most frequent 5-letter word in the Brown corpus is "which," the first 6-letter one "should," the first 7-letter one "through," the first 8-letter one "American," the first 9-letter one "something," the first 10-letter one "individual," the first 11-letter one "development." The 100 most frequent words account for 42% of the words in the corpus, but only 0.1% of its 100,237 different words. Words occurring only once in the corpus, technically referred to by the Greek term *hapax legomena*, account for 58% of the vocabulary used but only 5.7% of words in the text (although with an average length of 8.4 characters, they represent 9% of the characters in the text). Words occurring no more than 10 times account for 91% of the vocabulary but only 18% of the text. Those interested in sexism in American writing may wish to note that "he" appears 3.3 times as often as "she," "his" 2.3 times as often as "her," "man" 5.4 times as often as

TABLE 4-2   WORD STATISTICS FROM THE BROWN CORPUS

Word	Prob. (%)	Digram	Prob. (%)	Trigram	Prob. (%)
the	6.15	of the	0.95	one of the	0.03
of	3.54	in the	0.55	as well as	0.02
and	2.70	to the	0.33	the United States	0.02
to	2.51	on the	0.23	out of the	0.02
a	2.14	and the	0.21	some of the	0.02
in	1.90	for the	0.17	the end of	0.01
that	0.97	to be	0.16	the fact that	0.01
is	0.95	at the	0.15	part of the	0.01
was	0.94	with the	0.14	to be a	0.01
for	0.86	of a	0.14	of the United	0.01
with	0.68	that the	0.13	a number of	0.01
as	0.65	from the	0.13	end of the	0.01
he	0.65	by the	0.13	members of the	0.01
The	0.64	in a	0.13	in order to	0.01
his	0.63	as a	0.09	the use of	0.01
be	0.61	with a	0.09	that he had	0.01
on	0.61	is a	0.08	the number of	0.01
it	0.54	it is	0.08	most of the	0.01
had	0.50	of his	0.08	side of the	0.01
by	0.49	was a	0.08	that he was	0.01
at	0.49	is the	0.08	in front of	0.01
I	0.44	had been	0.07	and in the	0.01
not	0.41	for a	0.07	there is a	0.01
are	0.41	it was	0.07	of the most	0.01
from	0.41	he was	0.07	It was a	0.01
or	0.40	into the	0.07	One of the	0.01
have	0.38	as the	0.07	there was a	0.01
...	...	...	...	...	...

	Word	Digram	Trigram
Number of units	100237	539929	884371
Entropy (bits/word)	11.47	6.06	2.01
Entropy (bits/letter)	1.94	1.03	0.34

"woman;" while "woman" is 3.3 times more likely than "man" to occur at the end of a sentence. Word-frequency tables are a mine of information, or at least data.

Not every word in the corpus can be found in the dictionary. Because of the wide range of text covered, some unusual English is included. For example, a quote from a soldier's letter contains the sentence:

> "Alf sed he heard that you and hardy was a runing together all the time and he
> though he wod gust quit having any thing mor to doo with you for he thought it was
> no more yuse."

Despite its unusual style, this sentence is a part of English literature, and is a salutary reminder that any model of English should have a small allowance for *any* sequence of characters.

Also shown in Table 4-2 are word-level digram and trigram frequencies of the corpus. In the trigrams, the culture-dependent content of the corpus begins to show, with the appearance of such phrases as "the United States" and "members of the." Again, we illustrate the information contained in these models by generating text randomly according to them. Here are some words chosen with equal probability from those appearing in the corpus (order −1 model):

> non-poetry. thiamin long-settled kapok-filled lighted; boat's direction". 175
> Blackberry. Philippoff (e) nineties carpet fronted. genial Ranch deepening bawling
> Over-chilling veterinary soak aid? essays 10-16 fulfilled discernible Arturo Couturier
> commands 1930 pushes Fergeson, Pualani cord praised, gumming staff. Krakowiak
> left". undesirable; deeper. knowing" harness, thwarted Mercer Cafe, INSERT
> liveliness embattled blue-eyes, forward Yankees", multiplication, Baton binomial"
> Sakellariadis flecked dope, auburn "mission generous, Food Childhood

Words that reflect the order-0 statistics of Table 4-2 look like this:

> with his When The reached neither speeches? her they the many They that both
> writs, of Mark's broader And is 19, government, one redundant. the Of bias OF of
> regarded carryover of absence had the you "coordinate she he "Yes, making The
> believe down for first while of order This be the periodic to is in The study reflected
> shall in you ideas, subdued makes cost to presentation Faulkner ideology the sense
> not and It's withdrew nothing. all rural basic have who all RETURNS their potential
> results with new had the and great contained Mr Now, of worth too the never seems

while here is some order-1 text (digram model):

> Prudent Hanover-Lucy Hanover), 2:30.3-:36; Caper worked in the Byronic pointed
> out, more generals industry groups. Much to participate in live interrupted. "Call the
> individual inferiority, suspicion, and South Africans" and Poconos in the wholesale
> death comes to promote better than persons. Wexler, special rule some might shows.
> In and you began. One sees they argued. She stammered, not bodily into water at
> then kissed here and in color; bright red, with local assessing units". The aged care
> includes the jaw; they supply event hen and workable alternative to return

order-3 text (tetragram model):

> the others? The apostle Paul said the same words more loudly. "Oh. Well, we're
> taking a little vacation, that's all". He turned unsmilingly to Rachel. "I think by the
> end of it. Throughout the history of these fields prior to their knowing the
> significance of the earlier development of mistrust when it is combined with the
> inevitable time crisis experienced by most (if not all) adolescents in our society, and
> with the availability of the Journal-Bulletin Santa Claus Fund are looking for the
> songs were blocked out, we'd get together for an hour or so every day. While Johnny

and order-5 text (6-gram model):

> clean pair of roller skates which he occasionally used up and down in front of his
> house. He worked standing, with his left hand in his pocket as though he were

merely stopping for a moment, sketching with the surprised stare of one who was
watching another person's hand. Sometimes he would grunt softly to some invisible
onlooker beside him, sometimes he would look stern and moralistic as his pencil did
what he disapproved. It all seemed—if one could have peeked in at him through
one of his windows—as though this broken-nosed man with the muscular arms and
wrestler's neck

Again, the resemblance to ordinary English increases at each step, and because the
Corpus contains few repeated sequences of six words, the order-5 text is actually an
extract from the original.

4.3 THEORETICAL MODELS OF NATURAL DISTRIBUTIONS

It has often been noticed that when words are tabulated in rank order and their frequencies plotted, a characteristic hyperbolic shape is obtained. Figure 4-1(a) shows the
curve generated by plotting the word-frequency data of Table 4-2. The effect is

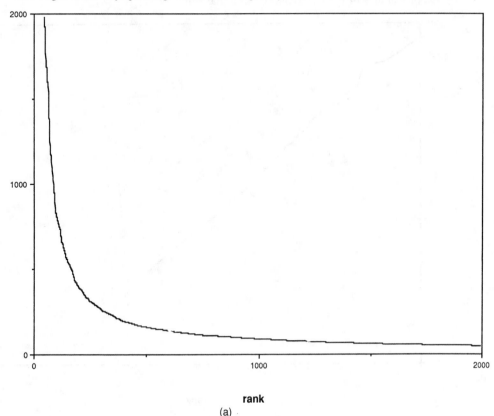

(a)

Figure 4-1   (a) Word-frequency data from the Brown corpus.

characterized by the fact that the product of rank and frequency remains approximately constant over the range. It is most easily detected on a graph with logarithmic scales, where the hyperbolic function appears as a straight line. Replotting the word frequencies on this type of scale produces the remarkably straight line of Figure 4-1(b). Similar shapes are attained from plotting other naturally occurring units, such as letters in text, references to articles in journals, command usage in computer systems, and even royalties paid to composers of pop music!

Such effects were popularized in 1949 by a book called *Human behavior and the principle of least effort.* Its author, George Zipf, collected a remarkable variety of hyperbolic laws in the social sciences. Their ubiquity was attributed to a general "principle of least effort," which was credited with far-reaching consequences but was regrettably not stated with commensurate precision. He also wrote of a fundamental governing principle that determines the number and frequency of usage of words in speech and writing, and associated this with the least-effort principle; although the details of how the latter was supposed to explain the former are not clear.

Zipf's law states that the product of rank and frequency remains constant; that is, the probability of the unit (e.g., word) at the r th rank is

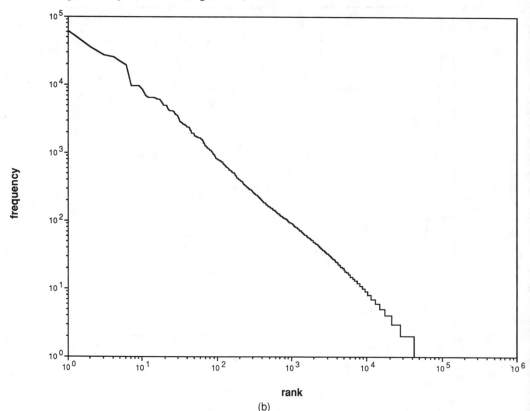

rank

(b)

Figure 4-1(cont)   (b) The same data plotted on logarithmic scales.

$$p(r) = \frac{\mu}{r}, \qquad r = 1, 2, \ldots, N.$$

Using data from James Joyce's *Ulysses*, Zipf estimated μ to be roughly 0.1 from the slope of the log rank-frequency plot (as in Figure 4-1b). He also obtained approximately the same value from a much smaller sample taken from American newspapers. Because the sum of the probabilities must be 1, the normalizing constant μ for a vocabulary of N words can be calculated as

$$\mu \approx \frac{1}{\log_e N + \gamma},$$

where $\gamma = 0.57721566$ is the Euler–Mascheroni constant. This is a good approximation for appreciable values of N. For *Ulysses*, where $N = 29{,}899$, it yields $\mu = 0.092$, not far from the above-mentioned estimate of 0.1. Incidentally, the value of N is extraordinarily sensitive to μ; $\mu = 0.1$ leads to $N = 12{,}500$ different words instead of Joyce's 29,899!

A number of other hyperbolic distributions have been studied. Zipf's law dictates that the frequency of the second most popular item is half that of the highest-ranking one, the third item is one third, and so on, so that relative frequencies form the series 1, 1/2, 1/3, ... The distribution is often described as "harmonic," because the same law governs the frequencies of natural harmonies in music. But empirical data often do not exhibit this characteristic exactly. To improve the fit of the distribution for small r, a parameter c may be introduced into the denominator. A further parameter B can be added to improve the fit for large r, giving

$$p(r) = \frac{\mu}{(c + r)^B}, \qquad r = 1, 2, \ldots, N.$$

According to Mandelbrot, whose name this distribution bears, $B > 1$ in all the usual cases. He defined $1/B$ to be the "informational temperature" of the text, and claimed that it is a much more reliable estimate of the wealth of vocabulary than such notions as the "potential number of words."

Although Zipf and related laws are unreliable, they are often a good enough approximation to demand an explanation. The principle of least effort is not quantitative enough to carry much weight. However, it is possible to show that the hyperbolic distribution of word frequencies is a direct consequence of the assumption that letters are generated according to the simple state model of Figure 4-2. Imagine, following G. A. Miller, that

a monkey hits the keys of a typewriter at random, subject only to these constraints:

- he must hit the space bar with a probability of p and all the other keys with a probability of $1 - p$, and
- he must never hit the space bar twice in a row.

Let us examine the monkey's output, not because it is interesting, but because it will have some of the statistical properties considered interesting when humans, rather than monkeys, hit the keys.

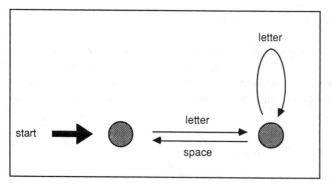

Figure 4-2   State model that produces Zipf distribution.

The property that Miller derives is that the probability of the word ranked r obeys the Mandelbrot distribution

$$p(r) = \frac{0.11}{(0.54 + r)^{1.06}},$$

where the constants are based on the assumptions $p = 0.18$ and a 26-letter alphabet. This is very close to Zipf's model for *Ulysses*. As Miller tartly observes, "research workers in statistical linguistics have sometimes expressed amazement that people can follow Zipf's law so accurately without any deliberate effort to do so. We see, however, that it is not really very amazing, since monkeys typing at random manage to do it about as well as we do." The result basically depends on the fact that the probability of generating a long string of letters is a decreasing function of the length of the string, while the variety of long strings is far greater than the variety of short strings that are available. Consequently, both the rank of a word and its frequency are determined by its length, for the monkeys, and—as Zipf and many others have observed—for English too. And the nature of the dependence is such that the product of rank and frequency remains roughly constant.

Miller's analysis of the text produced by monkeys is a trifle superficial. It assumes that letters are equiprobable, so the most common words are "a", "b", ..., "z", each of which is equally likely to occur. This means that the words of rank 1 to 26 have the same probability, whereas the Mandelbrot formula shows a steady decrease. Similarly, the two-character words, which have rank 27 to 702, are equiprobable, and so on. Thus the correct rank-frequency relationship is a series of plateaus, shown on the graph of Figure 4-3a. The function derived by Miller passes through the average rank of each plateau, as shown. If, instead, we train the monkeys to strike each key with a frequency corresponding to its probability in English text, the plateaus are eroded, so that the curve follows the Mandelbrot function very closely. Figure 4-3b shows the curve for a sample of 1,000,000 words produced in an actual experiment with specially trained monkeys,[1] with the Zipf–Mandelbrot relation superimposed (they are indistinguishable on this scale). The Zipfian behavior of this simple model is as remarkable as Miller's original observation, for it is based on order-0 random text,

---

[1] Computer-simulated ones.

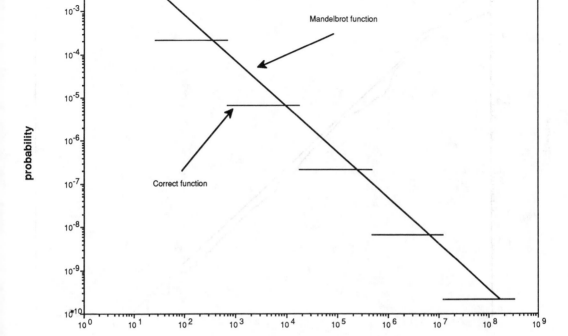

Figure 4-3   (a) Rank-probability graph for words generated by Miller's monkeys.

which bears little resemblance to English (see the second block of random text in Section 4-1 for an example). It seems that the Zipf curve is very easily achieved by simple random processes and does not need to be explained by an impressive-sounding teleological principle such as "least effort."

Despite its statistical explanation in terms of a random process, the fact remains that the Zipf law is a useful model of word frequencies. Figure 4-4 shows a graph of frequency against rank for the $N = 100,237$ different words in the Brown corpus, along with the Zipf model with normalizing constant calculated from $\mu = 1/(\log_e N + \gamma) = 0.08270$. Toward the end of the main line of data points the observed frequencies slope downward marginally more steeply than the model, indicating that the Mandelbrot distribution with B slightly greater than unity may provide a better fit. Moreover, the data seem flatter than the Zipf curve toward the left, an effect that could be modeled by choosing $c > 0$ but is more likely a remnant of the first plateau seen in Figures 4-3a and 4-3b.

The entropy of an order-0 model created from the Zipf distribution can be obtained from

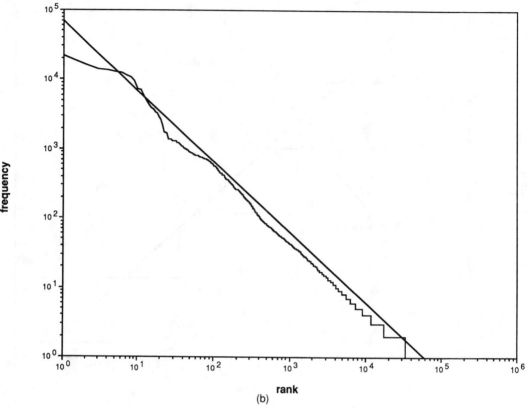

Figure 4-3(cont)   (b) Rank-frequency graph for words in order-0 random text.

$$\sum_{r=1}^{N} - \frac{\mu}{r} \log \frac{\mu}{r} \approx \frac{\mu(\log N)^2}{2 \log e} - \log \mu.$$

This leads to an estimate for the entropy of the word distribution in the Brown corpus of 11.51 bits/word, which is remarkably close to the value of 11.47 in Table 4-2. This contrasts with the 16.61 bits that would be required to specify one out of the 100,237 different words used in the Brown corpus if their distribution were uniform.

It is tempting to apply Zipf's law to all sorts of other rank-frequency data. For example, the letter, digram, trigram, and tetragram distributions of Table 4-1 are all hyperbolic in form. Despite this coincidence, the Zipf distribution is not a good model of the letter frequencies. For example, the Zipf distribution gives an entropy of 5.26 for the order-0 letter frequencies, whereas the observed value was 4.47.

For single-letter frequencies, a more accurate approximation is achieved when the probability interval between 0 and 1 is simply divided randomly and assigned to the letters "etaoin ...," respectively. Suppose that the unit interval is broken at random into N parts (in other words, $N-1$ points are chosen on it according to a uniform distribution). If the pieces are arranged in order beginning with the smallest, their expected sizes will be

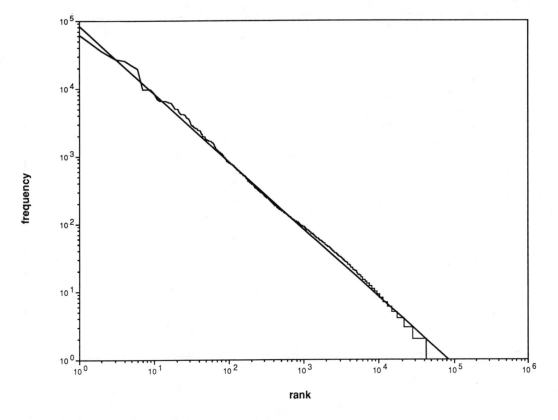

Figure 4-4   Word-frequency data from the Brown corpus with Zipf distribution (straight line).

$$\frac{1}{N}\cdot\frac{1}{N}, \quad \frac{1}{N}\left[\frac{1}{N}+\frac{1}{N-1}\right], \quad \frac{1}{N}\left[\frac{1}{N}+\frac{1}{N-1}+\frac{1}{N-2}\right], \quad \cdots .$$

It can be shown that this gives the rank distribution

$$p(r) = \frac{1}{N}\sum_{i=0}^{N-r}\frac{1}{N-i},$$

where $p(r)$ is the probability of the letter of rank r.

It has been observed that letter distributions (and, incidentally, phoneme distributions too) tend to follow this pattern. Figure 4-5 plots the letter probabilities of Table 4-1 (lowercase letters only) against rank, on logarithmic scales. The Zipf distribution appears as a straight line, while the dashed line is the distribution derived above, with $N = 26$. Although the latter appears to follow the data closely, the logarithmic scale masks sizable discrepancies. Nevertheless, it is clearly a much better fit than the Zipf distribution. For digrams, trigrams, and so on, the picture is similar, with the random distribution following the curve of the observed one in broad shape, while the Zipf plot is linear. However, the discrepancies are much greater, and neither model offers any reasonable fit to n-gram data.

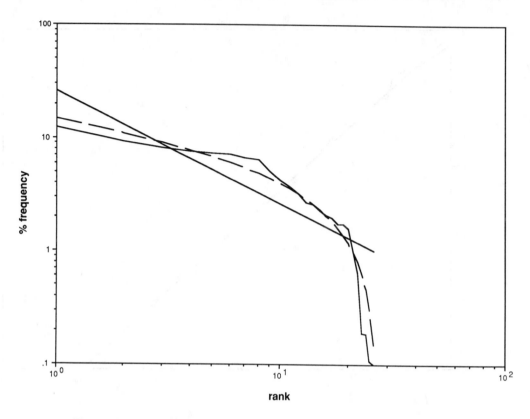

Figure 4-5   Letter-frequency data from the Brown corpus with Zipf distribution (straight line) and random distribution (dashed line).

To summarize, the Zipf distribution, rationalized by the principle of least effort, appears at first sight to be an attractive model for hyperbolic distributions such as the characteristic rank-frequency relations found throughout language. But in the two cases we have studied, letter and word frequencies, simple random models can match the data as well or better.

Other distributions have been studied. Linguists are often interested in the *type-token* relation. In the Brown corpus, the word *the* is a "type" of which 62,430 "tokens" appear. This constitutes a type-token pair (1, 62430). The words *year* and *less* both occur exactly 399 times, creating a type-token pair (2, 798). As words become rarer, the type-token relation becomes richer. For example, there are 747 words that occur exactly 10 times, and fully 58,141 *hapax legomena* (58% of the total), creating type-token pairs of (747, 7470) and (58141, 58141). The relationship can be modeled by a certain probability distribution, any particular corpus being regarded as a sample from it. Then statistical techniques can be employed to estimate the parameters of the distribution and hence the asymptotic vocabulary size.

For example, Shakespeare's 885,000 words include 31,500 different ones, of which 14,400 appear only once, 4300 twice, and so on. How many words did he know? It has been estimated that if another large body of work by Shakespeare were discovered, equal in size to his known writings, one would expect to find about 11,400 new words in addition to the original 31,500. Furthermore, according to the same estimate, he knew a total of at least 66,500 words. Although this work was done just for fun over a decade ago, the techniques have already found practical application in authorship ascription. Recently, a previously unknown poem, suspected to have been penned by Shakespeare, was discovered in a library in Oxford, England. Of its 430 words, statistical analysis predicted that 6.97 would be new, with a standard deviation of ±2.64. In fact, nine of them were (*admiration, besots, exiles, inflection, joying, scanty, speck, tormentor,* and *twined*). It was predicted that there would be 4.21 ± 2.05 that Shakespeare had previously used only once; the poem contained seven—only just outside the range. 3.33±1.83 should have been used exactly twice before; in fact, five were. Although this does not prove authorship, it does suggest it—particularly since comparative analyses of the vocabulary of Shakespeare's contemporaries indicate substantial mismatches.

Estimating the probability of previously unused words is related to the "zero-frequency problem" discussed in Section 3-1. However, let us move on from this digression, and look at the entropy of English and other languages.

4.4 THE INFORMATION CONTENT OF NATURAL LANGUAGE

In a classic paper published in 1951, Shannon considered the problem of estimating the entropy of ordinary English. In principle, this might be done by extending letter-frequency studies, like those of Table 4-1, to deal with longer and longer contexts until dependencies at the phrase level, sentence level, paragraph level, chapter level, and so on, have all been taken into account in the statistical analysis. In practice, however, this is quite impractical, for as the context grows, the number of possible contexts explodes exponentially. Although it is easy to estimate the distribution of letters following "t", "to", "to•", by examining a large corpus of text, trying to estimate the distribution following "to•be•or•not•to•b" by statistical methods is out of the question. The corpus needed for any reliable estimate would be huge.

To illustrate the problems, Figure 4-6 shows a graph obtained by plotting the entropy per letter from n-grams, where $n = 0$ to 12, for the Brown corpus. The entropy of English would correspond to a horizontal asymptote being reached, probably (as we shall see) at somewhere between 0.6 and 1.3 bits. However, it is certainly not feasible to predict the asymptote from this graph. Nor could it be possible. The corpus on which it is based is finite, and eventually, for large enough n, all n-grams will be unique. This could happen anywhere from $n = 4$ onwards, since there are 94 different characters in the corpus, and although 94^3 is less than the size of the corpus (1.6 million characters), $94^4 = 78$ million is greater. In fact, even at $n = 46$ and higher a very small proportion of n-grams are repeated—the phrase "the Government of the United States of America" occurs nine times, which one presumes says more about the material in the corpus than it does about the English language in general! Other large repeated phrases are supplied by the formalities of legal jargon; they include "in the year of Our Lord,

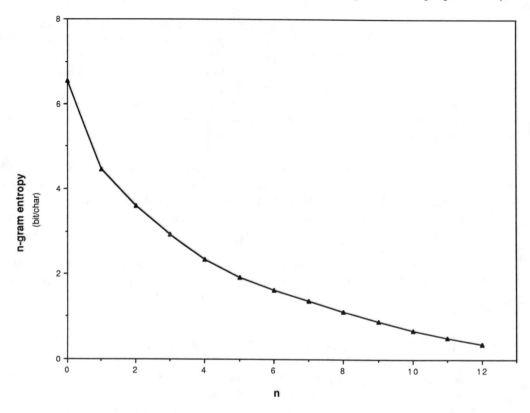

Figure 4-6   Entropy derived from *n*-grams, for *n* = 0 to 12.

one thousand nine hundred and" and "WHEREOF, I have hereunto set my hand and caused the seal of the State to be affixed" (both occurred seven times). Nevertheless, once *n* is so large that all *n*-grams are unique, each character can be predicted with certainty, so the entropy will be 0. It is clear that the experimental data converge on the *x*-axis rather rapidly. Consequently, no useful asymptotic entropy value can be obtained from this kind of approach.

Table 4-3 summarizes estimates of the entropy of natural languages that have been obtained by different researchers. The first two rows show the results Shannon obtained in 1951 by analyzing text. Using alphabets both with and without a space symbol, he got as far as trigrams (order 2, 3.1 bits/letter), and then went to a single-word model (2.14 bits/letter). (Note how similar his results are to those of Tables 4-1 and 4-2, notwithstanding the smaller alphabet he used.) The computational resources at his disposal did not permit examination of tetragrams or word pairs—but even if they had, he could not have gone much further before estimates became statistically unreliable due to the finite corpus available.

There followed several similar studies with different languages—French, German, Italian, Spanish, Portugese, Russian, Arabic, Malay, Samoan, Chinese, and three widely

TABLE 4-3 ESTIMATES OF THE ENTROPY OF NATURAL LANGUAGES

Language	Size of alphabet	Letter models with order:								Word model	Source
		−1	0	1	2	3	7	11	≥100		
From statistical analysis of text											
English	26	4.70	4.14	3.56	3.3					2.62	Shannon (1951)
	26+1	4.75	4.03	3.32	3.1					2.14	
English	26	4.70	4.12							1.65	Barnard (1955)
French	26	4.70	3.98							3.02	
German	26	4.70	4.10							1.08	
Spanish	26	4.70	4.02							1.97	
English	26+1	4.75	4.09	3.23	2.85	2.66	2.43	2.40			Newman and Waugh
Samoan	16+1	4.09	3.40	2.68	2.40	2.28	2.16	2.14			(1960)
Russian	35+1	5.17	4.55	3.44	2.95	2.72	2.45	2.40			
Portugese	26?	4.70?	3.92	3.51	3.15						Manfrino (1970)
Tamil	30	4.91	4.34								Siromoney (1963)
Kannada	49	5.61	4.55								Rajagopalan (1965)
Telugu	53	5.73	4.59	3.09							Balasubrahmanyam and Siromoney (1968)
Arabic	32	5.00	4.21	3.77	2.49						Wanas et al. (1976)
Chinese	4700	12.20	9.63								Wong and Poon (1976)
From experiments with subjects' best guesses											
English	26+1	4.75									
upper bound (smoothed)			4.0	3.4	3.0	2.6	2.1	1.9	1.3		Shannon (1951)
lower bound (smoothed)			3.2	2.5	2.1	1.8	1.2	1.1	0.6		
English	26+1	4.75				2.2	1.8	1.8	1.7		Jamison and Jamison
Italian	26+1	4.75				2.9	2.6	2.8	3.0		(1968)
Italian*	26+1	4.75				3.4	3.1	3.3	3.8		
French*	26+1	4.75				3.5	2.8	2.9	3.2		
From experiments with subjects using gambling											
English	26+1	4.75							1.25		Cover and King (1978)
Malay	26+1	4.75							1.32		Tan (1981)

spoken Indian languages, Tamil, Kannada, and Telugu. The entropy values obtained are summarized in the first block of Table 4-3. Using a different analysis technique, Newman and Waugh were able to get estimates with a much larger context size (but the statistical basis of this is dubious, and their method was not taken up by others). Given the variety of different languages represented, it would be interesting to study the influence of alphabet size on entropy, taking into account the expansion or contraction factors associated with translating one language into another.

Realizing that only a limited approximation to the true entropy of natural language could be obtained by this technique, Shannon proposed instead to use people as predictors and estimate the entropy from their performance. We all have an enormous knowledge of the statistics of English at a number of different levels—not just the traditional linguistic levels of morphology, syntax, semantics, but also knowledge of lexical structure, idioms, clichés, styles, discourse, and idiosyncrasies of individual authors, not to mention the subject matter itself. All this knowledge is called into play intuitively when we try to correct errors in text or complete unfinished phrases in conversation.

The procedure Shannon used was to show subjects text up to a certain point, and ask them to guess the next letter. If they were wrong, they were told so and asked to guess again, until eventually they guessed correctly. A typical result of this experiment is as follows, where subscripts indicate the number of the guess in which the subject got that letter correct.

$$T_1 H_1 E_1 R_5 E_1 \bullet_1 I_2 S_1 \bullet_1 N_2 O_1 \bullet_1 R_{15} E_1 V_{17} E_1 R_1 S_1 E_2 \bullet_1 O_3 N_2 \bullet_1 A_2 \bullet_2$$
$$M_7 O_1 T_1 O_1 R_1 C_4 Y_1 C_1 L_1 E_1 \bullet_1 A_3 \bullet_1 F_8 R_6 I_1 E_3 N_1 D_1 \bullet_1 O_1 F_1 \bullet_1 M_1 I_1$$
$$N_1 E_1 \bullet_1 F_6 O_2 U_1 N_1 D_1 \bullet_1 T_1 H_1 I_2 S_1 \bullet_1 O_1 U_1 T_1 \bullet_1 R_4 A_1 T_1 H_1 E_1 R_1 \bullet_1$$
$$D_{11} R_5 A_1 M_1 A_1 T_1 I_1 C_1 A_1 L_1 L_1 Y_1 \bullet_1 T_6 H_1 E_1 \bullet_1 O_1 T_1 H_1 E_1 R_1 \bullet_1 D_1 A_1$$
$$Y_1 \bullet_1$$

On the basis of no information about the sentence, this subject guessed that its first letter would be "T"—and in fact was correct. Knowing this, the next letter was guessed correctly as "H" and the one following as "E". The fourth letter was not guessed first time. Seeing "THE", the subject probably guessed space; then, when told that was wrong, tried letters such as "N" and "S" before getting the "R", which was correct, on the fifth attempt. Out of 102 symbols the first guess was correct 79 times, the second eight times, the third three times, the fourth and fifth twice each, while on only eight occasions were more than five guesses necessary. Shannon notes that results of this order are typical of prediction by a good subject with ordinary literary prose; newspaper writing and scientific work generally lead to somewhat poorer scores.

As material, 100 samples of English text were selected from Dumas Malone's *Jefferson the Virginian*, each 15 characters in length. The subject was required to guess the samples letter by letter, as described above, so that results were obtained for prior contexts of 0 letters, 1 letter, and so on up to 14 letters; a context of 100 letters was also used. Various aids were made available to subjects, including letter, digram, and trigram tables, a table of the frequencies of initial letters in words, a list of the frequencies of common words, and a dictionary. Another experiment was carried out with "reverse" prediction, in which the subject was required to guess the letter preceding those already known. Although this is subjectively much more difficult, performance was only slightly poorer.

Based on the data obtained in the experiment, Shannon derived upper and lower bounds for the entropy of 27-character English, shown in the first rows of the second block of Table 4-3. (These data are smoothed estimates based on experimental performance for contexts from 0 to 14 letters.) For 100-character contexts, the entropy was found to lie between 0.6 and 1.3 bits per character. Following Shannon's lead, other researchers performed similar experiments using different material and reached roughly similar conclusions. According to one study, increasing the context beyond about 30 letters produces no measurable gains in performance—subjects who were given 10,000 characters from a source were no better at guessing the next one than subjects who were required to predict the last letter of 33-letter sequences. The Jamisons, whose results are included in Table 4-3, were interested in the relation between linguistic knowledge and predictive success. The starred lines for Italian and French are for a subject who did not know these languages; not surprisingly, this caused poor performance (although the results seem to be less striking than one might have expected).

The guessing procedure gives only partial information about subjective probabilities for the next symbol. If the first guess is correct, as it is most of the time, all we learn is which symbol the subject believes is the most likely next one, not how much more likely it is than the others. For example, our expectation that "u" will follow "q" is significantly stronger than the expectation that "a" will follow "r"—yet both events, if they turn out to be correct, will appear the same in the experiment. The price paid for this loss of information is that the lower and upper bounds are widely separated and cannot be tightened by improved statistical analysis of the results. (The Jamisons' results, shown in Table 4-3, consist of a single figure rather than bounds because their analysis is less complete than Shannon's, not because their procedure is superior.)

The best way to elicit subjective probabilities is to put people in a gambling situation. Instead of guessing symbols and counting the number of guesses until correct, subjects wager a proportion of their current capital according to their estimate of the probability of a particular next symbol occurring. The capital begins at $S_0 = 1$, and at the nth stage S_n is set to $27pS_{n-1}$, where p is the proportion of capital assigned to the symbol that actually occurred. For an ideal subject who divides the capital on each bet according to the true probability distribution for the next symbol, it can be shown that the quantity

$$\log 27 - \frac{1}{n} \log S_n$$

approaches the entropy of the source as $n \to \infty$. Notice that to calculate the subject's winnings, it is not necessary to elicit an estimate of the probability of all 27 symbols in each situation, just the one that actually occurred. Since this information should obviously not be revealed until after the estimate has been made, the best procedure is to elicit the probability of the most likely symbol, the next most likely, and so on, until the correct one has been guessed. Only the last estimate is used by the procedure.

Cover and King, who developed this methodology, had 12 subjects gamble on a sample of text from the same source Shannon used—*Jefferson the Virginian*. About 250 words were presented to each subject, who had to guess the next 75 symbols one after another. Two subjects were also presented with a more contemporary piece of writing, from *Contact: the first four minutes,* by Leonard and Natalie Zunin, as a second text source. The passage used was

A handshake refused is so powerful a response that most people have never experienced or tried it. Many of us may have had the discomfort of a hand offered and ignored because it was not noticed, or another's hand was taken instead. In such an event, you quickly lower your hand or continue to raise it until you are scratching your head, making furtive glances to assure yourself that no one saw! When tw

and the subject had to guess the next 220 symbols, one by one.

This gambling procedure is very time consuming. Each subject worked with the *Jefferson* material interactively at a computer terminal for about 5 hours (4 minutes/letter). Subjects could read as much of the book as they liked, up to the point in question, to familiarize themselves with the subject matter and style of writing. They were provided with digram and trigram statistics for English; however, it was found that the best estimates came from subjects who did not use the tables as a crutch. Each subject was tested separately, but there was a definite air of competition.

When several subjects perform the experiment, an entropy estimate is obtained for each. Since we seek the minimum (best-case) entropy figure, it makes sense to select the results for the most successful gambler. However, this estimate is subject to statistical error—the best gambler might just have been very lucky. Cover and King analyzed several ways of combining individual results, and came up with a committee method that calculates a weighted average of each subject's betting scheme. Depending on the weights used, this may in fact do better than any individual gambler. Their results indicate an entropy of between 1.25 and 1.35 bits/symbol for both texts used, which is consistent (just) with Shannon's range of 0.6 to 1.3 bits/symbol and is by far the most reliable estimate available for any natural language.

NOTES

E. V. Wright's book *Gadsby*, a full-length novel that contains not a single "e", was published in 1939 by Wetzel and recently reprinted by Kassel Books, both in Los Angeles. Some of the information on letter frequencies (ETAOIN SHRDLU and his relatives) is from Atteneave (1953), Fang (1966), and Zettersten (1978).

Zipf's research on the statistics of natural phenomena is presented in Zipf (1949). Mandelbrot (1952) discusses shortcomings of the Zipf distribution and introduces the Mandelbrot distribution as a generalization of it. Miller et al. (1957) showed that the Zipf-like distribution of word frequencies is a direct consequence of a letters-and-space model, a result that was apparently known to Mandelbrot. Whitworth (1901) obtained the expected size of subintervals when the unit interval is split randomly into N parts, and discusses what it means to split an interval randomly. Good (1969) noticed that letter (and phoneme) distributions tend to follow this pattern. Carroll (1966, 1967) discusses how the log-normal distribution models the type-token relationship of words in the Brown corpus. Efron and Thisted (1976) used various statistical techniques to estimate Shakespeare's total vocabulary, and Kolata (1986) describes how their work was applied 10 years later to the identification of a newly discovered poem.

Shannon (1951) was the first to estimate the entropy of a natural language; Table 4-3 summarizes results of the research he stimulated. Despite this flurry of activity, there was no improvement in methodology over Shannon's procedure until Cover and King (1978) introduced the gambling approach. Their paper contains an extensive bibliography.

The continuation of the extract from *Contact* is

o people want to shake our hand simultaneously we may grab both one in a handshake and the other in a kind of reverse twist of the left hand which serves very well as a sign of cordiality and saves someone embarrassment.

45h[0j45thwGw45hqU9c
poejrg[4wky]p435q)b&
[0wejg[04jy42yj3*k!c
p0w4j5g[235-k6t0=w~n
[0ewjg04jy04jy4j;qmy
pmh][krty-jk46-[p"qb
p[jw435y   h[ps0%x
[psdhkj   8w34u5y9mwc
germhj-   j64k?ti
[ewjhj4wth5   0o#r0b
e[wmb[p h65 u;g4{@
65[];.9[   ]0.o~x6
germhj-53k=ukj64:3xf
[ewjhj4wth56430o*wm<
e[wmb[preh65,.u;aYlC
+[3fgm56rt0-"-23jsg!
[;jyt%ERghj(0;';Hd4=
1U5terEDghp=][>?kyeW

FROM PROBABILITIES TO BITS

5

In earlier chapters we emphasized an approach to text compression that separates the issue of modeling from that of coding a message with respect to the model. Creating models is a challenging activity, and in the bulk of this book we discuss and compare alternative modeling strategies. By now the groundwork is in place for this study. However, before getting to grips with practical modeling algorithms, it is worthwhile laying to rest the coding task. This will clarify how the two components interact in practice. Although essentially independent, they must be linked by an interface that transfers probability distributions from modeler to coder. Understanding the coder will help us design the modeler so that the interface can work efficiently. The problem of coding messages with respect to a probabilistic model is, in essence, completely solved. We present the solution in this chapter.

The basic problem is this: Given a probability distribution that is assumed to govern the choice of the next symbol, and the symbol that actually occurs (which of course may not be one that the distribution predicts as especially likely), find an algorithm to generate bits that specify the symbol to a decoder who is apprised of exactly the same distribution. For example, from a biased coin or die whose bias is known exactly, what is the best way to code a particular result, or, more appropriately, sequence of results, that actually turns up in a particular set of throws?

In principle, if the events really do occur in accordance with the specified distribution, it should be possible to encode each event in an average number of bits that is given by the entropy of the distribution. If they do not, the average number of bits per event will necessarily be greater. But getting distributions correct is the modeler's job. Here we are only concerned with coding with respect to one that is supplied.

Also in the modeler's domain is the choice of symbol to be used (bits, characters, words, or other units). This does not affect the coding problem, at least not in principle. In this chapter we develop the method of arithmetic coding using a single-character predictive model as an example, but the techniques apply quite generally to any other probabilistic model.

The best-known method for coding with respect to a probabilistic model is Huffman coding. This method is frequently advocated as the best possible technique for reducing the encoded data rate. But it is not. A more recent development, called arithmetic coding, is superior in almost all respects. It represents information at least as compactly—sometimes considerably more so. Its performance is optimal without the need for blocking of input data. It encourages a clear separation between the model for representing data and the encoding of information with respect to that model. It accommodates adaptive models easily. It is computationally efficient. Yet many authors and practitioners seem unaware of the technique. Indeed, there is a widespread belief that Huffman coding cannot be improved upon.

In previous chapters we have emphasized that adaptivity is an extremely powerful notion in modern data compression. It is usually important that coding methods accommodate adaptive models. Models adapt by changing probabilities according to that part of the message seen so far. This discourages the use of coding methods that take a probability distribution and embark on a large calculation to create a full code table. We need the flexibility to change the model frequently without expensive recalculation.

Because the existence of arithmetic coding guarantees that any message can be coded in the number of bits dictated by its entropy with respect to a model, the compression performance of any model can be evaluated without having to perform any coding. If the model estimates the probability of each symbol in an N symbol message to be $p_1, p_2, ..., p_N$, the message will be coded in $-\sum \log p_i$ bits.

While the method of arithmetic coding completely solves the coding problem in a way that is optimal from the point of view of the number of bits generated, there is always room for improved implementation techniques which improve the performance in terms of execution time. In particular, the implementation of adaptive models raises a number of important computational issues.

In the next section we describe the coding problem from a historical perspective. It is particularly curious that following the early and very influential ideas of Shannon and Huffman, the notion of arithmetic coding developed in erratic and tortuous fashion. With this background in place, in the next section we explain in detail how arithmetic coding works. A full software implementation, written in the C programming language, is included and documented in Appendix 5A; the main text explains the issues involved independently of programming language or other technical distractions. The Appendix also includes an implementation of an adaptive model. In Section 5-3 we describe the problems associated with the creation and maintenance of adaptive models, both for Huffman coding, to illustrate how tricky this is, and for arithmetic coding, where the task is much more straightforward. For large, unskewed alphabets the straightforward arithmetic coding solution is quite inefficient and can be improved by more sophisticated data structures. Moreover, for binary alphabets special tricks can be used to increase coding speed. Finally, we examine the efficiency of arithmetic coding, in terms of both compression performance and execution speed.

5.1 THE QUEST FOR OPTIMAL SOURCE CODING

A remarkable fundamental result of information theory relates the characteristics of an information source to the characteristics of a channel through which information from the source can be communicated. In Section 2-1 we introduced the notion of the *entropy* of a source of information. The *capacity* of a discrete communication channel quantifies its ability to carry information. This notion was first studied in the context of sampling analog waveforms in time—how many samples are necessary each second to preserve the fidelity of an analog signal like speech or music? In 1928, the American communications engineer Harry Nyquist analyzed and solved this problem (the answer is that the sampling rate must exceed twice the highest frequency in the signal, the so-called "Nyquist rate"). He had earlier wondered about the information content of each signal and decided on a logarithmic measure of information. But not until Shannon's work in the 1940s did the subject of information theory begin to blossom.

To us, with our present-day perspective of computers and information representation, it is manifest that a communication channel carrying n symbols per second, where each symbol can independently assume one of four values, transmits twice the information of a channel with the same rate but whose symbols are binary. The capacity of a channel is defined as the maximum rate at which information can be transmitted through it. In the case of a noiseless channel, this is just the number of samples that can be transmitted per second times the number of bits carried by each sample. When a modem enables a telephone line to carry 1200 one-bit symbols per second, its capacity is 1200 bits/s, but if the symbols are 2- or 4-bit ones, the capacity is doubled or quadrupled. The term "baud" refers to the channel capacity in *symbols* per second—the modem operates at 1200 baud regardless of whether the symbols are 1, 2, or 4 bits. However, the term is often used mistakenly as a synonym for bits/s.

Suppose that a source with entropy H bits/symbol feeds a channel with capacity C bits/s. Then Shannon showed in 1948 that if reception is to be error-free, (a) the transmission rate of the system cannot exceed C/H symbols/s, and (b) coding systems exist that approach this limit arbitrarily closely.

The first part of the result is a direct consequence of the definitions of entropy and channel capacity and simply confirms that these notions behave as one is entitled to expect from the way they are advertised—even in the realm of information you cannot get a quart into a pint pot. The second part is shown by considering sequences of N symbols from the source, enumerating all sequences in order of decreasing probability, and applying a simple coding scheme to the resulting possibilities. Although the resulting transmission rate is less than C/H symbols/s, it approaches it as $N \to \infty$.

While the coding scheme is quite practical (it is called Shannon–Fano coding and is described below), the requirement to enumerate all possible messages and sort them is certainly *not* feasible in any realistic coding situation. Nevertheless, given the statistics of the source, an approximation to an optimal coding scheme is to treat symbols as separate messages and to code them independently according to their zero-order probabilities. Successively better approximations can be obtained by taking digrams, trigrams, tetragrams, and so forth, as messages, and coding according to their probabilities (which can be calculated from the model). This idea of *blocking* input data into fixed-length groups of consecutive symbols, and coding each block as a unit independently of the others, is a most pervasive notion in coding theory and practice.

Only recently have people fought free from the shackles of the block-oriented approach and created true stream-oriented coding methods. This is perhaps the first really significant development in the field of coding that was not foreseen by Shannon. Blocking makes it easy to prove theorems about behavior in the limit as block size increases, but is inelegant in implementation. Considerable housekeeping is required to initialize and terminate blocks, and to keep track of position within a block, which is incidental to the primary task of coding. It is antithetical to real-time operation and modern interactive terminal protocols.

The stream-oriented method of arithmetic coding achieves the theoretical entropy bound to compression efficiency for any source without the need for blocking. In order to set the context, we review its predecessors and the historical development of the idea.

5.1.1 Shannon–Fano Coding

Shannon's idea for coding messages according to their probabilities, which was discovered independently at roughly the same time by R. M. Fano at M.I.T., was as follows:

- List all possible messages, with their probabilities, in decreasing probability order.

- Divide the list into two parts of (roughly) equal probability.

- Start the code for those messages in the first part with a 0 bit and for those in the second part with a 1.

- Continue recursively until each subdivision contains just one message.

Figure 5-1 illustrates the operation of this procedure on a small example with messages {*a, e, i, o, u, !*} and probabilities as shown. In Table 5-1 the average code length is compared across three different symbol-by-symbol methods. In the Shannon–Fano case, 2-bit codes occur half the time (*a* and *e*), while 3-bit codes appear the other half. Thus the average code length is 2.5 bits/symbol. The corresponding figure for the fixed-length code is 3 bits/symbol, while the entropy, which represents a lower bound that no code can possibly better, is 2.43 bits/symbol.

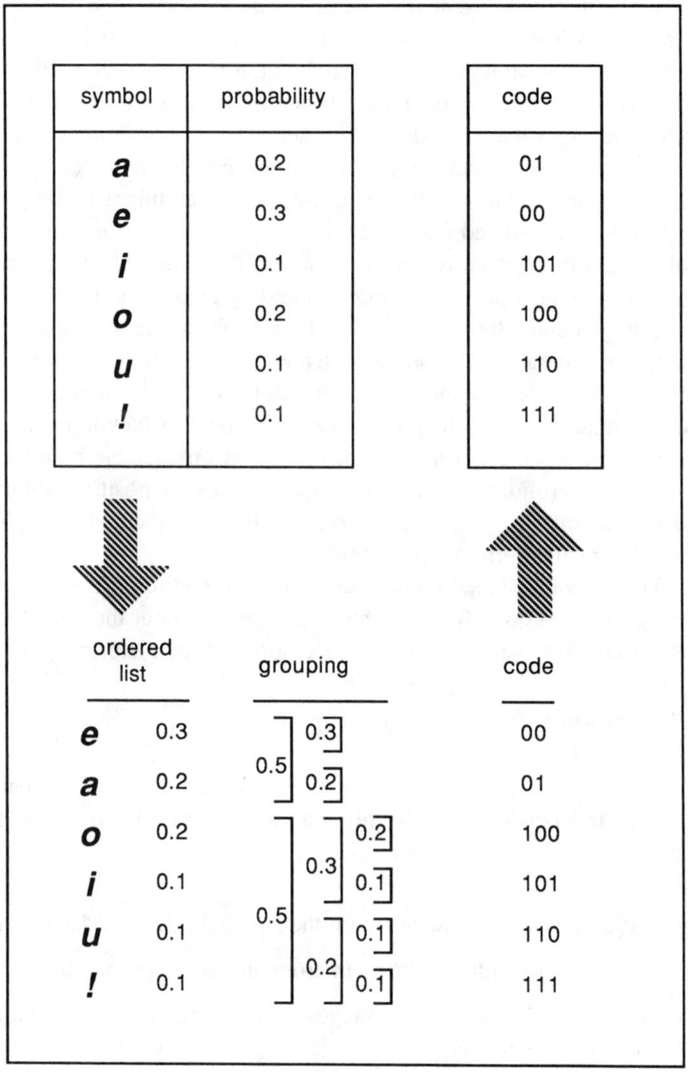

symbol	probability	code
a	0.2	01
e	0.3	00
i	0.1	101
o	0.2	100
u	0.1	110
!	0.1	111

ordered list		grouping		code
e	0.3	0.5 [0.3̄		00
a	0.2	[0.2̄		01
o	0.2	0.5 [0.3 [0.2̄		100
i	0.1	[0.1̄		101
u	0.1	[0.2 [0.1̄		110
!	0.1	[0.1̄		111

Figure 5-1   An example of Shannon–Fano coding.

The average code length of the Shannon–Fano scheme can be shown to lie within the range $[H, H+1)$,[1] where H is the entropy of the source according to the message probabilities used for coding. For example, using single-symbol probabilities as in Figure 5-1, the average code length of 2.5 is certainly within the range [2.43, 3.43). This was the result that Shannon required for his proof that the coding scheme approaches the optimal as the block length grows without bound.

[1]The notation [a, b) denotes the half-open interval $a \le x < b$.

TABLE 5-1   COMPARISON OF SYMBOL-BY-SYMBOL CODES ON A SMALL EXAMPLE

symbol	Source prob	$-p \times \log p$	Fixed-length code	$p \times length$	Shannon/Fano code	$p \times length$	Huffman code	$p \times length$
a	0.2	0.46	000	0.6	01	0.4	10	0.4
e	0.3	0.52	001	0.9	00	0.6	01	0.6
i	0.1	0.33	010	0.3	101	0.3	001	0.3
o	0.2	0.46	011	0.6	100	0.6	11	0.4
u	0.1	0.33	100	0.3	110	0.3	0000	0.4
!	0.1	0.33	101	0.3	111	0.3	0001	0.4
		2.43		3.0		2.5		2.5

5.1.2 Huffman Coding

Shortly after Shannon's work, D. A. Huffman of M.I.T. discovered a way of constructing codes from a set of message probabilities which gives greater compression.

- List all possible messages with their probabilities.
- Locate the two messages with the smallest probabilities.
- Replace these by a single set containing them both, whose probability is the sum of the individual probabilities.
- Repeat until the list contains only one member.

This procedure produces a recursively structured set of sets, each of which contains exactly two members. It can therefore be represented as a binary tree with the original messages at the leaves. Then to form the code for any particular message:

- Traverse the tree from the root to that message, recording 0 for a left branch and 1 for a right branch.

Figure 5-2 illustrates the process for our example message set. The messages are shown sorted by their probability, but a heap data structure is generally more efficient for finding the two items with the smallest probabilities. The coding produced is different from the Shannon–Fano case, there being three 2-bit codes, one 3-bit one, and two 4-bit ones. Nevertheless, the average code length, shown in Table 5-1, happens to be the same. In fact, there were many ties in the sorting process, and one way of resolving them would have produced precisely the Shannon–Fano code of Figure 5-1. In this case the Huffman procedure does not result in greater compression. But in general it does.

The three coding schemes of Table 5-1 share an important "prefix property": no code forms a prefix of any other. For example, 010 does *not* appear as a code in the Huffman column; if it did, it would violate the property since it contains 01, the code for *e*, as a prefix. The prefix property ensures that if a sequence of messages is coded,

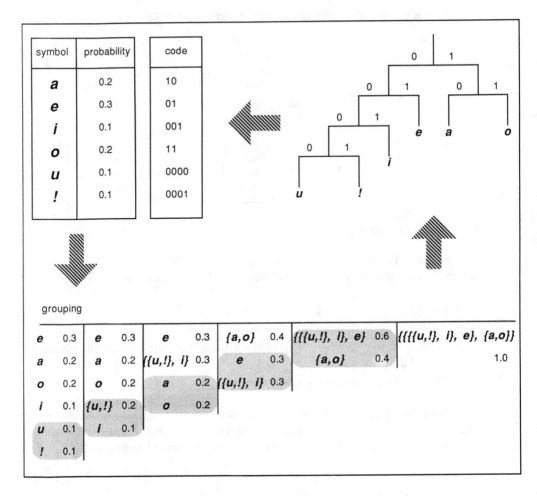

Figure 5-2   An example of Huffman coding.

the resulting code string can be parsed unambiguously into its constituents without the
need for any end markers. For example, the string

$$0100110001110000011110000 \cdots$$

is parsed as

010–011–000–111–000–011–110–000 $\cdots$	*ioa?ao?a* $\cdots$
01–00–110–00–111–00–00–111–100–00 $\cdots$	*aeue!ee!oe* $\cdots$
01–001–10–001–11–0000–11–11–0000 $\cdots$	*eiaiouoou* $\cdots$

using the fixed-length, Shannon–Fano, and Huffman codes, respectively. (Notice that
the codes 111 and 110 in the fixed-length case have no corresponding symbols; holes
like this in the code space indicate redundancy in the code.)

Coding schemes strive to give high-probability messages short codes and low-probability ones longer codes. But, in fact, the Shannon–Fano method sometimes assigns a longer code to a more probable message than it does to a less probable one. When this occurs, a more efficient code could be obtained by interchanging the two. Huffman coding does not suffer from this deficiency. It can be shown to generate "minimum-redundancy" codes that produce the shortest possible average code length given the message set's probability distribution. Although this is unquestionably true, when loosely rendered as a slogan such as "Huffman coding is optimal" it has led to the pervasive misconception that you cannot do better than Huffman coding. In most practical coding situations, you certainly can.

The misconception arises because in practice Huffman coding is not used to encode single, complete messages. To do so would require all possible messages to be enumerated, which is invariably quite out of the question. Instead, Huffman coding is applied to individual units, such as single symbols or n-gram blocks, and a stream of codes is transmitted. This is why the prefix property is important—if the entire message were encoded as one unit, the problem of parsing a sequence of codes would not arise (although you would still need to identify the end of the message). And while each unit, considered individually, is translated with minimum redundancy into an integral number of bits, the sequence of units taken together is not.

Given that each symbol in the alphabet must occupy an integral number of bits in the encoding, Huffman coding does indeed achieve "minimum redundancy." In other words, it performs optimally if all symbol probabilities are exact powers of $1/2$. But this is not normally the case in practice; indeed Huffman coding, like the Shannon–Fano method, can take up to one extra bit per symbol. The worst case is realized by a source in which there is a symbol whose probability approaches unity. Symbols emanating from such a source convey negligible information on average, but require at least one bit to transmit using any coding scheme that translates each symbol into a whole number of bits.

It can be shown that the redundancy of Huffman codes, defined as the average code length less the entropy, is bounded by $p + \log [2(\log e)/e] = p + 0.086$, where p is the probability of the most likely symbol. If there are many symbols of roughly equal probability, this is much better than the Shannon–Fano redundancy bound of 1. In the example of Table 5-1 the maximum probability is $p = 0.3$, so the average code length is guaranteed to lie within [2.43, 2.82), compared with Shannon–Fano's interval of [2.43, 3.43). In general, however, sophisticated models expose the deficiencies of Huffman coding more starkly than do simple ones. This is because they more often predict symbols with probabilities close to 1, the worst case for Huffman coding.

It is easy to make Huffman coding more effective—just block symbols into n-grams and use these as the units for coding. The larger the value of n (up to the length of the message itself), the lower the redundancy. While trivial in principle, this trick is inelegant in practice. Code tables grow. Padding the message to an integral number of blocks wastes bandwidth. The contextual information provided by the symbols toward the end of one block, which could help predict those at the beginning of the next, is wasted. Most important, continual adaptation to the source statistics becomes messy. The batch-oriented mentality brings its own problems.

5.1.3 The Birth of Arithmetic Coding

Arithmetic coding dispenses with the restriction that symbols translate into an integral number of bits, thereby coding more efficiently. It actually achieves the theoretical entropy bound to compression efficiency for any source, including one where each symbol conveys negligible information. It achieves the same effect as treating the message as one unit, yet the coding is performed incrementally, without the need to enumerate all possible messages in advance.

The details of the method are somewhat more intricate than Huffman coding, and because of its importance, a complete description, together with an analysis of implementation trade-offs, appears in the next section. However, arithmetic coding is certainly not a complicated idea, and considering its elegance and practical advantages over competing methods, it is quite surprising that it was not discovered until the late 1970s and popularized in the 1980s. It computes the code incrementally, one symbol at a time. This contrasts sharply with the Huffman method of blocking symbols into fixed-length n-grams and calculating a complete coding table. Right from Shannon's original work, the latter style thoroughly pervaded all thinking about coding methods, and this is presumably the reason why arithmetic coding had a long and tortuous gestation.

Shannon–Fano coding, described above, operates by sorting messages according to probability and then sending enough bits to specify one particular message in the ordering. In fact, Shannon noted explicitly in his 1948 paper that if the cumulative probability were expanded as a binary fraction to a precision sufficient to distinguish it from the next message, the code string could be decoded by magnitude comparison. This is the basic idea of arithmetic coding, and from it can be traced the developments that led to modern implementations. From this viewpoint, Huffman's method was a red herring!

In the early 1960s Elias realized first, that there is no need to sort the messages—any order will do providing encoder and decoder agree what it is—and second, that the cumulative probability can be calculated iteratively from individual symbol probabilities. Unfortunately, he did not publish his result. Abramson's 1963 text on information theory contains a brief reference to it, and it seems tantalizingly close to modern arithmetic coding. Some years later, Jelinek elaborated on Elias's code. However, as it was understood then, the method was quite impractical because the precision of the arithmetic required increased with message length. Consequently, even if the necessary storage were available, the time required for coding each symbol would increase linearly with message length.

The discovery that the calculation could be approximated in finite-precision arithmetic, creating a linear-time encoding method without any serious impact on compression efficiency, was made independently around 1976 by Pasco and Rissanen. Neither described particularly practical methods, however. Rissanen's was last-in first-out and produced the code in reverse order. Pasco's, although first-in first-out, retained the entire coded string in memory until the last symbol was encoded to permit carry propagation over the length of the coded message.

Three groups came up at about the same time with the modern concept of arithmetic coding, working with fixed-precision arithmetic and operating incrementally, symbol by symbol, in first-in, first-out fashion. Rubin, Guazzo, and Rissanen and Langdon all published papers describing the method. The first two papers were submitted for publication in 1977 but did not appear until 1979 and 1980, respectively. Rissanen and Langdon's description in 1979 was oriented very much toward hardware implementation. The same idea has been discovered independently, probably by many people (including one of the authors, JGC, regrettably much later!)

In view of the scattered and somewhat obscure nature of research publications on arithmetic coding, it is fortunate that a tutorial appeared by Langdon in 1981 as an IBM Research Report. A revised version was published in 1984, which included a brief history of the idea; our present discussion is based on it. Finally, Witten et al. made available a full software implementation of arithmetic coding in 1987. Despite these publications, however, the method is not widely known. A number of recent books and papers on data compression mention it only in passing, or not at all.

5.2 ARITHMETIC CODING

In arithmetic coding a message is represented by an interval of real numbers between 0 and 1. As the message becomes longer, the interval needed to represent it becomes smaller, and the number of bits needed to specify that interval grows. Successive symbols of the message reduce the size of the interval in accordance with the symbol probabilities generated by the model. The more likely symbols reduce the range by less than the unlikely symbols and hence add fewer bits to the message.

Before anything is transmitted, the range for the message is the entire half-open interval from zero to one, [0, 1). As each symbol is processed, the range is narrowed to that portion of it allocated to the symbol. For example, suppose that the alphabet is {a, e, i, o, u, !}, and a fixed model is used with the probabilities of Table 5-1, which are reproduced, along with ranges, in Table 5-2. Imagine transmitting the message *eaii!*. Initially, both encoder and decoder know that the range is [0, 1). After seeing the first symbol, *e*, the encoder narrows it to [0.2, 0.5), the range the model allocates to this symbol. The second symbol, *a*, will narrow this new range to the first one-fifth of it, since *a* has been allocated [0, 0.2). This produces [0.2, 0.26), since the previous range

TABLE 5-2 EXAMPLE FIXED
MODEL FOR ARITHMETIC
CODING

Symbol	Probability	Range
a	0.2	[0, 0.2)
e	0.3	[0.2, 0.5)
i	0.1	[0.5, 0.6)
o	0.2	[0.6, 0.8)
u	0.1	[0.8, 0.9)
!	0.1	[0.9, 1.0)

was 0.3 units long and one-fifth of that is 0.06. The next symbol, *i*, is allocated [0.5, 0.6), which when applied to [0.2, 0.26) gives the smaller range [0.23, 0.236). Proceeding in this way, the encoded message builds up as follows:

initially		[0,	1)
after seeing	*e*	[0.2,	0.5)
	a	[0.2,	0.26)
	i	[0.23,	0.236)
	i	[0.233,	0.2336)
	!	[0.23354,	0.2336)

Figure 5-3 shows another representation of the encoding process. The vertical bars with ticks represent the symbol probabilities stipulated by the model. After the first symbol has been processed, the model is scaled into the range [0.2, 0.5), as shown in Figure 5-3a. The second symbol scales it again into the range [0.2, 0.26). But the picture cannot be continued in this way without a magnifying glass! Consequently, Figure 5-3b shows the ranges expanded to full height at every stage and marked with a scale that gives the numeric values of endpoints.

Suppose that all the decoder knows about the message is the final range, [0.23354, 0.2336). It can immediately deduce that the first character was *e*, since the range lies entirely within the space the model of Table 5-2 allocates for *e*. Now it can simulate the operation of the *en*coder:

initially	[0, 1)
after seeing *e*	[0.2, 0.5).

This makes it clear that the second character of the message is *a*, since this will produce the range

after seeing *a*	[0.2, 0.26),

which entirely encloses the given range [0.23354, 0.2336). Proceeding like this, the decoder can identify the whole message.

It is not really necessary for the decoder to know both ends of the range produced by the encoder. Instead, a single number within the range—for example, 0.23355— will suffice. (Other numbers, such as 0.23354, 0.23357, or even 0.23354321, would do just as well.) However, the decoder will face the problem of detecting the end of the message, to determine when to stop decoding. After all, the single number 0.0 could represent any of *a*, *aa*, *aaa*, *aaaa*, ... To resolve the ambiguity, we ensure that each message ends with a special terminating symbol known to both encoder and decoder. For the alphabet of Table 5-2, *!* will be used to terminate messages, and only to terminate messages. When the decoder sees this symbol, it stops decoding.

Relative to the fixed model of Table 5-2, the entropy of the five-symbol message *eaii!* is

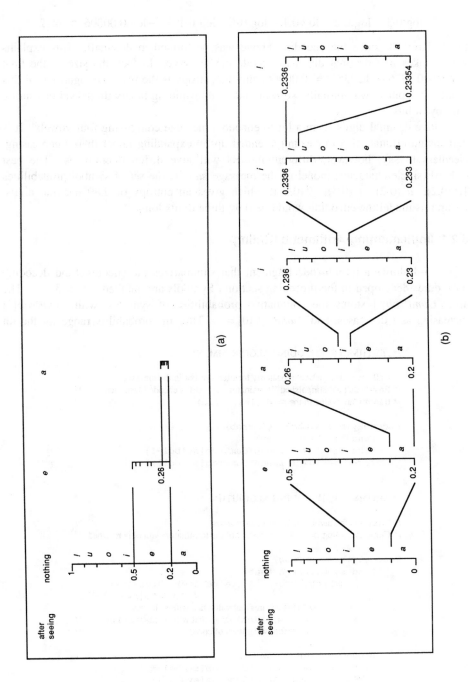

Figure 5-3 (a) Representation of the arithmetic coding process; (b) arithmetic coding with the interval scaled up at each stage.

$$-\log 0.3 - \log 0.2 - \log 0.1 - \log 0.1 - \log 0.1 = -\log 0.00006 \approx 4.22$$

(using base 10, since the encoding above was performed in decimal). This explains why it takes five decimal digits to encode the message. In fact, the size of the final range is $0.2336 - 0.23354 = 0.00006$, and the entropy is the negative logarithm of this figure. Of course, we normally work in binary, transmitting binary digits and measuring entropy in bits.

Five decimal digits seem a lot to encode a message comprising four vowels! It is perhaps unfortunate that our example ended up by expanding rather than compressing. Needless to say, however, different models will give different entropies. The best order-0 (single-character) model of the message *eaii!* is the set of symbol probabilities {*e* (0.2), *a* (0.2), *i* (0.4), *!* (0.2)}, which gives an entropy of 2.89 decimal digits. Using this model the encoding would be only three digits long.

5.2.1 Implementing Arithmetic Coding

Figure 5-4 shows a pseudocode fragment that summarizes the encoding and decoding procedures developed in the preceding section. Symbols are numbered 1, 2, 3, ... The array *CumProb*[ ] stores the cumulative probabilities of symbols, with *CumProb*[*i*] increasing as *i* decreases, and *CumProb*[0] = 1. Thus the probability range for the *i*th

```
/* ARITHMETIC ENCODING ALGORITHM. */

/* Call EncodeSymbol repeatedly for each symbol in the message.       */
/* Ensure that a distinguished "terminator" symbol is encoded last, then    */
/* transmit any value in the range [low, high).                        */

EncodeSymbol(symbol, CumProb)
    range := high - low;
    high  := low + range*CumProb[symbol-1];
    low   := low + range*CumProb[symbol];


/* ARITHMETIC DECODING ALGORITHM. */

/* Value is the number that has been received.                         */
/* Continue calling DecodeSymbol until the terminator symbol is returned. */

DecodeSymbol(CumProb)
    find symbol such that
        CumProb[symbol] ≤ (value-low)/(high-low)
                            < CumProb[symbol-1];
            /* This ensures that value lies within the new          */
            /* [low, high) range that will be calculated by         */
            /* the following lines of code.                         */

    range := high - low;
    high  := low + range*CumProb[symbol-1];
    low   := low + range*CumProb[symbol];
    return symbol;
```

Figure 5-4   Pseudocode for the arithmetic coding and decoding procedures.

symbol is from *CumProb* [*i*] to *CumProb* [*i* − 1]. (The reason for this "backwards" convention is that *CumProb* [0] will later contain a normalizing factor, and it will be convenient to have it begin the array.) The "current interval" is [*low*, *high*), and for both encoding and decoding this should be initialized to [0, 1).

Unfortunately, the algorithm in Figure 5-4 is overly simplistic. There are several factors that complicate both encoding and decoding in practice.

- Incremental transmission and reception.
  The encoding algorithm as described does not transmit anything until the entire message has been encoded; neither does the decoding algorithm begin to decode until it has received the complete transmission. In most applications an incremental mode of operation is necessary.
- The desire to use fixed-point arithmetic.
  The precision required to represent the [*low*, *high*) interval grows with the length of the message. Incremental operation will help overcome this, but the potential for overflow and underflow must still be examined carefully.
- Representing the model so that it can be consulted efficiently.
  The representation used for the model should minimize the time required for the decode algorithm to identify the next symbol. Moreover, an adaptive model should be organized to minimize the time-consuming task of maintaining cumulative frequencies.

A program for arithmetic coding appears in Appendix 5A. Because of the need to perform low-level operations such as bit shifting efficiently, it is written in the C programming language. Program documentation and all language-dependent technical details have been relegated to the appendix. The remainder of this section discusses the issues involved in going from the bare-bones sketch of Figure 5-4 to an actual implementation. Where necessary an informal notation like that of the figure is used to explain parts of the algorithm. Consideration of how adaptive models can be represented efficiently is postponed until Section 5-3.

5.2.2 Incremental Transmission and Reception

In the example of Figure 5-3, the message could be unambiguously coded as the number 0.23355. Notice that after the second character has been encoded, the range has been reduced to [0.2, 0.26). Since the final code must be within this range, we can guarantee that it begins "0.2 ...". Likewise, after the third character, we can be certain that it will begin "0.23 ...", and after the fourth, "0.233 ...". It is because of this that incremental transmission can be achieved—each digit is sent as soon as its value is known. The decoder can also interpret the codes incrementally; for example, after receiving the initial "0.23," the decoder can narrow the range sufficiently to determine the first three characters. If coding is incremental, it can be performed using finite-precision arithmetic, because once a digit has been transmitted, it will have no further influence on the calculations. For example, if the "0.23" of the interval [0.23, 0.236) has been sent, future output would not be affected if the interval were changed to [0.000, 0.006) or even [0.0, 0.6), thus decreasing the precision of the arithmetic required. We now look at how this is done in practice.

The quantities *low* and *high* of Figure 5-4 will be represented by integers, not real numbers. We will assume that a special data type, *CodeValue*, has been defined for these quantities; typically, the type *CodeValue* will be 16- or 32-bit integers. The cumulative probabilities will be represented as integer frequency counts in *CumFreq*[ ], instead of the probabilities of *CumProb*[ ]. The total frequency count, or number of symbols processed so far, is stored in *CumFreq*[0] as a normalizing factor. That is, $CumProb[i] = CumFreq[i]/CumFreq[0]$.

In Figure 5-4 the current interval is represented by [*low*, *high*), open at the upper end. It will henceforth be more convenient to represent it as [*low*, *high*], so that the range includes the value of *high*, which, like *low*, is now an integer. Actually, it is more accurate (although more confusing) to say that the interval represented is [*low*, *high* + 0.11111 ...), where the number 0.11111 ... is in binary notation. We can make our program reflect this convention by ensuring that when the bounds are scaled up to increase the precision, 0's are shifted into the low-order bits of *low* but 1's are shifted into *high*. Although it is possible to write a program to use a different convention, this one has some advantages in simplifying the implementation.

As the code range narrows, the top bits of *low* and *high* will become the same. Any bits that are the same can be transmitted immediately, since they cannot be affected by future narrowing. For encoding, since we know that *low* ≤ *high*, this requires code like

```
while high < Half or low ≥ Half do
    if high < Half then
            OutputBit(0);
            low := 2*low;
            high := 2*high + 1;
    if low ≥ Half then
            OutputBit(1);
            low := 2*(low - Half);
            high := 2*(high - Half) + 1;
```

where *Half* is the halfway point of the *CodeValue* range (for 16-bit operation it would be 32768, or 2^{15}). This code ensures that, upon completion, *low* < *Half* ≤ *high*. Notice how 1's are shifted in at the bottom when *high* is scaled, while 0's are shifted into *low*, to preserve the integrity of the [*low*, *high* + 0.11111 ...) interpretation.

In Figure 5-4, decoding is done using a number called *value*. To make the operation incremental, processed bits flow out the top (high-significance) end and newly received ones flow in the bottom of *value*. To begin, *value* is filled up with the first few received bits. Once the decoding procedure has identified the next input symbol, it shifts out now-useless high-order bits that are the same in *low* and *high*, shifting *value* by the same amount (and replacing lost bits by fresh input bits at the bottom end):

```
while high < Half or low ≥ Half do
    if high < Half then
            value := 2*value + InputBit();
            low := 2*low; high := 2*high + 1;
    if low  ≥ Half then
            value := 2*(value - Half) + InputBit();
            low := 2*(low - Half); high := 2*(high - Half) + 1;
```

5.2.3 Decoding Using Integer Arithmetic

At this point it is worth examining how the decoder can identify the next symbol correctly. Recall from Figure 5-4 that *DecodeSymbol( )* must use *value* to find the symbol that, when encoded, reduces the range to one that still includes *value*. Using the integer representation for the [*low*, *high*] interval and for the cumulative frequencies, the task of finding the symbol becomes

```
range := high - low + 1;
cum := ((value - low + 1)*CumFreq[0] - 1)/range;
symbol := 1;
while CumFreq[symbol - 1] > cum do
     symbol := symbol + 1;
high := low + (range*CumFreq[symbol - 1])/CumFreq[0] - 1;
low  := low + (range*CumFreq[symbol])/CumFreq[0];
```

The *while* loop identifies the symbol for which

$$CumFreq\,[symbol\,] \leq \left\lfloor \frac{(value - low + 1)*CumFreq\,[0] - 1}{high - low + 1} \right\rfloor < CumFreq\,[symbol - 1],$$

where $\lfloor \ \rfloor$ denotes the "integer part of" function that comes from integer division with truncation. It is shown in Appendix 5B that this implies

$$low + \left\lfloor \frac{(high - low + 1)*CumFreq\,[symbol\,]}{CumFreq\,[0]} \right\rfloor \leq value$$

$$\leq low + \left\lfloor \frac{(high - low + 1)*CumFreq\,[symbol - 1]}{CumFreq\,[0]} \right\rfloor - 1,$$

so *value* lies within the new [*low*, *high*] interval that is calculated above. This is sufficient to guarantee that the decoding operation identifies each symbol correctly.

5.2.4 Underflow and Overflow

As Figure 5-4 makes clear, arithmetic coding works by scaling the cumulative probabilities given by the model into the interval [*low*, *high*] for each character transmitted. Suppose that *low* and *high* become very close together—so close that this scaling operation maps some different symbols of the model on to the same integer in the [*low*, *high*] interval. That would be disastrous, because if such a symbol actually occurred, it would not be possible to continue encoding. Consequently, the encoder must guarantee that the interval [*low*, *high*] is always large enough to prevent this. This problem arises with symbols that have very low probabilities. The lowest probability that any symbol can have is 1/*CumFreq* [0]. One way to ensure that the range [*high*,*low*] has sufficient precision to encode such a symbol is to require that this interval is at least as large as the maximum allowed cumulative frequency count, which we will call *MaxFrequency*.

How could this condition be violated? The bit-shifting operation explained above ensures that *low* and *high* can only become close together when they straddle *Half*. Suppose that, in fact, they become as close as

$$FirstQtr \le low < Half \le high < ThirdQtr,$$

where, like *Half*, *FirstQtr* and *ThirdQtr* indicate positions within the *CodeValue* range (for 16-bit operation, *FirstQtr* = 16384, *Half* = 32768, *ThirdQtr* = 49152). Then the next two bits sent will have opposite polarity, either 01 or 10. For example, if the next bit turns out to be 0 (i.e., *high* descends below *Half* and [0, *Half*] is expanded to the full interval), the bit after that will be 1, since the range has to be above the midpoint of the expanded interval. Conversely, if the next bit happens to be 1, the one after that will be 0. Therefore, the interval can safely be expanded right now, if only we remember that whatever bit actually comes next, its opposite must be transmitted afterward as well. In this situation we simply expand [*FirstQtr*, *ThirdQtr*] into the whole interval, remembering in a variable—we will call it *BitsToFollow*—that the bit that is output next must be followed by an opposite bit.

```
if FirstQtr ≤ low and high < ThirdQtr then
    BitsToFollow := 1;
    low  := 2*(low - FirstQtr);
    high := 2*(high - FirstQtr + 1);
```

But what if, after this operation, it is *still* true that

$$FirstQtr \le low < Half \le high < ThirdQtr?$$

Figure 5-5 illustrates this situation, where the current [*low*, *high*] range (shown as a thick line) has been expanded a total of three times. Suppose that the next bit will turn out to be 0, as indicated by the arrow in Figure 5-5a being below the halfway point. Then the next *three* bits will be 1's, since not only is the arrow in the top half of the bottom half of the original range, it is in the top quarter, and moreover the top eighth, of that half—that is why the expansion can occur three times. Similarly, as Figure 5-5b shows, if the next bit turns out to be a 1, it will be followed by three 0's. Consequently, we need only count the number of expansions and follow the next bit by that number of opposites, replacing the code fragment above by

```
while FirstQtr ≤ low and high < ThirdQtr do
    BitsToFollow := BitsToFollow + 1;
    low  := 2*(low - FirstQtr);
    high := 2*(high - FirstQtr + 1);
```

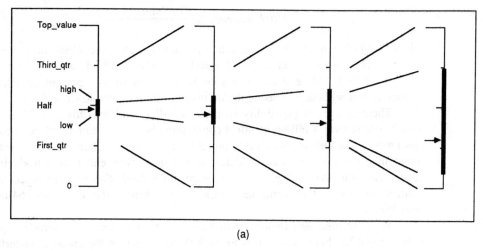

(a)

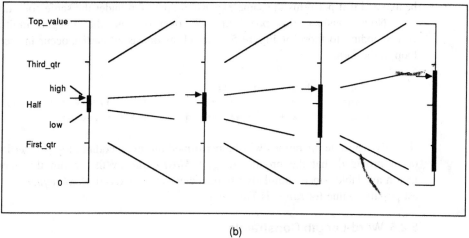

(b)

Figure 5-5   Scaling the interval to prevent underflow: (a) the situation where the next
bit will turn out to be 0: (b) the situation where the next bit will turn out to be 1.

Using this technique, the encoder guarantees that after the shifting operations, either

$$low < FirstQtr < Half \leq high \qquad (5\text{-}1a)$$

or

$$low < Half < ThirdQtr \leq high. \qquad (5\text{-}1b)$$

Therefore, as long as the integer range spanned by the cumulative frequencies fits into a
quarter of that provided by *CodeValue*, the underflow problem cannot occur. This
corresponds to the condition

$$MaxFrequency \leq \frac{TopValue + 1}{4} + 1,$$

where *TopValue* is the largest number permitted within the *CodeValue* range. For example, choosing a 16-bit *CodeValue* and $TopValue = 2^{16} - 1$, we could set *MaxFrequency* $= 2^{14} - 1$. More than 14 bits could not be used to represent cumulative frequency counts without increasing the number of bits allocated to *CodeValue*.

There is a small possibility that *BitsToFollow* will overflow. A 32-bit variable would require over 4 billion identical consecutive bits in the output before encountering this problem, but this is conceivably possible in a continuous transmission situation. To avoid this, the overflow can be detected and dealt with either by introducing some redundancy into the coding, or by supplementing *BitsToFollow* with a second 32-bit counter to ensure that centuries would elapse before the combined 64-bit count overflowed.

We have discussed underflow in the encoder only. Since the decoder's job, once each symbol has been decoded, is to track the operation of the encoder, underflow will be avoided if it performs the same expansion operation under the same conditions.

Now consider the possibility of overflow in the integer multiplications corresponding to those of Figure 5-4, which as discussed earlier occur in the decoding loop in the form

```
range := high - low + 1;
high  := low + (range*CumFreq[symbol - 1])/CumFreq[0] - 1;
low   := low + (range*CumFreq[symbol])/CumFreq[0];
```

(Exactly the same operations will be performed during encoding, too.) Overflow cannot occur provided that the product *range* × *MaxFrequency* fits within the integer word length available, since cumulative frequencies cannot exceed *MaxFrequency*. The largest possible value for *range* is *TopValue* + 1.

5.2.5 Word-Length Constraints

The constraints on word length imposed by underflow and overflow can be simplified by assuming that frequency counts are represented in f bits, and that *CodeValue* is c bits. The implementation will work correctly provided that

$$f \leq c - 2$$

$f + c \leq p,$ the precision to which arithmetic is performed.

Many computers provide hardware arithmetic operations on 32-bit signed integers. This corresponds to $p = 31$, for in arithmetic coding we deal only with positive quantities. Often, arithmetic operations on 32-bit unsigned integers are provided, too, in which case $p = 32$.

As an example, we have mentioned the use of 14-bit frequency counts and a 16-bit *CodeValue*, that is, $f = 14$ and $c = 16$. This satisfies the first inequality, and also the second if $p \geq 30$. Thus arithmetic coding with these parameters can be implemented correctly on a computer that provides arithmetic operations on 32-bit signed (31-bit unsigned) quantities. If arithmetic on 32-bit *unsigned* quantities is available, $f = 15$ and $c = 17$ could be used. In assembly-language implementations $c = 16$ is a natural choice because it expedites some comparisons and bit manipulations.

If p is restricted to 16 bits, the best values possible are $c = 9$ and $f = 7$, making it impossible to encode a full alphabet of 256 symbols, as each symbol must have a count of at least 1. A smaller alphabet (e.g., the 26 letters, or 4-bit nibbles) could still be handled.

5.2.6 Terminating the Message

To finish a transmission, it is necessary to send a unique terminating symbol and then follow it by enough bits to ensure that the encoded string falls within the final range. After the terminating symbol has been encoded, *low* and *high* are constrained by either (5-1a) or (5-1b) above. Consequently, it is only necessary to transmit 01 in the first case and 10 in the second to remove the remaining ambiguity.

The decoder's *InputBit* ( ) procedure will actually read a few more bits than were sent by the encoder's *OutputBit* ( ), as it needs to keep the low end of *value*, which receives input bits, full. It does not matter what value these bits have, because the terminating symbol is uniquely determined by the last two bits actually transmitted.

5.2.7 The Model

The program we have described must be used with a model that provides a cumulative frequency array *CumFreq* [ ]. For correct operation it is necessary that:

- $CumFreq[i-1] \geq CumFreq[i]$.
- There are no symbols i for which $CumFreq[i-1] = CumFreq[i]$.
- $CumFreq[0] \leq MaxFrequency$.

Provided that these conditions are satisfied, the values in the array need bear no relationship to the actual symbol frequencies in messages. Encoding and decoding will still work correctly, although encodings will occupy less space if the frequencies are accurate. (Recall our successfully encoding *eaii!* according to the model of Table 5-2, which certainly does not reflect the frequencies in the message.)

The simplest kind of model is one in which symbol frequencies are fixed. For English, one might choose symbol frequencies that approximate those of the Brown corpus. Table 5-3 shows such a model, in which counts have been normalized to total $2^{14} - 1$. To ensure that the second condition above is met, bytes that did not occur in the corpus have been given frequency counts of 1 in case they do occur in messages to be encoded. This ensures, for example, that the model will still work for binary files in which all 256 bytes occur. It will not give very good compression in this case, because the statistics are not those of binary files, but at least an encoding will be produced. This very simple model is introduced only so that we have something to drive the

TABLE 5-3 STATIC ORDER-0 MODEL GENERATED FROM THE BROWN CORPUS

nul	1	•	2575	@	1	`	1	128	1	160	1	192	1	224	1
soh	1	!	2	A	35	a	997	129	1	161	1	193	1	225	1
stx	1	"	48	B	19	b	178	130	1	162	1	194	1	226	1
etx	1	#	7	C	24	c	374	131	1	163	1	195	1	227	1
eot	1	$	1	D	14	d	495	132	1	164	1	196	1	228	1
enq	1	%	1	E	20	e	1582	133	1	165	1	197	1	229	1
ack	1	&	16	F	13	f	286	134	1	166	1	198	1	230	1
bel	1	'	30	G	11	g	239	135	1	167	1	199	1	231	1
bs	1	(	6	H	25	h	672	136	1	168	1	200	1	232	1
ht	1	)	7	I	41	i	893	137	1	169	1	201	1	233	1
nl	248	*	9	J	8	j	12	138	1	170	1	202	1	234	1
vt	1	+	1	K	5	k	80	139	1	171	1	203	1	235	1
np	1	,	159	L	13	l	518	140	1	172	1	204	1	236	1
cr	1	–	32	M	23	m	303	141	1	173	1	205	1	237	1
so	1	.	134	N	17	n	893	142	1	174	1	206	1	238	1
si	1	/	2	O	16	o	957	143	1	175	1	207	1	239	1
dle	1	0	12	P	16	p	243	144	1	176	1	208	1	240	1
dc1	1	1	14	Q	1	q	13	145	1	177	1	209	1	241	1
dc2	1	2	7	R	17	r	769	146	1	178	1	210	1	242	1
dc3	1	3	5	S	34	s	805	147	1	179	1	211	1	243	1
dc4	1	4	4	T	49	t	1137	148	1	180	1	212	1	244	1
nak	1	5	6	U	7	u	341	149	1	181	1	213	1	245	1
syn	1	6	4	V	4	v	124	150	1	182	1	214	1	246	1
etb	1	7	3	W	17	w	224	151	1	183	1	215	1	247	1
can	1	8	3	X	1	x	25	152	1	184	1	216	1	248	1
em	1	9	6	Y	6	y	215	153	1	185	1	217	1	249	1
sub	1	:	5	Z	1	z	12	154	1	186	1	218	1	250	1
esc	1	;	7	[	1	{	1	155	1	187	1	219	1	251	1
fs	1	<	8	\	1			1	156	1	188	1	220	1	252	1
gs	1	=	1	]	1	}	1	157	1	189	1	221	1	253	1
rs	1	>	8	^	1	~	6	158	1	190	1	222	1	254	1
us	1	?	6	_	6	127	1	159	1	191	1	223	1	255	1

arithmetic coder. Much more suitable models are described in Chapters 6 and 7. The entropy of the example model is about 4.7 bits per character (bits/char), while other models can compress English text to as little as 2.5 bits/char.

5.3 IMPLEMENTING ADAPTIVE MODELS

Generic models for English or other natural languages, for program files in a particular programming language, or even for binary files or digitized pictures, are unlikely to represent exactly the statistics of a particular message to be transmitted. Of course, for a given model structure it is always possible to calculate the probabilities exactly, so that the symbol frequencies in the message are precisely as prescribed by the model. For example, the model of Table 5-3 is close to an exact order-0 model for the Brown corpus from which it was taken. To be truly exact, however, symbols that did not occur in the corpus would be assigned counts of 0, rather than 1 (sacrificing the capability of transmitting messages containing those symbols). Moreover, the frequency counts would not be scaled to a predetermined cumulative frequency, as they have been in the table. The exact model can be calculated and transmitted before the message is sent. However, we saw in Section 3-2 that under quite general conditions, this will *not* give better overall compression than would utilizing an adaptive model.

In Chapter 3 we described how an adaptive model represents the changing symbol frequencies seen so far in the message. Initially all counts might be the same (reflecting no initial information), but they are updated as each symbol is seen to approximate the observed frequencies. Provided that both encoder and decoder use the same initial values (e.g., equal counts) and the same updating algorithm, their models will remain in step. The encoder receives the next symbol, encodes it, and updates its model. The decoder identifies it according to its current model, and then updates that model.

Arithmetic coding has some advantages over the Huffman method when used adaptively. The simplest forms of adaptive model suitable for use with it are more straightforward and efficient than those for adaptive Huffman coding. Unfortunately, worst-case behavior of these simple models can be unacceptable in some applications, particularly those with uniform symbol probabilities or large alphabets. Provably efficient algorithms are available for both Huffman codes and arithmetic coding, and in both cases they require relatively complex data structures. With Huffman coding the difficulty involves incrementally updating the coding tree, while in arithmetic coding it involves incrementally updating the counts and cumulative counts necessary for presentation to the coder. We describe an implementation of adaptive arithmetic coding that is efficient for large alphabets, and also show simplifications that are possible for binary alphabets.

5.3.1 Adaptive Huffman Coding

It is trivial to perform Huffman coding adaptively by recalculating the coding tree after each change to the model. However, this is inefficient. Recomputing the model for a q-character alphabet takes $q \log q$ operations. This is a high price to pay if the model is updated frequently, such as once for every character transmitted.

In 1978, in a paper written to honor the twenty-fifth anniversary of Huffman coding, a method was described for updating the coding tree incrementally. Consider the tree in Figure 5-2, but imagine that occurrence counts are stored at all nodes, including internal ones. For example, the node labeled u will contain the number of u's seen so far in the message, that labeled $!$ the number of $!$'s, and the parent node of these two will contain the sum of u's and $!$'s. Now suppose that another u is encountered, so that the count at that node must be incremented. This may require the tree to be rearranged. For example, u may now be more frequent than i, so it should occupy the latter's position. In this situation it would be adequate merely to exchange the two and update node counts appropriately, incrementing parents and grandparents up to the root of the tree to reflect the necessary changes in internal nodes.

Simply interchanging nodes cannot be sufficient to deal with the general case, however. If it were, the shape of the tree could never change—and it is clear that the shape of the optimal coding tree must depend on the frequency profile of the messages. In general, the update operation may involve interchanging several nodes' positions, and can be implemented effectively by rippling up the tree, swapping nodes as appropriate. This corresponds to following, in reverse, the path used to generate code bits for the particular symbol in question, so the time taken by the whole operation is proportional to the number of output bits generated. If counts are just incremented, however, they may overflow. Moreover, it is usually desirable to implement an aging policy which attempts to ensure that the statistics used are relevant to the portion of text being encoded. As the time constant for aging increases, the adaptation becomes slower, yielding better estimates for slowly varying statistics, but more irrelevant estimates for rapidly varying statistics.

The usual solution is to halve all counts at intervals—perhaps just on those occasions when some would overflow otherwise. More generally, they could be scaled by any constant less than 1. Because the relative magnitudes stay the same, this seems to involve no re-organization of the tree. Life, however, is unfortunately not so simple. Halving creates fractional parts, which cannot be handled using the incremental tree update algorithm because it relies on all increments being exactly 1. Counts must therefore be rounded or truncated to the nearest integer. But it is essential that internal nodes correctly reflect the total counts of their descendants, so they must be recalculated. And if several descendants have all been rounded in the same direction, an internal node's count could change significantly. Consequently, it is possible (if unlikely) that rounding could alter the structure of the tree drastically.

The simplest solution is just to recreate the tree from scratch whenever counts are rescaled. But this takes time and because rescaling happens periodically and perhaps at unpredictable intervals, the resulting algorithm could be unsatisfactory for real-time coding. Two other methods have been proposed, both of which require the coding algorithm to be generalized. First, one can implement exponential aging by incrementing by an amount that varies with time. For example, choosing s to be slightly greater than 1 (e.g., $s = 1.01$), increment the first transmitted character's count by 1, the second's by s, the third's by s^2, and so on. When the next power of s is so large that there is danger of overflow, all character frequencies can be divided by this power of s and the increment reset to 1. This requires that the incremental update algorithm can work with real numbers. A second method is to use statistics based on a window containing the last N characters only. This can be done by retaining these characters in a circular buffer, incrementing the count associated with a character when it joins the buffer and decrementing it when it leaves.

There is a generalization of the algorithm sketched above that allows noninteger counts and also permits them to be decremented as well as incremented. Call these counts *weight*s, and define the weight of an internal node to be the sum of the weights of its descendants. The method requires a list of all nodes in the tree to be maintained, either by threading pointers or by other means, which is ordered by node weight. When incrementing, we are given a leaf node—call it l—and the increment to be applied to its frequency. If *l*'s parent is the root, the tree can be updated directly, and this becomes the basis for a recursion. The recursion is rather involved and will not be described in detail. Suffice it to say that it scans up the above-mentioned ordering to find nodes with which *l* can safely be exchanged. The same method can be used when counts are decremented by scanning in the reverse direction.

For more sophisticated models than the preceding order-0 model assumed, a code tree must be maintained for each conditioning class in the model. Because an inordinate amount of memory would be consumed by a model containing many conditioning classes, Huffman coding is invariably used with an order-0 model.

5.3.2 Adaptive Arithmetic Coding

For arithmetic coding, the model must supply counts for each symbol, together with a total so that counts can be normalized into estimated probabilities. Such a model is updated simply by incrementing (or decrementing) the appropriate count by the appropriate amount. It may be necessary to store several arrays of these counts, one for each conditioning class in the model; but because arithmetic coding does not store any code tables, it is quite feasible to have several conditioning classes. In fact, even the arrays might not be stored in full, since the model need only supply the range of code space allocated to the symbol being coded, and this might be calculated on the fly.

The coding algorithm uses the cumulative total count up to the symbol being encoded, and up to the next symbol as well. Calculating such totals directly can be quite expensive, and it is best for the model to maintain cumulative values itself—the array *CumFreq* [ ] of Section 5-2. When necessary, rescaling is accomplished by multiplying all frequencies by the appropriate factor and recalculating cumulative values.

The cost of updating can be reduced by keeping the array in frequency order, an effective kind of self-organizing linear search. Whenever the model is updated, symbols are reordered if necessary to place the current one in its correct rank in the frequency ordering. This is done by maintaining an index to keep track of which symbol's count is where. Whenever a symbol changes rank, its entry in the index is simply swapped with the one that occupies the appropriate place. When a value is incremented, all those above it in the list are incremented by the same amount, to preserve cumulative totals. On average, much fewer than half the totals will need to be incremented because the array is in frequency order.

An implementation of such an adaptive model is given in Appendix 5A. For small alphabets the method is acceptably fast—particularly if symbols are accessed nonuniformly. For example, when single characters of text are being encoded from an order-0 model, the average number of values that must be incremented for each letter encountered is around nine; while for the complex models of later chapters, where the predictions are very good, performance is even better. However, if files of random data are encoded with a byte-oriented model, the alphabet contains 256 symbols and 128 values must be incremented on average for each byte encoded (of course, no compression would be achieved on completely random data!) In this case, as well as in the case of even larger alphabets, it becomes worthwhile to seek improved algorithms.

5.3.3 Efficient Adaptive Arithmetic Coding for Large Alphabets

The following more complex data structure for the model can give better performance with large alphabets or uniform access profiles. It was developed for adaptive arithmetic coding based on word, not letter, frequencies. With words as units, the coding table can have thousands of entries, and the penalty for keeping cumulative counts in a linear list becomes prohibitive, even if the list is kept sorted by frequency as described previously.

The basic idea is to store the frequencies for each conditioning class in the model as a binary tree, with a portion of the cumulative counts kept at each node. The full cumulative total for a node is obtained by summing the counts associated with some of its ancestors in the tree. When a node's count is incremented, only those counts stored with it and its ancestors need be updated. The maximum number of nodes that need be examined to accomplish either of these operations is log q, where q is the alphabet size. The linear storage scheme discussed previously would require q operations. However, this potential will not be realized unless the tree is kept balanced or approximately balanced, for if allowed to grow long and straggly, it could degenerate to a structure no better than the linear list. If the tree is to be manipulated to keep it balanced, we may as well improve performance by keeping frequently used symbols near the root.

The details of the data structure are best explained through an example. Figure 5-6a shows a small alphabet with frequency counts. A permutation of the alphabet is shown in Figure 5-6b, with counts preserved and cumulative counts calculated. Of course, the ordering of the alphabet does not matter with arithmetic coding provided that encoder and decoder agree on what it is at any time. The reason for this particular ordering will be explained later. The total range is recursively grouped into (approximately) equal parts in much the same way as it was for Shannon–Fano coding (Figure 5-1). However, there is a difference: The symbol at which the division occurs is singled out and does not appear in either group. Thus the first division is on letter h; the count above it (we call it the *above-count*) is 40 and that below (the *below-count*) is 26. The above- and below-counts apply only to the subset that they partition. Turned around, the grouping forms a tree with a symbol at each node, shown in part (c) of the figure. Associated with each node is a symbol, its count, and its above-count. For example, h has a count of 19 and an above-count of 40. It is not necessary to store below-counts. Note that the order of symbols in Figure 5-6b corresponds to an in-order traversal of the tree in Figure 5-6c.

For arithmetic coding, the following operations on the model are necessary.

- Given a symbol, determine the cumulative range that encompasses it.
- Given a value, determine the symbol whose cumulative range encloses it.
- Increment the count for a given symbol.

(The second operation is required when decoding only.) To find the range that encompasses a given symbol, trace the path down to it from the root, accumulating a number which will turn out to be the cumulative count up to that symbol. When a right branch

symbol	count
a	10
b	12
c	13
d	3
e	5
f	1
g	1
h	19
i	12
j	9

(a)

symbol	count	range	grouping
d	3	0 – 2	
b	12	3 – 14	
f	1	15 – 15	
c	13	16 – 28	
g	1	29 – 29	
a	10	30 – 39	
h	19	40 – 58	
j	9	59 – 67	
i	12	68 – 79	
e	5	80 – 84	

(b)

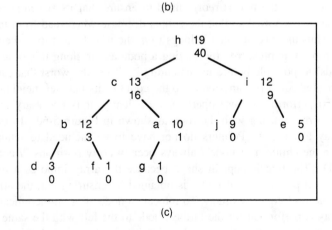

(c)

Figure 5-6   Tree-structured model for arithmetic coding: (a) example alphabet; (b) forming the tree; (c) tree representation.

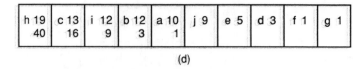

(d)

Figure 5-6(cont)   Tree structured model for arithmetic coding: (d) array representation.

is taken, add that node's symbol count and its above-count into the sum. When a left branch is taken, add nothing. Finally, when the node is reached, add in its above-count. For example, using Figure 5-6c to find the range for i, the first branch from the root is a right one, so the root's counts—$19+40$—are added. Next the target node i is reached, so its above-count of 9 is added. The result is $9+19+40 = 68$, which is indeed the beginning of the range for i. As another example, to find g's range the first branch is left, contributing nothing; the second is right, contributing $13+16$; the third is left, contributing nothing; while finally, g's node itself contributes 0. The result is 29, as it should be.

Determining a symbol given any value within its range involves a similar procedure. This time the value, and the number accumulated so far, govern whether the search should stop at the current node or whether one of the two subtrees should be explored. Suppose that we are given the value 64. The right branch must be taken from the root, for when $19+40$ is added to the initial total of 0, the result, 59, is less than the given value. At the node i the left branch is taken because otherwise at least 9 would be added to 59, exceeding the given value. At the node j the search terminates because the range at this point is $[59, 59+9]$, which includes the given value.

Finally, to increment the count for a given symbol involves not just incrementing the count at that node, but rippling up the tree to the root, adding one to the above-count of any node that is approached along a left branch. Thus, for example, incrementing the node for j involves incrementing that for i but not that for h. Before this is done, however, the tree is reorganized to ensure that its structure is not destroyed. In fact, the tree is sorted so that the counts decrease when read from top to bottom, left to right. Thus the largest count belongs to h, the next largest to c, then i, b, a, j, e, d, f, g. This property is preserved by moving a node as far along this ordering (to the left and upwards) as possible before incrementing it. Then the worst that can happen is that the incremented count becomes equal to the count of its new left neighbor.

To perform all these operations efficiently, it is necessary to transform the tree into an array, starting with the root, as shown in Figure 5-6d. In fact, this is an excellent way to store it. Pointers do not have to be included to retain the tree structure because the children of node i always occupy array positions $2i$ and $2i+1$ (numbering from 1). The tree is kept in shape because the array imposes a balanced form on it. The correct positioning of nodes is obtained by ensuring that the array is always sorted in decreasing frequency order. To relocate a node after an increment, a binary search of the array is performed for the farthest node to the left with the same count, and then the nodes are interchanged; the housekeeping involved in swapping is straightforward.

Using this data structure, the number of operations required for arithmetically coding n input bits into m output ones can be proven to grow linearly with $n+m$. It is obviously not possible to do better than this, since any algorithm will require some work to be performed on each input and output bit (even if it is only packing and unpacking them into a bit stream). Moreover, the constant of proportionality is small enough to make the method attractive whenever arithmetic encoding is done on alphabets containing more than the typical 128 characters, such as when the input alphabet is words rather than characters.

5.3.4 Efficient Adaptive Arithmetic Coding for Binary Alphabets

We have seen how to implement a cumulative probability distribution efficiently for large alphabets. At the other extreme are alphabets with only two symbols—0 and 1. This is a slightly special case for arithmetic coding because the cumulative frequency array has only one element, which specifies the breakpoint between the probability for 0 and that for 1. Clearly, this does not present the updating problem that was encountered with larger alphabets, and can be implemented very efficiently. It may even be worthwhile to decompose larger symbols into bits in order to use the binary encoder.

Figure 5-7 sketches the encoding and decoding procedures for binary arithmetic coding in a manner analogous to Figure 5-4. Developing them into proper algorithms requires attention to the issues discussed in Section 5-2. Since this is fairly routine, we will not do it here. Instead, we examine briefly an approximate algorithm that eliminates the time-consuming multiplication step required for both encoding and decoding and hence offers a much faster computer implementation.

The basic idea is to constrain the probability of the less probable symbol to the nearest integral power of $1/2$. The symbols will be ordered so that the less probable one comes first (the opposite to how they were ordered for our simple adaptive arithmetic coding implementation). Its probability is rounded to 2^{-Q}, where Q is an integer. This value is used as *CumProb*, and all multiplications in Figure 5-7 can then be performed by right-shift operations.

To choose an optimal way to round the probabilities, suppose that the true probability of the less frequent symbol is p and it is coded as though it had probability 2^{-Q}. Using arithmetic coding, this symbol will occupy Q bits. The other, more frequent,

```
EncodeSymbol(symbol, CumProb)
    if symbol=0 then
        high := low + (high-low)*CumProb;        /* leave low alone */
    if symbol=1 then
        low  := low + (high-low)*CumProb;        /* leave high alone */

DecodeSymbol(CumProb)
    if value < CumProb then
        symbol := 0;
        high   := low + (high-low)*CumProb;
    if value ≥ CumProb then
        symbol := 1;
        low    := low + (high-low)*CumProb;
```

Figure 5-7   Pseudocode for arithmetic coding with binary alphabet.

symbol has true probability $1-p$ and is coded with probability $1-2^{-Q}$; it will occupy $-\log(1-2^{-Q})$ bits. Hence the average code length per symbol is

$$pQ - (1-p) \log (1-2^{-Q}) \text{ bits.}$$

For each value of p in the range $[0, 0.5)$, this expression should be minimized by choice of Q. The breakpoint between $Q = r$ and $Q = r+1$ comes when

$$pr - (1-p) \log (1-2^{-r}) = p(r+1) - (1-p) \log (1-2^{-r-1}),$$

from which it is simple to show that

$$\frac{p}{1-p} = \log \frac{1-2^{-r-1}}{1-2^{-r}}.$$

From this the optimal probability ranges can be calculated; they are shown in Table 5-4.

This result is used as follows. In the model, an estimate of the probability of the less frequent symbol is maintained and updated as usual. However, the Q-value used for coding is obtained by consulting the table for the appropriate range. For example, if the estimated probability is anywhere between 0.0028 and 0.0056, $Q = 8$ will be used for coding, corresponding to an effective probability of $2^{-8} = 0.0039$.

Astonishingly little compression performance is lost by this approximation. Its coding efficiency is given by the entropy as a fraction of the average code length, which was calculated above:

$$\frac{-p \log p - (1-p) \log (1-p)}{p \, Q(p) - (1-p) \log (1-2^{-Q(p)})},$$

where $Q(p)$ is the value obtained from the table. The worst-case efficiency occurs at the first breakpoint, $p = 0.369$, and is about 95%. However, when $p < 0.33$ the worst

TABLE 5-4 OPTIMAL PROBABILITY
RANGES FOR APPROXIMATE
ARITHMETIC CODING

Probability range	Q	Effective probability
0.00018 – 0.00035	12	0.00024
0.00035 – 0.0007	11	0.00049
0.0007 – 0.0014	10	0.00098
0.0014 – 0.0028	9	0.0020
0.0028 – 0.0056	8	0.0039
0.0056 – 0.0113	7	0.0078
0.0113 – 0.0226	6	0.0156
0.0226 – 0.0452	5	0.0313
0.0452 – 0.0905	4	0.0625
0.0905 – 0.182	3	0.125
0.182 – 0.369	2	0.25
0.369 – 0.5	1	0.5

possible efficiency is 97.3%. In practice, an average of about 98.5% efficiency has been observed. In many applications, this is a small price to pay for coding without multiplication.

5.4 PERFORMANCE OF ARITHMETIC CODING

Now it is time to look at the performance of arithmetic coding in practice, in terms of both compression efficiency and execution speed. It has been argued that the method encodes messages "optimally" with respect to the model used; how true is this in actuality? (Recall that the same claim was made for Huffman coding!) We have examined ways of speeding up adaptive models without giving any real feeling for how fast arithmetic coding is on an absolute scale. Here we consider the performance of the algorithm developed in Section 5-2 and detailed in Appendix 5A.

5.4.1 Compression Efficiency

In principle, when a message is coded using arithmetic coding, the number of bits in the encoded string is the same as the entropy of that message with respect to the model used for coding. Three factors cause performance to be worse than this in practice:

- Message termination overhead
- Use of fixed-length rather than infinite-precision arithmetic
- Scaling of counts so that their total is at most *MaxFrequency*.

None of these effects is significant, as we now show. To isolate the effect of arithmetic coding, the model will be considered to be exact, in that it prescribes symbol frequencies which are precisely those of the message.

Arithmetic coding must send extra bits at the end of each message, causing a message termination overhead. As explained near the end of Section 5-2, two bits are needed to disambiguate the final symbol. In cases where a bit stream must be blocked into 8-bit characters before encoding, it will be necessary to round out to the end of a block. Combining these, an extra 9 bits may be required.

The overhead of using fixed-length arithmetic occurs because remainders are truncated on division. It can be assessed by comparing the algorithm's performance with the figure obtained from a theoretical entropy calculation which derives its frequencies from counts scaled exactly as for coding. Using a 16-bit *CodeValue*, as in the program of Appendix 5A, it is completely negligible—on the order of 10^{-4} bits/symbol. Thus it might add 0.002% to the length of an encoded message.

The penalty paid by scaling counts is somewhat larger, but still very small. For short messages (less than 2^{14} bytes) and a 16-bit *CodeValue*, no scaling need be done. Even with messages of 10^5 to 10^6 bytes, the overhead was found experimentally to be less than 0.25% of the encoded string. In fact, scaling the counts will often improve compression. It has the effect of weighting recent events more heavily compared with those earlier in the message. The statistics thus tend to track changes in the input sequence, which can be very beneficial. For example, we have encountered cases where limiting counts to 6 or 7 bits gives better results than working to higher precision. Of course, this depends on the source being modeled.

Although it would be nice to compare the compression performance of arithmetic coding with that of adaptive Huffman coding, this is rather difficult to do in general, for it depends critically on the modeling strategy. With a simple model such as one based on letter frequencies, the difference is usually very small. We noted earlier that the average code length for Huffman coding minus the entropy is bounded by $p + 0.086$, where p is the probability of the most likely symbol. For text this will be the space symbol, with a probability of around 0.18, which leads to a redundancy bound of just over 0.25 bits/symbol. Since the single-letter entropy of English is just over 4 bits/symbol, this is a worst-case redundancy of about 6%. In practice, however, this is a rather pessimistic bound for a single-symbol model of text, and we have observed an implementation of adaptive Huffman coding to perform only 1% worse than arithmetic coding in this situation. However, more sophisticated modeling strategies paint quite a different picture, for probabilities close to 1 evoke the worst performance from Huffman coding.

5.4.2 Execution Time

The program in Appendix 5A has been written for clarity, not execution speed. It contains easily avoidable overheads such as procedure calls, and some simple optimizations can be made to increase speed by a factor of 2 while still using the C programming language. A further factor of 2 can be gained by reprogramming in assembly language. Then full use can be made of any architectural features, such as registers that are provided by the machine available. Moreover, advantage can be taken of a 16-bit *Code-Value* to expedite some crucial comparisons and make subtractions of *Half* trivial. Although any hard performance figures are entirely technology dependent, to convey some idea of speed, a carefully optimized assembly language implementation takes in the region of 50 μs to encode each byte of text on a Motorola MC68020 microprocessor operating with a 16.67-MHz clock. Decoding is a little slower—around 60 μs per uncompressed byte—because it requires an extra division and a loop to identify the symbol from its cumulative frequency. These figures are averaged over a 100,000-byte file of plain English, and were obtained using the order-0 adaptive model.

Performance depends critically on the type of text encoded. If a large amount of compression is achieved, operations that process output bits are reduced because there is less output. More important, manipulation of the adaptive model is greatly affected by the distribution of the input data. Appendix 5A's adaptive model keeps symbols sorted in frequency order and updates cumulative counts by iterating through the list until the desired symbol is encountered. In the worst case, with random data, the loop will be executed 128 times on average if the alphabet contains 256 symbols. For English text the average number of executions was found to be 9 times, for program text 13 times, and for object code 35 times.[2] In the case of English, model updating accounts for just over 25% of encode time. When decoding, the model must be consulted to identify symbols, as well as being updated, and these operations together consume just over 50% of decode time for English. It is doubtful whether it is worth going to the more sophisticated tree data structure in this case. For purely random byte input it almost certainly would be. Between the two extremes is, for example, object code, which seems fairly random to human readers but still has a regular structure, and is likely to benefit from the tree data structure.

Even with a straightforward implementation of the model, adaptive arithmetic coding performs a lot faster than adaptive Huffman coding. Compared with an implementation (in the C language) of the latter, a mildly optimized version of the program in Appendix 5A (still in C) was twice as fast. It appeared that both programs had been optimized to roughly the same degree, although this is always difficult to tell. With a nonadaptive model, a carefully written implementation of Huffman coding, using table lookup for encoding and decoding, could be slightly faster than arithmetic coding because it avoids multiply and divide operations.

NOTES

Nyquist's research forms the basis for all digital signal processing work (including, for example, digital audio and digital telephone systems). As well as developing fundamentals of what is now known as information theory, he was a prolific inventor, and held many patents related to communications. He is also responsible for developing an important theory about thermal noise in electronic circuits, and for negative feedback amplifiers.

Shannon published his results on source entropy and channel capacity in a classic paper in the *Bell System Technical Journal* in 1948. This was republished as Shannon and Weaver (1949). Shannon's and Fano's coding methods are substantially the same but differ slightly in detail; what is presented here is actually Fano's, which appeared in an internal report from M.I.T. (Fano, 1949). Huffman's classic paper, "A method for the construction of minimum-redundancy codes," was published in 1952. The bound of $p + 0.086$ on the redundancy of Huffman codes is due to Gallager (1978).

Elias's insight into arithmetic coding appears in a brief note on pp. 61–62 of Abramson (1963). Jelinek (1968) describes it more fully. Other references relevant to the birth of arithmetic coding are Pasco (1976), Rissanen (1976, 1979), Rubin (1979), Rissanen and Langdon (1979), Guazzo (1980), and Langdon and Rissanen (1982). Tutorials can be found in Langdon (1981, 1984) and in Witten et al. (1987b), on which the development in this chapter is based. Martin (1979) and Jones (1981) published independent discoveries of the idea.

[2]These counts apply to the adaptive model only. For the nonadaptive model of Figure 5-9 the loop counts will be much higher, for no attempt has been made in that illustrative description to order the symbols according to expected frequency.

The fact that the Huffman coding tree can be updated incrementally was first noticed by Faller (1973) and independently by Gallager (1978). Their methods are restricted to incrementing counts by 1 only, and were generalized by Cormack and Horspool (1984) and, independently, by Knuth (1985). The former generalization caters for arbitrary increments, positive or negative, while the latter allows for increments and decrements of 1 only, but gives complete implementation details. Further work on adaptive Huffman coding can be found in Vitter (1987, in press). The use of splay trees to approximate adaptive Huffman coding is discussed by Jones (1988).

The efficient implementation of cumulative probability distributions for large alphabets, used by models for arithmetic coding, is due to Moffat (1988a). Jones (1988) achieves similar asymptotic runtime performance using a form of splay tree instead of a heap. The approximate arithmetic coding method for binary alphabets was developed by Langdon and Rissanen (1981). The observation that its efficiency is around 98.5% is based on their study of coding pixels in black-and-white documents. Witten et al. (1987b) give a much more detailed discussion of the performance of the program in Appendix 5A.

APPENDIX 5A   AN IMPLEMENTATION OF ARITHMETIC CODING

Figure 5-8 shows a working program, in C, for arithmetic encoding and decoding. It is considerably more detailed than the bare-bones sketch of Figure 5-4! Implementations of two different models are given in Figure 5-9; the encoding/decoding program can use either one. These models are provided only to obtain some sort of input to test the arithmetic coder. In practice, much better compression will be achieved by the models described in Chapters 6 and 7. This appendix, in which we briefly describe key portions of the code, should be read in conjunction with Section 5-2, which explains the general issues involved.

Encoding and Decoding

Consider first Figure 5-8. The interface to the model is defined in lines 20 to 38. In C, a byte is represented as an integer between 0 and 255 (call this a *char*). Internally, we represent a byte as an integer between 1 and 257 inclusive (call this an *index*), the message terminator, called EOF, being treated as a 257th symbol. As discussed in Section 5-3, it is advantageous to sort the model into frequency order, to minimize the number of executions of the decoding and cumulative update loops. To permit such reordering, the *char/index* translation is implemented as a pair of tables, *index_to_char* [ ] and *char_to_index* [ ]. In one of our models, these tables simply form the *index* by adding 1 to the *char*, but another implements a more complex translation which assigns small indexes to frequently used symbols.

The probabilities in the model are represented as integer frequency counts, and cumulative counts are stored in the array *cum_freq* [ ]. This array is "backwards," and the total frequency count—which is used to normalize all frequencies—appears in *cum_freq* [0]. Cumulative counts must not exceed a predetermined maximum,

```
arithmetic_coding.h

1    /* DECLARATIONS USED FOR ARITHMETIC ENCODING AND DECODING */
2
3
4    /* SIZE OF ARITHMETIC CODE VALUES. */
5
6    #define Code_value_bits 16        /* Number of bits in a code value  */
7    typedef long code_value;          /* Type of an arithmetic code value */
8
9    #define Top_value (((long)1<<Code_value_bits)-1)   /* Largest code value */
10
11
12   /* HALF AND QUARTER POINTS IN THE CODE VALUE RANGE. */
13
14   #define First_qtr (Top_value/4+1)    /* Point after first quarter    */
15   #define Half      (2*First_qtr)      /* Point after first half       */
16   #define Third_qtr (3*First_qtr)      /* Point after third quarter    */

model.h

17   /* INTERFACE TO THE MODEL. */
18
19
20   /* THE SET OF SYMBOLS THAT MAY BE ENCODED. */
21
22   #define No_of_chars 256        /* Number of character symbols */
23   #define EOF_symbol (No_of_chars+1)   /* Index of EOF symbol */
24
25   #define No_of_symbols (No_of_chars+1)   /* Total number of symbols */
26
27
28   /* TRANSLATION TABLES BETWEEN CHARACTERS AND SYMBOL INDEXES. */
29
30   int char_to_index[No_of_chars];    /* To index from character */
31   unsigned char index_to_char[No_of_symbols+1]; /* To character from index */
32
33
34   /* CUMULATIVE FREQUENCY TABLE. */
35
36   #define Max_frequency 16383    /* Maximum allowed frequency count */
37                                  /* 2^14 - 1                        */
38   int cum_freq[No_of_symbols+1]; /* Cumulative symbol frequencies   */
```

```
encode.c

39   /* MAIN PROGRAM FOR ENCODING. */
40
41   #include <stdio.h>
42   #include "model.h"
43
44   main()
45   {   start_model();
46       start_outputing_bits();
47       start_encoding();                    /* Set up other modules.      */
48       for (;;) {                           /* Loop through characters.   */
49           int ch; int symbol;
50           ch = getc(stdin);                /* Read the next character.   */
51           if (ch==EOF) break;              /* Exit loop on end-of-file.  */
52           symbol = char_to_index[ch];      /* Translate to an index.     */
53           encode_symbol(symbol,cum_freq);  /* Encode that symbol.        */
54           update_model(symbol);            /* Update the model.          */
55       }
56       encode_symbol(EOF_symbol,cum_freq);  /* Encode the EOF symbol.     */
57       done_encoding();                     /* Send the last few bits.    */
58       done_outputing_bits();
59       exit(0);
60   }

arithmetic_encode.c

61   /* ARITHMETIC ENCODING ALGORITHM. */
62
63   #include "arithmetic_coding.h"
64
65   static void bit_plus_follow();    /* Routine that follows */
66
67
68   /* CURRENT STATE OF THE ENCODING. */
69
70   static code_value low, high;      /* Ends of the current code region  */
71   static long bits_to_follow;       /* Number of opposite bits to output after */
72                                     /* the next bit.                     */
73
74
75   /* START ENCODING A STREAM OF SYMBOLS. */
76
77   start_encoding()
78   {   low = 0;                      /* Full code range.          */
79       high = Top_value;
80       bits_to_follow = 0;           /* No bits to follow next.   */
81   }
82
83
84   /* ENCODE A SYMBOL. */
85
86   encode_symbol(symbol,cum_freq)
87       int symbol;                   /* Symbol to encode                */
88       int cum_freq[];               /* Cumulative symbol frequencies   */
89   {   long range;                   /* Size of the current code region */
90       range = (long)(high-low)+1;
91       high = low +
92           (range*cum_freq[symbol-1])/cum_freq[0]-1;  /* Narrow the code region */
93       low = low +                   /* to that allotted to this */
94           (range*cum_freq[symbol])/cum_freq[0];      /* symbol. */
```

Figure 5-8 C implementation of arithmetic encoding and decoding.

133

```c
 95      for (;;) {                                    /* Loop to output bits. */
 96          if (high<Half) {
 97              bit_plus_follow(0);                   /* Output 0 if in low half. */
 98          }
 99          else if (low>=Half) {                     /* Output 1 if in high half.*/
100              bit_plus_follow(1);
101              low -= Half;
102              high -= Half;                         /* Subtract offset to top. */
103          }
104          else if (low>=First_qtr                   /* Output an opposite bit */
105                  && high<Third_qtr) {              /* later if in middle half.*/
106              bits_to_follow += 1;
107              low -= First_qtr;                     /* Subtract offset to middle*/
108              high -= First_qtr;
109          }
110          else break;                               /* Otherwise exit loop. */
111          low = 2*low;
112          high = 2*high+1;                          /* Scale up code range. */
113      }
114  }
115
116  /* FINISH ENCODING THE STREAM. */
117  done_encoding()                                   /* FINISH ENCODING THE STREAM. */
118  {
119      bits_to_follow += 1;                          /* Output two bits that */
120      if (low<First_qtr) bit_plus_follow(0);        /* select the quarter that */
121      else bit_plus_follow(1);                      /* the current code range */
122  }                                                 /* contains. */
123
124  /* OUTPUT BITS PLUS FOLLOWING OPPOSITE BITS. */
125  static void bit_plus_follow(bit)
126  int bit;
127  {
128      output_bit(bit);                              /* Output the bit. */
129      while (bits_to_follow>0) {
130          output_bit(!bit);                         /* Output bits_to_follow */
131          bits_to_follow -= 1;                      /* opposite bits. Set */
132      }                                             /* bits_to_follow to zero. */
133  }
134
135
```

```c
decode.c

/* MAIN PROGRAM FOR DECODING. */
#include <stdio.h>
#include "model.h"
main()
{
    start_model();                                    /* Set up other modules. */
    start_inputing_bits();
    start_decoding();
    for (;;) {                                         /* Loop through characters. */
        int ch; int symbol;
        symbol = decode_symbol(cum_freq);             /* Decode next symbol. */
        if (symbol==EOF_symbol) break;                /* Exit loop if EOF symbol. */
        ch = index_to_char(symbol);                   /* Translate to a character.*/
        putc(ch,stdout);                              /* Write that character. */
        update_model(symbol);                         /* Update the model. */
    }
    exit(0);
}
```

```c
arithmetic_decode.c

/* ARITHMETIC DECODING ALGORITHM. */

#include "arithmetic_coding.h"

/* CURRENT STATE OF THE DECODING. */

static code_value value;          /* Currently-seen code value */
static code_value low, high;      /* Ends of current code region */


/* START DECODING A STREAM OF SYMBOLS. */

start_decoding()
{
    int i;
    value = 0;
    for (i = 1; i<=Code_value_bits; i++) {            /* Input bits to fill the */
        value = 2*value+input_bit();                  /* code value. */
    }
    low = 0;
    high = Top_value;                                 /* Full code range. */
}

/* DECODE THE NEXT SYMBOL. */

int decode_symbol(cum_freq)
int cum_freq[];                                       /* Cumulative symbol frequencies */
{
    long range;                                       /* Size of current code region */
    int cum;                                          /* Cumulative frequency calculated */
    int symbol;                                       /* Symbol decoded */
    range = (long)(high-low)+1;
    cum =                                             /* Find cum freq for value. */
      (((long)(value-low)+1)*cum_freq[0]-1)/range;
    for (symbol = 1; cum_freq[symbol]>cum; symbol++); /* Then find symbol. */
    high = low +                                      /* Narrow the code region */
      (range*cum_freq[symbol-1])/cum_freq[0]-1;       /* to that allotted to this */
    low = low +                                       /* symbol. */
      (range*cum_freq[symbol])/cum_freq[0];
    for (;;) {                                        /* Loop to get rid of bits. */
        if (high<Half) {                              /* Expand low half. */
            /* nothing */
        }
        else if (low>=Half) {                         /* Expand high half. */
            value -= Half;
            low -= Half;
            high -= Half;                             /* Subtract offset to top. */
        }
        else if (low>=First_qtr                       /* Expand middle half. */
                && high<Third_qtr) {
            value -= First_qtr;                       /* Subtract offset to middle*/
            low -= First_qtr;
            high -= First_qtr;
        }
        else break;                                   /* Otherwise exit loop. */
        low = 2*low;
        high = 2*high+1;                              /* Scale up code range. */
        value = 2*value+input_bit();                  /* Move in next input bit. */
    }
    return symbol;
}
```

Figure 5-8(cont)   C implementation of arithmetic encoding and decoding.

bit_input.c

```c
216
217   /* BIT INPUT ROUTINES. */
218
219   #include <stdio.h>
220   #include "arithmetic_coding.h"
221
222   /* THE BIT BUFFER. */
223
224   static int buffer;          /* Bits waiting to be input        */
225   static int bits_to_go;      /* Number of bits still in buffer  */
226   static int garbage_bits;    /* Number of bits past end-of-file */
227
228
229   /* INITIALIZE BIT INPUT. */
230
231   start_inputing_bits()
232   {   bits_to_go = 0;         /* Buffer starts out with */
233       garbage_bits = 0;       /* no bits in it.         */
234   }
235
236   /* INPUT A BIT. */
237
238   int input_bit()
239   {   int t;
240       if (bits_to_go==0) {
241           buffer = getc(stdin);    /* Read the next byte if no */
242           if (buffer==EOF) {       /* bits are left in buffer. */
243               garbage_bits += 1;   /* Return arbitrary bits*/
244               if (garbage_bits>Code_value_bits-2) { /* after eof, but check */
245                   fprintf(stderr,"Bad input file\n"); /* for too many such. */
246                   exit(-1);
247               }
248           }
249           bits_to_go = 8;
250       }
251       t = buffer&1;           /* Return the next bit from */
252       buffer >>= 1;           /* the bottom of the byte.  */
253       bits_to_go -= 1;
254       return t;
255   }
256
```

bit_output.c

```c
257   /* BIT OUTPUT ROUTINES. */
258
259   #include <stdio.h>
260
261   /* THE BIT BUFFER. */
262
263   static int buffer;          /* Bits buffered for output      */
264   static int bits_to_go;      /* Number of bits free in buffer */
265
266
267
268   /* INITIALIZE FOR BIT OUTPUT. */
269
270   start_outputing_bits()
271   {   buffer = 0;             /* Buffer is empty to start */
272       bits_to_go= 8;          /* with.                    */
273   }
274
275   /* OUTPUT A BIT. */
276
277   output_bit(bit)
278   int bit;
279   {   buffer >>= 1;           /* Put bit in top of buffer.*/
280       if (bit) buffer |= 0x80;
281       bits_to_go -= 1;
282       if (bits_to_go==0) {    /* Output buffer if it is */
283           putc(buffer,stdout);  /* now full.            */
284           bits_to_go = 8;
285       }
286   }
287
288
289   /* FLUSH OUT THE LAST BITS. */
290
291   done_outputing_bits()
292   {   putc(buffer>>bits_to_go,stdout);
293   }
294
```

Figure 5-8(cont)   C implementation of arithmetic encoding and decoding.

135

Max_frequency, and the model implementation must prevent overflow by scaling appropriately. It must also ensure that neighboring values in the *cum_freq* [ ] array differ by at least 1; otherwise, the affected symbol could not be transmitted.

The program represents *low* and *high* as integers. A data type *code_value* is defined for these quantities, together with some useful constants: *Top_value*, representing the largest possible *code_value*, and *First_qtr*, *Half*, and *Third_qtr*, representing parts of the range (lines 6 to 16). Whereas in Figure 5-4 the current interval is represented by [*low*, *high*), in Figure 5-8 it is [*low*, *high* + 0.11111 ...).

As the code range narrows, the top bits of *low* and *high* will become the same. Any high-order bits that are the same are transmitted immediately by lines 95 to 113 of *encode_symbol* ( ), although there are some extra complications to protect against underflow (described shortly). Care is taken to shift 1's in at the bottom when *high* is scaled.

Incremental reception is done using a number called *value* as in Figure 5-4, in which processed bits flow out the top (high-significance) end and newly received ones flow in the bottom. Initially, *start_decoding* ( ) (lines 168 to 176) fills *value* with received bits. Once *decode_symbol* ( ) has identified the next input symbol, it shifts out now-useless high-order bits that are the same in *low* and *high*, shifting *value* by the same amount (and replacing lost bits by fresh input at the bottom end). This is done in lines 194 to 213, again complicated by precautions against underflow.

Decode_symbol ( ) must use *value* to find the symbol that, when encoded, reduces the range to one that still includes *value*. Lines 186 to 189 in *decode_symbol* ( ) identify this symbol, and lines 190 to 193 calculate the new interval that includes *value*. As described in the main text, arithmetic coding must expand up the new interval if it becomes too small. Lines 104 to 109 expand [*First_qtr*, *Third_qtr*] into the entire interval. *Bits_to_follow* records the number of expansions that take place, for afterward the next output bit must be followed by as many opposite bits as there were expansions. This explains why all output is done via *bit_plus_follow* ( ) (lines 128 to 135) instead of directly with *output_bit* ( ). This technique guarantees that as long as the integer range spanned by the cumulative frequencies fits into a quarter of that provided by *code_value*, underflow cannot occur. This condition is satisfied by the program since *Max_frequency* = $2^{14}-1$ and *Top_value* = $2^{16}-1$ (lines 36, 9). More than 14 bits cannot be used to represent cumulative frequency counts without increasing the number of bits allocated to *code_value*.

Underflow is avoided in the decoder since, once each symbol has been decoded, it tracks the operation of the encoder and performs the same expansion under the same conditions. Overflow cannot occur provided that the product *range* × *Max_frequency* fits within the integer word length available. *Range* might be as large as *Top_value* + 1, so the largest possible product is $2^{16}(2^{14}-1)$, which is less than 2^{30}. *Long* declarations are used for *code_value* (line 7) and *range* (lines 89, 183) to ensure that arithmetic is done to 32-bit precision.

In Figure 5-8, frequency counts are represented in 14 bits and *code_value* is 16 bits. With appropriately modified declarations, *unsigned long* arithmetic with 15-bit frequencies and a 17-bit *code_value* could be used. In assembly language 16 bits is a natural choice for *code_value* because it expedites the comparisons and bit manipulations of lines 95 to 113 and 194 to 213. To finish the transmission, a unique terminating symbol, *EOF_symbol*, is sent (line 56). *Done_encoding* (lines 119 to 123) follows this by two bits, 01 or 10, to ensure that the encoded string falls within the final range. It is convenient to do this using the *bit_plus_follow* ( ) procedure discussed earlier.

Implementing Models

The first model in Figure 5-9 has the symbol frequencies of Table 5-3, taken from the Brown corpus. The initialization procedure *start_model* ( ) simply computes a cumulative version of these frequencies (lines 48 to 51), having first initialized the translation tables (lines 44 to 47). Execution speed would be improved if these tables were used to reorder symbols and frequencies so that the most frequent came first in the *cum_freq* [ ] array. Since the model is fixed, the procedure *update_model* ( ), which is called from both *encode.c* and *decode.c*, is null.

The second half of Figure 5-9 is a simple adaptive model. Initialization is the same as for the fixed model, except that all frequencies are set to 1. The procedure *update_model* (*symbol*) is called by both *encode_symbol* ( ) and *decode_symbol* ( ) (Figure 5-8, lines 54 and 151) after each symbol is processed. *Update_model* ( ) first checks to see if the new model will exceed the cumulative-frequency limit, and if so, scales all frequencies down by a factor of 2 (taking care to ensure that no count scales to zero) and recomputes cumulative values (lines 29 to 37). Then, if necessary, *update_model* ( ) reorders the symbols to place the current one in its correct rank in the frequency ordering, altering the translation tables to reflect the change. Finally, it increments the appropriate frequency count and adjusts cumulative frequencies accordingly.

Of course, in practice the procedures *start_model* ( ) and *update_model* ( ) would be implementations of sophisticated adaptive modeling techniques such as PPM or DMC. These models will maintain several *cum_freq* [ ] arrays (either explicitly or implicitly), choosing the one most appropriate for each symbol according to the current context. The simple examples given should be sufficient to check that the arithmetic coding is functioning correctly.

APPENDIX 5B   PROOF OF DECODING INEQUALITY

Here we show, as promised in Section 5-2, that the condition which terminates the decoding loop is sufficient to guarantee that *value* lies within the new [*low*, *high*] interval that is calculated by both encoder and decoder. Using one-letter abbreviations for *CumFreq*, *symbol*, *low*, *high*, and *value*, suppose that

$$c[s] \le \left\lfloor \frac{(v - l + 1) \times c[0] - 1}{h - l + 1} \right\rfloor < c[s - 1];$$

in other words,

```
fixed_model.c

1   /* THE FIXED SOURCE MODEL */
2
3   #include "model.h"
4
5   int freq[No_of_symbols+1] = {
6       0,
7       1,  1,  1,  1,  1,  1,  1,  1,  1,  1,
8       1,  1,  1,  1,  1,  1,  1,  1,  1,  1,
9
10  /*       !    "    #    $    %    &    '    (    )    *    +    ,    -    .    / */
11      2575, 2, 48,  7,  1, 16, 30,  6,  4,  9, 248, 1, 159, 32, 134,  2,
12      1,  1,  1,  1,  1,  1,  1,  1,  1,  1,
13  /*  0    1    2    3    4    5    6    7    8    9    :    ;    <    =    >    ? */
14      12, 14,  7,  5,  4,  6,  3,  3,  6,  5,  7,  8,  1,  7,  1,  6,
15      1,  1,  1,  1,  1,  1,  1,  1,  1,  1,
16  /*  @    A    B    C    D    E    F    G    H    I    J    K    L    M    N    O */
17      1, 35, 19, 24, 14, 20, 13, 11, 25, 41,  8,  5, 13, 23, 17, 16,
18      1,  1,  1,  1,  1,  1,  1,  1,  1,  1,
19  /*  P    Q    R    S    T    U    V    W    X    Y    Z    [    \    ]    ^    _ */
20      16,  1, 17, 34, 49,  7,  4, 17,  4,  6,  1,  1,  1,  1,  1,  6,
21      1,  1,  1,  1,  1,  1,  1,  1,  1,  1,
22  /*  `    a    b    c    d    e    f    g    h    i    j    k    l    m    n    o */
23      1, 997, 178, 374, 495,1582, 286, 239, 672, 893, 12, 80, 518, 303, 893, 957,
24      1,  1,  1,  1,  1,  1,  1,  1,  1,  1,
25  /*  p    q    r    s    t    u    v    w    x    y    z    {    |    }    ~      */
26      243, 13, 769, 805,1137, 341, 124, 224, 25, 215, 12,  1,  1,  6,  1,
27      1,  1,  1,  1,  1,  1,  1,  1,  1,  1,
28      1,  1,  1,  1,  1,  1,  1,  1,  1,  1,
29      1,  1,  1,  1,  1,  1,  1,  1,  1,  1,
30      1,  1,  1,  1,  1,  1,  1,  1,  1,  1,
31      1,  1,  1,  1,  1,  1,  1,  1,  1,  1,
32      1,  1,  1,  1,  1,  1,  1,  1,  1,  1,
33      1,  1,  1,  1,  1,  1,  1,  1,  1,  1,
34      1,  1,  1,  1,  1,  1,  1,  1,  1,  1,
35      1,  1,  1,  1,  1,  1,  1,  1,  1,  1,
36      1
37  };
38
39  /* INITIALIZE THE MODEL. */
40
41  start_model()
42  {   int i;
43      for (i = 0; i<No_of_chars; i++) {   /* Set up tables that        */
44          char_to_index[i] = i+1;         /* translate between symbol  */
45          index_to_char[i+1] = i;         /* indexes and characters.   */
46      }
47
48      cum_freq[No_of_symbols] = 0;
49      for (i = No_of_symbols; i>0; i--)   /* Set up cumulative         */
50          cum_freq[i-1] = cum_freq[i] + freq[i];  /* frequency counts. */
51      if (cum_freq[0] > Max_frequency) abort();   /* Check counts within limit*/
52  }
53
54
55  /* UPDATE THE MODEL TO ACCOUNT FOR A NEW SYMBOL. */
56
57  update_model(symbol)
58      int symbol;
59  {                                       /* Do nothing. */
60  }
61
```

```
adaptive_model.c

1   /* THE ADAPTIVE SOURCE MODEL */
2
3   #include "model.h"
4
5   int freq[No_of_symbols+1];              /* Symbol frequencies        */
6
7
8   /* INITIALIZE THE MODEL. */
9
10  start_model()
11  {   int i;
12      for (i = 0; i<No_of_chars; i++) {   /* Set up tables that        */
13          char_to_index[i] = i+1;         /* translate between symbol  */
14          index_to_char[i+1] = i;         /* indexes and characters.   */
15      }
16      for (i = 0; i<=No_of_symbols; i++) {   /* Set up initial frequency */
17          freq[i] = 1;                    /* counts to be one for all  */
18          cum_freq[i] = No_of_symbols-i;  /* symbols.                  */
19      }
20      freq[0] = 0;                        /* freq[0] must not be the   */
21  }                                       /* same as freq[1].          */
22
23
24  /* UPDATE THE MODEL TO ACCOUNT FOR A NEW SYMBOL. */
25
26  update_model(symbol)
27      int symbol;
28  {   int i;                              /* Index of new symbol       */
29      if (cum_freq[0]==Max_frequency) {   /* See if frequency counts   */
30          int cum;                        /* are at their maximum.     */
31          cum = 0;
32          for (i = No_of_symbols; i>=0; i--) {   /* If so, halve all the */
33              freq[i] = (freq[i]+1)/2;    /* counts (keeping them      */
34              cum_freq[i] = cum;          /* non-zero).                */
35              cum += freq[i];
36          }
37      }
38      for (i = symbol; freq[i]==freq[i-1]; i--) ;  /* Find symbol's new index. */
39      if (i<symbol) {
40          int ch_i, ch_symbol;
41          ch_i = index_to_char[i];
42          ch_symbol = index_to_char[symbol];   /* Update the translation */
43          index_to_char[i] = ch_symbol;        /* tables if the symbol has */
44          char_to_index[ch_symbol] = i;
45          index_to_char[symbol] = ch_i;        /* moved.                */
46          char_to_index[ch_i] = symbol;
47      }
48      freq[i] += 1;                       /* Increment the frequency   */
49      while (i>0) {                        /* count for the symbol and  */
50          i -= 1;                          /* update the cumulative     */
51          cum_freq[i] += 1;               /* frequencies.              */
52      }
53  }
```

Figure 5-9   Fixed and adaptive models for use with Figure 5-8.

$$c[s] \le \frac{(v-l+1) \times c[0] - 1}{r} - \varepsilon \le c[s-1] - 1, \qquad (5\text{B-}1)$$

where $r = h - l + 1$, $0 \le \varepsilon \le (r-1)/r$. (The last inequality of (5B-1) derives from the fact that $c[s-1]$ must be an integer.) Then we need to show that $l' \le v \le h'$, where l' and h' are the updated values for *low* and *high* as defined below.

(a) $l' \equiv l + \left\lfloor \dfrac{r \times c[s]}{c[0]} \right\rfloor \le l + \dfrac{r}{c[0]} \left[\dfrac{(v-l+1) \times c[0] - 1}{r} - \varepsilon \right]$ from (5B-1)

$$\le v + 1 - \frac{1}{c[0]},$$

so $l' \le v$ since both v and l' are integers and $c[0] > 0$.

(b) $h' \equiv l + \left\lfloor \dfrac{r \times c[s-1]}{c[0]} \right\rfloor - 1 \ge l + \dfrac{r}{c[0]} \left[\dfrac{(v-l+1) \times c[0] - 1}{r} + 1 - \varepsilon \right] - 1$ from (5B-1),

$$\ge v + \frac{r}{c[0]} \left[-\frac{1}{r} + 1 - \frac{r-1}{r} \right] = v.$$

Taking (a) and (b) together, we have $l' \le v \le h'$, as desired.

45h[0j45thwGw45hqU9d
poejrg[4wky]p435q)b&
[0wejg[04jy42yj3*k!c
p0w4j5g[235-k6t0=w~n
[0ewjg04jy04jy4j;qmy
pmh][krty-jk46-[p"qb
p[jw435y43 ,h[ps0%x
[psdhkj0- 34u5y9mwq
germhj-   j64k?ti
[ewjh4 h56 0o#r0b
e[wmb[p h65 u;g4{@
65[];.9[   ]0.o~x6
germhj-53k=ukj64:3xf
[ewjh4wth56430o*wm<
e[wmb[preh65,.u;aYlC
+[3fgm56rt0-"-23jsg!
[;jyt%ERghj(0;';Hd4=
1U5terEDghp=][>?kyeW

CONTEXT MODELING

Now the scene has been set to look at how to construct models of text that can be used for efficient compression. Given a predictive model that generates a probability distribution for each character as it appears in the text, arithmetic coding is able to code the actual sequence of characters effectively—so effectively that the number of bits used for transmission is only marginally greater than the entropy of the text with respect to the model. The secret of good compression, therefore, is coming up with ways of building suitable models. In Chapter 5 we said a little about adaptive modeling, but the models discussed there are very simple ones that do not give nearly as much compression as can be achieved using more sophisticated techniques. In this chapter we show how finite-context adaptive models can be used to construct a number of different compression algorithms.

Finite-context models, which were introduced in Section 2-2, use the preceding few characters to predict (estimate the probability of) the next one. The size of the context is fixed, typically comprising 1 to 10 characters. The modeler estimates probabilities conditioned on this context and uses them to predict the next character. In an adaptive model, the probability estimates are simply frequency counts based on the text seen so far.

The main obstacle to this procedure for adaptive modeling is the zero-frequency problem. In finite-context models it is desirable to have a long context, to take into account as much relevant information as possible when making predictions. However, this means that most contexts will never have been seen. For example, if a 10-character context is used, it will be many millions of characters before more than a tiny fraction of the trillions of possible 11-character strings have been encountered. But in Chapter 3 we explained the importance of assigning a nonzero probability to each character that can possibly occur, so the probability estimation procedure must take care to reserve some probability space for each character in each context. This means that initially the compression algorithm will have to rely solely on zero-frequency estimates of probabilities, which are not based on the text being coded. The alternative is to make the context very short, but then compression will be be poor in the long term, because little of the structure of the text will be available for making predictions.

The solution to this dilemma is to use a *blending* strategy, where the predictions of several contexts of different lengths are combined into a single overall probability. A number of ways of performing this blending will be examined, although like the zero-frequency problem, there are many different plausible solutions, no one of which stands out as the best.

The structure of this chapter is as follows. In the next section we present a general blending technique, together with three specific methods that are used in practice. As it stands, full blending is usually too slow to be useful, but two highly practical approximations are also presented—*exclusions* and *lazy exclusions*. Following that, different ways of constructing the models are discussed and parallels drawn with the dictionary approach, which is examined in Chapter 8. In Section 6-3 we describe practical finite-context algorithms in detail. We call the general blending scheme PPM for "prediction by partial match"; and particular implementations are identified by a suffix. Next we present the results of some experiments, although a general evaluation and comparison of the coding schemes is deferred until Chapter 9. In the concluding section we introduce a number of useful techniques and data structures for implementing the algorithms.

6.1 BLENDING

Context models condition the probability that a particular symbol will occur on the sequence of characters that immediately precede it. The order of the model, which we represent by the symbol o, is the number of characters in the context used for prediction. For example, suppose that an order-2 model is selected and the text that has just been processed is "$\cdots\bullet$and$\bullet$the$\bullet$text$\bullet$that$\bullet$has$\bullet$just$\bullet$been$\bullet$processed$\bullet$i". Since the model has $o = 2$, the next character, denoted by ϕ, is predicted on the basis of occurrences of trigrams "$\bullet$iϕ" earlier in the message. A scan through an English dictionary will show that ϕ = "e", ϕ = "h", ϕ = "i", ϕ = "j", ϕ = "k", ϕ = "q", ϕ = "u", ϕ = "w", ϕ = "y", and ϕ = "z" are unlikely in this context; while the high frequency of the word "is" will give ϕ = "s" a reasonably high probability.

Blending strategies use a number of models with different values of o in consort. For example, an order-1 model may be used, which predicts ϕ on the basis of the digrams encountered in the text so far, as well as an order-0 model, which predicts according to the unconditioned character probabilities. One way to combine these predictions is to assign a weight to each model and calculate the weighted sum of the probabilities. Many different blending schemes can be expressed as special cases of this general mechanism.

To express this more precisely we need to introduce some notation. Let $p_o(\phi)$ be the probability assigned to ϕ by the finite-context model of order o, for each character ϕ of the input alphabet A. This probability is assigned adaptively and will change from one point in the text to another. If the weight given to the model of order o is w_o, and the maximum order used is m, the blended probabilities $p(\phi)$ are computed by

$$p(\phi) = \sum_{o=-1}^{m} w_o p_o(\phi).$$

The weights should be normalized to sum to 1. To calculate both probabilities and weights, extensive use will be made of the counts associated with each context. Let $c_o(\phi)$ denote the number of times that the symbol ϕ occurs in the current context of order o. Denote by C_o the total number of times that the context has been seen; that is,

$$C_o = \sum_{\phi \in A} c_o(\phi).$$

6.1.1 A Simple Blending Algorithm

We are now ready to describe the first of many possible blending schemes. Its chief virtue is simplicity; some ways to improve its performance will be examined later. In this simple method, the individual contexts' prediction probabilities are

$$p_o(\phi) = \frac{c_o(\phi)}{C_o}.$$

This means that they are zero for characters which have not been seen before in that context. However, it is necessary that the final blended probability be nonzero for every character. To ensure this, an extra model is introduced which predicts every character with the same probability $1/q$ (where, as usual, q is the number of characters in the alphabet A). As mentioned in Chapter 2, this is referred to as an order -1 model. Providing its predictions are included with a nonzero weight, each of the final blended probabilities is guaranteed to be nonzero.

A second problem is that C_o will be zero whenever the context of order o has never occurred before. In a range of models of order $0, 1, 2, \ldots, m$, there will be some largest order $l \leq m$ for which the context has been encountered previously. All shorter contexts will necessarily have been seen too, because the context for a lower-order model is a substring of that for a higher-order one. Giving zero weight to models of order $l+1, \ldots, m$ ensures that only contexts that have been seen will be used.

Table 6-1 shows an example of a blending calculation that predicts the character following the sequence "cacbcaabca." For simplicity, the five-character alphabet $A = \{a, b, c, d, e\}$ is assumed. The order-4 context "abca" has never occurred before and therefore receives a weight of 0. The context "bca" has occurred just once; it was followed by "a". Since this order-3 model makes a prediction, it receives nonzero

TABLE 6-1 CALCULATION OF BLENDED PROBABILITIES (SIMPLE SCHEME AND ESCAPE METHOD A) FOR THE MESSAGE "cacbcaabca"

o	Context	Counts C_o	Predictions — $p_o(\phi)$ $c_o(\phi)$										Weight w_o	Escape e_o
			a		b		c		d		e			
4	abca:	0	—	0	—	0	—	0	—	0	—	0	0	—
3	bca:	1	1	1	0	0	0	0	0	0	0	0	$\frac{1}{2}$	$\frac{1}{2}$
2	ca:	2	$\frac{1}{2}$	1	0	0	$\frac{1}{2}$	1	0	0	0	0	$\frac{1}{3}$	$\frac{1}{3}$
1	a:	3	$\frac{1}{3}$	1	$\frac{1}{3}$	1	$\frac{1}{3}$	1	0	0	0	0	$\frac{1}{8}$	$\frac{1}{4}$
0	:	10	$\frac{4}{10}$	4	$\frac{2}{10}$	2	$\frac{4}{10}$	4	0	0	0	0	$\frac{5}{132}$	$\frac{1}{11}$
−1	—	—	$\frac{1}{5}$	—	$\frac{1}{5}$	—	$\frac{1}{5}$	—	$\frac{1}{5}$	—	$\frac{1}{5}$	—	$\frac{1}{264}$	0
Blended probabilities			$\frac{956}{1320}$		$\frac{66}{1320}$		$\frac{296}{1320}$		$\frac{1}{1320}$		$\frac{1}{1320}$			

weight. The context "ca" has occurred twice and predicts the characters "a" and "c". Each of "a", "b", and "c" have occurred following "a" and are predicted by the order-1 model. The order-0 model shows that just the characters "a", "b", and "c" have occurred so far in the message; the only model that predicts "d" or "e" is the default model of order −1. Combining these probabilities with the weights shown in Table 6-1 finally predicts "a" with probability 1176/1320 and "b", "c", "d", and "e" with probabilities 66/1320, 76/1320, 1/1320, and 1/1320, respectively.

6.1.2 Escape Probabilities

Where do the weights come from? One possibility is to assign a fixed set of weights to the models of different order. Another is to adapt weights as coding proceeds to give more emphasis to high-order models later. However, neither of these takes account of the fact that the relative importance of the models varies with the context and its counts.

A more pragmatic approach, which at first might seem quite different to blending, is to allocate some code space in each model to the possibility that a lower-order model should be used to predict the next character. The motivation for this is to allow for the coding of a novel character in a particular model by providing access to lower-order models, although we shall see that it is effectively giving a weight to each model based on its usefulness.

This approach requires an estimate of the probability that a particular context will be followed by a character that has never before followed it, since that determines how much code space should be allocated to the possibility of shifting to the next smaller context. The probability estimate should decrease as more characters are observed in that context. Each time a novel character is seen, a model of lower order must be consulted to find its probability. Thus the total weight assigned to lower-order contexts should depend on the probability of a new character. For example, if it is estimated that there is a 25% chance that a new character will occur in the longest context, that context might be weighted at 0.75 and all the remaining contexts together at 0.25. Note, however, that arguments such as this do no more than confirm the plausibility of a particular technique—its actual worth can only be assessed in the heat of real compression.

The probability of encountering a previously unseen character is called the *escape probability*, since it governs whether the system escapes to a smaller context to determine its predictions. This escape mechanism has an equivalent blending mechanism as follows. Denoting the probability of an escape at level o by e_o, equivalent weights can be calculated from the escape probabilities by

$$w_o = (1 - e_o) \times \prod_{i=o+1}^{l} e_i, \qquad -1 \leq o < l$$

$$w_l = 1 - e_l,$$

where l is the highest-order context making a nonnull prediction. In this formula, the weight of each successively lower order is reduced by the escape probability from one order to the next. The weights will be plausible (all positive and summing to 1) provided only that the escape probabilities are between 0 and 1 and it is not possible to escape below order -1, that is, $e_{-1} = 0$. The advantage of expressing things in terms of escape probabilities is that they tend to be more easily visualized and understood than the weights themselves, which can become small very rapidly. We will also see that the escape mechanism is much more practical to implement than weighted blending.

If $p_o(\phi)$ is the probability assigned to the character ϕ by the order-o model, the weighted contribution of the model to the blended probability of ϕ is

$$w_o p_o(\phi) = \prod_{i=o+1}^{l} e_i \times (1 - e_o) \times p_o(\phi).$$

In other words, it is the probability of decreasing to an order-o model, *and* not going any further, *and* selecting ϕ at that level. These weighted probabilities can then be summed over all values of o to determine the blended probability for ϕ. Specifying an escape mechanism amounts to choosing values for e_o and p_o, and this is how the mechanisms are characterized in the descriptions that follow.

6.1.3 Determining Escape Probabilities: Method A

An escape probability is the probability that a previously unseen character will occur, so the business of estimating it brings us back to our old friend the zero-frequency problem (see Section 3-1). There is no theoretical basis for choosing the escape probability optimally. However, it does seem intuitively reasonable that it should decrease as the number of times the context has been seen increases. After encountering just one character, it is more than likely that the next one will be different; whereas after 1000 characters it is quite unlikely that something new will turn up.

The first method of probability estimation, unimaginatively dubbed "method A," allocates one additional count over and above the number of times the context has been seen, to allow for the occurrence of new characters.[1] This gives the escape probability

$$e_o = \frac{1}{C_o + 1}.$$

For example, if a particular context has occurred three times before (excluding the present occurrence), the escape probability will be $e_o = 1/4$. The probability assigned to each character (ignoring the escape symbol) is simply its relative frequency,

$$p_o(\phi) = \frac{c_o(\phi)}{C_o}.$$

For example, if the above-mentioned context was followed by an "a" twice and a "b" once, then the probability for "a" is 2/3 and for "b" is 1/3.

Allowing for the escape code, the code space allocated to ϕ in the order-o model is $(1 - e_o)p_o(\phi)$. The formula simplifies to

$$\frac{c_o(\phi)}{C_o + 1},$$

which is useful because in practice the code space is calculated very frequently. The escape probabilities and weights in Table 6-1 were computed using this method.

6.1.4 Determining Escape Probabilities: Method B

As noted above, there can be no theoretical justification for choosing any particular escape mechanism as the optimal one. Here is another equally plausible method. Consider a context that has appeared 20 times. If "a" is the only character to have followed the context in all these occurrences, the probability of the next character being different should be low. However, if 10 different characters had followed, it would seem that the text being compressed is quite variable and that some new character is fairly likely to appear next time. If the appearance of a new character is considered a special type of event, then in the first scenario it has occurred once out of 20 cases and in the second, 10 times out of 20 cases. Accordingly, the escape probability is estimated as 1/20 in the first situation and 10/20 in the second. Methods B and C are both based on this approach.

Method B refrains from predicting characters unless they have occurred more than once in the present context. This is done by subtracting one from all counts. For instance, if a context has occurred three times with "a" following twice and "b" once, then "a" is predicted with a weighted probability of $(2-1)/3 = 1/3$ and "b" is not predicted at all. The two unused counts are assigned to the escape probability, making it 2/3. This technique provides a filter against anomalous or unusual events—until something is seen twice, it is not "believed."

---

[1]Method A described here is similar to solution A for the zero-frequency problem in Chapter 3. Method B is *not* the same as method B of Chapter 3, but we have preserved the labeling to correspond with the original papers.

To be more precise, let q_o be the number of different characters that have occurred in some context of order o. The escape probability used by method B is

$$e_o = \frac{q_o}{C_o},$$

which increases with the proportion of new characters observed. Before allowing code space for the escape character, the estimated probability of each character is

$$p_o(\phi) = \frac{c_o(\phi) - 1}{C_o - q_o},$$

so a character is not predicted until it has occurred twice. After allowing for the escape code, the code space allocated to ϕ is $(1 - e_o)p_o(\phi)$, which is simply

$$\frac{c_o(\phi) - 1}{C_o}.$$

6.1.5 Determining Escape Probabilities: Method C

Method C is similar to method B, but begins predicting characters as soon as they have occurred once, giving

$$p_o(\phi) = \frac{c_o(\phi)}{C_o}.$$

The escape probability still increases with the number of different characters in the context, but needs to be a little smaller to allow for the extra code space allocated to characters, so

$$e_o = \frac{q_o}{C_o + q_o}.$$

This gives each character a code space of

$$\frac{c_o(\phi)}{C_o + q_o}$$

in the order-o model.

6.1.6 Exclusion

In a fully blended model, the probability of a character includes predictions from contexts of many different orders, which makes it very time consuming to calculate. Moreover, an arithmetic coder requires *cumulative* probabilities from the model. Not only are these slow to evaluate (particularly for the decoder), but the probabilities involved can be very small, and therefore high-precision arithmetic is required. Full blending is not a practical technique for finite-context modeling.

The escape mechanism can be used as the basis of an approximate blending technique called *exclusion*, which eliminates these problems by decomposing a character's probability into several simpler predictions. It works as follows. When coding the character ϕ using context models with a maximum order of m, the order-m model is first consulted. If it predicts ϕ with a nonzero probability, it is used to code ϕ. Otherwise, the escape code is transmitted, and the second longest context attempts to predict ϕ. Coding proceeds by escaping to smaller contexts until ϕ is predicted. The context of order -1 guarantees that this will happen eventually. In this manner each character is coded as a series of escape codes followed by the character code. Each of these codes is over a manageable alphabet of no more than $q+1$ symbols, where q is the size of the input alphabet.

The exclusion method is so named because it excludes lower-order predictions from the final probability of a character. Consequently, all other characters encountered in higher-order contexts can safely be excluded from subsequent probability calculations because they will never be coded by a lower-order model. This can be accomplished by effectively modifying counts in lower-order models by setting the count associated with a character to zero if it has been predicted by a higher-order model. (The models are not permanently altered, but rather the effect is achieved each time a particular prediction is being made.) Thus the probability of a character is taken only from the highest-order context that predicts it. Table 6-2 shows the predictions of Table 6-1 recalculated using exclusions. Table 6-3 shows the sequence of codes generated in practice. The character probabilities from Table 6-2 have been multiplied by $1 - e_o$ to allow for the escape. For example, the character "d" is coded as the five symbols <esc><esc><esc><esc>"d" with probabilities 1/2, 1/2, 1/2, 1, and 1/2, respectively. The first <esc> indicates a transition from the "bca" context to "ca", the second from "ca" to "a", and so on. The "d" is predicted in the order -1 context. Notice that since the order-0 context does not predict

TABLE 6-2 CALCULATION OF BLENDED PROBABILITIES (USING EXCLUSIONS AND ESCAPE METHOD A) FOR THE MESSAGE "cacbcaabca"

o	Context	Counts C_o	a p_o	a c_o	b p_o	b c_o	c p_o	c c_o	d p_o	d c_o	e p_o	e c_o	Weight w_o	Escape e_o
4	abca:	0	—	0	—	0	—	0	—	0	—	0	0	—
3	bca:	1	1	1	0	0	0	0	0	0	0	0	$\frac{1}{2}$	$\frac{1}{2}$
2	ca:	1	x		0	0	1	1	0	0	0	0	$\frac{1}{4}$	$\frac{1}{2}$
1	a:	1	x		1	1	x		0	0	0	0	$\frac{1}{8}$	$\frac{1}{2}$
0	:	0	x		x		x		0	0	0	0	0	1
-1	—	—	x		x		x		$\frac{1}{2}$	—	$\frac{1}{2}$	—	$\frac{1}{8}$	0
Blended probabilities			$\frac{1}{2}$		$\frac{1}{8}$		$\frac{1}{4}$		$\frac{1}{16}$		$\frac{1}{16}$			

TABLE 6-3 EXAMPLE OF ESCAPE MECHANISM
(WITH EXCLUSIONS) CODING THE FIVE CHARACTERS
THAT MIGHT FOLLOW THE STRING "cacbcaabca"
OVER THE ALPHABET {a, b, c, d, e}

Character	Coding	Total code space
a	a $\frac{1}{2}$	(total = $\frac{1}{2}$; 1 bit)
b	\<esc> \<esc> b $\frac{1}{2}$ $\frac{1}{2}$ $\frac{1}{2}$	(total = $\frac{1}{8}$; 3 bits)
c	\<esc> c $\frac{1}{2}$ $\frac{1}{2}$	(total = $\frac{1}{4}$; 2 bits)
d	\<esc> \<esc> \<esc> \<esc> d $\frac{1}{2}$ $\frac{1}{2}$ $\frac{1}{2}$ 1 $\frac{1}{2}$	(total = $\frac{1}{16}$; 4 bits)
e	\<esc> \<esc> \<esc> \<esc> e $\frac{1}{2}$ $\frac{1}{2}$ $\frac{1}{2}$ 1 $\frac{1}{2}$	(total = $\frac{1}{16}$; 4 bits)

any new characters, it has an escape probability of 1, so coding this escape will cost nothing.

The disadvantage of exclusion is that statistical sampling errors are emphasized by using only higher-order contexts. However, experiments to assess the impact of exclusions indicate that compression is only fractionally worse than for a fully blended model. Furthermore, execution is much faster and implementation is simplified considerably.

There is a small flaw in each of methods A, B, and C when they are used with exclusions. If all the characters of the alphabet have been encountered in a particular context, no new one can possibly occur, and there will be no need to escape to smaller contexts. However, each method continues to assign a nonzero escape probability. This is not a severe problem if the alphabet is of reasonable size, for the context's count must have grown large before all characters have been seen, making the escape probability small. The effect therefore has little influence on the final efficiency of compression. However, when the alphabet is small—say, two characters—it will be much more significant. A simple modification is then advisable to decrease the escape probability as the number of characters approaches the maximum possible.

A further simplification of the blending technique is *lazy exclusion*, which uses the escape mechanism in the same way as exclusion to identify the longest context that predicts the character to be coded, but does not exclude the counts of characters predicted by longer contexts when making the probability estimate. This will always give worse compression (typically, about 5%) because such characters will *never* be predicted in the lower-order contexts, so the code space allocated to them is completely wasted. However, it is significantly faster because there is no need to keep track of the characters that need to be excluded. In practice, this can halve the time taken, which may well justify the relatively small decrease in compression performance.

In a fully blended model, it is natural to update counts in all the models of order 0, 1, ..., m after each character is coded, since all contexts were involved in the prediction. However, when exclusions are used, only one context is used to predict the character. This suggests a modification to the method of updating the models, called *update exclusion*, where the count for the predicted character is not incremented if it is already predicted by a higher-order context. In other words, a character is counted only in the context used to predict it. This can be rationalized by supposing that the correct statistic to collect for the lower-order context is not the raw frequency, but rather the frequency with which a character occurs when it is not being predicted by a longer context. This generally improves compression slightly (about 2%), and also reduces the time consumed in updating counts.

6.2 BUILDING MODELS

The blending approach demands that a set of models of different orders be maintained. The most straightforward way to accomplish this is to fix on a maximum allowed order, say m, and build a set of contexts and their predictions for each model from 0 to m. This is what is done, in fact, for all the compression techniques described in the next section. The sets can be represented abstractly as dictionaries of *traces*, where each trace comprises a context with one prediction appended. For example, if the context "ab" predicts the characters "b", "c", or "d", then the three traces "abb", "abc", and "abd" will be stored. All that is required to support the necessary probability calculations is to record the number of times each trace has occurred. Efficient data structures for storing traces are considered in Section 6-5.

6.2.1 Contexts and Dictionaries

There are other options for constructing the suite of models. For example, there might be no predetermined limit on the model orders. Of course, the length of individual traces does need to be restricted, so that models can be stored in a finite amount of memory. One way to accumulate arbitrarily long traces is to record them only when an occurrence is already recorded in the model one order lower. The null string, which constitutes the single trace of length 0, is assumed always to have occurred. For example, the trace "abc" would be recorded only if there was a record of the trace "bc". Thus an order-1 model is built up first, then an order-2 model, and so on. This scheme removes the need for the user to choose the maximum order in advance. Instead, it adapts to the file being compressed.

Unfortunately, experiments indicate that this approach causes compression to deteriorate significantly. By the time the system embarks on the construction of a particular model, relevant statistics from the early part of the file have already been discarded. This affects compression performance because the probability estimates are less reliable than they would be otherwise. Modifications such as recording a prediction whenever a context two characters shorter has been recorded (rather than just one character shorter) may help to alleviate this.

The main reason for introducing this technique is to motivate a different view of the information stored in the models. By constructing successively longer traces, one effectively accumulates a list of the substrings that occur in the text. This is exactly what the dictionary techniques of Chapter 8 do. For example, the center column of Table 6-4 shows the traces built up for the message "cacbcaabca" by models of order 0, 1, and 2 together. To the left and right are dictionaries constructed by two different encoders which are described in Chapter 8. The one on the left splits the text into nonoverlapping strings, and as a result, the dictionary is smaller. The one on the right records all strings of up to three characters which occur at least once, whether they overlap or not, and so it builds the same dictionary as the first technique but with each string counted only once.

This view helps to decouple the process of building a model from that of encoding using a given model. For example, both of the dictionary encoders mentioned above use the same encoding process but different dictionary construction mechanisms. One could perfectly well employ blended probabilistic predictions with either mechanism. In fact, the scheme described earlier, which builds up traces of steadily increasing orders, effectively couples a blended probability encoder with a set of traces constructed using a standard dictionary-building technique. This view of the encoding process points to

TABLE 6-4   DICTIONARIES BUILT
UP BY DIFFERENT SYSTEMS
FOR THE MESSAGE "cacbcaabca"

LZ78 encoder	Finite context orders 0, 1, and 2		LZ77 encoder (with $F = 3$)
a	a	(4)	a
c	b	(2)	b
ab	c	(4)	c
ca	aa	(1)	aa
cb	ab	(1)	ab
	ac	(1)	ac
	bc	(2)	bc
	ca	(3)	ca
	cb	(1)	cb
	aab	(1)	aab
	abc	(1)	abc
	acb	(1)	acb
	bca	(2)	bca
	caa	(1)	caa
	cac	(1)	cac
	cbc	(1)	cbc

promising areas of research for new compression techniques, perhaps ones that combine the high speed of dictionary coding with the excellent compression of finite-context probabilistic schemes.

6.2.2 Scaling Counts

While the models are being constructed, the counts associated with each context, C_o and $c_o(\phi)$, are also being incremented. In any practical implementation these will be stored as fixed-width binary integers. For example, 32-bit values could be used and putative data compressors instructed not to compress files of more than 4×10^9 characters. However, the frequency counts that can be used by an arithmetic encoder may be much narrower—14 bits is typical—and it is convenient to store the counts in the same width. This makes it likely that they will overflow occasionally. An easy way of preventing this is to halve C_o and all of the $c_o(\phi)$ whenever C_o threatens to exceed the maximum allowed integer. It is important to ensure that none of the $c_o(\phi)$ are left at 0, which can be done either by rounding up or by deleting the reference to ϕ when $c_o(\phi) = 0$.

Retaining frequencies to low precision does little harm because small errors in predicted frequencies have almost no effect on the average code length. Consider a set of characters with true probabilities p_i and predicted probabilities $p_i + \varepsilon_i$. The expected code length will then be

$$-\sum p_i \log(p_i + \varepsilon_i) = -\sum p_i \log p_i - \sum \varepsilon_i + \sum \frac{\varepsilon_i^2}{2p_i} - \sum \frac{\varepsilon_i^3}{3p_i^2} + \cdots .$$

Since the predicted probabilities sum to 1, $\sum \varepsilon_i = 0$, so, assuming that the errors are smaller than the probabilities p_i, the increase over entropy is approximately

$$\sum \frac{\varepsilon_i^2}{2p_i} .$$

If the maximum allowed count is C, the errors will be of order $1/C$ and the increase in the average code length of order $1/C^2$.

A curious consequence of scaling the counts is that it often improves compression! This is rather counterintuitive, as probabilities are less accurate when smaller counts are involved. The resolution of the paradox is that in natural text the model does not converge to some final, "correct" version, but rather follows a moving target. The statistics toward the end of a book may differ significantly from those at the beginning. (For an example, compare the popular words in Chapter 10 of this book with those of Chapter 1.) Hence recent statistics are often a better guide to the next character than those accumulated from long ago. Periodic scaling effectively gives recent traces a larger weight than those from the distant past, resulting in better compression. In some experiments, investigators have found that restricting counts to maximum values as low as 32 (five bits) is optimum, and others have reported that 8-bit counts are suitable.

It should be noted, however, that for any given text there always exist models that predict equally well at the beginning and end. By having contexts that are sufficiently finely distinguished, it is possible to condition predictions on the current position in the text. The problem is that to learn such very precise models would take countless examples of texts that exhibit a similar evolution of patterns from start to finish.

6.2.3 Alphabets

Clearly, at least one parameter must be specified to a blended finite-context coder—the maximum order of the models that are constructed (or, more generally, the maximum amount of storage available). There is, however, a more subtle parameter: the alphabet that is used. The most natural choice is the input alphabet implied by the compression domain—for example, 7-bit ASCII characters for text. However, any alphabet will suffice provided that the original text can be transformed unambiguously into it. For example, 8-bit characters might be split into two 4-bit characters, or even single bits. In general, the impact of such recoding is far from clear. The operation of blending is affected, for if contexts are held at an equivalent length, there will be more models of different orders to blend. In text the obvious alphabet is so natural that splitting it seems unlikely to give any benefit. However, in binary files such as executable images of computer programs or numeric data, there does seem to be some advantage. Such files tend to use all possible 256 eight-bit characters. Splitting the alphabet into 4-bit ones reduces diversity and increases the lengths of contexts that can be stored. This often improves the blending operation, giving better compression.

It is also possible to recode data into larger alphabets. For example, natural-language text can be split into words that are viewed as single symbols. For this to work in practice, the set of words must be adaptive, so the alphabet grows as the message proceeds. This requires some way of specifying previously unseen words and building up the alphabet.

6.3 DESCRIPTION OF SOME FINITE-CONTEXT MODELS

Now we describe six coding schemes, which between them encompass all significant finite-context models we are aware of (and for which we have been able to find full details). The methods are evaluated in Chapter 9, which presents an extensive set of performance results. Unless otherwise noted, they all use models of order −1, 0, ... up to a maximum allowed value m.

PPMA (for "prediction by partial match, method A") uses method A to assign escape probabilities, blends predictions using the exclusion technique, and does not scale character counts.

PPMB is the same as PPMA but uses method B to assign escape probabilities.

PPMC is a more recent version of the PPM technique that has been carefully tuned to improve compression and increase execution speed. It deals with escapes using method C, uses update exclusion and scales counts to a maximum precision of about 8 bits (which was found suitable for a wide range of files).

PPMC' is a streamlined descendant of PPMC, built for speed. It deals with escapes using method C but uses lazy exclusion for prediction (as well as update exclusion) and imposes an upper bound on memory by discarding and rebuilding the model whenever space is exhausted.

DAFC is one of the first schemes to blend models of different orders and to adapt the model structure. It includes order-0 and order-1 predictions, but instead of building a full order-1 model it bases contexts only on the most frequent characters, to economize on space. For example, in the experiments of Chapter 9, the first 31 characters to reach a count of 50 are used adaptively to form order-1 contexts. Method A is used as the escape mechanism. The use of low-order contexts ensures that DAFC uses a bounded (and relatively small) amount of memory and is very fast. A special "run mode" is entered whenever the same character is seen more than once consecutively, which is effectively an order-2 context. In this mode only two symbols are possible—a "1" if the next symbol is the same as the last two, and a "0" to mark the end of the run. These two symbols are coded adaptively for each of the 32 contexts.

WORD uses an alphabet of "words"—comprising alphabetic characters—and "nonwords"—comprising nonalphabetic ones. The original text is recoded by expressing it as an alternating sequence of words and nonwords. Thus the string "A•variable•name:$A_23" would be decomposed into the sequence "A", "•", "variable", "•", "name", ":$", "A", and "_23". Separate finite-context models, each combining orders 0 and 1, are used for words and nonwords. A word is predicted by preceding words, and a nonword by preceding nonwords. Method B is used for estimating probabilities, and because of the large alphabet size lazy exclusions are appropriate for prediction; update exclusion is also employed. The model stops growing once it reaches a predetermined maximum size, whereupon statistics are updated but no new contexts are added.

Whenever novel words or nonwords are encountered, they must be specified in some way. This is done by first transmitting the length (chosen from the numbers 0 to 20) using an order-0 model of lengths. Then a finite-context model of the letters (or nonalphabetic characters, in the case of nonwords) with contexts of order −1, 0, and 1 is used, again with escape probabilities computed using method B. In total, 10 different models are stored and blended, five for words and five for nonwords, comprising in each case models of order 0 and 1, a length model of order 0, and character models of order 0 and 1.

6.4 EXPERIMENTAL PERFORMANCE

In practice, none of the methods described in Section 6-3 consistently outperforms the others (except that DAFC is almost always inferior). Each one does better on some files and worse on others. It is interesting to evaluate different aspects of the techniques used for finite-context models, as well as their overall performance.

6.4.1 Blending

The first question is whether blending does any good. The answer is an unequivocal "yes": a blended model is much better than a single fixed-order one. Figure 6-1 plots compression against number of characters for "book1" (described in Appendix B). One curve shows the results for a single model of order 4 with an escape to order –1. The other shows the same data compressed using PPMC with orders –1, 0, 1, 2, 3, and 4. Clearly, blending (in this case, using exclusions) has improved performance dramatically, especially in the earlier part of the data when the order-4 model has few predictions.

6.4.2 Escape Probabilities

The second question is how best to calculate the escape probabilities. As noted earlier, there is no theoretical basis to choose between the different methods, and there are files on which each is better than all the others—although we have noticed a general tendency for methods B and C to outperform method A. PPMC and PPMC′ are a little faster than PPMA and PPMB because the statistics are simpler to maintain due to the use of update exclusions. It is actually quite satisfying that compression performance is insensitive to the exact escape probability calculation. It illustrates that the coding method is robust and gains its power from the idea of the escape mechanism rather than the precise details of the algorithm used to implement it. This is fortunate in view of the fact that particular escape algorithms cannot be justified theoretically.

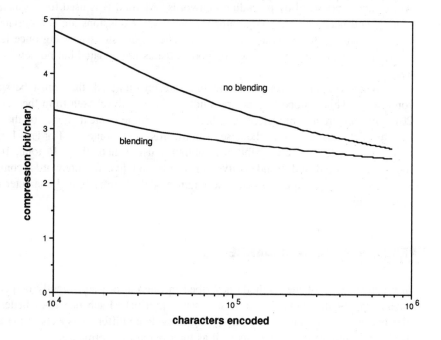

Figure 6-1   Comparison of blended and non-blended compression.

How robust are the various escape mechanisms to the choice of maximum order? Figure 6-2 shows the compression given by methods A, B, and C on two files from the corpus in Appendix B: "paper1," a text file of 53,161 characters, and "geo," which is 102,400 bytes of numeric geophysical data. These two have quite different properties and the compression algorithms differ sharply in their relative performance. Nevertheless, it can be seen that beyond the optimum order, performance remains flat for both files with the exception of PPMA, which fared rather badly on the geophysical data. This has two implications. First, it shows that the blending methods are able to accommodate the presence of higher-order models that contribute little or nothing to the compression. Second, if the optimum order is not known beforehand, it is better to err on the high side. The penalty in compression performance will be small, although time and space requirements will increase.

6.5 IMPLEMENTATION

Finite-context methods give the best overall compression of all techniques examined in this book, but they can be slow. As with any practical scheme, the time required for encoding and decoding grows only linearly with the length of the message. Furthermore, it grows at most linearly with the order of the largest model. However, to achieve an effective implementation, close attention must be paid to details, and this section assesses the resources required by these methods. Any balanced system will represent a complex trade-off between time, space, and compression efficiency. All we can do here is give some idea of the trade-offs involved, and outline what techniques are most important for achieving efficient implementations.

Any coding scheme that yields good compression must use very large models which typically consume more space than the data being compressed. Indeed, a major part of the advance in coding over the past decade can be attributed to the ready availability of large amounts of memory. Because of adaptation this memory is relatively cheap, for the models themselves are not transmitted and remain in existence only for the period of the actual compression. All that is required is empty storage, which is becoming increasingly cheap as technology advances. Regrettably it is not infinite, so care must be exercised when designing the data structures to ensure that no waste occurs. In situations where the model eventually fills available memory, there is a direct relationship between efficiency of the data structure in storing the model, speed of operation, and coding performance. The more efficient the data structure, the larger the model that can be stored. As a result, the predictions are better, but the speed is lower.

The most practical method for achieving blending is using exclusions (or lazy exclusions), and for these the execution time can be broken down into three major components:

- The time to find the prediction with the longest match to the current context.

- The time to compute the probability of the next character in that context.

- The time to perform arithmetic coding using the probability.

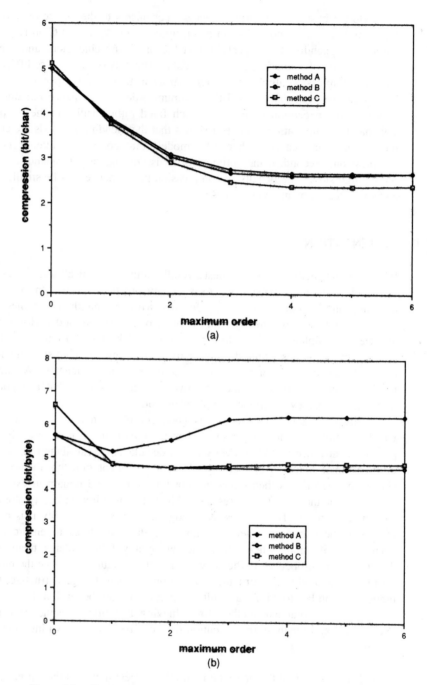

Figure 6-2   Compression by methods A, B, and C plotted against order for (a) file "paper1" and (b) file "geo."

The third component has been dealt with in Chapter 5, and is around 100 to 200 μs on a 1-MIP machine. In finite-context coding it is necessary to perform at least one arithmetic coding operation for each symbol encoded, which limits speed to at most 5000 to 10,000 symbols/s. A further arithmetic coding operation is required for every escape transmitted. If the model is predicting well and the highest matching context usually succeeds in finding a prediction, this overhead will be small. On the other hand, when the model is predicting poorly, it will be much greater. It is difficult to see how to reduce the number of these operations without significantly changing the basic algorithm. The next two sections explore the first two components of execution time.

6.5.1 Finding Contexts

Forward trees.   One appealing aspect of using all models of orders 0, 1, ..., m is that they need not be stored and accessed independently but can be combined together into a single integrated data structure, since an order-o model contains all the information required by an order $o-1$ model. Figure 6-3 shows one way of doing this. A tree is used to record all strings in the dictionary together with the number of times they have occurred (this kind of structure is more accurately called a "trie"). Each node is labeled with a symbol and carries one count. A node represents a single trace in the dictionary and unless it is a leaf, corresponds to a context in one of the models; its depth is the order of that model.

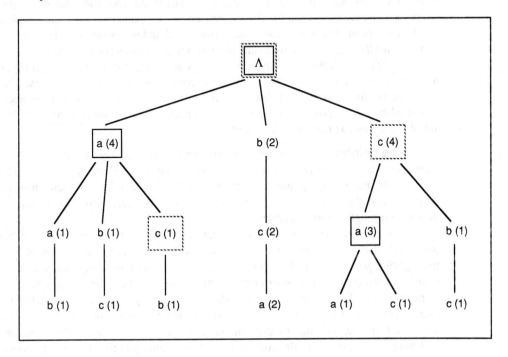

Figure 6-3   Structure of a forward tree for the message "cacbcaabca."

For example, consider the context "ca" followed by "c". The order-0 context is represented by the root node. The order-1 context ("a") is found at the child of the root labeled "a". The order-2 context ("ca") is found by moving from the root to its child labeled "c", and from there to the appropriate grandchild labeled "a". The tree is therefore constructed with traces growing forward in time from root to leaves. We refer to this as a *forward tree*. Because of this organization, the number at a node gives the total count C_o for that context (except that it will be $C_o + 1$ for contexts adjacent to the coding position; see below). Also, the numbers at a node's descendants record how often the corresponding characters have occurred in that context [the value $c_o(\phi)$ for character ϕ]. For example, below the node for the context "ca", the characters "a" and "c" are both recorded as having occurred once. The message from which this was taken ends with "...ca". Since "ca" has just occurred, its node has been updated, but the sequel has not yet been seen, so none of the children have been incremented; therefore, the count on this node is $C_o + 1$ rather than C_o. In fact, all the current contexts will have a count one larger than might be expected.

To calculate a fully blended probability, it is necessary to locate each current context (these are marked with solid boxes in Figure 6-3) and examine their counts and each of their descendants' counts. If exclusions are used, some of the lower-order contexts will not always need to be located. Defer for a moment the question of how to represent individual nodes, and just assume that from any node one can locate that descendant which is tagged with a particular symbol—call this an *index* operation. The simplest way to find a particular context is to start at the root and scan down the tree, indexing successive nodes until the desired one is encountered. To locate each of the $m + 1$ contexts in this way would take $m(m + 1)/2$ index operations. But this can be reduced to $O(m)$ operations by using the last set of current contexts and moving each down one level, with the next input character as an index. For example, if in Figure 6-3 the next character to occur after the current context is "c", the new contexts "c" and "ac" can be found one level down from the marked nodes. These new nodes are identified by dotted boxes. Note that the root node is always current, and the descendant of a leaf context need not be sought.

Vine pointers. A further economy can be made by keeping an extra pointer at each node which points back to the node whose trace is one character shorter. Thus the node for the trace "cac" points back to that for "ac" (the oldest character having been dropped), and the node for "ac" points back to "c". We call these *vine pointers*, since they loop through the tree structure.

Vine pointers have two important features. First, given a pointer to the highest-order node that matches the current context, all other matching contexts can be found by tracing vine pointers until the root is reached. It is no longer necessary to explicitly store or to search for these other contexts, since they can be located when necessary by a single pointer dereference. Figure 6-4 shows how vine pointers can be used to find the current contexts of Figure 6-3. The second feature is that the new current context can be found from the node that predicts the next character. For instance, the node for "cac" will have a vine pointer to the context node "ac". Consequently, it is never necessary to search for contexts, but only to follow pointers. Figure 6-5 shows the vine pointers used to find the contexts of the trace "cac".

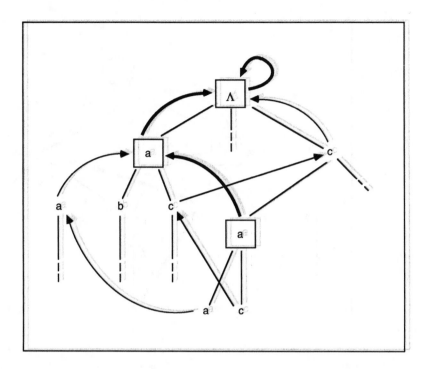

Figure 6-4   Vine pointers (shown bold) linking current contexts in the forward tree of Figure 6-3.

The upshot is that index operations are needed only when checking to see whether a context predicts the next character. In the worst case, when each context is checked unsuccessfully, this may involve $m+1$ index operations. In the long run, however, things are significantly better. To see this, note that two cases can occur when moving to a new set of contexts. When the longest matching context is equal to the maximal order, a single vine pointer will locate the first of the next contexts. When the longest matching context is shorter than the maximal order, nothing at all need be done as the node containing the predicted character is the required context node!

In fact, every case where it is necessary to escape down one level and do an index is matched with a corresponding case where nothing need be done to find the next starting context—otherwise, the order of the longest match would steadily increase or decrease. The result is that in the best case, when every character is predicted by the maximal context, one index operation together with one vine dereference is needed for each character encoded. In the worst case, where an escape is used on average for every second character, $1\frac{1}{2}$ index operations and $\frac{1}{2}$ a dereference are required per character.

Updating the tree structure.   To update the tree structure involves both incrementing node counters and adding any new traces that have not occurred before. The relevant counters are found by following the vine pointers from the pointer

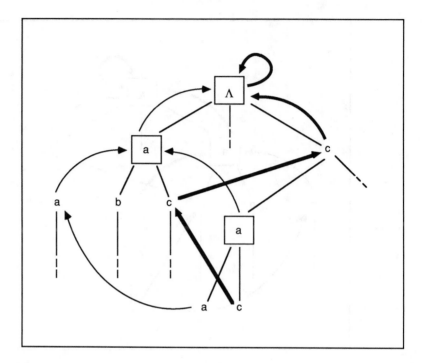

Figure 6-5   Vine pointers used to locate next contexts and to update counts in the forward tree of Figure 6-3.

predicting the next character (these are the same pointers needed to locate the next set of contexts, shown in bold in Figure 6-5). This is an $O(m)$ operation, although the individual steps are very quick. It may also be necessary to rearrange or update the data structure used to record the node's descendants, depending on what structure is used. This rearrangement usually costs about the same as an index operation.

The whole business is avoided by using update exclusions, for this technique does not increment any counter other than that for the longest match. This can actually improve compression performance by around 5%. Unfortunately, it destroys the simple relationship whereby the count at a node is the sum of its descendants' counts (possibly plus 1). To accommodate this it is necessary to preserve two counts at each node: One is the count for the node when viewed as a prediction by the parent context, while the other is the sum of its own descendants' counts. This kind of incrementing is used in PPMC and PPMC′.

Adding new traces to the tree is more expensive than updating the counters. At each step, up to $m+1$ new nodes may need to be created and linked into their parents. This will involve operations about as expensive as an index. As more of the input is seen, the model becomes more comprehensive, and new traces are added less frequently. Nevertheless, in the early stages of compression, and whenever the input changes radically in form, execution speed will tend to be dominated by the time required to add new nodes.

Backward trees.   Backward trees are alternative structures that have advantages under some circumstances. As before, each nonleaf node corresponds to a context in one of the models. However, as Figure 6-6 shows, the nodes are related differently. If the context is "ca", then starting from the root the node labeled "a" is located, then its descendant labeled "c". This is the opposite order from the forward trees discussed above. To each node is attached a separate structure with the predicted characters and their frequencies. All the current contexts lie along the path from the root to the longest matching one.

The advantage of this structure is that it can be used for prediction problems where contexts are not taken just from the most recent characters. For example, if the problem is the compression of DNA sequences introduced in Section 2-2, it may be desirable to slip into the context a number that indicates whether the next base pair is the first, second, or third pair in a triplet. Figure 6-7 shows such a sequence and the fabricated contexts. Neither forward trees nor the many other methods discussed in this

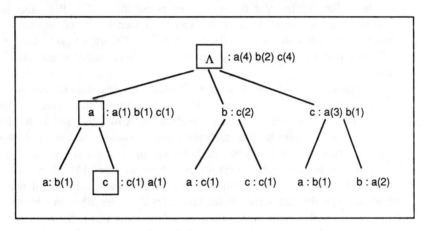

Figure 6-6   Structure of a backward tree for the message "cacbcaabca."

DNA sequence	C	G	A	T	A	A
position information		1	2	3	1	2	3

contexts generated		3 A G C	1 T A G	2 A T A	3 A A T

Figure 6-7   Inclusion of position information in a DNA sequence.

book can deal easily with this situation, for they assume that the input is a totally ordered sequence of characters. However, backward trees match context against models anew for each prediction, so any desired information can be added to the context. The end of Chapter 10 contains a brief discussion of another compression problem, picture compression, which breaks out of the strictly sequential mode. Vine pointers can be reintroduced if the backward tree structure is used with purely sequential input, although they are of no value for nonsequential contexts.

6.5.2 Computing Probabilities

Once the context(s) have been located, the final probability must be determined and presented to the arithmetic encoder. With full blending the raw frequencies of each model must be calculated and blended together. When exclusions are used, the character is predicted in just one context. The arithmetic encoder needs not only the probability of the next character but also the sum of the probabilities of all those that precede it. Precedence assumes some ordering that can be chosen in any convenient way, although it must be consistent in both encoder and decoder. The use of exclusions creates the complication that a list of excluded characters must be consulted when calculating probabilities.

The following three subsections consider the best data structures to use for nodes under three different conditions. The first performs fully correct blending without exclusions; the second implements exclusions; while the third is for lazy exclusions. The descriptions assume that each node takes a small fixed amount of space and that forward trees are used. There are faster techniques that require a large array at each node or which use variable-sized nodes. These are unwieldy when new nodes are being created frequently, but appropriate for large alphabets and a small maximum context. For example, the data structure for large alphabets described in Section 5-3 is ideal for the WORD algorithm. The data structures described below are appropriate for medium-sized alphabets, such as the ASCII character set. Table 6-5 shows the fields in these data structures. The first three fields have already been described: the *down pointer* records the first descendant of the node, *symbol* is the character that labels the node, and *count* is the number of times the trace associated with the node has occurred.

Full blending.   First we consider the least tractable approach, which blends probabilities with a weighted sum as described in the first section of this chapter. All contexts must be scanned before the next character's probability can be calculated. A simple ordered binary tree can be used to organize nodes. It is only necessary to find the sum of the raw probabilities of all characters that precede the next character in each of the contexts, as well as the probability of the character itself. This can be accomplished by storing at each node the total count of nodes in the left (or right) subtree of siblings. The required sum can then be accumulated while scanning down the tree to the sought character.

Provided that trees are balanced, the time for scanning, accumulating sums, and updating counters will all be logarithmic in the number of sibling nodes. The simplest

TABLE 6-5 SUMMARY OF FIELDS USED IN NODE DATA STRUCTURES

Present In All Structures

down pointer	Pointer to node of next higher order (null at leaf).
symbol	Symbol labeling this node.
count	Number of times this node has occurred.

Optional Items Depending On Implementation Techniques

vine pointer	Pointer to context of next lower order (see text for full description). Necessary only to speed execution.
child counter	Sum of counters on all nodes descended from this. Necessary if counts are being scaled or if update exclusions are used.

Used to Access Sibling Nodes Descended From Common Parent

Linked list

next pointer	Next sibling node.
previous pointer	Needed to make a doubly linked list if all contexts have counters incremented, vine pointers are used, and the move-to-front heuristic is used.

Binary tree

left pointer	Points to left subtree of siblings.
right pointer	Points to right subtree of siblings.
left count	Sum of counts on all nodes in left subtree.
elder sibling pointer	Points to the sibling node with a left pointer to this node (this would be called a parent pointer except that that hopelessly tangles the genealogy). Improves performance if vine nodes are being used to locate lower-order contexts, so all counts can be updated.

way to build a tree is to allocate nodes in the order that characters are inserted, but then it may become unbalanced. However, in real text it is unlikely that the ordering will be so perverse as to cause a severe imbalance, especially since most trees will be fairly small. In fact, experiments using sophisticated balancing algorithms such as splay trees indicate that the time gained through better balance is outweighed by the extra overhead incurred to perform the balancing.

Difficulties arise when vine pointers are used to locate nodes whose counts are to be incremented in lower-order contexts, for the *left counts* on all nodes that point to the incremented one must be updated. To do so requires an additional pointer back from any node that has a left subtree pointer aimed at it, namely the *elder sibling pointer*. Then the necessary adjustments can be made in logarithmic time.

With exclusion. Full blending is computationally very expensive. Exclusion is far more practical because it avoids scanning lower-order contexts by stopping immediately as soon as the next character is predicted with a nonzero probability. The search starts at the longest matching context and moves to lower-order contexts (following vine pointers if they are available) until the next character is predicted. This will be much more efficient than searching all contexts of orders -1 to m, for often—particularly when predictions are accurate—the next character will be found in the longest one or two contexts. During the scan all characters seen so far are recorded in an array with one flag for each character so that they can be excluded if they recur. For reasonable alphabets (such as ASCII characters, or bytes) this involves negligible overhead. However, resetting the entire array of flags can be expensive, and rather than resetting them all it may be faster to rescan the list of characters to find which ones to reset.

For exclusions, the natural data structure is a linked list of sibling nodes. A node's *down pointer* leads to its first descendant, while *next pointers* link the chain of sibling nodes. During the scan, the probability of all characters less than the target character can be accumulated. The counter on the parent node (minus 1) gives the total for the context. Recall that the notion of "less than" is arbitrary (provided that encoder and decoder agree). By defining the ordering to put all predicted characters whose longest match is order o before those whose longest match is order $o-1$, all excluded counts will have been accumulated (to subtract from the total) by the time the next character is found. At worst this scanning could take $q(m+1)$ steps, but as noted above, this will rarely be the case and most searches will terminate very quickly.

An excellent heuristic that helps the scanning process is to move the node with the highest count to the front of the list. Characters that occur often will then be located sooner, reducing the average time spent scanning. A complication arises when vine pointers are used to locate contexts. In order that characters in lower contexts can be moved to the front, siblings need to be connected in a doubly linked list with an additional *previous pointer* at each node. The "move-to-front" heuristic will be even more helpful when update exclusions are used, for in lower-order contexts the characters that are predicted often, but tend not to occur in higher contexts, will migrate to the front of the list.

The cost of scanning through sibling nodes can be significant if vine pointers are not used. In this case it is necessary to search through each context of order 0 to $m-1$ to find the contexts for the next round of predictions. The low-order models typically predict many, if not all, of the characters in the alphabet, so scans become lengthy. The problem can be alleviated by storing sibling nodes in a more complex data structure such as a binary tree. When small alphabets are used, this takes more space, is significantly more complex, and is almost certain to be slower than using vine pointers. However, in schemes such as WORD, where the effective alphabet size may be many thousands, and lazy exclusions are used, a binary tree works well. When using exclusions it is still necessary to scan all nodes that precede the next character. So the only operation that is accelerated by a binary tree is the indexing of lower-order contexts not used in predicting the next character but which must be located so that their counts can be updated. If vine pointers or update exclusions are used even this advantage vanishes, and a list is the only suitable data structure.

Lazy exclusions.   The very fast PPMC′ algorithm employs a third way of dealing with exclusions. The probability $(1-e_l)p_l(\phi)$, where l is the length of the longest matching context that predicts ϕ, is taken as the final blended probability. This means that contexts need only be scanned until the first prediction is found. The complete scan required by a full blending calculation is unnecessary and no account need be taken of exclusions, so that maximum advantage is gained from the self-organizing nature of the lists. Either a linear list or an ordered binary tree as described for the previous two alternatives is appropriate. For large alphabets, the binary tree is significantly faster.

The drawback of this approach is that it wastes code space because the probabilities sum to less than 1. This stems from the fact that whereas the final blended probability should contain contributions from the weighted probabilities at each level, only one of them is used. Arithmetic coding still behaves correctly, but the encoding is longer than necessary. Experiments indicate that the degradation in compression is usually between 5 and 10%. The only file in the corpus of Appendix B which exceeds this range is "geo," at 13%.

6.5.3 Space

The space needed for the different techniques varies considerably. The smallest possible implementation uses a simple linked list and no vine pointers, and requires at each node two pointers, one counter, and a symbol. A straightforward implementation of this would consume 13 bytes, and these could be packed into perhaps 10 bytes. The largest node described requires five pointers, three counters, and one symbol, for a total of between 25 bytes (packed) and 33 bytes.

6.5.4 Small Alphabets

If the alphabet is very small, say two or three symbols, a different representation of nodes, where all descendants are packed in a single record structure, becomes attractive. This eliminates the need for pointers between siblings but does waste space if many nodes are left empty. Note that splitting an alphabet of 8-bit characters into eight 1-bit characters will not necessarily decrease storage, as the number of nodes could increase eightfold. However, in cases where most symbols are predicted at least once in each context, the trade-off could be attractive.

For example, for a 1-bit alphabet, a node and its descendants can be represented with one vine pointer plus two down pointers and two counters. If all nodes are full, this averages $20/2 = 10$ bytes per node compared with 33 bytes for a correspondingly quick implementation using sibling pointers. If at worst half the nodes are empty, the original 33 bytes for 8-bit characters would require $8 \times 21 = 168$ bytes to represent. Clearly, this scheme could prove superior in some cases, but would perform badly whenever characters become very predictable. It might be appropriate in the case of data such as object files or floating-point numbers.

NOTES

General references to the kinds of data structures used for realizing trees and tries are Aho et al. (1983) and Knuth (1973). The earliest reference to combining models of different orders for the purpose of prediction is Cleary (1980). Their first use for compression was by Rissanen and Langdon (1981) and Roberts (1982). DAFC was described by Langdon and Rissanen (1983) and is patented (U.S. patent 4,494,108). The PPMA and PPMB encoders were described by Cleary and Witten (1984b). A series of improvements and careful implementations, culminating in the PPMC and PPMC' algorithms, are given by Moffat (1988b). The WORD algorithm is described in Moffat (1987). Other methods of prediction based on varying contexts are proposed by Rissanen (1983) and Williams (1988). A prediction technique using hash tables rather than tries is given in Raita and Teuhola (1987). An extensive series of experiments about scaling counters and the resulting improvements in compression has been reported by Darragh et al. (1983).

45h[0j45thwGw45hqU9d
poejrg[4wky]p435q)b&
[0wejg[04jy42yj3*k!d
p0w4j5g[235-k6t0=w~n
[0ewjg04jy04jy4j;qmy
pmh][krty-jk46-[p"qb
p[jw435y   n[ps0%x
[psdhkj0-8w   u5y9mwq
germhj-53k   kj64k?ti
[ewjhj4wth 5430o#r0b
e[wmb[pre 5,.u;g4{@
65[];.9[.8[]0.o~x6
germhj-53k=ukj64:3xf
[ewjhj4wth56430o*wm<
e[wmb[preh65,.u;aYld
+[3fgm56rt0-"-23jsg!
[;jyt%ERghj(0;';Hd4=
lU5terEDghp=][>?kyeW

STATE-BASED MODELING

7

Context-based models such as those studied in Chapter 6 are resource-hungry. For one thing, they grow very large very quickly. For another, they can be quite slow unless close attention is paid to the details of the data structure in which they are stored and the algorithms that access and update it. Naturally, there is a trade-off between speed and amount of memory used, which further complicates the design and implementation of a satisfactory system.

From a practical point of view, it is worth contemplating ways of reducing the storage space needed for a given amount of compression. A few years ago this would have been of paramount importance, for the volume of memory consumed in coding a tract of text using context-based modeling is often several times bigger than the size of the text itself. (It is obvious that no method need ever consume more storage than would be occupied by the input text, for all necessary information can be derived on demand directly from the input. However, continually rescanning the input would make for exceedingly slow coding.) In these days of Mbit chips, storage is not necessarily an overriding problem. Nevertheless, it is a consideration.

Slow execution is another drawback to the partial-match context method, particularly with a simple implementation. As we have seen in Chapter 6, this problem can be attacked by using more sophisticated data structures, setting up extra links in the trie to obviate the need to re-traverse it from top to bottom for each character read. Of course, these links consume additional storage space—once again we are faced with the classic time-space trade-off.

Another approach is to use a different level of abstraction for the models. Instead of thinking of nodes and pointers, we can work instead with states and transitions between them. In the actual implementation, of course, a state model will have to be represented in terms of nodes and pointers. Moreover, there will be many alternatives and trade-offs to be evaluated when designing such a representation, just as there are for context-based models. But it is profitable to forget all that for the moment and remain at the higher level of abstraction offered by a finite-state model.

Finite-state models were introduced in Section 2-2, and examples appear in Figures 2-1 and 2-2. Recall that several transitions lead from each state, one for each letter of the alphabet. Each transition is labeled with a letter, and a count is recorded that shows how often the transition has been traversed. Probabilistic predictions can be calculated for each state, based on these counts. When a new letter is processed, the state changes accordingly, and so does the probability distribution. Thus states play the role of conditioning the distribution, just as contexts do in finite-context models.

In principle, state-based implementations are speedy. To process each new symbol necessitates traversing a single link. Moreover, the number of states in a model is a natural measure of its space complexity, and the measure is independent of implementation details. This provides a higher level of abstraction, which allows one to examine the trade-off between the size of a model and its compression performance without getting bogged down in alternative data structures. Thus state models seem to be a good way to talk about the economics of coding.

Implementation efficiency is not the only reason for considering state-based models. In principle they are able to capture structures that a finite-context model cannot. Such structures generally involve counting. For example, we saw in Figure 2-2 how a state model could be used to capture the triplet structure of a DNA sequence by counting in modulo 3. Thus state models are attractive because they are more powerful than the finite-context models considered so far.

Unfortunately, state modeling turns out to be much less useful than one might expect. In this chapter we present some results on state-based modeling techniques, each of which is a little disappointing in its own way. First, we look at *optimal* state modeling. Suppose that we are given a particular piece of text and that resource considerations restrict the model to a certain number of states. Then of all possible models with that number of states, there must be one that gives the best compression performance when the text is coded with respect to the model. The catch?—not only must the model be precalculated for that particular piece of text and somehow transmitted to the decoder, but more important, it is computationally infeasible to produce anything but the smallest, most approximate models. Although in some situations these can provide interesting insights into the structure of the text, they are unsuitable for practical coding. There may be alternative ways to find approximations to the optimal model, but no really good methods have surfaced yet. Because the results are essentially negative, the practically oriented reader may wish to skim or skip Sections 7-1 and 7-2. Although they enrich our understanding of the prediction problem, they do not lead to feasible compression techniques.

An important method of adaptive data compression is described in Section 7-3, which constructs a state model incrementally. It uses a heuristic criterion to decide when to create a new state by "cloning" an existing one. The model grows through continued cloning, adapting to fit the characteristics of the sequence that is being modeled. In conjunction with arithmetic coding it produces excellent compression results, comparable with those from the partial match technique described in Chapter 6. However, on closer analysis it turns out to be equivalent to a context-based predictive modeler. This is disappointing since, as mentioned in Chapter 2 and illustrated more amply in Section 7-1, finite-state models are potentially more powerful than context ones. But in this case—contrary to first appearances—the potential is not realized. Despite this, the method is an eminently practical one for text compression and is among the top performers in terms of compression ability.

The upshot is that prediction techniques which exploit the full power of finite-state models seem to be completely impractical for data compression. However, the state-model formalism can provide an attractive implementation base for finite-context modeling methods. It may be that in practice the difficulty in tapping the full potential of finite-state models is unimportant, because the performance of any such model can be approximated by a finite-context one with a large enough context.

7.1 OPTIMAL STATE MODELS

Imagine generating models one by one and evaluating how well each performs when predicting a given text sequence. This is a tedious procedure, but a powerful one. It obviously guarantees, for any given number of states, to get the best model of that size for the particular sequence in question. "Best" is measured in terms of predictive ability—how well does the model predict each character in the sequence? This in turn is measured by entropy, the entropy of the sequence with respect to the model. Note that the modeling method is nonincremental in that it requires advance knowledge of the entire text. Furthermore, it is not clear how best to transmit the model, since the adaptive transmission method used in earlier chapters works only on an incremental basis. However, let us ignore these problems, for things are difficult enough without worrying about how to create and transmit models on the fly.

There is a trade-off between *model complexity* and *goodness of fit*. We define complexity as the number of states in the model, and goodness of fit as the entropy of the text sequence with respect to the model (the lower the entropy, the better the fit). Alternative measures could be used instead. For example, complexity might be characterized by the number of transitions, or the product of states and transitions. Goodness of fit might be measured in terms of a least-squares fit rather than a logarithmic entropy-based one. Modeling is a kind of induction, and like all induction problems is heavily underconstrained. It is necessary to make choices in advance about how to measure complexity and goodness of fit which cannot possibly be justified within the theory.

Because the process of enumeration and evaluation is so computation-intensive, we can consider only small, artificial examples. Figure 7-1a shows such an example, which is a sequence of 101 letters. A *model* of the sequence is a state-transition network that allows the sequence to be traced through it, starting at a designated start state. Each transition is labeled with a letter, which must match the letter in the sequence at the point where the transition is traversed. For example, Figure 7-1b shows four models. In each one, the starting state is marked with an arrow. Each model can be evaluated by calculating the entropy of the sequence of letters with respect to it. To accomplish this, we need to associate probabilities with transitions. It turns out that the

a d b a d a c b d c b a c b d b a c b a c d c d a c b a d a c b d b a
c b a c b a c d b a d a c b a c b a c b a d a c b a c b a c b a d c d
b a c b a d b a c d b d c b a c d a c b a c b a c b a c d d a

(a)

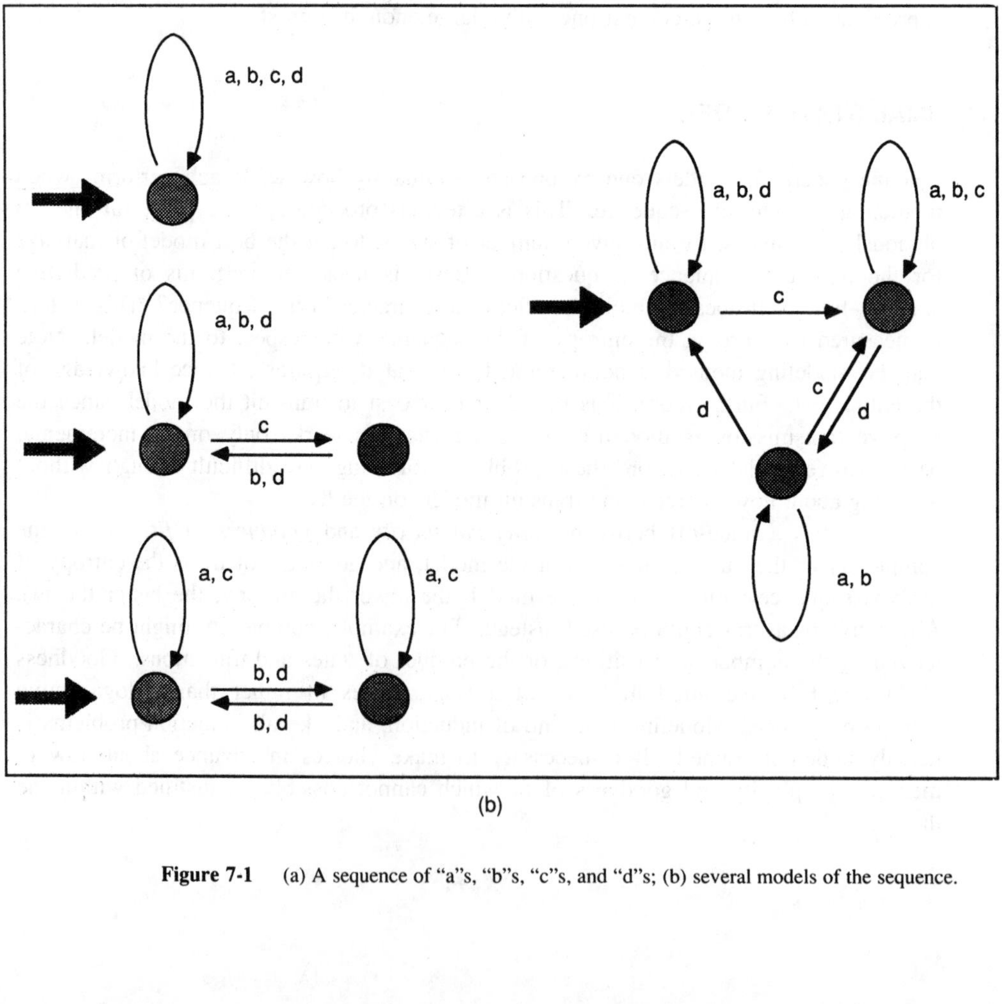

(b)

Figure 7-1   (a) A sequence of "a"s, "b"s, "c"s, and "d"s; (b) several models of the sequence.

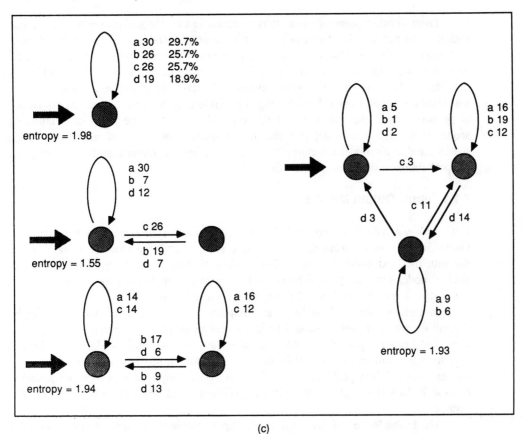

Figure 7-1(cont)   (c) Models augmented by transition counts and entropies.

best way to estimate probabilities—the way that minimizes the entropy—is to pass the sequence through the model, counting how often each transition is used, and to calculate probabilities according to these frequency counts. Part (c) of the figure shows the same models annotated with transition counts and, for the first model, probabilities. It also gives the entropy of the sequence with respect to each model.

To find the best model with a given number of states, all models of that size are generated and evaluated. We will discuss the result of this process on our example sequence, and the trade-off between complexity and goodness of fit, shortly. Here, let us contemplate what an arduous undertaking it is! The number of possible models with n states, for an alphabet of q symbols, is n^{nq}, so the search grows superexponentially with model size. Actually, many of these models can be ruled out of court without being evaluated, because some smaller model exists with identical behavior. This occurs when some states can never be reached from the start state and are therefore entirely redundant. So n^{nq} is a pessimistic figure for the number of models that have to be evaluated. Nonetheless, the superexponential growth with increasing n remains.

From another point of view, it is remarkable that the search for the best model with a given number of states can be carried out at all. The models are *probabilistic* in that probabilities are associated with each transition. Since these are real numbers, when they are taken into account, the space of possible models is continuous rather than discrete. It therefore does not permit exhaustive search at all—there are just too many real numbers to try them all! Searching is possible only because an optimal assignment of probabilities to the transitions of this type of model may be made by running the sequence through the model and making frequency counts. It is necessary only to search through all model structures, which are enumerable, rather than through all possible probability assignments, which are not.

7.1.1 Input–Output Models

Until now we have been considering only *input* models, in which each transition is labeled, and an input string defines a unique path through the model. At each step in the path the next symbol in the string is used to determine which transition to take. Such a model can equally well be viewed as an *output* model. At each step we choose a transition at random and output the symbol corresponding to it.

In contrast, this section looks at *input–output* models, where the input symbol determines which transition should be taken *and* an output corresponding to the transition. Unlike the input models considered earlier, input–output models are relatively easy to infer from examples of their behavior. Although this is not directly relevant to the text compression problem, we will present an example of input–output modeling because it does shed light on the difficult problem faced when this situation cannot be assumed.

The example we will use to illustrate input–output modeling is a simple insertion sort algorithm. The object is to automatically generate a machine that will sort any list, given the sequence of behavior required to sort a few example lists. The inputs will be symbols in the list, and the outputs are actions to perform on the list. Figure 7-2 illustrates the action of a simple machine when sorting the list "baa" into alphabetical order, "aab". In each cycle of operation the machine looks at a single symbol in the list and takes an appropriate action. Each action replaces the symbol in that position of the list, and moves to the neighboring one, either right or left. Thus an action might be "bR", which replaces the current symbol with "b" and moves to the right. A record of the operations performed during the sort of Figure 7-2 is

b bR a bL b bL # –R b aR b bR a bL b bL a aR b aR b bR
       5   10   15   20

Single "a"s and "b"s represent the symbol in the current position of the list. Two-letter symbols represent actions. The "#" input signifies that the end of the list has been reached; nothing can be written in that position, so a null writing action "–" is specified.

Given that the model should be input–output, with "a"s, "b"s, and "#"s as inputs and the two-letter symbols as outputs, a data-driven, simplest-first search with recursive backtracking finds it very quickly. Figure 7-3 shows the sequence of models that lead to the solution. Input symbols are associated with transitions and actions are associated

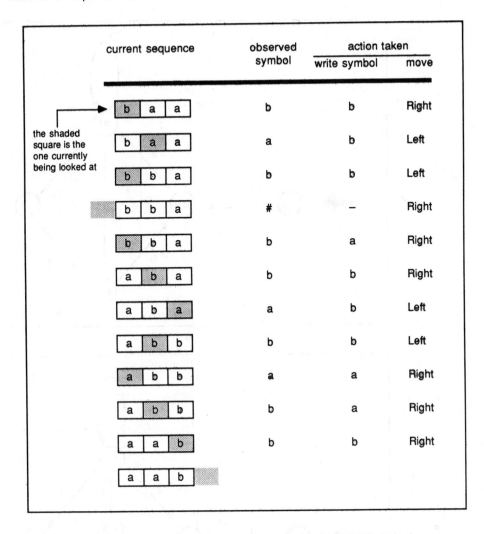

current sequence	observed symbol	action taken write symbol	move
b a a	b	b	Right
b a a	a	b	Left
b b a	b	b	Left
b b a	#	–	Right
b b a	b	a	Right
a b a	b	b	Right
a b a	a	b	Left
a b b	b	b	Left
a b b	a	a	Right
a b b	b	a	Right
a a b	b	b	Right
a a b			

the shaded square is the one currently being looked at

Figure 7-2   Operations required when sorting the list "baa" into alphabetical order.

with states. Model (a) is constructed by following the sequence, filling in symbols on the transitions, and creating new states whenever a new composite action is encountered. At position 6 in the sequence we had a choice between creating a new state with the action "bL" or reusing the existing "bL" state. The latter action was chosen because it generated a simpler model, but the decision must be noted so that we can backtrack to that point should the simplest decision lead to a stalemate later. Similar choices must be made on symbols 12 and 18. By symbol 20 the model is as shown in Figure 7-3a, and here we discover that it is inadequate, for the model, seeing a "b" transition from state aR, predicts bR next, while the sequence shows aR at that point. Backtracking to symbol 18 and making a new state for the aR leads to model (b). When we get to the "b" transition (symbol 20) we must choose which of the two aR states to send it to.

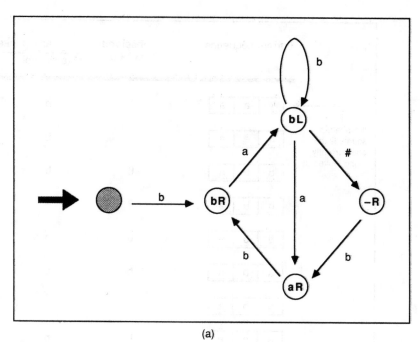

(a)

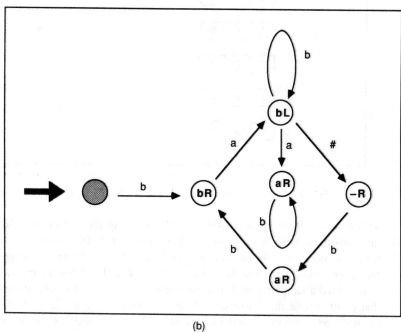

(b)

Figure 7-3   Input–output models for a particular sorting sequence: (a) fails on symbol 20; (b) fails on symbol 22.

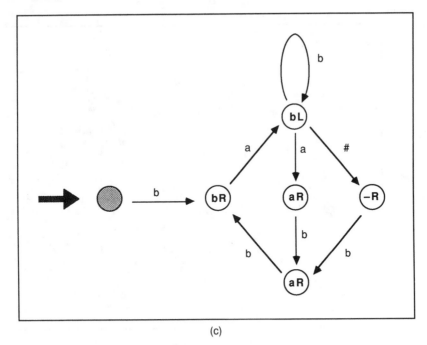

(c)

Figure 7-3(cont)   Input–output models for a particular sorting sequence: (c) correct model for the sequence.

The figure shows an unlucky choice, which is found inadequate on symbol 22. Backing up to symbol 20 and making the alternative choice leads to the correct model (c).

The reason for creating this kind of model is to produce a program that will sort a general string of "a"s and "b"s from examples of execution of the program with specific strings. Figure 7-3c is not yet such a model. However, with the addition of one more transition, shown in Figure 7-4, it will serve to sort a general string of "a"s and "b"s, provided that the string starts with "b". That transition would be created by the method just described if a trace were presented that sorted a string containing more than one "b" (e.g., "bbaa"). To create a model that sorts strings even if they start with "a", the trace for a string like "aabbaa" would have to be presented.

The model of Figure 7-4 works as follows. Suppose that any string is presented which begins with "b". Then state 1 scans right, skipping over consecutive "b"s until the first "a" is found. That "a" is overwritten by "b", and state 2 scans left, back over the run of "b"s, until either "a" (state 3) or the end of the string (state 4) is encountered. Moving right to the first of the string of "b"s, state 5 replaces it with "a". Now the number of "a"s and "b"s is the same as it was before starting, but the first "b" has been moved rightward. Repeating this operation will sort the string.

Only a very small number of alternative models had to be evaluated to create this one. This is because each output is assumed to be determined unambiguously by the previous state and input. Many differently labeled transitions may emanate from a single state, reflecting the fact that elements of the input sequence are inherently unpredictable. However, any given transition leads to a definite state. It is because sequence

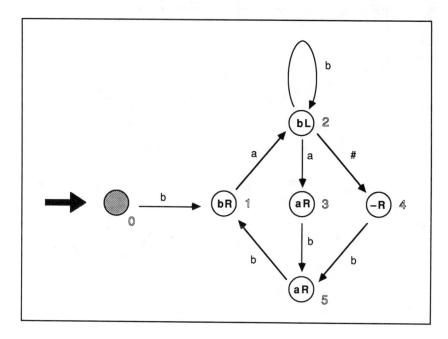

Figure 7-4   Input–output model which correctly sorts strings of "a"s and "b"s.

elements can be stratified into inputs and outputs, and because the models are assumed to be input–output, that the search can be so economical.[1]

7.1.2 General Models

Consider what would happen if the same sequence were modeled without the assumption that the inputs and outputs are distinguished in the example. Figure 7-5 shows the single one-state model (a) and a couple of the 1379 two-state ones (b), as well as the two-state one that has the best entropy evaluation (c). Despite the fact that a vastly larger search space has been explored, much less structure has been discovered than in the input–output models of Figure 7-3. Note, however, that the best two-state model correctly distinguishes inputs from outputs—even though it was not given this information to begin with.

Now let us return to the example of Figure 7-1. Input–output modeling would be fruitless on this sequence. The "a"s, "b"s, "c"s, and "d"s it contains cannot be divided into inputs and outputs. To regard them all as inputs would be senseless, for the input–output modeling procedure does not attempt to predict inputs and would contentedly generate the trivial 1-state structure, all of whose transitions lead back to

[1]While the search is economical compared with that undertaken by the more general methods considered next, it is certainly not economical in absolute terms. It can be shown that the problem of finding input–output models is NP-complete in terms of the number of states required, although it is polynomial time in terms of the size of the input–output sequence.

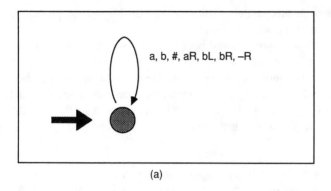

(a)

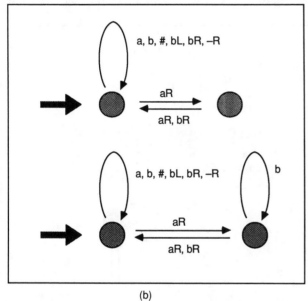

(b)

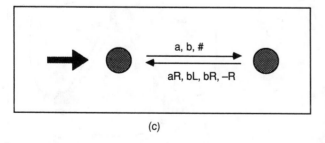

(c)

Figure 7-5   General models for a sorting sequence: (a) the one-state model; (b) two two-state models; (c) the optimal two-state model.

the same state. Suppose, therefore, that they were all regarded as outputs. The input–output modeling procedure insists that the model predicts each output correctly, as a function of the previous state and input. Since inputs are null, the model must reproduce the sequence exactly. This requires a model with 101 states, one for each letter of the sequence. Although this model is entirely accurate, it has no predictive power at all—it is just a record of the sequence itself!

Exhaustive searching, despite—or rather, because of—its enormous computational demands, does succeed in finding some structure in the sequence. Figure 7-1 shows a number of representative models. In contrast, Figure 7-6a shows the *best* models with one, two, three, and four states. For example, the four-state optimal model clearly identifies the cycle-of-3 pattern which is evident when you read through the original sequence. In fact, the sequence was generated by taking the cycle

c b a c b a c b a . . .

and sampling it in short segments of arbitrary length, with the symbol "d" inserted at segment boundaries. The delimiting role of "d" can be seen in the four-state model, for

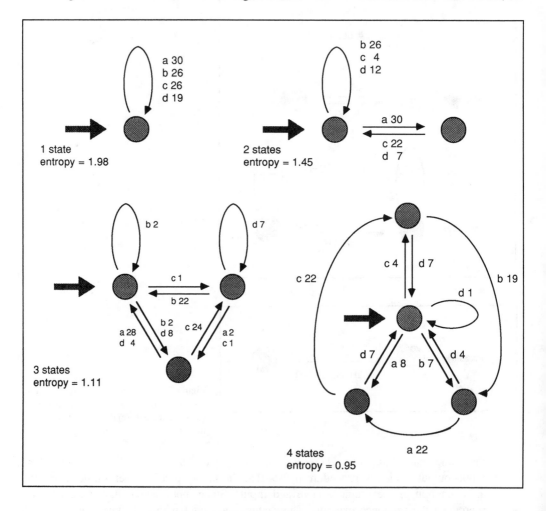

Figure 7-6   (a) Optimal models for the sequence of Figure 7-1.

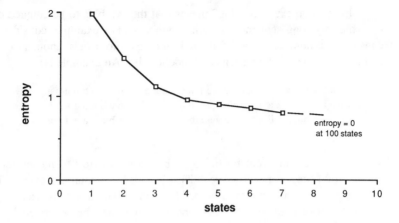

Figure 7-6(cont)   (b) How entropy of the optimal model decreases with its size.

after that symbol the center state is always reached. This is the only one that gives immediate access to all other states. Notice that the fact that "d" is a delimiter is inferred but not imposed. In general, this type of modeling is capable of inferring inputs from their regularity and delimiters from the unpredictability of what follows them.

It is often interesting to plot the performance of the optimal models against the number of states they contain. Figure 7-6b shows how the entropy decreases steadily, and hence performance increases, as model complexity increases. Eventually, at 100 states, the model will record the sequence exactly and deterministically, and the entropy evaluation will be zero. The fact that there are no abrupt breaks indicates a steady improvement in performance. For this sequence, there is no particular point at which radically new structure is discovered.

7.1.3 State versus Context Models

Context models effectively split an input sequence into overlapping substrings of length k, where $k - 1$ is the context length. The first $k - 1$ characters of each substring predict its last character. The partial-match strategy does not change the picture radically; it just provides a way of supplying predictions in situations where the full context has not yet been seen.

The *sequence* of k-tuples that occur in a particular string fully characterizes that string. However, context models discard the sequential information and store just the *set* of k-tuples encountered. This means that certain kinds of finite-state structure cannot be modeled.

In order to consider the power of the modeling method independently of the particular input sequence that occurs, it is necessary to characterize the set of potential input sequences. In the terminology of automata theory, such a set is called an *event*. A *k-testable event* is one that is completely determined by the k-tuples contained in the sequences. It can be shown that some events are not k-testable. Such events are those in which "counting" occurs.

In this context, "counting" means that the symbols to be counted can be separated by arbitrarily long sequences of other symbols. For example, consider a sequence that consists of a number of "a"s followed by a "b", more "a"s, another "b", yet more "a"s, and a "c"; the whole being repeated indefinitely. An example is

```
a a a b a b a a a a c a a b a a a b a a c a a a a a b a a a a b a c a
a b a a a b a a a a c a a a b a a a a b a a c a b a a a a a a a a b a
a c a a a b a a a b a a a a c a a a b a b a c a a a a b a a a a a b a
a a c.
```

We denote such an event by (a* b a* b a* c)*, where "*" means repeat an arbitrary number of times, zero or more. This is indeed a counting event. To discover the repeating "bbc" pattern that is embedded within the "a"s, it is necessary to count "b"s up to 2 before predicting a "c"—and the "b"s may be separated by arbitrarily long strings of "a"s. In contrast, the event (a b a a b a a a c)*, of which an example is

```
a b a a b a a a c a b a a b a a a c a b a a b a a a c a b a a b a a a
c a b a a b a a a c a b a a b a a a c a b a a b a a a c a b a a b a a
a c a b a a b a a a c a b a a b a a a c a b a a b a a a c a b a a b a
a a c
```

is *not* a counting event, for no matter whether we are counting "a"s, "b"s, or "c"s, the separating strings have a fixed length.

Counting events can be characterized by finite-state models but not by finite-context ones. First, look at the models of the second sequence above, the *noncounting* one, which are shown in Figure 7-7. The finite-state model in the first part of the figure characterizes the sequence exactly, as do the order-5 predictions in the second part. Now consider the other, counting, event. The model in the first part of Figure 7-8 captures its structure exactly, although of course it does not predict the sequence deterministically—no model could. But consider the context-based predictions in the second part. The list is incomplete because arbitrarily long contexts are needed to capture the structure of the input—the left-hand side of the predictions must contain an example for every number of "a"s that can occur in between "b"s and "c"s. A context-based model will never fully account for the input because the list of predictions can be carried on indefinitely with the left-hand side getting longer and longer, and still continue to improve.

Here is another example of the impotence of context-based models to deal with sequences that require counting. It is taken from a delightful anecdote by John Andreae about a gaming club owner who suspected a penny-tossing machine of being rigged. Figure 7-9a shows a sample of the observed behavior for 100 tosses. Can you spot the pattern? Study the sequence for a few minutes before reading on.

Figure 7-9b shows the best models with one, two, three, four, and five states. Even the two-state model demonstrates some regularity in the sequence, because transitions occur from each state to itself much more frequently than to the other state. It is rather hard to see at first whether the three-state, four-state, and five-state models incorporate significant additional structure.

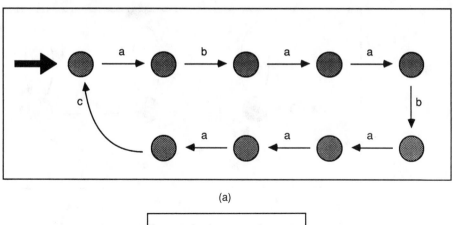

(a)

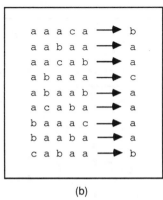

(b)

Figure 7-7   Models of a noncounting event: (a) state model; (b) context model.

However, the graph of entropy against number of states in part (c) of the figure tells us where to look. There is a significant decrease in entropy going from the three-state to the four-state model. And indeed, when we look at that model, we see that it has two deterministic transitions (out of the top and bottom states). This shows that some symbols in the sequence are completely predictable. Indeed, it can be deduced from this model that every third symbol—number 2, 5, 8, 11, ...—is completely predictable. It is just a repetition of the previous symbol.

Context-based modeling is not capable of discovering this regularity, at least, not in its entirety. Figure 7-10a shows context models with increasing context length, along with their entropy evaluation; while Figure 7-10b plots the entropy of these and larger context models against the number of contexts they contain, the order-1 model having two contexts, the order-2 one four, the order-3 one eight, and so on. While the entropy steadily decreases as the context grows, there is no point at which the models capture the structure in the sequence exactly. By the time the order-3 model is reached, Figure 7-10a shows that there are some unique predictions (from context "hth", which predicts "h", and context "tht", which predicts "t"). However, we know that every third symbol is uniquely predictable, and this model accounts for only 8 out of a possible 33

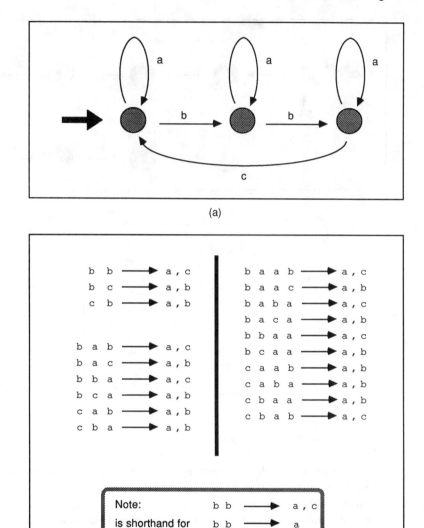

(a)

(b)

Figure 7-8   Models of a counting event: (a) state model; (b) incomplete context model.

predictable ones. As the length is increased, the number of uniquely predictable symbols will gradually grow as more of the infinity of possible contexts can be taken into account. But at no stage will the models reflect the actual structure of the sequence, for it is a "counting" event, requiring the ability to count up to three to flag every third

```
h h t h h t h h h t t h h h h t t h t t t h h h h h t h h h t t t h
h h t t t h h h h h h t t h t t t t t h t t h t t t h h h t t h h h
t h h h h h h h h h t t h h h t t t t h h h h h t t t t t t t h
```

(a)

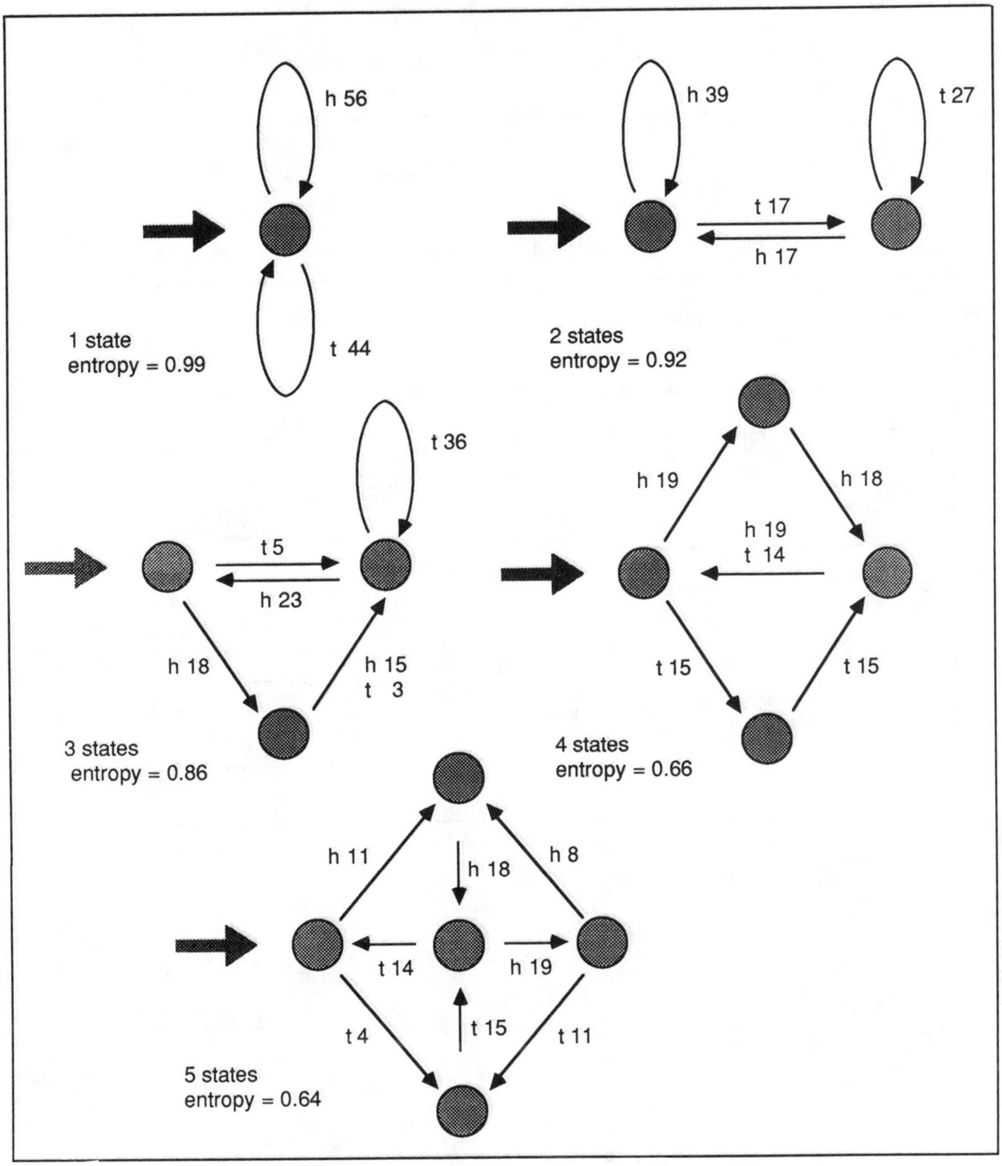

h 56
t 44
1 state
entropy = 0.99
h 39
t 27
t 17
h 17
2 states
entropy = 0.92
t 36
t 5
h 23
h 18
h 15
t 3
3 states
entropy = 0.86
h 19
h 18
h 19
t 14
t 15
t 15
4 states
entropy = 0.66
h 11
h 18
h 8
t 14
h 19
t 4
t 15
t 11
5 states
entropy = 0.64

(b)

Figure 7-9 (a) A coin-tossing sequence; (b) Optimal models for the sequence.

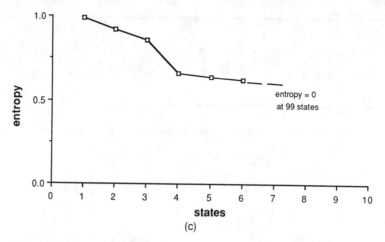

(c)

Figure 7-9(cont)   (c) How the entropy of optimal models decreases with their size.

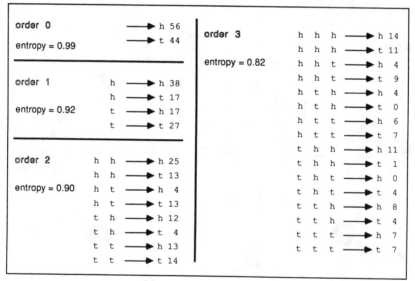

(a)

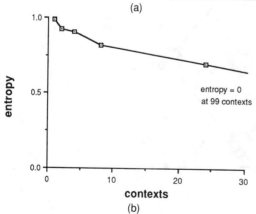

(b)

Figure 7-10   (a) Context models for the coin-tossing sequence; (b) how the entropy of context models decreases with their size.

184

symbol even if the sequence is actually a long string of consecutive "h"s or "t"s. The context models simply become gradually better approximations.

The enumeration methodology is a very powerful way of finding structure in sequences. Perhaps you feel in hindsight that the pattern in the heads and tails sequence is "obvious"—although it is unlikely that you spotted it before reading the preceding paragraphs. Just imagine, though, if every third symbol had a strong bias but was not completely predictable. For example, instead of being a repetition of the preceding one, it might be a repetition 90% of the time and a completely random toss the remaining 10%. The enumeration method would discover this regularity just as easily, but a person would be very unlikely to discover it at all no matter how hard they tried. And when we reverse the probabilities from 90% and 10% to 10% and 90%, so that every third symbol had just a slight chance of being a repetition, enumeration would find that just as easily too (provided that the sequence was long enough to allow the bias to be detectable).

7.2 APPROXIMATE STATE MODELS

Finding optimal state models for sequences is very difficult. Are there efficient ways of obtaining good approximations to such models? Unfortunately, the only really practical approximate construction techniques sacrifice the cardinal advantage of finite-state models—namely, that they can characterize counting events.

7.2.1 Limited-Context State Modeling

If one is prepared to forgo the ability to model counting events, compact state models can easily be created from the set of k-tuples that occur in the string being modeled. This set, which contains all the information used by a partial-match modeling method, can be massaged into the form of a finite-state model as follows. The method is most transparent if we use a slightly different way of expressing the model. Although previous models were written with symbols on the *transitions*, in this case symbols will be associated with *states*.[2] This is not an important difference. Each type of model can be translated into an equivalent one in the other formulation. It does affect the number of states needed, though. The result will be expressed as an output model, although of course it can be used as an input model.

First, create a state for each k-tuple and give it transitions that reflect the succession of tuples in the behavior sequence. Only the last element of a tuple is recorded as the output of its state. This model, which is very large (having one state for each k-tuple), is then subjected to a reduction process which coalesces states in a way that does not destroy information about the k-tuples that occurred in the behavior.

The reduction process is quite straightforward. For each pair of states with the same output, see if the transitions out of them are the same. If so, these two states can

[2]This type of model is called a *Moore* machine. The models we have used elsewhere are *Mealy* machines.

be coalesced without losing information about the original k-tuples. The process continues until no more pairs of states can be merged. The models formed in this way have the property that any sequence of k symbols from the alphabet determines just one state of the model (or no states, if that sequence has not appeared in the input string).

Figure 7-11 shows models created by this process before and after reduction. Model (a) was obtained from the succession of 2-tuples in the coin-tossing data. Since this contains information about which 2-tuples follow which, it is effectively constructed from the 3-tuples in the sequence, which constitute the order-2 model of Figure 7-10. However, the reduction process manages to collapse the eight predictions of this model down to just two states. This is because all eight possible combinations occur in the order-2 model.

The model of Figure 7-11b is more interesting. The initial model is derived from the succession of 3-tuples—effectively the same information as in the order-3 model of Figure 7-10. Two transitions are prohibited by this model. For example, the succession "tht" followed by "hth", which would result from an occurrence of "thth", corresponds to the prediction tht→h, which has a count of zero. The absence of this subsequence is a manifestation of the fact that for any three consecutive symbols, at least one must be the same as its predecessor. Consequently, the reduced model of Figure 7-11b has some interesting structure. In particular, two states—the one directly below the start state and the one diagonally opposite it—have deterministic transitions, corresponding to the unique predictions following the contexts "tht" and "hth" in Figure 7-10. However, the self-loops on the top and bottom states of Figure 7-11b indicate that not all the structure has been extracted from the sequence, for although every third symbol is in fact predictable exactly, these self-loops allow indefinite numbers of symbols to go by without any deterministic predictions being made.

This method is called *length-k* modeling, k being the size of the tuples from which the model is formed. An interesting property is that reduction can be performed incrementally as the input sequence unfolds. Each new element of the input sequence can be incorporated into an already reduced model to form an updated version of it. Suppose that a new input symbol appears. This creates a k-tuple, with the new symbol at its end, that must be incorporated into the model. If that k-tuple has never occurred before, a new state is added to the model, labeled with the new symbol, with an appropriate transition leading to it. (A transition out of the state will be generated when the next symbol is processed.) If the k-tuple has occurred before, it uniquely determines a state of the model. However, it may call for a new transition to be created into that state. If so, it will be necessary to expand the model around the state, add the new transition, and reduce the model again, to ensure that extraneous sequences are not created by the inclusion of the new transition.

The ability to update the model incrementally gives an advantage over other methods of state modeling which require the complete input sequence to be stored, and remodel it from scratch when new information shows the current model to be inadequate. However, the price paid is high. Length-k models correspond in predictive power to order-k context models. They are generally much more compact, but their

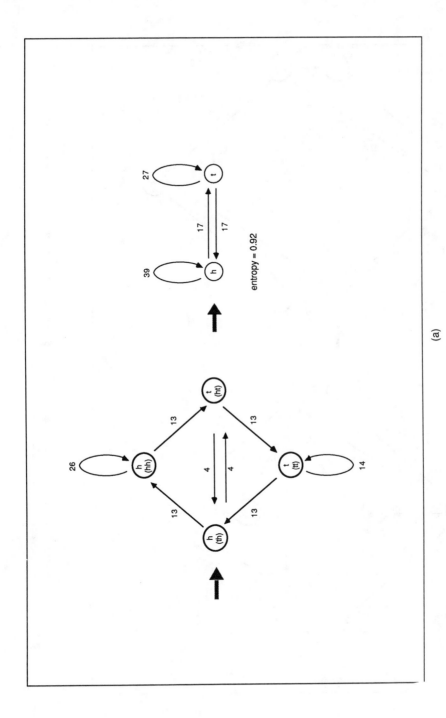

Figure 7-11 Length k state models. The string shown in brackets is the context represented by the state (a) $k = 2$.

(a)

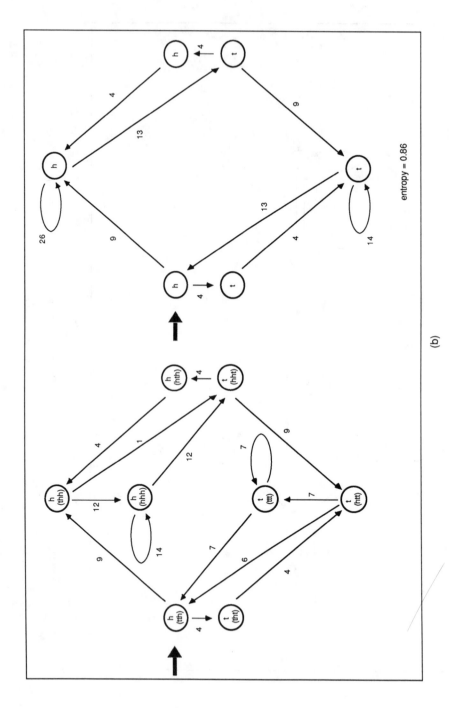

entropy = 0.86

(b)

Figure 7-11(cont) Length k state models. The string shown in brackets is the context represented by the state (b) $k = 3$.

performance is slightly worse. For example, the entropy of the length-3 model in Figure 7-11b is 0.86, compared with 0.82 for the order-3 model in Figure 7-10.

Length-k models, like context models, do not permit counting events to be described properly. However, when implemented suitably, they are much more space efficient than equivalent context-based models. This can be seen most readily by considering their behavior when subjected to a stream of random inputs. If the stream is long enough, the number of different k-tuples that are seen will approach q^k (where q is the alphabet size), so the storage required by a context model grows exponentially with context length. In contrast, the length-k model will collapse into a mere q states after the reduction process, once a sufficient variety of k-tuples has been encountered. Thus although an increased value of k normally provides a larger, more accurate, model, it does not necessarily do so if structure does not exist in the behavior sequence—as in this example. Moreover, it is very quick to follow a sequence through the model, since at each stage one need only consider transitions out of the current state. On the other hand, the update procedure is considerably more complex than with a straightforward context trie, so adaptation will be time consuming.

7.2.2 Reduction and Evaluation

The enumeration approach investigates models starting from the smallest up. One way to avoid the exponential search that this entails is to employ a method of reduction, starting with a large model and successively merging states until the desired size is reached. The initial model could be a direct representation of the sequence itself, that is, an n-state model of an n-element sequence. If this is too long, other methods of generating large, approximate models, like the length-k technique, could be used to create the initial model. This large model is reduced by repeatedly coalescing pairs of states. The most straightforward way to determine which states should be merged is to evaluate separately the models that result from merging each pair of states and select that giving the best evaluation.

Suppose that we begin with an n-state initial model. Then the number of models that need to be evaluated to produce the $(n-1)$-state model is

$$ ^nC_2 = \frac{n(n-1)}{2}. $$

To create a set of models with $n-1$, $n-2$, ..., 2, 1 states takes $n(n^2-1)/6$ operations—a polynomial rather than exponential complexity.

Figure 7-12 shows the results of some experiments with this reduction technique on the coin-tossing data. Several approximate models for a given behavior sequence were generated by the length-k method, for different values of k. The entropy evaluation of these is plotted against their size, measured by the number of states. For each model except the smallest, a series of models was calculated by successively merging pairs of states, chosen to give the lowest entropy at each stage. It can be seen that these new models are sometimes better and sometimes worse than the original length-k ones.

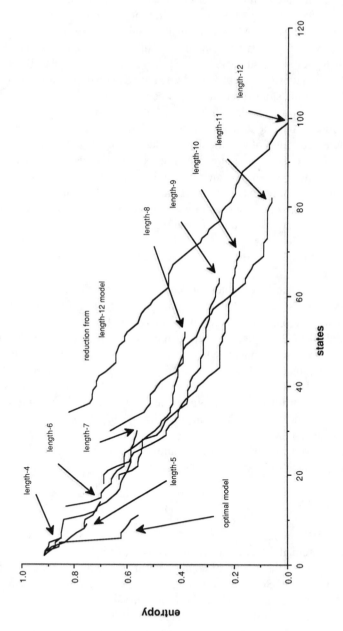

Figure 7-12   Entropy of successive reductions of models by pairwise merging of states.

For example, the line beginning at 100 states passes well above the 82-state length-11 model, the 70-state length-10 model, the 64-state length-9 model, and so on, indicating considerably worse performance. On the other hand, reduction from the length-8, length-9, and length-10 models produces better 30-state models than does reduction from the length-7 one.

Instead of successively merging states in a pairwise fashion, one could generate an n-state model directly from an N-state model ($n < N$) by identifying the best set of $N - n + 1$ states to coalesce. To do this, $^{N}C_{n}$ models would need to be considered. In fact, to generate the full set of one-state, two-state, ..., $(n-1)$-state models from an N-state model by this method would require the evaluation of 2^{N-1} models—a return to exponential complexity.

Consequently, while the reduction technique may prove valuable in certain special cases, it does not constitute a good general-purpose finite-state modeling method.

7.3 DYNAMIC MARKOV MODELING

A quite different state-modeling technique has been developed which is adaptive, beginning with a small initial model and growing it by adding new states when needed. A heuristic criterion is used to determine when to create a state. The method, dubbed DMC for "dynamic Markov coding," provides an efficient way of building complex state models that fit a particular sequence, and is the first (and only) technique described in this chapter which works fast enough to support practical text compression.

In contrast with most other text compression methods, DMC is normally used to process one bit of the input at a time rather than one symbol at a time. In principle, there is no reason why a symbol-oriented version of the method should not be used; it is just that in practice symbol-oriented models of this type tend to be rather greedy in their use of storage unless a sophisticated data structure is used. State-based models with bit-wise input have no difficulty finding the next state—there are only two transitions from the previous state, and it is simply a matter of following the appropriately labeled one. It is also worth noting that if a model works with one bit at a time, its prediction at any stage is in the form of the two probabilities p(0) and p(1) (these two numbers must sum to 1). As explained in Chapter 5, adaptive arithmetic coding can be made particularly efficient in this case.

7.3.1 How DMC Works

The basic idea of DMC is to maintain frequency counts for each transition in the current finite-state model, and to "clone" a state when a related transition becomes sufficiently popular. Figure 7-13 illustrates the cloning operation. A fragment of a finite-state model is shown in which state t is the target state for cloning. From it emanate two transitions, one for symbol 0 and the other for 1, leading to states labeled x and y. There may well be several transitions into t. Three are illustrated, from states u, v, and

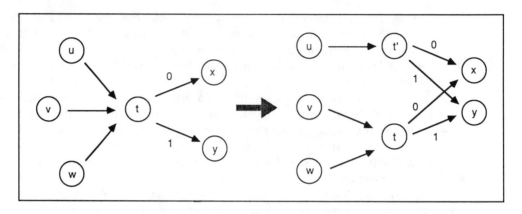

Figure 7-13   The DMC cloning operation.

w, and each will be labeled with 0 or 1 (although, in fact, no labels are shown). We will assume that the transition from state u has a large frequency count.

Because of the high frequency of the $u \rightarrow t$ transition, state t is cloned to form an additional state t'. The $u \rightarrow t$ transition that caused the change is redirected to t', while other transitions into t are unaffected by the operation. Otherwise, t' is made as similar to t as possible by giving it t's (new) output transitions.

The point of the exercise is that in the original model, whenever state t is entered, some contextual information is lost. Thereafter it is not known whether t was entered from the $u \rightarrow t$ transition or along some other one, $v \rightarrow t$ or $w \rightarrow t$. But it is quite possible that the best prediction for the next symbol, 0 or 1, is influenced by the previous state. The simplest way to determine whether significant correlation exists is to clone state t as shown. After cloning, the counts for transitions from t' to x and y will be updated only when t' is reached from u; otherwise, the counts for the original t transition will be updated. The operation of cloning is analogous to increasing the context length for some particular prediction in a blended context model.

If, in fact, the previous states (u, v, and w) have no influence on the next states (x and y), the cloning operation was pointless. However, it does not do a great deal of harm; it simply makes the model more complicated and renders the transition counts from states t and t' more susceptible to statistical fluctuation because each state is visited less often. If, on the other hand, such influence does exist, we can expect a dramatic improvement in performance. Moreover, if there are longer-range correlations, say between u and x or y's successors, further cloning of x and/or y will discover them.

There is a small question of how to determine transition counts for the newly created $t' \rightarrow x$ and $t' \rightarrow y$ transitions. Ideally, the original two output transition counts for state t would be apportioned between the four new output transition counts for states t' and t to reflect what had actually happened in the past following state u and states v/w, respectively. Unfortunately, this information is not available since no record is kept with t's output transitions of how state t was entered—rectifying this is precisely the purpose of the cloning operation. The best guess is to divide t's output transition counts between t' and t in proportion to the input counts from states u and v/w, respectively.

Cloning consumes resources by creating an extra state, and should not be performed unless it is likely to be productive. High-frequency transitions have, by definition, been traversed often in the past and are therefore likely to be traversed often in the future. Consequently, they are likely candidates for cloning, since any correlations discovered will be utilized frequently. However, cloning is only worthwhile if the *other* transitions into the state are traversed a significant number of times too. For example, suppose that the $u \rightarrow t$ transition had been taken 100 times while the $v \rightarrow t$ and $w \rightarrow t$ ones had only be taken twice. Clearly, little benefit is likely to be gained by cloning t.

In fact, experience shows that cloning is best done very early. In other words, the best performance is obtained when the model grows rapidly. Typically, t is cloned on the $u \rightarrow t$ transition when that transition has occurred once and t has been entered a few times from other states, too. This somewhat surprising experimental finding has the effect that statistics never settle down. Whenever a state is used more than a few times, it is cloned and the counts are split. It seems that it is preferable to have unreliable statistics based on long, specific, contexts than reliable ones based on short, less specific ones.

7.3.2 Initial Models

To start off, the DMC method needs an initial model. It need only be a simple one, since the cloning process will tailor it to the specific kind of sequence encountered. However, it must be able to code all possible input sequences. The simplest choice is the one-state model shown in Figure 7-14, and this is a perfectly satisfactory initial model. Once cloning begins, it grows rapidly into a complex model with thousands of states.

In practice, some benefit can be gained by priming the initial model to give it some information about any known structure in the sequence. For text compression, where characters usually arrive as 8-bit bytes, correlations will tend to occur between

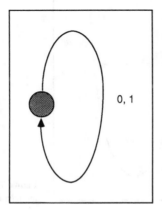

0, 1

Figure 7-14   The DMC one-state initial model.

adjacent bytes rather than between adjacent bits. If we begin with a model that exhibits byte structure, the process of adapting to message statistics gets off the ground faster, improving compression slightly. The simplest initial model with this property is a "chain" of eight states, shown in Figure 7-15a. Slightly better performance is achieved using a simple binary tree with a total of 255 nodes. Figure 7-15b illustrates a small version of this model with 15 states, designed for 4-bit characters rather than 8-bit bytes. The tree has a unique path for each different byte that can occur, so is able to

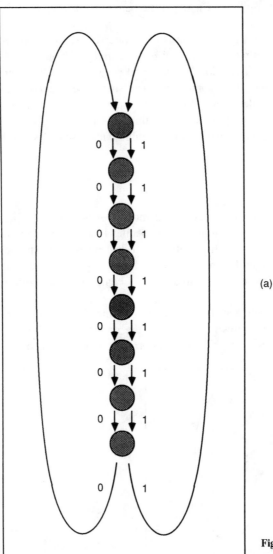

(a)

Figure 7-15   More sophisticated initial models: (a) chain (8-bit characters).

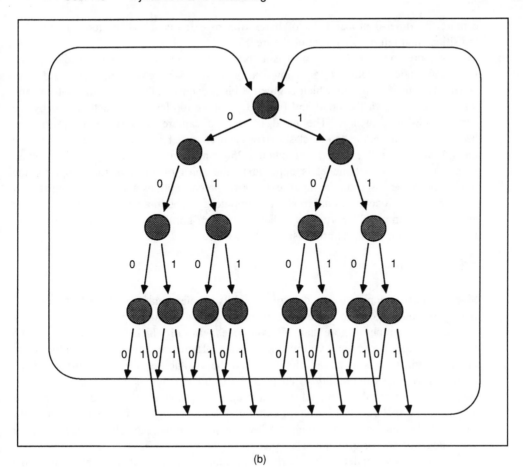

(b)

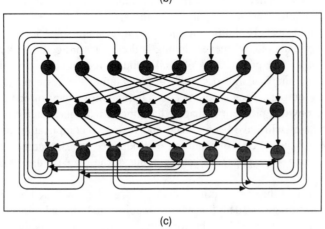

(c)

Figure 7-15(cont)   More sophisticated initial models: (b) tree (4-bit characters); (c) braid (3-bit characters).

capture the order-0 probabilities of bytes (the byte frequencies are stored in the 256 transitions that return to the root of the tree).

A more complex initial model is a "braid" structure, which has eight levels, each with 256 nodes. Figure 7-15c shows a braid for 3-bit characters. A braid is a generalization of a tree in which a given 8-bit sequence follows transitions from any top-level node down the braid and back to a *unique* top-level node determined by the particular 8-bit sequence. The braid is able to capture some order-1 information because it has a unique top-level state for each character in the alphabet. To capture order-1 statistics fully, a model containing 256 binary trees could be used. However, such a complex initial model is opposed to the spirit of adaptive modeling, for the model should be based on the input text, not on preconceptions about it. We must trust that DMC will clone the initial model appropriately to obtain a structure suitable for the text being compressed. Fortunately, these ideals are borne out in practice, and a braid initial model rarely outperforms a simple binary tree.

7.3.3 Forgetting

Since with early cloning the model grows rapidly, implementations of the DMC method rapidly run out of storage space. For example, coding 100,000 characters of text typically creates a graph of more than 150,000 nodes, each of which require storage of two pointers to other nodes and two transition counts. There are various simple solutions to this problem. One is to curtail cloning when the available space is exhausted. However, this sacrifices the ability to adapt if the characteristics of the input text change. Another is to discard the model and start again. Although this sounds drastic, it is surprisingly effective. The hiccup in compression efficiency that occurs upon reinitialization can be ameliorated by saving the last few hundred message characters in a buffer and using this to perform initial adaptation of the model whenever it is reinitialized. This yields a new model with a fairly small number of states that corresponds to the characteristics of the most recent part of the message.

More sophisticated solutions might try to implement some form of "forgetting" in the model. For example, whenever cloning is done a record could be kept of the resulting pair of states. The productivity of each could be measured relative to what it would have been if cloning had not occurred, by calculating the corresponding reduction in entropy of the output. Then clonings could be undone if they turned out to be unproductive. The obvious problem is that by the time reliable measures could be estimated, the relevant states will have been cloned and recloned, complicating the assessment of productivity and the process of reuniting unproductive states. Moreover, keeping additional information to expedite forgetting reduces the size of the model that can be stored.

It is clear that the cost of implementing "forgetting" will be high, in terms of both the additional storage needed for record keeping and the additional execution time needed to work out what should be forgotten. It seems quite likely that this cost will outweigh any benefits that might be obtained. However, this is conjecture and proper studies have yet to be done.

7.4 THE POWER OF DMC

The DMC method is potentially more powerful than the blended context models of Chapter 6 because it creates finite-state models, and as we have discussed, these can represent regularities in the text sequence that cannot be captured by finite-context methods. In this section we show that, surprisingly, the DMC scheme does not use the full power of a finite-state model but is actually a variable-order context model.

DMC is a successful data compression technique, and the fact that it fails to offer the full power of finite-state models does not detract from its proven high performance. It does, however, explain why in practice it gives about the same compression as finite-context models, as we will see in Chapter 9. It does have certain potential advantages in implementation (principally speed) which spring from the use of state rather than context models.

First, we formally define finite-context models as a subset of finite-state models. The idea of the proof is to show that the initial model for DMC is a finite-context model, and that cloning states in a finite-context model always produces another finite-context model. This is first done using the simplest, one-state, initial model of Figure 7-14. It is subsequently extended to other initial models by viewing models as having transitions on symbols rather than bits, where a symbol is a fixed-size string of bits (typically, 8 bits).

The development will, of necessity, be somewhat formal. First we need to characterize the essential difference between finite-state and finite-context models, and for this we need some definitions.

7.4.1 Distinguishing Finite Context Models

A finite-state model has an input alphabet A, a state set S, an identified starting state within S, and a state-transition function μ. In the case of DMC, the input alphabet is normally binary, $A = \{0, 1\}$. The state-transition function takes a state and a symbol and produces another state:

$$\mu: S \times A \to S.$$

Let A^* be the set of all strings, including the empty string, with elements drawn from the input alphabet A. The empty string is denoted as Λ. For convenience, the state-transition function is extended in an obvious way to act on strings of symbols as well as individual ones:

$$\mu: S \times A^* \to S.$$

Given a state and input string, μ produces the new state that would be obtained by starting with the original state and applying the input string.

For any finite-state model there may be certain input strings that have the special property of forcing the model into a particular state, no matter which state it is originally in. These are called *synchronizing* strings. For a synchronizing string x, $\mu(s, x)$ is independent of the state s; in other words, $\mu(s, x) = \mu(r, x)$ for any states $s, r \in S$.

Strings that do *not* have the synchronizing property are of special interest and will be denoted by the set N:

$$N = \{x \in A^* : \mu(s,\, x) \neq \mu(r,\, x) \text{ for some } s,\, r \in S\}.$$

For example, the model in Figure 7-16a, which might have been generated using the DMC algorithm, has $N = \{\Lambda, 0\}$, while the model in Figure 7-16b, which in fact could not have been generated by DMC, has $N = \{\Lambda, 0, 00, 000, \dots, 0^k, \dots\}$.

The distinguishing feature of finite-*context* models is that the set N of nonsynchronizing strings is finite. For example, the model of Figure 7-16a is of finite context while that of Figure 7-16b is not. The reason is that when N is finite, there is some upper limit, say k, to the length of nonsynchronizing strings (since there are only finitely many of them). Any string longer than k must be a synchronizing string. Thus

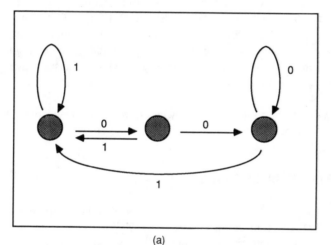

(a)

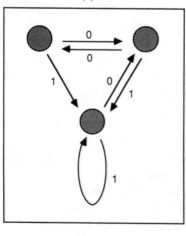

(b)

Figure 7-16   (a) A model with finite N set; (b) a model with infinite N set.

if we know the previous $k+1$ symbols of the input sequence, we know what state the model must be in. This is exactly what is meant by a finite-context model.

7.4.2 Proof That DMC Models Are Finite Context

We will prove that DMC models have finite N sets and are therefore finite-context models, by induction. The 1-state initial model certainly has a finite N, for its state is completely determined by the previous zero symbols!—there is only one state. In fact, for this model, N is the empty set. It is now only necessary to show that cloning a model with a finite set of nonsynchronizing strings produces another model with a finite set of nonsynchronizing strings.

To do this we must formally characterize the cloning operation. Cloning takes a finite-state model and produces a new model with an augmented state set and transition function. It is performed on a particular state–symbol pair, say the state $u \in S$ and symbol $b \in A$. Denote the state to be cloned by t, where $\mu(u, b) = t$. Then cloning produces the new state t', so that the new state set is

$$S' = S \cup \{t'\}$$

and the new transition function is μ'. This is just the same as μ except that it takes state u and symbol b into state t':

$$\mu'(u, b) = t',$$

and gives the new state t' the same output transitions as t:

$$\mu'(t', a) = \mu(t, a) \qquad \text{for each } a \in A.$$

What does the cloning operation do to the set of nonsynchronizing strings? The new set N' is defined by

$$N' = \{x \in A^* : \mu'(s, x) \neq \mu'(r, x) \text{ for some } s, r \in S\}.$$

This differs from N because for some states s and strings x, $\mu'(s, x) \neq \mu(s, x)$. However, this is possible only if $\mu(s, x) = t$ and $\mu'(s, x) = t'$, for transitions on strings in the cloned model that do not end at the state t' end up at the same state as they did before cloning. This happens because on each transition, μ' is only different from μ when the transition is to t'. Because the new transitions out of t and t' are the same as the old transitions out of t, strings that pass through those states in the cloned model go to the same state as they did in the original model. The upshot is that the new nonsynchronizing set N' differs from the old one N only because it has the new members

$$\{x : \mu'(s, x) = t, \ \mu'(r, x) = t' \text{ for some } s, r \in S'\}.$$

It remains only to show that this set is finite. We will do so by exhibiting a larger set that includes this one, and showing that set to be finite.

What we must do first is somehow get rid of the prime on the μ' in the definition of the preceding set, so that it is expressed in terms of the old state-transition function rather than the new one. Suppose that s and r are states with $\mu'(s, x) = t$ and $\mu'(r, x) = t'$. Denote by b the very last symbol of the string x, and call y the substring up to that point, so that $x = y \cdot b$, where the "$\cdot$" denotes string concatenation. Now we will show that $\mu(s, y)$ and $\mu(r, y)$ must be different. First, notice that $\mu'(s, y)$ and $\mu'(r, y)$ must be different, since $\mu'(s, y \cdot b)$ and $\mu'(r, y \cdot b)$ are. As we have already observed, the only way that these could be the same before cloning and different afterward is that their targets are t and t'. If this is so, it must have been that $\mu(s, y) = \mu(r, y) = t$. But from this we get the contradiction that

$$
\begin{aligned}
t &= \mu'(s, y \cdot b) = \mu'(\mu'(s, y), b) = \mu'(t, b) \\
&= \mu'(t', b) \quad = \mu'(\mu'(r, s), b) = \mu'(r, y \cdot b) = t',
\end{aligned}
$$

so it must be that $\mu(s, y) \neq \mu(r, y)$, which is just what we set out to show.

Since whenever $\mu'(s, x) = t$ and $\mu'(r, x) = t'$ it must be that $\mu(s, y) \neq \mu(r, y)$, the set of all strings $y \cdot b$ in which y satisfies the latter condition must be a superset of the set of strings x that satisfy the former. Consequently, the set

$$
\{x: \mu'(s, x) = t, \mu'(r, x) = t' \text{ for some } s, r \in S'\}
$$

is included in the larger set

$$
\{y \cdot a: \mu(s, y) \neq \mu(r, y) \text{ for some } s, r \in S \text{ and } a \in A\}.
$$

We will now show that this larger set is finite. It is a set of strings of the form $y \cdot a$ for some $a \in A$, where y satisfies the stated condition. It is certainly included in the set of strings $\{y \cdot a_1, y \cdot a_2, y \cdot a_3, \ldots\}$, where $a_1, a_2, a_3, \ldots$ are all the members of A. For convenience, we extend the concatenation operation "$\cdot$" to sets of strings, where the concatenation of two sets is the set containing each string of the first concatenated with each string of the second. Then we can write this larger set as

$$
\{y: \mu(s, y) \neq \mu(r, y) \text{ for some } s, r \in S\} \cdot A,
$$

which is just

$$
N \cdot A.
$$

This is finite because N is finite by our inductive hypothesis, and A is certainly finite. This completes the proof.

7.4.3 Extending the Proof to Other Initial Models

We noted earlier that although the one-state Markov model is a suitable initial model, slightly better compression can be obtained by starting with a model that reflects the byte structure of the text. Such structures are shown in Figure 7-15. These initial models contain cycles of h bits, where h is typically 8. In the figure, the chain is shown with $h = 8$, the tree with $h = 4$, and for the braid, $h = 3$.

We will now consider the behavior of DMC at the h-bit symbol level. Of course, h is usually chosen to be the size of input symbols. Therefore, we redefine the transition function to operate on symbols rather than bits. The input alphabet is now A^h, which we will call A_h since we will use subscript h to identify symbol-level constructs. The transition on a symbol from A_h is equivalent to h-bit transitions, except that the intermediate states are ignored. The symbol-level equivalent models for those in Figure

7-15a and 7-15b are simply order-0 Markov models; the braid model translates to an order-1 Markov model. Figure 7-17 shows the tree-structured initial model and its symbol-level equivalent.

Viewing DMC models at the symbol level is possible because cloning only creates cycles with lengths that are multiples of h. For example, only nodes cloned from the starting state are visited after each h bits of input. This can be verified by considering the effect of cloning a state that is part of a cycle (see Figure 7-13)—if the state t is part of a cycle, then cloning does not increase the length of the cycle. Figure 7-18a shows how cloning the initial state of Figure 7-17a is reflected in the symbol-level equivalent. Cloning other states has no effect on the symbol-level equivalent. For example, Figure 7-18b shows a state within the tree being cloned, but this does not affect the symbol model. The symbol view ignores dependencies between bits but retains the model structure as far as h-bit symbols are concerned.

This means that for the chain and tree initial models of Figure 7-15, the only states that will appear in the symbol-level model are the initial state and those cloned from it. In general, the set of nodes cloned from the initial state s_1 is the set of all nodes visited from s_1 after a multiple of h bits:

$$S_h = \{s \in S : s = \mu(s_1, x) \text{ for some } x \in A_h{}^* \}.$$

The same definition applies to the braid model because the nodes that can be visited after a multiple of h bits are those at the same level as the starting state. The symbol-level transition function is

$$\mu_h : S_h \times A_h{}^* \rightarrow S_h$$

defined by $\mu_h(s, x) = \mu(s, x)$, where the first x is treated as a member of $A_h{}^*$ and the second is the same string viewed as a member of A^*. A bit-level cloning results in a change at the symbol level only when the cloning is on a transition that is the last bit of a symbol. Thus the bit-level cloning on the state $u \in S$ and bit $b \in A$ affects the symbol-level model only if $\mu(u, b) \in S_h$. If so, it produces the new state set

$$S_h{}' = S_h \cup \{t'\},$$

where t' is the new state created by cloning. The new transition function $\mu_h{}'$ is just the same as μ_h except for the following two things. First, it gives the new state t' the same output transitions as t:

$$\mu_h{}'(t', a) = \mu_h(t, a) \qquad \text{for each } a \in A_h.$$

Second, if v was the last member of S_h encountered before cloning, and $\mu(v, y) = u$, then

$$\mu_h{}'(v, y \cdot b) = t'.$$

For example, in Figure 7-18a, v and t' are the two states in black, while y is 000 and b, the input that caused the cloning, is 0.

We have seen that the initial models suggested for DMC translate into two types of model at the symbol level, with the new alphabet A_h. The "tree" and "cycle" structures both correspond to the one-state model

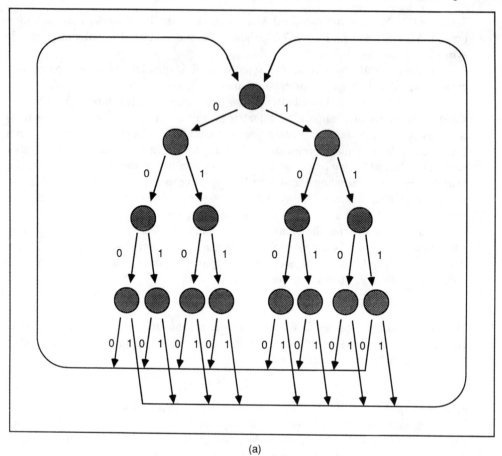

(a)

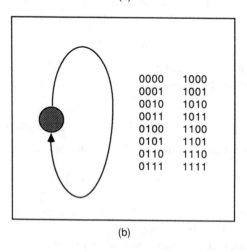

(b)

Figure 7-17   (a) The tree-structured initial model; (b) its symbol-level equivalent.

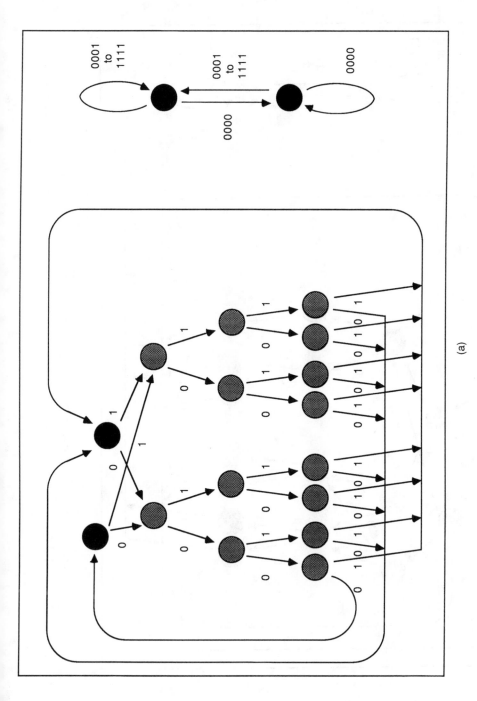

(a)

Figure 7-18 The effect of cloning on a symbol-level equivalent model: (a) cloning the initial state of Figure 7-17a.

203

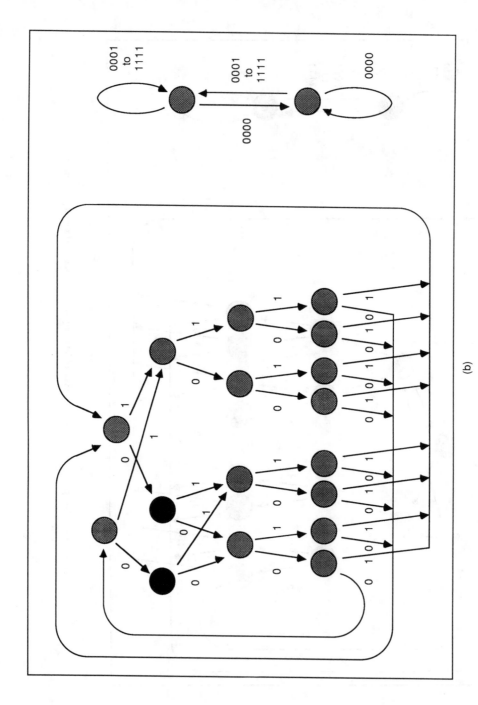

Figure 7-18(cont) The effect of cloning on a symbol-level equivalent model: (b) cloning another state of (a).

(b)

204

$$S_h = \{s\} \qquad \text{with } \mu_h(s, a) = s \text{ for all } a \in A_h.$$

The "braid" structure corresponds to a 2^h-state model with one state for each symbol in the alphabet:

$$S_h = \{s_a : a \in A_h\} \qquad \text{with } \mu_h(s, a) = s_a \text{ for all } s \in S_h \text{ and } a \in A_h.$$

In the first case, the set N of nonsynchronizing strings is certainly finite, for there are none—the state the model occupies is completely determined by the previous zero symbols. In the second case, N contains just the null string Λ, for any input string of one or more symbols dictates the new state according to the last symbol in the string.

Because the new cloning function is defined identically to that used in the proof earlier, the result obtained there holds for the symbol-level model. In other words, all models generated by DMC are finite-context models at the symbol level when started with any of the suggested initial models. For example, with an 8-bit initial model, every byte is predictable from some finite number of preceding bytes. The probabilities used for prediction will be affected by interactions within the bit patterns of the symbols, but the overall probability used to encode any symbol is dictated entirely by a finite-context process.

Although the DMC scheme models text with a finite-state model, that model is in fact restricted to be equivalent to a finite-context one. DMC is in effect another version of the methods developed in Chapter 6 (although it might have practical advantages, such as speed). The use of unrestricted finite-state models for text compression still awaits exploration.

NOTES

The idea of enumeration and evaluation for discovering optimal general state models was explored by Gaines (1976, 1977). He discusses the utility of the method and alternative formulations of it, along with a host of examples, some of which are included in this chapter, in considerably more detail than we have been able to here. Biermann (1972) showed how input–output machines can be inferred from samples of their behavior, and introduced the sorting example presented here. Gold (1978) discusses the computational complexity of the problem of identifying input–output machines from behavior sequences.

A formal discussion of k-testable and counting events can be found in McNaughton and Papert (1971). The anecdote about the rigged penny-tossing machine is introduced and discussed by Andreae (1977) as an example of a simple stochastic machine. The method of length-k modeling is explored by Witten (1979, 1980), while a similar idea for use with input–output models is due to Biermann and Feldman (1972). The use of reduction and evaluation was pioneered by Evans (1971) when attempting to infer picture grammars from examples. Dynamic Markov modeling is due to Horspool and Cormack (1986) and Cormack and Horspool (1987); while Bell and Moffat (1989) proved that the method is equivalent to a finite-context predictive modeler.

45h[0j45thwGw45hqU9d
poejrg[4wky]p435q)b&
[0wejg[04jy42yj3*k!d
p0w4j5g[235-k6t0=w~n
[0ewjg04jy04jy4j;qmy
pmh][krty-jk46-[p"qb
p[jw435y‎‎‎‎h[ps0%x
[psdhkj‎‎3w‎‎u5y9mwq
germhj-5‎‎‎j64k?ti
[ewjhj4‎‎n5‎‎0o#r0b
e[wmb[p‎‎h65‎‎u;g4{@
65[];.9[‎‎‎‎]0.o~x6
germhj-53k=ukj64:3xf
[ewjhj4wth56430o*wm<
e[wmb[preh65,.u;aYlC
+[3fgm56rt0-"-23jsg!
[;jyt%ERghj(0;';Hd4=
1U5terEDghp=][>?kyeW

DICTIONARY TECHNIQUES

8

Approaches to text compression can be divided into two classes: *statistical* and *dictionary*. So far we have considered only statistical methods, where a probability is estimated for each character, and a code is chosen based on the probability. Dictionary coding achieves compression by replacing groups of consecutive characters (phrases) with indexes into some dictionary. The dictionary is a list of phrases that are expected to occur frequently. Indexes are chosen so that on average they take less space than the phrase they encode, thereby achieving compression. This type of coding is also known as "macro" coding or a "codebook" approach. As an example, Figure 8-1 shows how some compiler error messages can be compressed using a dictionary containing common words. The Telegraph and Braille systems in Chapter 1 use forms of dictionary coding, in contrast to Morse, which uses a statistical approach.

Dictionary encoding has enjoyed popularity for several reasons. First, it is intuitive, and the same principle is used in contexts removed from computers. We are happy to encode the phrases "January," "February,"…, "December," as the numbers 1, 2, …, 12; and are accustomed to supermarkets using a bar code (UPC) to represent a complete description of a product. We talk about "Chapter 8" rather than "the chapter about dictionary techniques," and when dealing with large organizations, it is inevitable that our entire identity (name, address, etc.) will be represented as a single number (account number, tax number, etc.) which can be uniquely decoded to yield useful information about us.

Dictionary:	Code	String
	%001	"EXTRA·"
	%002	"MISSING·"
	%003	"IMPROPER·"
	%004	"SEMI-COLON"
	%005	"EXPRESSION"

Sample encodings:	String	Encoded form
	EXTRA·(.	%001(.
	MISSING·(.	%002(.
	EXTRA·).	%001).
	MISSING·).	%002).
	EXTRA·SEMI-COLON.	%001%004.
	MISSING·SEMI-COLON.	%002%004.
	MISSING·EXPRESSION.	%002%005.
	MISSING·VARIABLE.	%002VARIABLE.

Figure 8-1   Compression of compiler error messages.

Another reason for the popularity of dictionary coding is that the size of indexes to the dictionary can be chosen to align with machine words, expediting an efficient implementation. This contrasts with statistical coding, which inevitably requires manipulation of various-sized groups of bits within a machine word. The codes for many dictionary schemes are multiples of 4 or 8 bits.

Dictionary schemes can achieve good compression given only a modest amount of computer time and memory because one dictionary reference may encode several characters. The compression achieved by the better ones is outperformed only by statistical schemes using high-order context models, and these require considerably more computing power because effort must be put into coding each *character* rather than each *phrase*. The better compression performance of statistical schemes is not a coincidence. In Chapter 9 we show that all the dictionary schemes described here have an equivalent statistical scheme which achieves exactly the same compression. This means that the compression achieved by dictionary schemes can always be equaled, and usually improved on, by statistical ones. Dictionary schemes are still useful for their speed and economy of memory, but we predict that the improvement of computing technology will make high performance statistical schemes feasible for general use, and that dictionary coding will eventually be of historical interest only.

The central decision in the design of a dictionary scheme is the selection of entries in the coding dictionary. Some designers impose a restriction on the length of phrases stored. For example, in digram coding they are never more than two characters long. Within this restriction the choice of phrases may be made by static, semiadaptive, or adaptive algorithms. The simplest dictionary schemes use static dictionaries containing only short phrases. However, the best compression is achieved by adaptive schemes that allow large phrases. Ziv–Lempel coding is a general class of compression methods that fit the latter description, and because it outperforms other dictionary schemes, this approach will be emphasized. Brief descriptions of other methods are given mainly to provide a foil to the elegance of Ziv–Lempel coding.

One saving grace of static and semiadaptive dictionary coding techniques is that they are especially suited to the coding of records within a file, such as a bibliographic database, where records are to be decoded at random but the same phrase often appears in different records. For example, in a file of periodical references, the phrases "Journal of" and "Association" will be common. Provided that the same dictionary is used for an entire file, decoding can begin at any phrase boundary in the file. For a dictionary coder that outputs only 8-bit codes, decoding may start at the beginning of any byte in the coded file. Also, fast searching may be possible if the code for a search key can be obtained from the dictionary and used to search the compressed text. Adaptive techniques are more applicable to a file that will be compressed and decompressed as a whole, since the decoding of any particular character requires all prior text to have been decoded first.

Formally, a dictionary $D = (M, C)$ is a finite set of phrases M and a function C that maps M onto a set of codes. The phrases in M are generated from the input alphabet A. Without loss of generality, the output codes will be assumed to be strings over the binary alphabet $\{0,1\}$. The set M is *complete* if every infinite string over the input alphabet A^* is also in M^*; that is, any input string can be made up of phrases from M. The function C obeys the *prefix property* if no string $C(m)$ is a prefix of another string $C(s)$, for $s, m \in M$ and $s \neq m$. For reversible compression of any input to be possible, the set M must be complete and C must obey the prefix property. We will use the function $L(m)$ to denote the length of $C(m)$ in bits.

8.1 PARSING STRATEGIES

Once a dictionary has been chosen, there is more than one way to choose which phrases in the input text will be replaced by indexes to the dictionary. The task of splitting the text into phrases for coding is called *parsing*. The most practical approach is *greedy* parsing, where at each step the encoder searches for the longest string $m \in M$ that matches the next characters in the text, and uses $C(m)$ to encode them. For example, if $M = \{a,b,ba,bb,abb\}$, and $C(a) = 00$, $C(b) = 010$, $C(ba) = 0110$, $C(bb) = 0111$, and $C(abb) = 1$, then "babb" is coded in 8 bits as $C(ba).C(bb) = 0110.0111$.

Unfortunately greedy parsing is not necessarily optimal. For example, the string "babb" could have been coded in only 4 bits as $C(b).C(abb) = 010.1$. However, determining an optimal parsing can be difficult in practice, because there is no limit to how far ahead the encoder may have to look. This is illustrated by coding the string with prefix $(ba)^i b$ (i.e., bababa $\cdots$ bab) using $M = \{a,b,ab,ba,bb\}$, and $C(a) = 000$, $C(b) = 001$, $C(ab) = 10$, $C(ba) = 11$, $C(bb) = 0100000$. If the string being encoded is followed by the character "a", the best parsing is "ba, ba, ba, ..., ba, ba" ($2i + 2$ bits), but if the next character is "b", the best parsing would be "b, ab, ab, ab, ..., ab, b"

(3 + 2*i* + 3 bits). To ensure optimal parsing in this situation, the encoder must look ahead 2*i* + 1 characters, where *i* can be arbitrarily large. So although the greedy approach is not optimal, it is used widely in practical schemes because it allows single-pass encoding with a bounded delay. The furthest a greedy scheme needs to look ahead is the length of the longest string in *M*.

The task of optimal parsing can be transformed to a shortest-path problem, which can then be solved by existing algorithms. The transformation is performed for a string $x[1..n]$ as follows. (As an example, Figure 8-2 shows the parsing of a short string using this technique.) A graph is constructed which contains $n+1$ nodes, numbered from 1 to $n+1$. For every pair of nodes i and j, a directed edge is placed between them if the substring $x[i..j-1]$ is in the dictionary. The edge is given a weight equal to the length of the code $C(x[i..j-1])$. The shortest path from node 1 to node $n+1$ then represents the optimal parsed sequence for **x**. Note that the graph generated is acyclic and has other properties that make the power of a general shortest-path algorithm something of a sledgehammer for solving the problem.

Two algorithms have been proposed for optimal parsing which provide solutions to the shortest-path problem in the specific case of graphs generated as above. One approach is to perform a breadth-first search through the coding space. This algorithm keeps track of all possible encodings until a point is reached where one is known to be better than all others. Such a point corresponds to a node in the graph through which every possible path must pass, and is known as a *cut* node. The better encoding can be applied, and the encoding position shifts to the end of the characters just encoded. Of

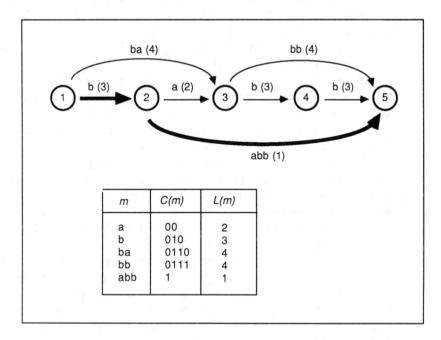

Figure 8-2   Optimal parsing using a shortest path algorithm; the path weights are shown in brackets and the shortest path is shown in boldface type.

course, there is no guarantee that a parsing decision can be made until the entire text has been seen, but in practice there are often cut points along the way where the different codings synchronize, and an optimal decision can be made before proceeding.

Another way to generate an optimal encoding is by working backward through the text. The approach, which is a kind of dynamic programming, is inductive. For a string $\mathbf{x}[1..n]$, the optimal coding for $\mathbf{x}[n]$ is found, then for $\mathbf{x}[n-1..n]$ given the optimal coding for $\mathbf{x}[n]$, then for $\mathbf{x}[n-2..n]$, and so on, until the optimal coding is known for the entire text. The corresponding shortest-path algorithm would be to take advantage of the acyclic nature of the graph, which allows the nodes to be sorted topologically. The shortest path is evaluated for node n, then node $n-1$, $n-2$, and so on. The shortest path from any node can be determined by examining the cost of each edge and the cost of the shortest path for the node at the end of that edge.

As well as suffering from the problem that the encoding delay is not bounded, all these optimal parsing algorithms are slow, and to be sure of working for any input, enough memory must be available to cope with parsing the entire input in one bite. A compromise between greedy and optimal parsing is the longest fragment first (LFF) heuristic. This approach searches for the longest substring of the input (not necessarily starting at the beginning) which is also in M. This phrase is then coded, and the algorithm repeats until all substrings have been coded. For example, for the dictionary $M = \{$a,b,c,aa,aaaa,ab,baa,bccb,bccba$\}$, where all dictionary strings are coded in 4 bits, the LFF parsing of the string "aaabccbaaaa" first identifies "bccba" as the longest fragment. The final parsing of the string is "aa,a,bccba,aa,a" and the string is coded in 20 bits. Greedy parsing would give "aa,ab,c,c,baa,aa" (24 bits) while the optimal parsing is "aa,a,bccb,aaaa" (16 bits). In general, the compression performance and speed of LFF lie between greedy and optimal parsing. As with optimal parsing, LFF needs to scan the entire input before making parsing decisions.

Another approximation to optimal parsing works with a buffer of, say, the last 1000 characters from the input. In practice, cut points (points where the optimal decision can be made) almost always occur well under 100 characters apart, so the use of such a large buffer almost guarantees that the entire text will be encoded optimally. This approach can achieve coding speeds almost as fast as greedy coding.

Many theoretical results have been derived that compare the compression performance of greedy and optimal parsing, generally giving tight bounds for how far greedy coding can be from optimal. Although these bounds turn out to be large, the strings that attain the bounds are pathological. An average case analysis would be more relevant, but since there is no "average case" for text, it is usually more worthwhile to evaluate performance from practical experiments.

One interesting theoretical result is that although greedy parsing is not necessarily optimal for a general dictionary, it is optimal for some dictionaries that are used in practice. It can be shown that greedy parsing is optimal for a dictionary where the codes $C(m)$ are all the same length, provided either that no $m \in M$ is longer than two characters, or that every suffix of m is also in the dictionary. A proof for the case where m can only be one or two characters is sketched below in the description of digram coding. The proof for a suffix dictionary is similar.

Practical experiments have shown that optimal encoding can be two to three times slower than greedy encoding, but improves compression by only a few percent. The LFF and bounded buffer approximations improve the compression ratio a little less, but also require less time for coding. In practice the small improvement in compression is usually outweighed by the extra coding time and effort of implementation, so the greedy approach is by far the most popular. Most dictionary compression schemes concentrate on choosing the set M and assume that greedy parsing will be applied.

8.2 STATIC AND SEMIADAPTIVE DICTIONARY ENCODERS

Countless papers have been published proposing compression schemes using dictionary coding, although it transpires that a high proportion of them represent independent inventions of essentially the same idea. This probably indicates the intuitive nature of dictionary coding as well as the variety of different places these schemes have been published. We have classified such schemes according to whether the dictionary is static, semiadaptive, or adaptive. As with statistical coding, the adaptive approach is much more attractive than the others, so these schemes are described in the most detail.

8.2.1 Static Dictionary Encoders

Static dictionary encoders are useful for achieving a small amount of compression for very little effort. One fast algorithm that has been proposed several times in different forms is *digram coding*, which maintains a dictionary of commonly used digrams, or pairs of characters. At each coding step the next two characters are inspected to see if they correspond to a digram in the dictionary. If so, they are coded together; otherwise, only the first character is coded. The coding position then is shifted by one or two characters as appropriate.

Digram schemes are built on top of an existing character code. For example, the ASCII alphabet contains only 96 text characters (including all 94 printing characters, space, and a code for newline) and yet is often stored in 8 bits. The remaining 160 codes are available to represent digrams—more will be available if some of the 96 characters are unnecessary. This gives a dictionary of 256 items (96 single characters and 160 digrams). Each item is coded in one byte, with single characters being represented by their normal code. Because all codes are the same size as the representation of ordinary characters, the encoder and decoder do not have to manipulate bits within a byte, and this contributes to the high speed of digram coding.

More generally, if q characters are considered essential, then $256 - q$ digrams must be chosen to fill the dictionary. Two methods have been proposed do this. One is to scan sample texts to determine the $256 - q$ most common digrams. The information in Table 4-1 would augment the character set with the digrams { •e, •t, s•, th, •a, he, ... }. The list may be fine tuned to take account of situations such as "he" being used infrequently because the "h" is usually coded as part of a preceding "th".

A simpler approach is to choose two small sets of characters, d_1 and d_2. The digrams to be used are those generated by taking the cross-product of d_1 and d_2, that is, all pairs of characters where the first is taken from d_1 and the second from d_2. The dictionary will be full if $|d_1| \times |d_2| = 256 - q$. Typically, both d_1 and d_2 contain common characters, so Table 4-1 gives the digrams $\{\bullet, e, t, a, \ldots\} \times \{\bullet, e, t, a, \ldots\}$, that is, $\{\bullet\bullet, \bullet e, \bullet t, \ldots, e\bullet, ee, et, \ldots\}$. Another possibility, based on the idea that vowel–consonant pairs are common, is to choose d_1 to be $\{a, e, i, o, u, y, \bullet\}$.

The parsing used by digram coding is greedy, but it turns out that its use of fixed-length codes and the maximum phrase size of 2 ensure that the size of the output is the same as for optimal parsing. This can be proved by induction as follows. Suppose that the string $\mathbf{x}$ has been parsed optimally by the greedy algorithm up to character $\mathbf{x}[i-1]$. Consider the parsing of the next few characters. If the optimal parsing is $\mathbf{x}[i, i+1]$, $\mathbf{x}[i+2\ldots]$, the greedy algorithm will choose it. If the optimal parsing is $\mathbf{x}[i], \mathbf{x}[i+1\ldots]$ but the greedy algorithm chooses $\mathbf{x}[i, i+1]$, $\mathbf{x}[i+2\ldots]$, it has coded more input characters for the same amount of output as the optimal. Of course, the optimal coding will eventually catch up, and at that point the induction step can be reapplied.

This argument does not work for a dictionary that contains phrases of three (or more) characters. Consider the situation where the greedy parsing has got one character ahead of the optimal but has generated the same amount of output. If the optimal parsing now overtakes it with a three-character phrase, the optimal will be two characters ahead, and to catch up, the greedy might be forced to code those two characters as two phrases, generating one more output code than the optimal.

The compression achieved by digram coding can be improved by generalizing it to "n-grams"—fragments of n consecutive characters. The problem with a static n-gram scheme is that the choice of phrases for the dictionary is critical and depends on the nature of the text being encoded, yet we want phrases to be as long as possible. As an extreme example, there are very few 100-grams common to any texts! A safe approach is to use a few hundred common words from a list like Table 4-2. It is reasonable to expect these words to occur frequently in many texts. Even many programming languages are covered by this approach, since keywords are often common English words (such as "while," "and," "for," "repeat"). Unfortunately, the brevity of the words prevents any dramatic compression being achieved, although it certainly represents an improvement on digram coding.

Figure 8-3 shows an example of a static n-gram coding scheme. The first 4 bits of a code either represent a common character or escape to a different code. Only 13 common characters are represented this way, leaving three escape codes (indicated by the three arrows in the figure). Escape code "0" indicates that the next 4 bits identify a common word, which is assumed to begin with a blank except at the beginning of a line. Escape code "1" indicates that the next 4 bits identify one of 16 less common characters. Escape code "2" indicates that the next 8 bits identify either a rare character or a less common word. So the total length of a code can be 4, 8, or 12 bits, depending on the rank of the phrase it encodes. For example, "e" occupies 4 bits, while "u" occupies 8, "the" 8, and "have" 12.

8.2.2 Semiadaptive Dictionary Encoders

A natural development of the static n-gram approach is to generate a dictionary specific to the particular text being encoded. The dictionary will accumulate idiosyncratic phrases that occur frequently in the text, such as technical terms that would not be

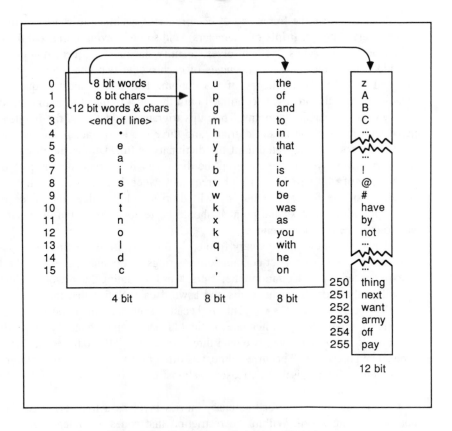

Figure 8-3   Static *n*-gram dictionary coding scheme.

found in other texts. For example, if this chapter were to be compressed, the phrase "dictionary encod" would be useful, yet we would not expect it to be much help for compressing, for example, Shakespeare. Since technical words and phrases tend to be longer than common English words, we would expect this approach to offer good compression. A drawback is that the dictionary must now be stored or transmitted with the compressed form of the text. The dictionary itself might be compressed using one of the differential techniques outlined in Section 1-3.

The task of determining an optimal dictionary for a given text is known to be NP-complete in the size of the text. The proof of this shows that the problem of finding an optimal dictionary can be solved using a form of the *node (vertex) cover problem*, and vice versa. However, many heuristics have sprung up that find near-optimal solutions to the problem, and most are quite similar.

Usually a maximum number of entries in the dictionary is chosen, which we denote as $|M|$. Each entry will be coded with $\lceil \log |M| \rceil$ bits, so the coding will be optimal if the phrases in the dictionary are equifrequent. The heart of dictionary generation is an algorithm that attempts to identify suitable phrases in the text. A typical algorithm to do this proceeds as follows.

First calculate the frequency of occurrence of each single character, digram (pair of characters), trigram (triple of characters), and so on. Having initialized the dictionary to include all characters by themselves, identify the most frequent digram (say "e•") and add it in, reducing the frequencies of each of the two characters that compose it ("e" and "•") by the frequency of the digram. The second most frequent digram is added next, and the process is continued until the most frequent trigram exceeds the frequency of the remaining digrams. Then this trigram is added, and the frequencies associated with its two constituent digrams and three single characters are reduced accordingly. The process is repeated until the dictionary is full. During the process it may be necessary to remove an element from the dictionary if its frequency drops too low. For example, "•of•th" will have a high frequency when it is added, but if "•of•the" is included too, the former's frequency will drop to a low value since it nearly always occurs preceding "e". At that point it should be removed from the dictionary to make way for a more productive entry.

Table 8-1 shows a dictionary formed in this way from the Brown corpus. As one might expect, the symbol set contains those strings that come naturally to the fingers of an experienced typist. Common letter pairs, word beginnings, and word endings appear, as well as the most frequent words and a word pair. Notice that the phrases ".•" and ".•••" appear, but not ".••". This is because sentences in the sample were almost exclusively separated by either one or three spaces—the frequency with which a "." was followed by *exactly* one, two, and three spaces was 74%, 0.008%, and 18%, respectively. The phrase ".••" occurred almost as often as ".•••", but it was eliminated from the dictionary for precisely this reason—almost every occurrence of a ".••" would be coded as part of ".•••".

Choosing the codes for dictionary entries involves a trade-off between compression and coding speed. Within the restriction that codes are integer-length strings of bits, Huffman codes generated from the observed frequencies of phrases will give the best compression. However, if the phrases are nearly equifrequent, then variable-length codes have little to offer, and a fixed-length code is appropriate. If the size of codes aligns with machine words, the implementation will be faster and simpler. A compromise is to use a two-level system, such as 8 bits for phrases of one character, and 16 bits for longer phrases, with the first bit of each code distinguishing between the two.

8.3 ADAPTIVE DICTIONARY ENCODERS: ZIV–LEMPEL CODING

A 1967 paper describing a semiadaptive dictionary coding technique closed with the remark that better compression could be obtained by "replacing [a] repeated string by a reference to [an] earlier occurrence." This idea was not pursued until 1977, when Jacob Ziv and Abraham Lempel described an adaptive dictionary encoder in which they "employ the concept of encoding future segments of the [input] via maximum-length copying from a buffer containing the recent past output."

Almost all practical adaptive dictionary encoders are encompassed by a family of algorithms derived from Ziv and Lempel's work. This family is called Ziv–Lempel

TABLE 8-1   DICTIONARY FORMED FROM THE BROWN CORPUS

•	•that•	9	Z	e•a	ic	na	s
••	•the•	:	{	e•o	id	nc	s•
•A	•to•	;	\	e•s	ie	nd	s,•
•S	•u	<	]	e•t	il	nd•	se
•a	•w	>	^	ea	im	ne	si
•a•	!	?	_	ec	in	ng	ss
•an	"	@	'	ed	ing	ng•	st
•and	#	A	a	ed•	ing•	ni	st•
•b	$	B	a•	ee	ir	ns	t
•be	%	C	ac	el	is	nt	t•
•c	&	D	ad	em	is•	o	ta
•co	'	E	ai	en	it	o•	te
•d	(	F	al	en•	j	of•	ter
•e	)	G	al•	ent	k	ol	th
•f	*	H	am	er	ke	on	the•
•g	+	I	an	er•	l	oo	ti
•h	,	J	an•	es	l•	or	to
•i	,•	K	and•	es•	la	os	to•
•in	-	L	ar	et	le	ou	u
•in•	.	M	as	f	li	ow	un
•is•	.•	N	at	f•	ll	p	ur
•l	.•••	O	b	g	lo	pe	us
•m	/	P	be	g•	ly	pl	v
•n	0	Q	c	ge	ly•	q	w
•o	1	R	ce	h	m	r	x
•of•	2	S	ch	h•	m•	r•	y
•of•the•	3	T	d	ha	ma	ra	y•
•p	4	U	d•	he	me	re	z
•r	5	V	de	he•	mi	re•	{
•re	6	W	di	hi	n	ri	|
•s	7	X	e	ho	n•	ro	}
•t	8	Y	e•	i	n•a	rt	~

coding, abbreviated as LZ coding.[1] The essence is that phrases are replaced with a pointer to where they have occurred earlier in the text. Figure 8-4 illustrates how well this approach works for a variety of texts by indicating some of many instances where phrases could be replaced in this manner. A phrase might be a word, part of a word, or several words. It can be replaced with a pointer as long as it has occurred once before in the text, so coding adapts quickly to a new topic. For example, the phrases "dictionary," "fact," and "Loonquawl" occur frequently in the particular examples given in Figure 8-4, yet they are not particularly common in general. In fact, the source of the third quote is probably the only place that the word "Loonquawl" has been used in the history of written English (apart from the present book!) More common words are also susceptible to this type of coding because repetitions are never far apart—examples in Figure 8-4 are the phrases "an," "integer," and "the."

[1]The reversal of the initials in the abbreviation is a historical mistake that we have chosen to perpetuate.

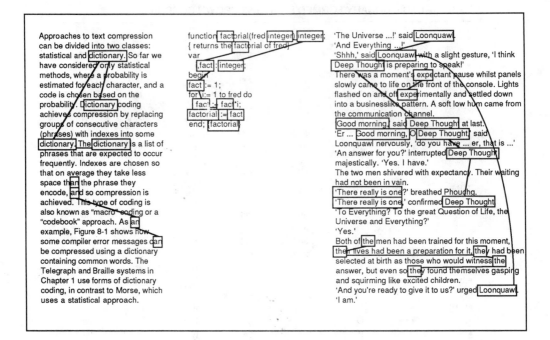

Figure 8-4   The principle of Ziv–Lempel coding—phrases are coded as pointers to earlier occurrences.

Decoding a text that has been compressed in this manner is straightforward; the decoder simply replaces a pointer by the already decoded text to which it points. In practice LZ coding achieves good compression, and an important feature is that decoding can be very fast.

One form of pointer is a pair (m,l) that represents the phrase of l characters starting at position m of the input string, that is, $\mathbf{x}[m..m+l-1]$. For example, the pointer $(7,2)$ refers to the seventh and eighth characters of the input string. Using this notation, the string "abbaabbbabab" could be coded as "abba(1,3)(3,2)(8,3)," as shown in Figure 8-5. Notice that despite the last reference being recursive, it can still be decoded unambiguously as follows. When the pointer $(8,3)$ is to be decoded, the string up to that point will have been decoded as "abbaabbba." The next two characters ("ba") are available immediately, and once they have been appended to the decoded string, the final character ("b") is now available.

It is a common misconception that LZ coding is a single, well-defined algorithm. The original LZ papers were highly theoretical, and subsequent accounts by other authors give more accessible descriptions. Because these expositions are innovative to some extent, a very blurred picture has emerged of what LZ coding really is. With so many variations on the theme, it is best described as a growing family of algorithms, with each member reflecting different design decisions. The main two factors that differ between versions of LZ coding are whether there is a limit to how far back a pointer

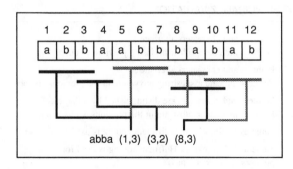

Figure 8-5   Example of Ziv–Lempel coding.

can reach, and which substrings within this limit may be the target of a pointer. The reach of a pointer into earlier text may be unrestricted (growing window), or it may be restricted to a fixed-size window of the previous N characters, where N is typically several thousand. The choice of substrings can either be unrestricted, or limited to a set of phrases chosen according to some heuristic.

Each combination of these choices represents some compromise between speed, memory requirements, and compression. The growing window offers better compression by making more substrings available. However, as the window becomes larger, the encoding may slow down because of the time taken to search for matching substrings; compression may get worse because pointers must be larger; and if memory runs out the window may have to be be discarded, giving poor compression until it grows again. A fixed-size window avoids all these problems but has fewer substrings available as targets of pointers. Within the window chosen, limiting the set of substrings that may be the target of pointers makes the pointers smaller and encoding faster. However, considerably fewer substrings are available this way than when any substring can be referenced.

We have labeled the most significant variations of LZ coding, described below, to discriminate between them. Table 8-2 summarizes the main distinguishing features. These algorithms are generally derived from one of two different approaches published by Ziv and Lempel in 1977 and 1978, labeled LZ77 and LZ78, respectively. The two approaches are quite different, although some authors have perpetuated their confusion by assuming they are the same. Labels for subsequent LZ schemes are derived from their proposers' names.

The design decisions that distinguish the LZ algorithms amount to choosing a dictionary (the substrings available for coding) and a code function (the representation of a pointer). The dictionary will change as coding proceeds but can be identified at any time during coding. It is informative to identify the dictionary for the different LZ schemes, as this crystalizes the differences, which are normally hidden in the pointers. The descriptions below identify the dictionary, M, implied by each scheme; $|M|$ is the number of phrases in the dictionary. Rather than include details of the code function $C(m)$, we give the length function $L(m)$, which is the number of bits in $C(m)$. The symbol A represents the input character set (such as ASCII), and contains q characters.

Ziv–Lempel techniques require a method to encode the components of a pointer. It is not always desirable (or even possible) to use a fixed-width binary representation

TABLE 8-2 SUMMARY OF PRINCIPAL LZ VARIATIONS

LZ77	Ziv and Lempel (1977)	Pointers and characters alternate Pointers indicate a substring in the previous N characters
LZR	Rodeh et al. (1981)	Pointers and characters alternate Pointers indicate a substring anywhere in the previous characters
LZSS	Bell (1986)	Pointers and characters are distinguished by a flag bit Pointers indicate a substring in the previous N characters
LZB	Bell (1987)	Same as LZSS, except a different coding is used for pointers
LZH	Brent (1987)	Same as LZSS, except Huffman coding is used for pointers on a second pass
LZ78	Ziv and Lempel (1978)	Pointers and characters alternate Pointers indicate a previously parsed substring
LZW	Welch (1984)	The output contains pointers only Pointers indicate a previously parsed substring Pointers are of fixed size
LZC	Thomas et al. (1985)	The output contains pointers only Pointers indicate a previously parsed substring
LZT	Tischer (1987)	Same as LZC but with phrases in a LRU list
LZMW	Miller and Wegman (1984)	Same as LZT but phrases are built by concatenating the previous two phrases
LZJ	Jakobsson (1985)	The output contains pointers only Pointers indicate a substring anywhere in the previous characters
LZFG	Fiala and Greene (1989)	Pointers select a node in a trie Strings in the trie are from a sliding window

for this, and a variety of alternative representations are available. These are collected in Appendix A. Some of the Ziv–Lempel schemes use simple codes for pointers, while others exploit the more complex ones to obtain better compression.

8.3.1 LZ77

LZ77 was the first form of LZ coding to be published (1977). In this scheme pointers denote phrases in a fixed-size window that precedes the coding position. There is a maximum length for substrings that may be replaced by a pointer, given by the parameter F (typically, 10 to 20). These restrictions allow LZ77 to be implemented using a "sliding window" of N characters. Of these, the first $N - F$ have already been encoded and the last F constitute a *lookahead buffer*. For example, if the string "abcabcbacba-babcabc..." is being encoded with the parameters $N = 11$ and $F = 4$, and character number 12 is to be encoded next, the window is as shown in Figure 8-6. Initially, the first $N - F$ characters of the window are (arbitrarily) spaces, and the first F characters of the text are loaded into the lookahead buffer.

To encode the next character, the first $N - F$ characters of the window are searched to find the longest match with the lookahead buffer. The match may overlap

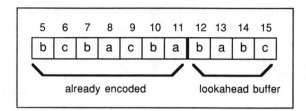

Figure 8-6   The LZ77 sliding window.

the buffer, but obviously cannot be the buffer itself. In Figure 8-6 the longest match for the "babc" is "bab", which starts at character 10.

The longest match is then coded into a triple $<i, j, a>$, where i is the offset of the longest match from the lookahead buffer, j is the length of the match, and a is the first character that did not match the substring in the window. In the example, the output triple would be $<2, 3, c>$. The window is then shifted right $j + 1$ characters, ready for another coding step. Attaching the explicit character to each pointer ensures that coding can proceed even if no match is found for the first character of the lookahead buffer.

A window of moderate size, typically $N \leq 8192$, can work well for a variety of texts for the following reasons.

- Common words and fragments of words occur regularly enough in a text to appear more than once in a window. Some English examples are "the," "of," "pre-," "-ing"; while a source program may use keywords such as "while," "if," "then."

- Specialist words tend to occur in clusters: for example, words in a paragraph on a technical topic, or local identifiers in a procedure of a source program. Examples of this from Figure 8-4 are the words "dictionary," "fact," and "Loonquawl."

- Less common words may be made up of fragments of other words. For example, in Figure 8-4 "experimentally" could be constructed from "expectant" and other suitable words.

- Runs of characters are coded compactly. For example, k spaces may be coded recursively as $<?, ?, \text{'} \bullet \text{'}> <1, k-1, ?>$, the first triple establishing the space character, and the second repeating it $k - 1$ times.

The amount of memory required for encoding and decoding is bounded by the size of the window. The offset (i) in a triple can be represented in $\lceil \log(N - F) \rceil$ bits, and the number of characters (j) covered by the triple in $\lceil \log F \rceil$ bits. The time taken at each step is bounded to $N - F$ substring comparisons, which is constant, so the time used for encoding is $O(n)$ for a text of n characters.

Decoding is very simple and fast. The decoder maintains a window in the same way as the encoder, but instead of searching it for a match it copies the match from the window using the triple given by the encoder.

Ziv and Lempel showed that LZ77 could give at least as good compression as any semiadaptive dictionary designed specifically for the string being encoded, if N is sufficiently large. This result is confirmed by intuition, since a semiadaptive scheme must include the dictionary with the coded text, while for LZ77 the dictionary and text are the same thing. The space occupied by an entry in a semiadaptive dictionary is no less than that consumed by its first (explicit) occurrence in the LZ77 coded text. This was one of the earliest indications of the promise of adaptive coding and signaled that the nonadaptive approach might not be worthy of the attention it was receiving at that time (1977).

The main disadvantage of LZ77 is that although each encoding step requires a constant amount of time, the constant can be large, and a straightforward implementation can require up to $(N-F) \times F$ character comparisons per fragment produced. As fragments are typically only a few characters in length, this represents a vast number of comparisons per character coded. This property of slow encoding and fast decoding is common to many LZ schemes. The encoding speed can be increased using data structures described in Section 8-4, but the amount of memory required also increases. This type of coding is therefore best for situations where a file is to be encoded once (preferably on a fast computer with plenty of memory) and decoded many times, possibly on a small machine. This occurs frequently in practice, for example, on-line help files, manuals, news, teletext, and electronic books.

The dictionary, M, implied by the design of LZ77, changes at each coding step. It comprises the set of strings in the window with length up to the size of the lookahead buffer, concatenated with the alphabet.[2] The code for each phrase can be viewed in two ways. As an index to the dictionary, it must select one of the $(N-F) \times F \times q$ phrases in M. As a pointer, it has three components, which specify one of $N-F$ positions in the window, a length from 0 to $F-1$, and a character from the alphabet. The length of the code works out to be the same in both cases. Formally, the dictionary and length function for LZ77 are as follows:

$$M = \{\text{every string beginning in the previous } N - F \text{ characters of length } 0$$
$$\text{to } F - 1\}.A,$$

$$L(m) = \lceil \log N - F \rceil + \lceil \log F \rceil + \lceil \log q \rceil.$$

8.3.2 LZR

LZR is the same as the LZ77 algorithm, except that it allows pointers to denote any position in the already encoded part of the text. This is the same as setting the LZ77 parameter N to exceed the size of the input text. Because the values of i and j in the $<i, j, a>$ triple can grow arbitrarily large, they are represented by a variable-length coding of the integers. The method used can be found in Appendix A-1, labeled $C_{\omega'}$. It is capable of coding any positive integer, with the length of the code growing logarithmically with the size of the number being represented. For example, the codes for 1, 8, and 16 are 0010, 10010000, and 101100000, respectively.

---

[2] By the "concatenation" of two sets we mean the set of strings obtained by concatenating each string in the first set with each string in the second.

There are drawbacks to LZR, principally because the dictionary grows without bound. First, more and more memory is required as encoding proceeds. Once the memory becomes full either no more of the input can be remembered, or the memory must be cleared and coding started from scratch. Second, the size of the text in which matches are sought increases continually. If a linear search is used, the time taken to code a text of n characters will be $O(n^2)$. Data structures have been developed to achieve coding in $O(n)$ time and $O(n)$ memory, but other LZ schemes offer similar compression to LZR for much less effort.

The coding dictionary implied by LZR at each step has

$$M = \{\text{every substring of the input seen so far}\}.A.$$

The length of the code for phrase m is a function of the position of the previous occurrence of the substring m in the input, which decreases with the distance from the coding position and increases with the length of the substring.

8.3.3 LZSS

The output of LZ77 and LZR is a series of triples, which can also be viewed as a series of strictly alternating pointers and characters. The use of the explicit character following every pointer is wasteful in practice because it could often be included as part of the next pointer. LZSS addresses this problem by using a free mixture of pointers and characters, the latter being included whenever a pointer would take more space than the characters it codes. A window of N characters is used in the same way as for LZ77, so the pointer size is fixed. Suppose that a pointer occupies the same space as p unencoded characters. The LZSS algorithm is

```
while lookahead buffer not empty do
    get a pointer (offset, length) to the longest match
                in the window for the lookahead buffer[3]
    if length > p then
        output the pointer (offset, length)
        shift window length characters
    else
        output first character in lookahead buffer
        shift window one character.
```

An extra bit is added to each pointer or character to distinguish between them, and the output is packed to eliminate unused bits.

Implementations of LZSS encoders and decoders (and other schemes that use a window) can be simplified by numbering the input text characters modulo N (Figure 8-7). The window is an array of N characters. To shift in character number r (modulo N), it is simply necessary to overwrite element r of the array, which implicitly shifts out character $r-N$ (modulo N). Instead of an offset, the first element of an (i, j) pointer can be a position in the array $(0 \cdots N-1)$. This means that i is capable of indexing

[3]The length may be zero.

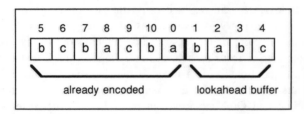

Figure 8-7 Modulo N numbering of window ($N = 11$).

substrings that start in the lookahead buffer. These F unused values of i cause negligible deterioration in the compression ratio provided that $F \ll N$, and they can be employed for special messages, such as *end of file*.

The first element of a pointer can be coded in $\lceil \log N \rceil$ bits. Because the second element can never have any of the values $0, 1, \ldots, p$, it can be coded in $\lceil \log (F - p) \rceil$ bits. Including the flag bit to distinguish pointers from characters, a pointer requires $1 + \lceil \log N \rceil + \lceil \log (F - p) \rceil$ bits. An output character requires one flag bit plus 7 bits to represent an ASCII character, a total of 8 bits. Experiments show that using $N = 8192$ and $F = 18$ typically yields good compression for a range of texts, and that the choice of N and F is not too critical.

The dictionary that LZSS uses has

$$M = A \cup \{ \text{every string beginning in the previous } N \text{ characters of length } p$$

$$\text{to } p + F - 1 \},$$

$$L(m) = \begin{cases} 1 + \lceil \log q \rceil & \text{if } m \in A \\ 1 + \lceil \log N \rceil + \lceil \log (F - p) \rceil, & \text{otherwise.} \end{cases}$$

8.3.4 LZB

Every LZSS pointer is the same size regardless of the length of the phrase it represents. In practice some phrase lengths are much more likely to occur than others, and better compression can be achieved by allowing different-sized pointers. LZB is the result of experiments that evaluated a variety of methods for encoding pointers, as well as explicit characters, and the flags that distinguish between them. It turns out that alternative codings for the characters and flags do not offer much improvement in compression, but by using a different coding for both components of a pointer, LZB achieves significantly better compression than LZSS and has the added virtue of being less sensitive to the choice of parameters.

The first component of a pointer is the location in the window of the beginning of the match. If fewer than N characters have been read from the input, it is wasteful to reserve $\log N$ bits to encode this component. Since the number of bits used is rounded up to the next higher integer, it is actually wasteful only if less that $N/2$ characters have been read. In particular, if the whole input string contains fewer than $N/2$ characters, the full capacity of a pointer is never used. LZB corrects for this by phasing in this component of the pointer using the first method described in Appendix A-2. The size starts at 1 bit until there are two characters in the window, then increases to 2 bits until the window contains four characters, and so on, until it is up to full steam with N characters in the window. In general, when encoding a substring beginning at character n, this component of the pointer can be transmitted in the minimum of $\lceil \log n \rceil$ and $\lceil \log N \rceil$ bits. With this modification, there is no penalty in compression efficiency for choosing N to be much larger than the number of characters in the input text.

LZB uses the variable-length coding scheme C_γ (explained in Appendix A-1) to code the j component of an (i, j) pointer. If the minimum number of characters represented by a pointer (i.e., minimum value of j) is p, a match of j can be coded as $\gamma(j - p + 1)$. C_γ codes $j - p + 1$ in $2 \lfloor \log(j - p + 1) \rfloor + 1$ bits. Since any length of match can be represented by this code, LZB does not impose the limit of F on the size of a match, although for practical purposes it might be helpful to restrict it to some sufficiently large ceiling, such as N.

The parameter F is no longer necessary, although a value must be obtained for p, the minimum useful match length. Although the minimum length of a pointer is $2 + k$ bits (where $k = \lceil \log n \rceil$, the current size of the first component of the pointer), suggesting that p should be $\lfloor (2 + k)/8 \rfloor + 1$ for 8-bit characters, this is not the case in practice. For example, if the smallest pointer is 15 bits and characters are 8 bits, it would appear worthwhile to encode two characters as a pointer ($p = 2$). However, if we set $p = 3$ then although character pairs may be coded using one more bit, the code for triples is shorter, and for the distribution of phrase lengths found in practice the latter choice gives slightly better compression. The best value for p must be determined by experiment, but experience has shown that it is around $\lfloor (3 + k)/8 \rfloor + 1$ for 8-bit characters, and that this value is not critical.

Figure 8-8 shows how LZB coding works for the first 12 characters of the string "ababbabbbabcaa…," with $N = 8$. For such a small window, p is always equal to 1. A pointer is represented as (i, j), where i is the location of the match (coded in binary) and j is the adjusted length of the match (coded using C_γ). The "match location" and "match length" always specify i and j, while the "output" column shows their encodings.

The dictionary that LZB is using after coding n characters has

$$M = A \cup \{\text{every string beginning in the previous } N \text{ characters of more}$$

$$\text{than } p \text{ characters}\},$$

$$L(m) = \begin{cases} 1 + \lceil \log q \rceil & \text{if } m \in A \\ 1 + \lceil \log \min(n, N) \rceil + 2 \lfloor \log |m| \rfloor + 1, & \text{otherwise.} \end{cases}$$

8.3.5 LZH

LZB uses some simple codes to represent pointers, but the best representation of pointers can only be determined from their probability distributions using arithmetic or Huffman coding. It turns out to be difficult to improve compression by applying one of these statistical coders to LZ pointers because of the cost of transmitting the codes, and in addition, the resulting scheme lacks the speed and simplicity of LZ coding.

Number of characters encoded	Input string and window	Match location	Match length	Output
0	|a b a b b a b b b a b c a a ⋯	?	0	a
1	[a] b a b b a b b b a b c a a ⋯ 0	?	0	b
2	[a][b] a b b a b b b a b c a a ⋯ 0 1	0	2	<0,001>
4	[a][b][a][b] b a b b b a b c a a ⋯ 0 1 2 3	1	4	<01,00001>
8	[a][b][a][b][b][a][b][b] b a b c a a ⋯ 0 1 2 3 4 5 6 7	4	3	<100,011>
11	a b a[b][b][a][b][b][b][a][b] c a a ⋯ 3 4 5 6 7 0 1 2	?	0	c
12	a b a b[b][a][b][b][b][a][b][c] a a ⋯ 4 5 6 7 0 1 2 3			

Figure 8-8   LZB coding of the string "ababbabbbabcaaaaa."

LZH is one of these schemes that combine the Ziv–Lempel and Huffman techniques. Coding is performed in two passes. The first is essentially the same as LZSS, while the second uses statistics measured in the first to code pointers and explicit characters using Huffman coding. This means that for LZH, the dictionary M is the same as that of LZSS, but the length function $L(m)$ is determined by Huffman's algorithm.

The difficulty is that the encoder must transmit the Huffman codes to the decoder, but there could be up to $N+F+q$ codes—typically, several thousand. LZH avoids having such a large code table by splitting the first component of pointers into two numbers (with values now ranging to the square root of N) and then using a single code table with only a few hundred entries for these two codes and the length and character codes. Considerably less space is needed for the code table, but the codes are now only approximations to the optimum since they are influenced by four different probability distributions—in fact, in practice they are not usually better than the approximate codes used by LZB.

The transmission of the code tables could be eliminated altogether with an adaptive Huffman or arithmetic code, but it is difficult to get this to work efficiently because the large range of values accentuates the zero-frequency problem. In Chapter 9 we show that LZ coders (including hybrid schemes such as LZH) can be simulated by a predictive model driving an arithmetic coder anyway, so it would be much cleaner to go directly to this type of system if statistical coding is to be employed.

8.3.6 LZ78

LZ78 is a fresh approach to adaptive dictionary compression and is important from both the theoretical and practical points of view. Instead of allowing pointers to reference any string that has appeared previously, the text seen so far is parsed into phrases, where each phrase is the longest matching phrase seen previously plus one character. Each phrase is encoded as an index to its prefix, plus the extra character. The new phrase is then added to the list of phrases that may be referenced.

For example, the string "aaabbabaabaaabab" is divided into seven phrases as shown in Figure 8-9. Each is coded as a phrase that has occurred previously, followed by an explicit character. For instance, the last three characters are coded as phrase number 4 ("ba") followed by the character "b". Phrase number 0 is the empty string.

There is no restriction on how far back a pointer may reach (i.e. no window), so more and more phrases are stored as encoding proceeds. To allow for an arbitrarily large number of them, the size of a pointer grows as more are parsed. When p phrases have been parsed, a pointer is represented in $\lceil \log p \rceil$ bits. In practice the dictionary cannot continue to grow indefinitely. When the available memory is exhausted, it is simply cleared, and coding continues as if starting on a new text.

An attractive practical feature of LZ78 is that searching can be implemented efficiently by inserting each phrase in a trie data structure. A trie is a multiway tree where the node associated with each phrase is the one at the end of the path from the root described by that phrase. Each node in the trie contains the number of the phrase it represents. The process of inserting a new phrase will yield the longest phrase previously seen, so for each input character the encoder must traverse just one arc down the trie. Figure 8-10 shows the data structure generated while parsing the string from Figure 8-9. The last phrase to be inserted was "bab", and this process has identified node 4 as the longest match and caused the creation of node 7.

An important theoretical property of LZ78 is that when the input text is generated by a stationary, ergodic source, compression is asymptotically optimal as the size of the input increases. That is, LZ78 will code an indefinitely long string in the minimum size dictated by the entropy of the source. Very few coding methods enjoy this property. Recall from Chapter 2 that a source is ergodic if any sequence it produces becomes entirely representative of the source as its length grows longer and longer. Since this is a fairly mild assumption, it would appear that LZ78 is *the* solution to the text compression problem. However, the optimality occurs as the size of the input tends to infinity, and most texts are considerably shorter than this! It relies on the size of the

Input:	a	aa	b	ba	baa	baaa	bab
Phrase number:	1	2	3	4	5	6	7
Output:	(0,a)	(1,a)	(0,b)	(3,a)	(4,a)	(5,a)	(4,b)

Figure 8-9   LZ78 coding of the string "aaabbabaabaaabab"; the notation (i,a) means copy phrase i followed by character a.

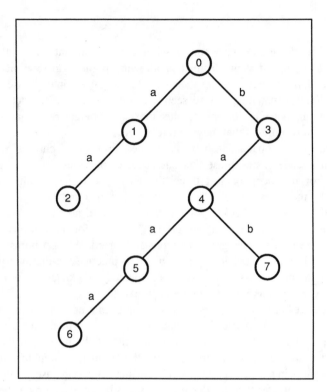

Figure 8-10   Trie data structure for LZ78
coding of Figure 8-9.

explicit character being significantly less than the size of the phrase code. Since the
former is about 8 bits, it will still be consuming 20% of the output when 2^{40} phrases
have been constructed. Even if a continuous input were available, we would run out of
memory long before compression became optimal.

The real issue is how fast LZ78 converges toward this limit. In practice
convergence is relatively slow, and performance is comparable to that of LZ77. The
reason why LZ techniques enjoy so much popularity in practice is not because they are
asymptotically optimal, but for a much more prosaic reason—that some variants lend
themselves to highly efficient implementation.

For LZ78 the dictionary has

$$M = \{\text{all phrases parsed so far}\}. A$$

$$L(m) = \lceil \log |M| \rceil + \lceil \log q \rceil.$$

8.3.7 LZW

The transition from LZ78 to LZW parallels that from LZ77 to LZSS The inclusion of
an explicit character in the output after each phrase is often wasteful. LZW manages
to eliminate these characters altogether, so that the output contains pointers only. This
is achieved by initializing the list of phrases to include every character in the input

alphabet. The last character of each new phrase is encoded as the first character of the next phrase. Figure 8-11 shows the dictionary created and the output generated for the LZW encoding of the string "aabababaaa".

In Figure 8-11 the coding of the phrase "aba" illustrates a tricky situation that arises during decoding if a phrase has been encoded using the phrase immediately preceding it. Before the "aba" string comprising the fifth unit is decoded, the dictionary contains phrases 0 to 4, and an incomplete phrase 5. It is waiting for one more character to be decoded to complete phrase 5. However, what it receives next is the code for phrase 5! Consequently, it needs to know phrase number 5 to decode that phrase because its first character must be concatenated to the phrase "ab" to construct the new one, yielding a chicken-and-egg situation trying to work out what that character is. However, things are not as bad as they look because the first and last characters of the unknown phrase must be the same in this situation, so decoding is possible provided that this special case is detected and dealt with.

LZW was originally proposed as a method of compressing data as they are written to disk, using special hardware in the disk channel. Because of the high data rate in this application it is important that compression be very fast. Transmission of pointers can be simplified, and hastened, by using a constant size of (typically) 12 bits. After 4096 phrases have been parsed, no more can be added to the list and coding becomes static. Despite this move for the sake of practicality, LZW achieves reasonable compression and is very fast for an adaptive scheme.

The dictionary used by LZW is

$$M = A \cup \{\text{the first } 4096 - q \text{ phrases parsed}\}, \qquad |M| \leq 4096$$

$$L(m) = \log 4096 = 12 \text{ bits.}$$

Input:	a	a	b	ab	aba	aa
Output:	0	0	1	3	5	2

Phrase list:

Phrase number	Phrase	Derived from phrase
0	a	initial
1	b	
2	aa	0+a
3	ab	0+b
4	ba	1+a
5	aba	3+a
6	abaa	5+a

Figure 8-11   LZW coding of the string "aabababaaa" (phrases 0 and 1 are present before coding begins).

8.3.8 LZC

LZC is the scheme used by the program "compress" available on UNIX systems. It began as an implementation of LZW and has been modified several times to achieve better and faster compression. The result is a high-performance scheme that is one of the most practical currently available.

An early modification was to return to pointers of increasing size, as in LZ78. The section of the program that manipulates pointers is coded in assembly language for efficiency. The maximum length for pointers (typically 16 bits, but less for small machines) must be given as a parameter to prevent the dictionary overflowing memory. Rather than clearing the memory when the dictionary is full, LZC monitors the compression ratio. As soon as it starts deteriorating, the dictionary is cleared and rebuilt from scratch.

The dictionary being used by LZC has

$$M = A \cup \{\text{all phrases parsed so far}\},$$

$$L(m) = \lceil \log |M| \rceil.$$

8.3.9 LZT

LZT is based on LZC. The main difference is that once the dictionary is full, space is made for new phrases by discarding the least recently used phrase (LRU replacement). This is performed efficiently by maintaining phrases in a self-organizing list indexed by a hash table. The list is designed so that a phrase can be replaced in a small, bounded number of pointer operations. Because of the extra housekeeping, this algorithm is a little slower than LZC, but the more sophisticated choice of phrases in the dictionary means that it can achieve the same compression ratio with less memory.

The LRU replacement is effectively imposing the same system as the window used by LZ77 and related schemes. When a phrase is encoded it becomes the most recently used (enters the window), and is discarded (leaves the window) only when it is the oldest one to have appeared in the input. This type of adaptation ensures that the memory available is well utilized, and it adapts well to changes in subject or style.

LZT also codes phrase numbers slightly more efficiently than LZC by using the second method of phasing the binary encoding described in Appendix A-2. (This improvement could also be applied to several other LZ algorithms.) A little extra effort is required of the encoder and decoder, but it is insignificant compared with the task of searching and maintaining the LRU list.

For LZT,

$$M = \{\text{all phrases in the self organizing list}\},$$

$$L(m) = \begin{cases} k-1 & \text{if } i < 2^k - \rho \\ k, & \text{otherwise,} \end{cases}$$

where i is the phrase number, $\rho = |M|$ and $k = \lceil \log \rho \rceil$.

8.3.10 LZMW

All of the algorithms derived from LZ78 have generated a new phrase for the dictionary by appending a single character to an existing phrase. This method of deriving a new phrase is rather arbitrary, although it certainly makes implementation simple. LZMW uses a different approach for generating dictionary entries. At each coding step a new phrase is constructed by concatenating the last two *phrases* encoded. This means that long phrases are built up quickly, although not all the prefixes of a phrase will be in the dictionary. To bound the size of the dictionary and maintain adaptivity, infrequently used phrases are discarded as for LZT. The faster phrase construction strategy of LZMW generally achieves better compression than the strategy of increasing phrases one character at a time, but a sophisticated data structure is required for efficient operation. The dictionary implied by LZMW is essentially the same as that of LZT, except for the different heuristic for selecting phrases in the dictionary.

8.3.11 LZJ

LZJ introduces a new approach to LZ coding that fills an important gap in the range of variations, as well as having the rare property that encoding is easier than decoding. This balance is valuable in situations where a text is not likely to be used again, such as backups and archives, or when a small remote device is sending data to a major facility, such as a deep space probe transmitting to earth. However, LZJ will not necessarily be the most suitable choice here because, although the encoder/decoder balance is ideal, encoding might be performed as economically by other methods.

Basically, the implied dictionary of LZJ contains every *unique* string in the previously seen text, up to a maximum length h ($h \approx 6$ works well). Each dictionary phrase is assigned a fixed-length identification number in the range 0 to $H - 1$ ($H \approx 8192$ is suitable). The character set is included in the dictionary to ensure that any string can be encoded. When the dictionary is full, it is pruned by removing *hapax legomena*, that is, substrings which have only occurred once in the input. Figure 8-12 shows an example of LZJ coding. Note that several phrases may be added to the dictionary at each coding step.

The LZJ encoder and decoder are implemented using a trie data structure to store the substrings from the already encoded part of the text (Figure 8-13). The depth of the trie is limited to h characters, and it may contain no more than H nodes. Each node has a unique number between 0 and $H - 1$. Initially, the trie contains every character in the alphabet. At each encoding step it is searched using the characters about to be encoded. When the path down the trie is blocked, the number of the last node encountered is transmitted (using $\lceil \log H \rceil$ bits), from which the decoder can deduce the path down the trie. For each *character* encoded, the substring of length h which is terminated by that character is then inserted in the trie.

This encoding step is repeated until the trie contains H nodes. At this point it is full, and it is pruned by removing all nodes that have been visited only once. Encoding proceeds, and whenever the trie becomes full, it is pruned again. Pruning will yield fewer and fewer nodes each time, until eventually coding becomes nonadaptive.

Input:	a	a	b	ab	aaba
Output:	0	0	1	3	9

Phrases:

Phrase number	Phrase
0	a
1	b
2	aa
3	ab
4	aab
5	ba
6	bab
7	aba
8	abab
9	aaba
10	baa
11	baab
12	abaa
13	baba

Figure 8-12   LZJ coding of the string "aababaaba" for $h = 4$ (the table groups phrases generated in the same coding step).

LZJ encoding has the advantage of a fixed-size output code and a fast trie data structure for encoding. However, the pruning algorithm slows down the operation considerably, and large amounts of memory are required for good compression. Experiments have shown that good compression is achieved when a few thousand nodes are available for the trie, but the best performance usually occurs when H is the same order of magnitude as the number of characters in the text being compressed.

The dictionary used by LZJ has

$$M = A \cup \{\text{every } \textit{unique} \text{ string of length 2 to } h \text{ in the previous text}\}, \qquad |M| \le H$$

$$L(m) = \log H.$$

When $|M| = H$, M is reduced by extracting *hapax legomena*.

A simple improvement to the compression (but not the speed) of LZJ is to represent the output codes using the efficient system for phasing in binary numbers (Appendix A-2). This variation is labeled LZJ'.

8.3.12 LZFG

This is one of the most practical LZ variants. It gives fast encoding and decoding, and good compression, without undue storage requirements. It is similar to LZJ in that the

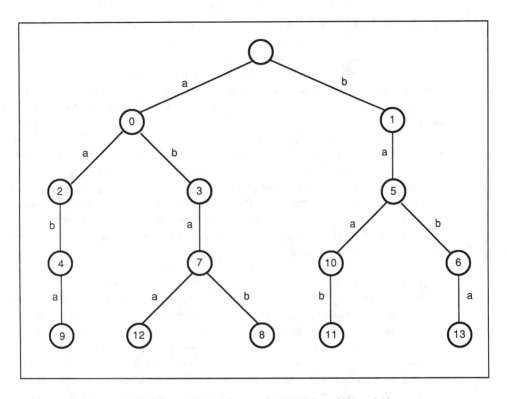

Figure 8-13   Trie data structure for LZJ coding of Figure 8-12.

waste of having two different pointers capable of encoding the same phrase is eliminated by storing the encoded text in a type of trie[4] and transmitting positions in the trie.
Of course, the decoder must maintain an identical data structure, so the resources
required for encoding and decoding are similar.

LZJ is slow because every position in the encoded text is the potential target of a
pointer, and one phrase must be inserted into the trie for every character encoded.
LZFG achieves faster compression by using the technique from LZ78, where pointers
can only start at the boundary of a previously parsed phrase. This means that one phrase
is inserted into the dictionary for every *phrase* encoded. Unlike LZ78, pointers include
an (essentially) unbounded length component to indicate how many characters of the
phrase should be copied. The encoded characters are placed in a window (in the style of
LZ77), and phrases that leave the window are deleted from the trie.

Figure 8-14 shows the LZFG data structure for a window of 25 characters that
have just been encoded as six phrases. The commas in the window indicate phrase
boundaries, although in practice these positions are determined from the trie. The data
structure is a little more sophisticated than the tries we have encountered previously.
The main difference is that each arc between nodes can represent more than one character, with a node inserted only where two strings differ. The characters are not stored

[4]It is actually a *Patricia* trie.

explicitly in the trie, but each node contains a pointer (i, j) to the window, identifying the characters on the path to the node. For example, node 3 contains the pointer (21,2) to the phrase "ab". The implicit arc labels are shown in parentheses in Figure 8-14, but are not stored explicitly in the data structure. Using this representation the arcs to leaves of the trie are able to represent an unbounded number of characters, so there need not be a restriction on match lengths. The trie contains one leaf node for each phrase in the window.

Two separate numbering systems are used to identify nodes in the trie, one for interior nodes and one for leaves. The leaves are maintained in an LRU list, with smaller numbers identifying more recently used leaves. An LZFG pointer essentially identifies a position in the trie, and this corresponds to a unique phrase. Like LZB, the coding of pointers has been fine tuned with shorter representations for more likely values. In fact, when LZFG was designed the best codes were evaluated using Huffman's algorithm, and then the most similar start–step–stop codes (see Appendix A-3) were identified and fine tuned.

LZFG employs two main methods to code a phrase: one for phrases that terminate on an arc into an internal node (coded as a "NodeCopy") and those associated with a leaf node ("LeafCopy"). The first bit of a pointer identifies which of these two codes has been used. In Figure 8-14, if the next few characters to be encoded begin "abcc...," then a NodeCopy will be used because the longest match for it in the trie is "abc", which ends one character after node 3 on the right-hand arc. A NodeCopy is encoded as two numbers (n,d), where n is the number of the node that will next be encountered after the mismatched character and d is the number of characters successfully matched down the arc into that node. In our example the pointer will be (2,1). If the match ends exactly at the node n, then d is set to zero. Both n and d are encoded using the improved binary phase-in code of Appendix A-2 [which can also be expressed as a $(k, 1,k)$ start–step–stop code as described in Appendix A-3]. It turns out that most of the time the arc into n represents only one character, and in this case there is no need to transmit d at all.

In Figure 8-14, a LeafCopy is required if the next few characters are "abcaaacb...," because the longest match ends on the arc between node 2 and leaf 3. The LeafCopy has two components, (d, l). The value l identifies the leaf node that follows the mismatch (in the example, leaf 3), and d has the same meaning as for NodeCopy, except notice that it is transmitted first. In the example the LeafCopy is (2,3). The components of a LeafCopy are coded with start–step–stop codes—d is represented by a (1,1,10) code (giving a maximum match length of 2046), and l has a (10,2,14) code phased in from (1,2,5), as described in Appendix A-3.

A LeafCopy will never use a value of zero for d, but LZFG uses this value to flag the special case where the longest match in the trie is less than two characters. After this flag a "literal" string of characters is transmitted, ending when a phrase of more than one character is encountered which can be encoded using a NodeCopy or LeafCopy. The literal is coded as a character count followed by the characters themselves. The count is represented by a (0,1,5) code. In Figure 8-14 a literal is required if the next few characters are "cacbaac...", for none of the strings starting at the first three characters prefix a phrase in the trie of more than two characters. The output would be

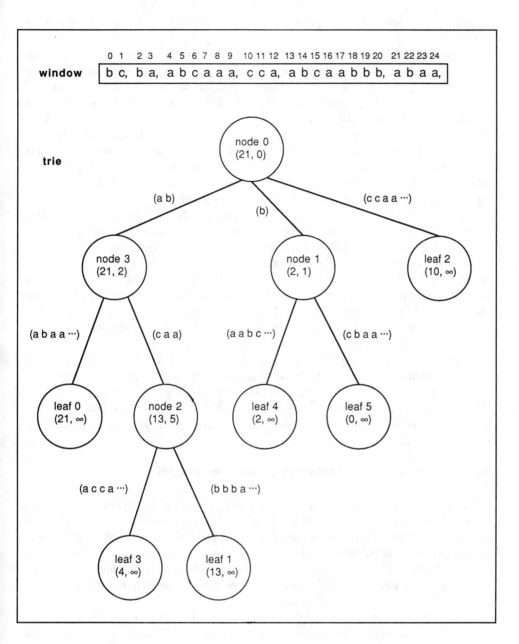

Figure 8-14   The LZFG data structure.

the number 3 followed by the characters "cac", and then the code for the phrase "baa", and so on. The (0,1,5) code for the literal length allows for literals of up to 63 charac- ters. Most of the time they will be considerably smaller than this. In this case, another literal cannot occur next, and if a LeafCopy follows immediately, its d component cannot be zero. Some extra compression is achieved by coding $d-1$ instead of d when this occurs.

After a phrase has been coded (whether as a NodeCopy, LeafCopy, or literal) the trie is updated to include it. Each literal character is inserted as it is processed, which in fact may cause the availability of a phrase to end the literal. During the search all i values in the nodes' (i, j) pointers are set to the starting position of the new phrase to ensure that they point to the most recent occurrence of their phrases. Then the arc on which the mismatch occurred is split at the last character that matched, and a new leaf is added for the new phrase. The decoder can follow suit because it knows the position of the split, and it can put in an (i, j) pointer to the new phrase even though that phrase is not yet known! The remainder of the phrase will be added to the window before the pointer might be required, so synchronization is maintained.

There are some more details to the algorithm that we have ignored. LZFG operates with a bounded amount of memory, so some maximums must be specified in advance. The maximum number of phrases in the window determines the number of leaf nodes that will be required. The maximum number of characters in the window depends on the size of phrases in it; a reasonable limit is 12 times the maximum number of phrases. If at any stage the window cannot hold all the phrases, the oldest phrases must be removed from the trie. This is expedited by maintaining an LRU list of leaf nodes. A maximum must also be placed on the number of internal nodes, and if this is reached, old phrases must be removed from the window.

The implicit dictionary M used by an LZFG encoder is easily identified to be the set of all substrings beginning at phrase boundaries (up to 2046 characters long), plus all possible literals (strings over the alphabet up to length 63). The length function is quite complex because of the variety of start–step–stop codes employed, but it can easily be determined for the phrases in any given window by constructing the corresponding trie.

8.3.13 Compression Performance of Ziv–Lempel Coding

All of the LZ schemes described above use greedy parsing, and theoretical results have been derived comparing this with optimal parsing. For example, for the LZSS scheme it has been shown that if a pointer is represented in p bits and a character in c bits, greedy parsing generates output at most $(2p-c)/p$ times that of optimal parsing. This tells us that if pointers and characters are the same size, greedy parsing is optimal, but in the more usual case where $p=2c$, the output may be 50% longer than necessary. In practice, a difference of a few percent is more typical.

In Section 8-1 we mentioned that greedy parsing is optimal for suffix dictionaries with a fixed code length. This applies to the LZ77 and LZJ schemes, and also to LZSS if pointers are the same size as characters. It may be satisfying to know that these compression schemes use optimal parsing, but it is not necessarily worthwhile to manipulate the dictionary to achieve this situation. For example, LZ77 and LZSS (with $p=2c$) use similar dictionaries but different output representations. Theory shows that LZ77 uses optimal parsing and that LZSS may use 50% more space than optimal, yet LZSS invariably outperforms LZ77 in practice.

A practical comparison of the LZ schemes for encoding a variety of texts is given in Chapter 9. The best compression is generally achieved by LZFG. The speed of encoding and decoding depends on the implementation, and the next section suggests some suitable data structures to obtain good performance.

8.4 DATA STRUCTURES FOR DICTIONARY CODING

All the practical compression schemes described above use greedy parsing, and in the majority of cases the most time-consuming task is finding the longest match in the dictionary for the next few characters of input. Each decoding step usually requires only a table lookup to find the string identified by a pointer or index. Here we will look at some data structures that can perform the encoding step efficiently. Data structures for locating *exact* matches, such as search trees and hash tables, are well known, and it transpires that these can be adapted to locate the *longest* matches needed for encoding.

The most demanding dictionary compression schemes are those that are adaptive, use a window, and allow pointers to reference anywhere in the window (LZ77, LZSS, LZB, and LZH). A new potential starting point for a longest match is introduced with each input character entering the window. Potential starting points are removed at the same rate as characters leaving the window. The data structures given below apply to this situation, but can be adapted for other forms of dictionary coding. For further details the reader should consult a book on algorithms and data structures.

8.4.1 Unsorted List

A trivial way to find a longest match is to perform a linear search of the text in the window. Since the window has a fixed size, the time this algorithm takes to find a longest match is independent of the size of the text; furthermore, it requires relatively little memory. However, the approach is slow since a window of N characters requires at least N character comparisons. Speed can be increased by maintaining a suitable index for the window using one of the following more sophisticated data structures, although in general the more efficient the index, the more memory that is consumed.

8.4.2 Sorted List

Suppose that a string l is inserted at its correct position in a sorted list, and it falls between the strings x_a and x_b. Then the longest match for l in the list will be a prefix of either x_a or x_b. Figure 8-15 shows a sorted list that corresponds to the window of Figure 8-7. It contains an entry for all strings of four characters in the window (which is the maximum length of a match). The string in the lookahead buffer, $l =$"babc", has just been inserted between $x_a =$"baba" and $x_b =$"bacb", and we can see that the longest match for the inserted string is "bab", the prefix of x_a. Finding the point of insertion can be achieved by a binary search, using about $\log N$ substring comparisons, but insertion and deletion require $O(N)$ operations.

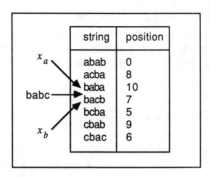

Figure 8-15   The longest match in a sorted list.

8.4.3 Binary Tree

It is possible to use a binary search tree to find x_a and x_b, making the insertion and deletion of substrings more efficient than for the list. Figure 8-16 shows a binary tree containing the strings of the previous example. When the string "babc" is inserted, the two longest match candidates will be on the path from the root to the point of insertion.

This can be proved for the general case by considering the situation after l has been inserted. If x_a is not on the path to l, then l and x_a must have at least one common ancestor. If x_p is the most recent common ancestor, it must have x_a in its left subtree and l in its right subtree, which implies that $x_a < x_p < l$. This is a contradiction because x_a and l are adjacent, so x_a must be on the path to l. A similar argument shows that x_b must be, too. It follows that either x_a or x_b will be the parent of l, and the other candidate for the longest match is found using the rule (see Figure 8-17):

> If x_a is the parent of l, then x_b is the node where the insertion path last turned left; otherwise, x_a is the node where the insertion path last turned right.

To index a window of N characters, the tree contains at most N nodes. This simplifies implementation because the nodes for the tree can be drawn from an array of length N,

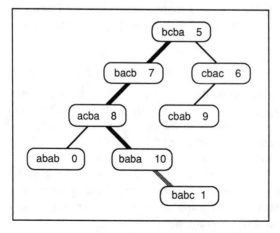

Figure 8-16   Using a binary tree to find the longest match.

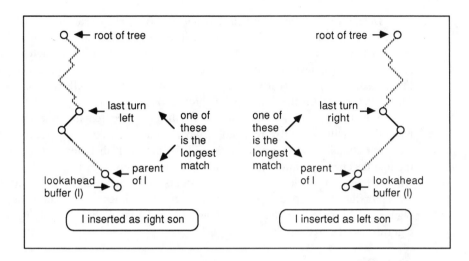

Figure 8-17   Using a binary tree to find a longest match in the general case.

whose *i*th element stores the string at position *i* in the window. A node need only store the position in the window of the string it represents, rather than the string itself. In fact, there is no need to store even this, because the position of the string in the window is the same as the corresponding node's index in the array, so each node need only contain the two pointers to its children.

Figure 8-18 shows the resulting data structure for the tree of Figure 8-16. It comprises two arrays: the window of *N* characters, and an array of *N* nodes. Each node contains pointers (two children and one parent) to other nodes. The parent node is included to provide efficient deletion, as follows.

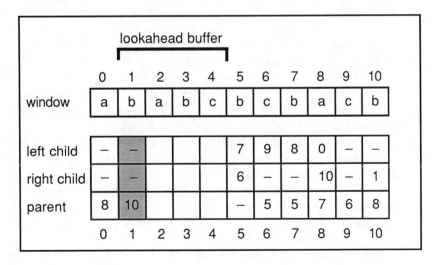

Figure 8-18   Using two arrays to implement the tree of Figure 8-16.

Deletion in a binary tree is traditionally performed by searching for the node to be deleted and then adjusting the tree around it. Because the node representing the string at position i can be located directly at element i of the tree array, there is no need to search the tree. However, because deletion requires access to the parent of the node to be deleted, each node must store a pointer to its parent, as well as to its two children. This is the reason for the third, "parent" row in Figure 8-18.

Sometimes it is necessary to ensure that the tree remains reasonably balanced. Natural text will generally create a fairly balanced tree without any special effort, but if the input contains too many regularities, it is important that steps are taken to prevent the tree degenerating into a linked list. A binary tree gives particularly bad performance when a long run of identical characters occurs in the input and phrases are inserted in the order that they appear. This can be prevented either by permuting the order that phrases are inserted in the tree, by using a splay tree, or by applying a balancing algorithm to the tree.

8.4.4 Trie

A trie, or digital search tree, is a multiway tree with a path from the root to a unique node for each string represented in the tree. Figure 8-19 gives an example of a trie indexing a window. Note that only the unique prefix of each string is stored, as the suffix can be determined by looking up the string in the window. A longest match is found by following down the tree until no match is found, or the path ends at a leaf. As with the binary tree algorithm, the longest match can be found at the same time as inserting a new string.

There are many ways to implement the nodes of a trie. Some were discussed in Chapter 6 with regard to context modeling; here we outline methods relevant to dictionary coding. The fastest approach is to create an array of pointers for each node in the trie, with one pointer for each character of the input alphabet (Figure 8-20a). Unfortunately, this can waste considerable space, particularly if some characters of the alphabet are rarely used. An alternative is to use a linked list at each node, with one item for each possible branch (Figure 8-20b). This uses memory economically, but can be slower because of the time taken to search the list. Some improvement may be achieved by moving an item to the front of the list each time it is used. The design of nodes in the trie is rapidly turning into a subproblem in searching, and we might even consider using a binary tree or a hash table to implement each node.

A trie can also be implemented as a single hash table with an entry for each node. To determine the location of the child of the node at location n in the table for input character c, the hash function is supplied with both n and c. This algorithm is used successfully by the program "compress" (LZC). The memory consumed by a trie can be reduced by truncating it prematurely at a shallow depth, and using some other data structure for subsequent characters. Also, a chain of nodes will frequently have only one child, and such nodes can be collapsed into one, as in Figure 8-21. The resulting data structure is sometimes referred to as a *Patricia* tree (Practical Algorithm To Retrieve

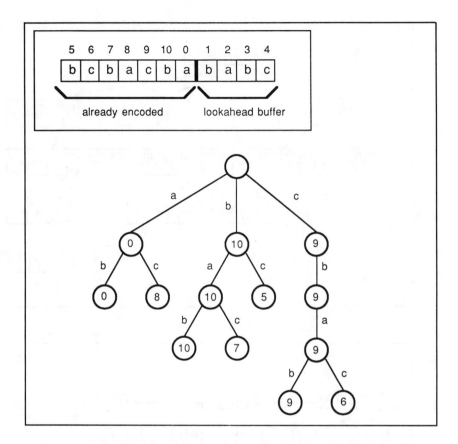

Figure 8-19   Using a trie to find a longest match.

Information Coded In Alphanumeric). The description of LZFG includes details of a more advanced implementation of this type of structure.

As more and more strings are inserted in a trie, the time to process each increases. There is a data structure called a position (or prefix) tree, which by maintaining suitable auxiliary data structures for the trie is able to perform insertions in constant time regardless of the amount of input. However, although position trees have been suggested for text compression applications, they are rather complicated and do not appear to be used in practice.

8.4.5 Hash Table

Hash tables are normally associated with exact matches. It is possible to use them to find longest matches if all prefixes of each substring are inserted in the hash table. Then to find the longest match of the string $\mathbf{x}$, we first test whether $\mathbf{x}[1]$ is in the table, then $\mathbf{x}[1..2]$, then $\mathbf{x}[1..3]$, and so on. If $\mathbf{x}[1..i + 1]$ is the first such string not found, the

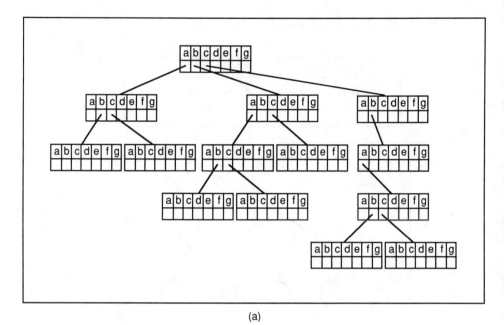

(a)

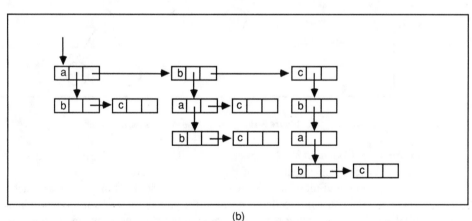

(b)

Figure 8-20   Implementations of trie nodes for Figure 8-19: (a) array; (b) linked list.

longest match must be $\mathbf{x}[1..i]$. This approach is really equivalent to the implementation of a trie using a single hash table, mentioned above.

It is often the case that there is a minimum length that a substring must be before it will be used as a match, typically about two characters. In this case a hash table could be used to index all strings with the same first two characters, and some other search could be used to check subsequent characters. An extreme case of this which avoids any hashing collisions is to have a slot for every possible pair of characters. If the input alphabet contains q characters, then q^2 slots would be required.

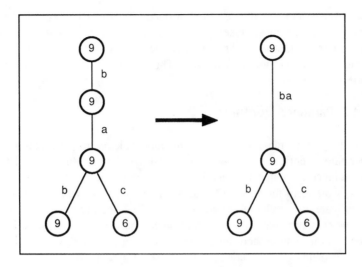

Figure 8-21   Collapsing a trie.

8.4.6 Coping With Data Structures Where Deletion Is Difficult

One of the major difficulties presented by LZ schemes which use a window is that strings leaving the window must be deleted from the data structure which indexes it, and deletion is not always simple for structures such as hash tables and position trees. One solution is to maintain several indexes to the window. Each one covers blocks of N characters, and these blocks overlap so that the characters in any window of size N are in no more than three indexes. Figure 8-22 shows a window covered by indexes number 2, 3, and 4. Characters are added to the one or two relevant indexes when they enter the window. An index is discarded when none of its characters are in the window, so at

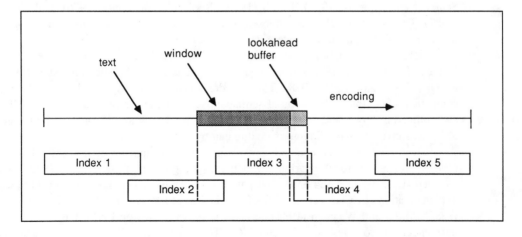

Figure 8-22   Using several indexes to achieve deletion.

most three indexes must be stored at once. To find a longest match in the window, the
first two indexes must be searched (the overlapping ensures that the third index is useful
only after the first is discarded). A probe into the first index must be careful to ignore
strings no longer in the window. The better of the matches produced by the two
indexes is chosen.

8.4.7 Parallel Algorithms

The longest match problem is quite amenable to multiprocessor implementation, as
there are essentially N independent matchings to be evaluated. A different processor can
be assigned to perform comparisons for each of the N characters in the window. These
processors form the leaves of a binary tree containing a further $N - 1$ processors, which
coordinate the results of the comparisons. The average time taken to encode each input
character is essentially the time for one comparison, plus $O(\log N)$ time for communication to propagate up and down the tree of processors. Other parallel algorithms can be
used, depending on the layout and number of processors available.

NOTES

Figure 8-1 is from Wagner (1973). The use of shortest paths for optimal parsing was
proposed by Schuegraf and Heaps (1974). The most practical optimal parsing algorithm
is by Katajainen and Raita (1987a), which includes the bounded buffer approximation.
Other optimal algorithms are given by Wagner (1973), Rubin (1976), and Storer and
Szymanski (1982). The LFF parsing is due to Schuegraf and Heaps (1974). Theoretical
comparisons of parsing techniques can be found in Storer and Szymanski (1982),
Gonzalez-Smith and Storer (1985), and Katajainen and Raita (1987b).

    Digram coding techniques have been suggested by Snyderman and Hunt (1970),
Schieber and Thomas (1971), Jewell (1976), Bookstein and Fouty (1976), and Cortesi
(1982). The use of vowels was proposed by Svanks (1975). The static n-gram scheme is
that of Pike (1981); a similar system has been proposed by Tropper (1981).

    Heuristics for building semiadaptive dictionaries are given by White (1967),
Schuegraf and Heaps (1973), Wagner (1973), Lynch (1973), Mayne and James (1975),
Rubin (1976), and Wolff (1978). The one described is from Lynch (1973). The NP-
completeness of finding the optimal semiadaptive dictionary is proved in Storer (1977)
and outlined in Storer and Szymanski (1982). Further discussion of some of the theoretical issues involved with dictionary coding can be found in Storer (1988).

    The prophetic remark about Ziv–Lempel coding appears at the end of White
(1967). References for the various LZ schemes are given in Table 8-2. LZ78 has been
patented (U.S. patent 4,464,650). The patent includes details of software and hardware
implementation. LZC is version 4.0 of the UNIX utility *compress*, by Thomas et al.
(1985). Miller and Wegman (1984) describe three variations on LZ78; the first two are
independent discoveries of LZW and LZT. The third is LZMW, and an efficient data

structure to implement it is given. LZFG is algorithm C2 from Fiala and Greene (1989); it has been patented (U.S. patent applied for).

The use of sorted lists and binary trees for finding a longest match is from Bell (1986). Algorithms using hashing can be found in Thomas et al. (1985) and Brent (1987). An adaptation of position trees is given by Rodeh et. al. (1981). A more practical use of position trees is described by Fiala and Greene (1989). The method for avoiding deletion using three indexes was proposed by Rodeh et. al. (1981). Parallel algorithms for data compression are given by Gonzalez-Smith and Storer (1985). More general information on algorithms and data structures is available in Aho et al. (1983) and Knuth (1973).

CHOOSING
YOUR WEAPON

From the preceding chapters it is clear that a great variety of methods are available to compress text. But which compression scheme is the best? Are any fundamentally superior to others? Is there a relationship between the dictionary and statistical approaches? This chapter contains many comparisons that answer these questions. However, comparing two compression schemes is not as simple as finding the one that yields better compression. Even leaving aside the conditions under which compression is measured—the kind of text, the questions of adaptivity and versatility in dealing with different genres—there are many other factors to consider, such as how much memory and time is needed to perform the compression. The task of evaluation is compounded because these factors must be considered for both encoding and decoding, and they may depend on the type of text being compressed.

A competition was held in Australia early in 1988 with the object of finding the "best" text compression program. A prize of $30,000 was offered for the program that obtained the greatest data reduction over an undisclosed set of test files. The main restrictions were that it had to run faster than 1 Kbyte/min on a personal computer, with around 1/2 Mbyte of memory available for the program to use. Some 50 programs were entered in the competition, ranging from ad hoc contrivances to variations of Ziv–Lempel coding, and PPM modeling driving an arithmetic coder. It took 4 months for the organizers to evaluate all the different methods, highlighting the difficulty of comparing compression schemes. In the end, the prize was split between two entries which both used PPM models—which in fact agrees with the conclusion of this chapter.

This chapter compares compression schemes from several points of view in order to show the different strengths and weaknesses of the methods. Section 9-1 shows how the two main approaches to compression—statistical and dictionary coding—can be compared by recasting a dictionary algorithm as a statistical model. Then, in contrast to looking at the methods of constructing models, Section 9-2 offers unusual insight into the quality of the models built by different methods by using them "backwards" to *generate* text rather than code it. The main part of the chapter is Section 9-3, which evaluates the practical performance of all the significant schemes described in this book by observing the compression achieved for a variety of files, and measuring speed and memory requirements. Section 9-4 looks at how the compression of some adaptive schemes varies as encoding proceeds and how quickly they form an accurate model of the input. In Section 9-5 we conclude by discussing some considerations that arise in practical implementations of text compression.

9.1 DICTIONARY CODING VERSUS STATISTICAL CODING

Within the two main classes of dictionary and statistical coding it is possible to discern those schemes that are likely to give the best compression. For dictionary coding we favor methods that use larger, sensibly chosen dictionaries, and for statistical coding, those that use long, specific contexts for prediction. Comparing dictionary coding with statistical coding is difficult without practical experiments because two fundamentally different paradigms are involved. Nevertheless, principled comparison between the two classes is in fact possible. This is because of the remarkable fact that an algorithm exists which takes a greedy dictionary scheme and generates a predictive model that achieves exactly the same compression as the dictionary scheme. The contexts used for prediction can then be compared with those used by statistical schemes. A consequence of this is that it is always possible to design a statistical coder which compresses as well as any greedy dictionary coder (although it may be slower), and so it follows that the greedy dictionary coding paradigm cannot be more powerful than the statistical coding one. Of course, a dictionary coder need not use greedy parsing, but it is clear from Chapter 8 that this is by far the most practical approach.

Before giving the general algorithm for converting a dictionary coder to a statistical model, here is an example to illustrate what is involved. Consider a digram coder (Section 8-2) with the set of digrams chosen as the product of the sets { •,a,e,i,n,o,t,u} and { •,e,t,a,o,n,r,i,s,h,d,l,f,c,m,u}. This generates a dictionary of 8 × 16 = 128 digrams. With an 8-bit representation, 128 codes can be allocated to the digrams, and the remaining 128 to individual characters. At each compression step, if the next pair of input characters is one of the chosen digrams, it is coded in 8 bits; otherwise, the next single character is coded in 8 bits. Figure 9-1 shows an example of this.

Figure 9-2 shows a two-state model designed to give the same compression as the digram scheme. The example of Figure 9-1 is coded using the new model to illustrate how this is achieved. Each character on the same transition is allocated the same

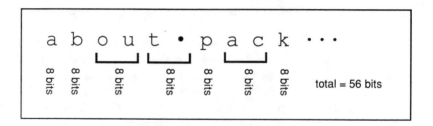

Figure 9-1   Digram coding.

probability. The probabilities in the model drive an arithmetic coder, so a character with probability p will be coded in $-\log p$ bits. Coding begins in state 1 of the model, and from here, characters that cannot begin a digram are coded in 8 bits ($-\log 1/256$). A character that *can* begin a digram is coded in 3.96 bits ($-\log 33/512$). In this case, we move to state 2, and the coding of the next character depends on whether or not it could be the second character of a digram. If it could, it is coded in 4.04 bits ($-\log 2/33$), otherwise in 12.04 bits ($-\log 1/4224$). In either case, we return to state 1. Consequently, there are two paths that can be followed on an excursion to state 2, and either way two characters are coded. In the first case, where the two characters correspond to a dictionary digram, a total of 8 (3.96 + 4.04) bits are consumed, while in the second, 16 (3.96 + 12.04) bits are used. Either way, the length of the output is exactly the same as it would be for digram coding.

This finite-state model may not be as practical as the original digram coder, but it has theoretical significance which can be generalized into a result that applies to all greedy dictionary encoders. First note that the model is very simple, with only two contexts, so it has little predictive power—which explains why digram coding is not very effective. Second, recall that the digram coder often looks at the next *two* characters before generating a code for the first. The finite-state model has decomposed the digram codes into single character codes, so it never has to "look ahead." Because of this, the statistical model is sometimes called the *symbol-wise equivalent* of the original digram model.

Finally, the probabilities in the decomposed model do not cover the entire code space. For example, state 1 has 120 transitions with probability 1/256, and 8 with probability 33/512. The total code space consumed is 504/512, so the unused space of 8/512 could be distributed among the transitions, decreasing the code lengths. The reason for the waste is that the original digram scheme has codes that are never used; there were codes available to represent the two characters in each digram as two single, explicit characters. For example, the phrase "aa" could be coded in 8 bits as a digram, or in 16 bits as two characters. Of course, the former option is always chosen, so the latter code is never used. This redundancy is easily removed from the finite-state model, but not from the original dictionary scheme.

The remainder of this section gives a general algorithm that can generate a symbol-wise finite-state model for *any* dictionary coder, provided that the coder uses greedy parsing. The inputs to the algorithm are the set M of strings in the dictionary,

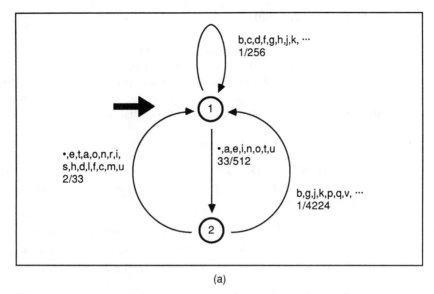

(a)

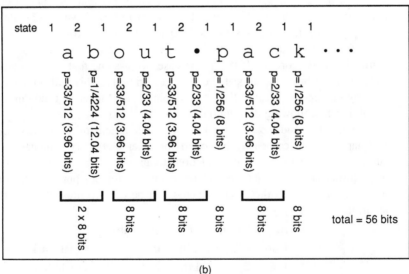

(b)

Figure 9-2   (a) A state model that is equivalent to digram coding; (b) example coding.

and the function L(m), the length of the code allocated to the string $m \in M$. The output of the algorithm is a finite-state model that can be used to supply probabilities to an arithmetic coder, and achieves exactly the same compression as the original dictionary coder. The description of the algorithm and its proof of correctness is necessarily formal, and the reader may be content to skip the remainder of this section and take our word that greedy dictionary coding cannot outperform statistical coding.

9.1.1 General Algorithm

Recall from Chapter 8 that greedy dictionary coding maps a set of strings M onto a set of codes by the function $C(m)$, $m \in M$. The function $L(m)$ is the length of $C(m)$ in bits. For any string m we define the amount of code space allocated to it, $R(m)$, to be the probability of m that is implied by the length of its code. Code space is related to code length by the entropy formula $L(m) = -\log R(m)$, that is,

$$R(m) = 2^{-L(m)}.$$

The three functions C, L, and R can be extended recursively to the set of strings in M^*. If the greedy algorithm parses the prefix u from the string $u.v$, $u \in M$, $v \in M^*$, and Λ is the empty string, define

$$C(\Lambda) = \Lambda, \quad C(u.v) = C(u).C(v) \qquad \text{(concatenation of codes)}$$
$$L(\Lambda) = 0, \quad L(u.v) = L(u) + L(v) \qquad \text{(addition of code lengths)}$$
$$R(\Lambda) = 1, \quad R(u.v) = R(u) \times R(v) \qquad \text{(multiplication of code spaces).}$$

For the encoding to be uniquely decodable, the total amount of code space must not exceed unity, that is, $\Sigma\, R(m) \leq 1$. In what follows it will be assumed that the dictionary scheme fully utilizes the code space, so that $\Sigma\, R(m) = 1$. For some schemes, $\Sigma\, R(m) < 1$ (e.g., a Ziv–Lempel scheme with 12-bit pointers but fewer than 4096 entries in the dictionary). If this is the case, we assume that an extra artificial phrase is added to M to bring the allocated code space to unity. This will not alter the code space used by the scheme because the artificial phrase will never be used during coding, but it simplifies the following descriptions.

The set M and the function $L(m)$ were identified for all the Ziv–Lempel schemes in Chapter 8 and can easily be found for other dictionary schemes. M and $L(m)$ are sufficient for the following construction because they abstract the information relevant to performance analysis and are of more interest for our purposes than $C(m)$. The following simple greedy dictionary scheme will be used to illustrate how the construction algorithm works.

$$A \quad = \{a,b\}, \quad M \quad = \{a,b,aab\},$$
$$C(a) = 01, \quad C(b) = 00, \qquad C(aab) = 1,$$
$$L(a) = 2, \quad L(b) = 2, \qquad L(aab) = 1,$$
$$R(a) = \tfrac{1}{4}, \quad R(b) = \tfrac{1}{4}, \qquad R(aab) = \tfrac{1}{2}.$$

Recall that greedy parsing is assumed throughout, so there is no ambiguity in parsing a string like "aab".

A finite-state machine will be constructed, with set of states S, input alphabet A, transition function μ, and starting state s_0. Its basis is a directed multiway tree (a trie) that is formed by adding transitions from the root for each string $s \in M$ (Figure 9-3). Each node is a state, labeled by its path from the root. The root itself is labeled with the empty string Λ and is the initial state s_0. At this stage S contains a node labeled with every prefix of strings in M, including the strings themselves. When the machine is

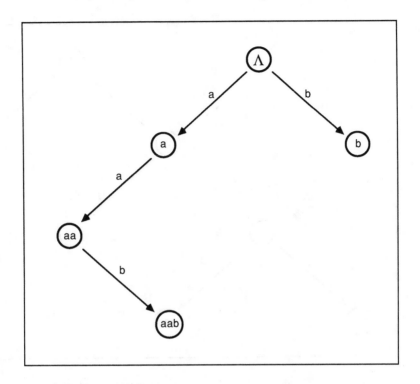

Figure 9-3   A directed multiway tree for the example dictionary scheme.

complete, the label of each state will turn out to be a context which uniquely identifies that state.

We now ensure that every nonleaf node has a transition for each character in the alphabet. For each nonleaf node $s \in S$, with a transition on $x \in A$ not yet defined, add a new leaf node, $s.x$, to S, and the transition $\mu(s, x) = s.x$ (Figure 9-4). Next, it is necessary to add some "escape" transitions. For each leaf node s, define u to be the longest prefix of s uniquely parsed by the greedy algorithm. The choice of leaf nodes ensures that $|u| > 0$, because a leaf node is never a proper prefix of a string in M. Let t be the remaining part of s, so that $s = u.t$. Add the escape transition $\mu(s, <\text{esc}>) = t$ to each leaf node (Figure 9-5). Note that u may be a succession of several words from the vocabulary, while t cannot be parsed without more information about what follows.

Each node s is assigned code space $P(s)$, to allow for each transition out of s (Table 9-1). $P(s)$ is defined to be the code space assigned by the function R to all infinitely long strings from M^* with s as a prefix. Although the sum is infinite, it can be evaluated in a finite amount of time, as illustrated by the following example. Consider the evaluation of $P(aa)$ for the example scheme. The only infinite strings in M^* with "aa" as a prefix are those of the form "aab.v_k", "a.aab.v_k", or "a.a.v_k", where v_k is any string in M^*. The total code space allocated to these three forms is obtained by multiplying the code space of the phrases in a string, and summing over each possible string, giving

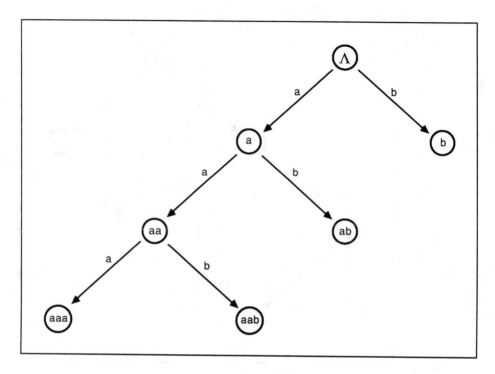

Figure 9-4   Addition of transitions from nonleaf nodes.

$$P(aa) = R(aab)\sum_k R(v_k) + R(a)R(aab)\sum_k R(v_k) + R(a)R(a)\sum_k R(v_k).$$

Because $\Sigma\, R(v_k)$ is the code space allocated to all strings, it is unity, so

$$P(aa) = R(aab) + R(a)R(aab) + R(a)R(a) = \frac{1}{2} + \frac{1}{4}\cdot\frac{1}{2} + \frac{1}{4}\cdot\frac{1}{4} = \frac{11}{16}.$$

For the general case, the function $P(s)$ can be calculated recursively in finite time by the following algorithm.

```
function P(s):
  P := 0
  for each m ∈ M do
    if s is a prefix of m (including s = m), m = s.v,
      P := P + R(m)
    else if m is a prefix of s, s = m.v,
      P := P + R(m) · P(v).
```

$P(s)$ allows space for every string beginning with s that might follow. By definition, $P(\Lambda) = \Sigma\, R(m) = 1$. Table 9-1 gives the function P for the example scheme.

In the machine, every nonleaf node $s \in S$ has a transition for every $x \in A$, $\mu(s,x) = s.\,x$. Each of these transitions is assigned code space using

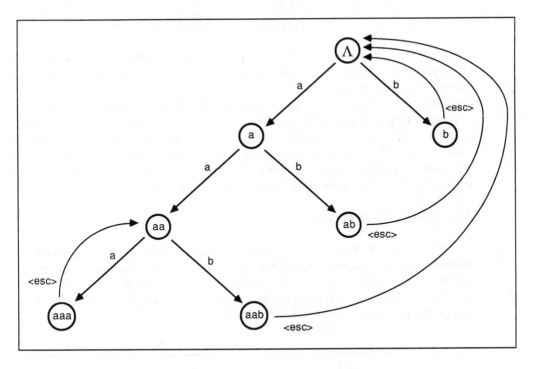

Figure 9-5   Addition of escape transitions.

$$P(x \mid s) \doteq \frac{P(s.\,x)}{P(s)}.$$

Every leaf node $s \in S$ has only one outgoing transition, $\mu(s, <\text{esc}>) = t$, and this transition is assigned the code space

TABLE 9-1   ALLOCATION
OF CODE SPACE TO NODES
FOR EXAMPLE SCHEME

$P(\Lambda)$	1
$P(a)$	$\frac{3}{4}$
$P(aa)$	$\frac{11}{16}$
$P(aaa)$	$\frac{11}{64}$
$P(aab)$	$\frac{33}{64}$
$P(ab)$	$\frac{1}{16}$
$P(b)$	$\frac{1}{4}$

$$P(<esc>|s) = \frac{R(u)P(t)}{P(s)},$$

where $s = u.t$ and u is the longest prefix parsed from s by the greedy algorithm. The machine is now complete (Figure 9-6). A proof that this algorithm works for the general case will be given shortly.

Note that the construction above does not allow the set M to change during encoding, except in special cases. This means that for the LZ schemes, where the vocabulary is adaptive, the existence of a statistical equivalent can only be shown independently for each coding step. Whether the general machine can be re-structured to accommodate incremental adaptation is still unknown, although this has been done for the specific cases of LZ77 and LZ78, and the other LZ schemes are closely related to these two.

9.1.2 Proof of Equivalence

To demonstrate that the code space used by the machine is the same as that used by the original dictionary scheme, consider coding the string $\mathbf{x}[1..n]$. The idea of the proof is that if u is the first string that the greedy algorithm would parse from $\mathbf{x}$, then the machine will code $\mathbf{x}$ in $L(u)$ more bits than it codes $\mathbf{x}$ with the prefix u removed. Induction on this result leads to the desired equivalence.

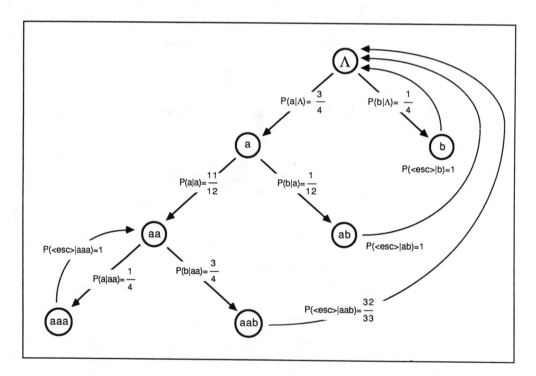

Figure 9-6   The final automaton with transition probabilities.

When coding **x**, the machine follows transitions down the tree from the root until a leaf node is reached, say at character $\mathbf{x}[\,j]$. The transitions followed are

$$\mu(\Lambda, \mathbf{x}[1]) = \mathbf{x}[1], \quad \mu(\mathbf{x}[1], \mathbf{x}[2]) = \mathbf{x}[1..2], \quad \ldots, \quad \mu(\mathbf{x}[1..j-1], \mathbf{x}[\,j]) = \mathbf{x}[1..j].$$

At this point the transition $\mu(\mathbf{x}[1..j], <\text{esc}>) = t$ is taken, where $\mathbf{x}[1..j] = u.t$, and u is the longest prefix of $\mathbf{x}[1..j]$ parsed by the greedy algorithm. Now let $u = \mathbf{x}[1..i]$ and $t = \mathbf{x}[i+1..j]$. Recall that the choice of leaf nodes ensures that $|u| > 0$. The code space used by the transitions up to the point immediately before encoding $\mathbf{x}[\,j+1]$ is

$$P(\mathbf{x}[1]\,|\,\Lambda)\,P(\mathbf{x}[2]\,|\,\mathbf{x}[1])\,P(\mathbf{x}[3]\,|\,\mathbf{x}[1..2]) \cdots P(\mathbf{x}[\,j]\,|\,\mathbf{x}[1..j-1])\,P(<\text{esc}>\,|\,\mathbf{x}[1..j])$$

$$= \frac{P(\mathbf{x}[1])}{P(\Lambda)} \cdot \frac{P(\mathbf{x}[1..2])}{P(\mathbf{x}[1])} \cdot \frac{P(\mathbf{x}[1..3])}{P(\mathbf{x}[1..2])} \cdots \frac{P(\mathbf{x}[1..j])}{P(\mathbf{x}[1..j-1])} \cdot \frac{R(u)P(t)}{P(\mathbf{x}[1..j])}$$

$$= R(u)P(t).$$

Now consider the action of the machine encoding the string **x**, but with the prefix u removed, in other words, the string $\mathbf{x}[i+1..j..n]$. Immediately after the character $\mathbf{x}[\,j]$ is encountered, it is in state $t\ (= \mathbf{x}[i+1..j])$, and the code space used is

$$\frac{P(\mathbf{x}[i+1])}{P(\Lambda)} \cdot \frac{P(\mathbf{x}[i+1..i+2])}{P(\mathbf{x}[i+1])} \cdots \frac{P(\mathbf{x}[i+1..j])}{P(\mathbf{x}[i+1..j-1])} = P(t).$$

In other words, the machine will be in the same state whether it had coded $u.t$ or t, but in the former case will consume the extra code space $R(u)$, which is the same as the code space allocated by the dictionary scheme to the prefix u. This means that the output contains $L(u)$ more bits. Encoding proceeds for the remainder of **x** in a similar manner, parsing off prefixes and moving to an appropriate state to allow for the delay in recognizing parsed phrases.

9.1.3 Equivalent Statistical Compression

The main consequence of the existence of the algorithm just presented is that a decomposed greedy dictionary coding method can be regarded as a statistical encoder whose probabilities are conditioned on differing amounts of prior context. The probabilities used for coding are the code spaces associated with transitions. (The arithmetic coding technique guarantees that these probabilities can be used for coding in a way that preserves the original code lengths.) The contexts used to condition these probabilities are the labels associated with the relevant states. For each input character the current state moves down the tree, determining a longer context for encoding the next character. The escape character resets the machine to a shorter context when a leaf is reached and there is no longer context in the tree.

In the finite-state model, the context normally increases by one character for each character encoded, but is periodically reset to a smaller context. For example, in Figure 9-6, the string "aaba" would have successive predictions based on the contexts Λ, "a", and "aa". Then the context reverts to Λ, completely removing all contextual information. There is no attempt to maximize the context used to predict *each* character, so the greedy dictionary approach is inferior to that of statistical modeling techniques such as PPM and DMC, which seek the longest reasonable context available in their model to encode each character.

To illustrate how the task of looking ahead to determine the encoding is implemented in symbol-wise fashion, follow the action of the machine of Figure 9-6 with the input string "aaaaaaab". After the first two "a"s are encountered the machine cycles on subsequent "a"s, giving each "a" a code space of 1/4 (2 bits) until the "b" is encountered. Thus the encoder effectively associates the first two "a"s with the final "b" to encode the phrase "aab".

Notice that as for the digram example presented earlier, the transitions out of each node will not necessarily use all of the code space—interpreted statistically, the probabilities do not sum to 1. This is because the original scheme may contain redundant codes. For example, the scheme used to illustrate the construction algorithm will never code the sequence "aab" as C(a).C(a).C(b), which accounts for the unused code space out of node "aab" in the machine.

The algorithm to generate a symbol-wise equivalent is quite general and applies to any modification to dictionary schemes as long as greedy parsing is retained. For example, the list of variations on Ziv–Lempel coding will probably continue to grow, but since greedy parsing is essential to the efficiency of this type of coding, symbol-wise equivalents will still exist.

The converse of the result above, that any statistical scheme can be simulated by an equivalent dictionary scheme, is well established but does not generally lead to practical algorithms. An equivalent dictionary scheme is generated using "blocking," where the dictionary vocabulary contains many large phrases (blocks). As the size of these blocks increases, the coding rate approaches the entropy of a statistical model, given a suitable choice of codes. For example, the coding rate of LZ78 asymptotically approaches the source entropy under quite general conditions. Unfortunately, in practice the phrases must be very large, leading to unwieldy dictionaries and large coding delays. Even if the compressor has seen more text than has been written throughout the history of the human race, the amount of compression will still be a significant distance from the asymptote. Thus the symbol by symbol statistical approach is more attractive.

We conclude that, in principle, statistical and greedy dictionary schemes are equivalent in their potential for compression performance. However, in practice, superior compression will more easily be achieved by statistical schemes. In particular, the compression achieved by dictionary schemes suffers because of the loss of context at phrase boundaries. The advantage of dictionary encoding schemes is usually their high speed and modest memory required to achieve a reasonable rate of compression.

9.2 LOOKING INSIDE MODELS

It should be clear by now that the essence of good compression is to construct a good model for the text being compressed. A multitude of modeling algorithms have been presented, and in the preceding section we were able to compare the quality of the construction techniques employed by different algorithms. What really counts, of course, is the quality of the models that a particular method builds in practice. For example, if English text is being compressed, the question is how well a particular model reflects the rules of English. Unfortunately, the models generated are usually so large and complex that to look at all the rules embodied in them would be prohibitively time consuming, and besides, there is no really well-defined set of "rules for English" to compare the model with.

However, there is a way to obtain a "feel" for how good a model is, and that is to *generate* text based on the rules it contains, in the same way that we examined "random" text from the finite-context models in Chapter 4. For example, to produce text from a DMC state model, one simply moves among states by following transitions randomly according to their probabilities. As each transition is followed, the symbol that labels it is added to the output.

The same effect could be achieved with a decoder that has created a model (presumably by decompressing a text) by sending it random bits. This ties in with the idea that the output of a perfect compressor should be completely random (if this is not the case, there is an opportunity for further compression). Consequently, in the ideal case, random input to the decompressor will generate sensible output, since the coding should treat meaningless text as highly improbable! For models that are less than ideal, the more the output resembles the style of text being modeled, the better the model is. Creativity in the output is also of merit, for a model that simply reproduces the input text is not very powerful in general, despite its high-quality output!

As an example of a very poor model, here is some text generated using the digram coding scheme described at the beginning of Section 9-1.

>QiuilpZtsuhif=ec8 rCuuun sueii7m nafoataeoanocos{SeaFYu

noafnf;6utecmOtr 0oot ictftltn{ilaeaeN fBltsoaistdAetlHarat3ututeibFtih

otu7bcna?orvylufooSntHefeo lohuuicasLopLF5ahaoncilRn nu mYetaie

ioatoctromocncuaFnf{}ad ganmiles?gntiuodod+@bUonk<au%uuernrw

oid9imI*utuoih@ueioictl]@olru in$toeaneof!Qic.haaW3Koa2nrvoi

ovno'oi9tcm4af0un2faluia m>4?Fic tndj c l6oiie)nro celufRi_e

Although it bears little resemblance to English, it is considerably better than completely random text, for about two-thirds of the characters are parts of digrams, which in turn are constructed from the 16 most common characters. The low quality of the output corresponds to the relatively poor compression achieved by digram coding.

To generate text using adaptive schemes, a model must first be created using some representative English text. For this the Brown corpus was used, so that the outputs can be compared with those in Chapter 4. The size of the corpus usually meant that memory was exhausted before it had all been read; in this case the remaining text was ignored. About 4 megabytes of memory were available, so the models formed were very large.

Here is some text generated by the DAFC model described in Section 6-3.

Halincas iny ort wangonetouridasharsthe patived. selar ad byetleed os ce
tisel, ace his tharidicutet prabof ill rareposh wad aiede bes n
anombenedowonshethe d Pt thay. ", Ie thatrasitol wasutoonged pre peshe
isin ma Dpalz4 bus>ivereass ontesthen ttive y. w re tilsslin ast <; e stour
hearen ac ft e Ioff C5ureille, ewace tonged ad KHeme aleas as C& inse a
beedobe th itoue purinishidoutiadesis. Be L0omepelind. onk. erstherecr "I
pliton t chere.

The resemblance to English is considerably greater than in the previous excerpt, but it is
not very striking because DAFC is based on an order-1 model only. (The fact that it
superficially resembles a cross between Welsh and Icelandic is probably entirely coin-
cidental.)

The next excerpt was generated by a DMC model (Section 7-3) with 312,579
states.

Soos of chos of joint performine the wonse in the 192:   Minion.
Incoughavatems, by he at their lleappption. The mediff DELELD
BUNuence-evight bries/ The sales tax politest a ht 4-:   The supich he
addtion gttorouble time.   Bepartment payuron that the brax syear. "weary,
hoth setturomportative rever deleventugh spon innedy saustrate.

The resemblance to English has increased from DAFC. Sentences now begin with capital letters, and small phrases such as "sales tax" have been picked up. Comparing it to
the random samples in Chapter 4, it appears to resemble the order-2 text, indicating that
the model has picked up information of this order.

Next, some text generated by a PPMA model (Section 6-3).

substiclear immed and Statutiven which cal objecting has because, of
theygrought days statesmily proxico won to commission on youndays?
Morse, upons of that in 1959, 55,000, whichards homah Thur.), diffens of
the good-1960.   His cons took sligation publin in that meet, to is eace in
home ching imp}.   Bue.   Memocration the minianages witteen the
Besidently not in fromothe come been her Kored day, the mations is a such.

It appears to be of similar quality to the preceding excerpt, indicating that the two
methods are comparable. This ties in with the proof in Section 7-4 that DMC uses a
finite-context model similar to PPM.

To represent the LZ schemes, we used LZC (Section 8-3-8) to generate text. This
was done by constructing a list of 385,152 phrases from the input. Since each phrase is
coded by a pointer of the same length, they are all equally likely, so generating text
amounts to choosing phrases at random. This procedure underlines the loss of context at
phrase boundaries, because while individual phrases may be sensible, there is no relationship between consecutive phrases. Clearly, the resemblance to English will increase
as phrases become arbitrarily long, and this reflects the optimality of this type of coding
in the limit—as the input grows, the average phrase's length increases, and therefore the

random text will contain longer and longer excerpts from the input. Here is some text generated using the LZC model.

> nd desa privn grater who slectorswell. Ind reacdsuere actuaand lefeasness
> that evisi, watcf chanarent issionedne partdemande disceintelligentYEDlso
> sp the Holys yourkolovume less whMervnside ofed, wo he'en
> dismunning,ied in DISn termvoices.n adved steffaxactly eonstrher letruits,
> lla sATHncey Decinjoyment t, then, your igequestionsidationhat the Aing
> jetn, Mrability

Despite the sophisticated modeling techniques and large tracts of memory consumed, none of the texts reproduced above could be construed as lucid fragments of written English! This indicates that there is still plenty of room for improvement in modeling methods.

9.3 PRACTICAL COMPARISONS

The practical performance measure for a text compression scheme that strikes one first is the amount of compression it achieves. However, there are other factors that are important in practice—namely, the amount of time and memory used by the encoding and decoding algorithms. It is necessary to ensure that the requirements of the compression program do not exceed the capacity of the host machine, and that the expenditure of resources is justified by the expected savings.

What is more, the resources available may be different for encoding and decoding. In a system where news is distributed electronically it might be reasonable to expend a lot of effort compressing the news once, but the decoding process should be simple, as it will be performed at many different sites, possibly on small machines. This situation contrasts with a file backup program, where many files will be backed up, but (we hope!) they will rarely be accessed after that. When compressing such files the encoding should be fast, but it does not matter so much if decoding is slow.

It is difficult to present a definitive practical comparison of different compression methods because of the large range of variable factors. All aspects of performance (i.e., compression, speed, and memory) depend on the type and size of the text being compressed. Moreover, each of these three aspects is interdependent; if more memory is available for modeling, better compression will usually result; on the other hand, if a model consumes too much memory (perhaps because of a search tree), space might be saved by using a more compact model representation (possibly requiring a linear search), with a concomitant decrease in speed. Apart from the choice of data structure, the trade-off between compression, speed, and memory is usually determined by the choice of parameters for a scheme, such as window size (for Ziv–Lempel coding) or maximum context size (for context modeling). In this section we examine the trade-off for some of the better schemes and present comparative results from practical implementations.

9.3.1 Measuring Compression

The inevitable question that is asked about a compression scheme is: What compression does it achieve? Unfortunately, this has no simple answer. In an extreme case where the input text is random, compression simply cannot be done. On the other hand, there will be texts that can be compressed by a remarkable factor: for example, a file of 1 million "a"s. For this reason, claims such as "our method has reduced the size of files by up to 98%" are of little consequence.

If the *type* of text being compressed is specified, results are more meaningful. In Chapter 4 we observed many features that are shared by different English texts, despite having different authors. Some simple examples are that the most common letter in most texts is "e" and that the average length of words is usually about 4.5 letters; more complex ones are the detailed distributions of letters, groups of letters, and words—and it is these that are used to achieve compression. The remarkable consistency between texts means that a scheme can be expected to achieve similar compression for two different English texts (of the same length), so it is reasonable to quote the performance of a scheme for, say, "English text." Another consequence of this is that if one scheme consistently outperforms another for a few texts, it is likely to be better for most other texts of the same type. Of course, it may be difficult to decide if two texts are the same type because of the many formats in which English text can be stored on a computer. One text might contain detailed typesetting commands, while another might be completely in upper case with no punctuation. Or one might contain tab characters, while in another these may be represented as multiple consecutive spaces—as might be expected, this can make a dramatic difference to compressibility.

9.3.2 The Schemes

Every significant compression method described in this book has been evaluated on the corpus of Appendix B. The methods are listed in Table 9-2. The Ziv–Lempel schemes are heavily represented because a wide range of variations has been published; all share the idea of replacing phrases with a pointer to where they have occurred earlier in the text. They are divided into two families: those derived from LZ77 and those from LZ78. The main distinction is that the first type uses pointers with two components to select a string and specify its length, whereas pointers in the second family contain just one integer which identifies a string previously parsed from the input. All of these schemes are described in Chapter 8 and their main features are summarized in Table 8-2.

The third family in Table 9-2 comprises the statistical coders, which are based on the modeling/coding paradigm. Huffman coding is generally used with an order-0 model, and is represented by the adaptive scheme labeled HUFF. The other statistical schemes use arithmetic coding. DAFC, DMC, PPMC, and WORD employ forms of finite-context modeling. MTF uses the "bookstack" model described in Chapter 1, but it has been set up to code the position in the stack as efficiently as possible by having an adaptive order-0 model driving an arithmetic coder. Other events, such as new words, are coded from their own adaptive order-0 models. This achieves better compression

TABLE 9-2   COMPRESSION SCHEMES AND PARAMETERS USED IN EXPERIMENTS

Family	Scheme	Described in Section:	Parameters used for experiments	
LZ77	LZ77	8-3-1	$N = 8192$	characters in window
(Ziv–Lempel)			$F = 16$	maximum length of match
	LZR	8-3-2	–	unbounded memory
	LZSS	8-3-3	$N = 8192$	characters in window
			$F = 18$	maximum length of match
	LZB	8-3-4	$N = 8192$	characters in window
			$p = 4$	determines minimum length of match
	LZH	8-3-5	$N = 16384$	characters in window
	LZJ'	8-3-11	$H = 8192$	nodes in trie
			$h = 6$	maximum length of match
LZ78	LZ78	8-3-6	–	unbounded memory
(Ziv–Lempel)	LZW	8-3-7	$M = 4096$	maximum phrases in dictionary
	LZC	8-3-8	$M = 4096$	maximum phrases in dictionary
	LZT	8-3-9	$M = 4096$	maximum phrases in dictionary
	LZMW	8-3-10	$M = 4096$	maximum phrases in dictionary
	LZFG	8-3-12	$M = 4096$	maximum phrases in dictionary
statistical	HUFF	5-3-1	–	no parameters
	DAFC	6-3	contexts = 32	number of order-1 contexts
			threshold = 50	occurrences before character becomes a context
	PPMC	6-3	$m = 3$	maximum size of context
				unbounded memory
	WORD	6-3	–	no parameters
	DMC	7-3	$t = 1$	prerequisite transitions on current path for cloning
			$T = 8$	prerequisite transitions on other paths for cloning
	MTF	1-3-7	$size = 2500$	number of words in list

than the simple codes suggested for MTF in Chapter 1, but we shall see that even with all this improvement it cannot compete with other models.

9.3.3 Parameters for the Schemes

Most compression schemes require one or two parameters that must be selected before compression is performed. For the experiments below, parameters have been chosen to give good compression without using an inordinate amount of memory or time. The resulting values are shown in Table 9-2.

For the LZ77 family the main parameter is the size of the window on the text. In general, compression is best if the window is as large as possible (but no bigger than the text itself!) Nevertheless, larger windows yield diminishing returns, and a window as small as 8000 characters will often perform nearly as well as much bigger ones. An advantage of keeping the window small is that encoding is faster (unless a complex data structure such as a position tree is being used). Some of the LZ77 family require a second parameter which limits the number of characters that a pointer can represent. A limit of around 16 generally works well; if it is smaller, two pointers may be needed where one would have sufficed; if it is larger, the capacity of the pointer will often be wasted. For the experiments, most of the LZ77 family were given just 8 Kbytes of storage, except that the LZH scheme was given 16 Kbytes because the coding of pointers was designed for a window of this size. Since LZJ′ always outperforms LZJ, only results for the former are given.

Most of the LZ78 family require one parameter to specify the maximum number of phrases that can be stored. This determines the amount of memory required. The speed is not usually affected by the number of phrases stored because a constant amount of effort is expended for each character encoded. A limit of 4096 phrases was used for these schemes. Slightly better compression can often be achieved with larger lists, but this size translates into an amount of memory comparable to the 8-Kbyte windows of the LZ77 family.

The parameters for the statistical schemes govern how quickly the models adapt, as well as how sophisticated they can become. The two parameters for DAFC specify the memory size in terms of the number of order-1 contexts to allow for and how quickly to choose the contexts. The two parameters for DMC determine how quickly the model grows. More precisely, they specify how often a target state must have been visited before it may be cloned. The first parameter, t, is the minimum number of visits from the current state, and the second, T, is the minimum number of visits from states other than the current one. The optimal values are usually around 1 and 8, respectively, indicating that states should be cloned readily, provided that they have been visited a few times from different contexts. Slightly higher values for the parameters give better compression for the non-ASCII files, indicating that adaptation should be curbed because DMC could not detect so much structure in them.

PPMC has one parameter, which limits the number of characters in the context used for prediction. If the limit is too low, only small contexts will be used, but if it is too high, PPMC will expend code space escaping to smaller contexts (and waste a lot of memory). A maximum context of three or four characters is usually best for ASCII files, but for the others, a value of 1 can be better, indicating that PPMC had the same difficulty as DMC in detecting structure in those files.

The MTF scheme requires a limit on the number of distinct words in the list, principally to bound the memory requirement. A limit of 2500 words was used, since a list this size is large enough to hold a high proportion of words that occur more than a couple of times in a text.

The parameters that have been chosen for the experiments are nearly optimal for a variety of texts, and fortunately the amount of compression achieved rarely seems to be overly sensitive to the exact parameter values. Little research has been performed to determine how parameters should be chosen, and an area that particularly needs exploration is how they might be varied as coding proceeds. If compression is important and speed is not, a file (or sample of it) might even be compressed with a variety of parameters to determine which is best for that particular text.

9.3.4 Compression Experiments

There are several ways to measure the amount of compression achieved in an experiment, and each is widely used. If a text of 1000 8-bit ASCII characters is compressed to 250 bytes, this could be expressed as a compression ratio of 25% (or 0.25), a reduction of 75%, a factor of 4:1, or even a ratio of 28.57% (since ASCII only uses 7 out of each 8 bits in the original file). We prefer yet another measure, which is a rate of 2 bits per character (bits/char), since this depends less on the format of the original file. Also, it is the common unit of entropy, generated when calculations are based on character probabilities and logarithms are to base 2. If characters are stored in 8-bit bytes, then 4 bits/char is a saving of half the space, and 0 bits/char is ideal! In the case of the binary files, the compression is measured in bits/byte.

The saving obtained in practice will not always correspond to the amount of compression achieved in our experiments if the space for the data being stored or transmitted is allocated in blocks. For example, if disk blocks contain 1024 bytes, then compressing an 800-byte file will achieve nothing; it still consumes one block. On the other hand, reducing a 1025-byte file by only one byte will halve the disk requirement of 2048 bytes!

To evaluate the 18 schemes in Table 9-2, we compressed each of the 14 files in Figure B-1 (Appendix B) with each scheme. Because of the large amount of data generated, the results are organized as a tournament. In the first round the best of each of the three families (LZ77, LZ78 and statistical) are determined, and these three winners are compared in a final.

Figure 9-7 compares the performance of the LZ77 family.[1] The schemes are shown in the order of the average compression that they achieve. Most of the files have been compressed to a little less than half their original size, with the exception of the non-ASCII files—"geo" is particularly hard to compress, while "pic" can be condensed to under 25% of its original size. For a given type of file each scheme is quite consistent in amount of compression and relative ranking. For example, the graphs for "paper1" and "paper2" are about the same height and have a similar shape.

Most of the schemes have been evaluated with only 8-Kbyte windows, with the exception of LZR (which was unbounded) and LZH (16 Kbytes). Despite these head starts, LZB gives the best compression for 12 of the 14 files and has the best average. It is surprising that LZB outperforms LZH because the main difference is that LZH generates an optimal Huffman code for pointers, while LZB uses a fixed code. It seems that the cost of transmitting the Huffman code is greater than the inefficiency of the fixed code. Another surprise is the performance of LZR—this scheme is optimal for a sufficiently large input, and uses far more memory than the others, yet it gives the worst performance. The test files are too short for it to achieve good compression, but for larger files, correspondingly more storage would be required.

LZB was designed as an improvement of LZSS, which in turn was an improvement of LZ77. Figure 9-7 shows that the design decisions are justified because LZB is consistently better than LZSS, and likewise for LZSS and LZ77 (except for the file

---

[1]The values plotted here are given in Appendix B, Table B-1.

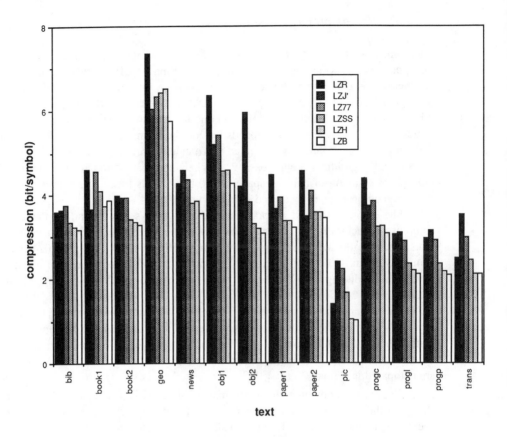

Figure 9-7   Compression performance of the LZ77 family.

"geo"). Overall, LZB gives the best performance and will represent the LZ77 family in the final of the tournament.

Figure 9-8 shows the compression performance of the LZ78 family. Again, most of the ASCII files are compressed to just less than half of their original size, and the amount of compression and ranking is consistent within each file type. All schemes have a maximum of 4096 phrases, except for LZ78, which has no limit. Like LZR, the unbounded memory and theoretical optimality of LZ78 are not reflected in impressive practical performance.

The LZW scheme ceases adaptation after 4096 phrases have been built up, and the weakness of this approach is dramatically exposed in the coding of "obj2", where the initial part of the file is not representative of the remainder and compression actually expands the file by 25%! LZT improves on LZW by adapting continuously, and Figure 9-8 shows how this pays off in practice. LZMW is a refinement of LZT, constructing phrases more rapidly. The results demonstrate the value of this improvement. The best performance of the LZ78 family is achieved by LZFG, which, like the best scheme in the LZ77 family, uses carefully selected codes to represent pointers.

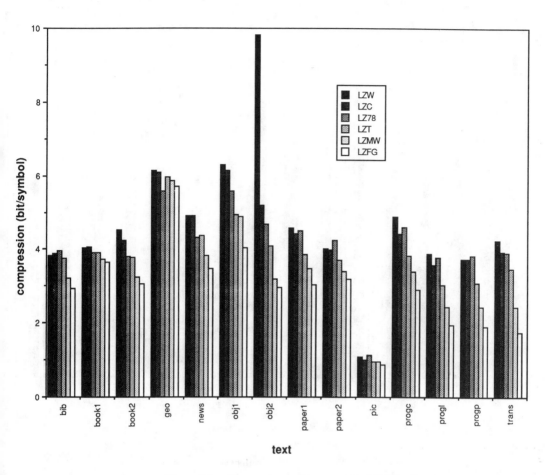

Figure 9-8   Compression performance of the LZ78 family.

The statistical family of compression methods gives a greater range of compression performance (Figure 9-9), which correlates with their sophistication—the more complex the model, the better the compression. The "geo" file provides the only exception because a simple model captures its main features adequately.

The HUFF scheme uses a simple order-0 model, requiring only a few hundreds of bytes of memory, and consequently gives poor compression performance. DAFC is a little more sophisticated, with order-1 contexts being used frequently, yielding better results than HUFF.

The remaining four schemes build considerably more complex models, and this generally leads to much better compression. The MTF method is best suited to English and other languages because it breaks the text up into words. However, it works quite well on other files because then it spends most of its time transmitting new words with a simple character model, and this model happens to work well for those files. Nevertheless, MTF does not perform as well as WORD, which also breaks the input

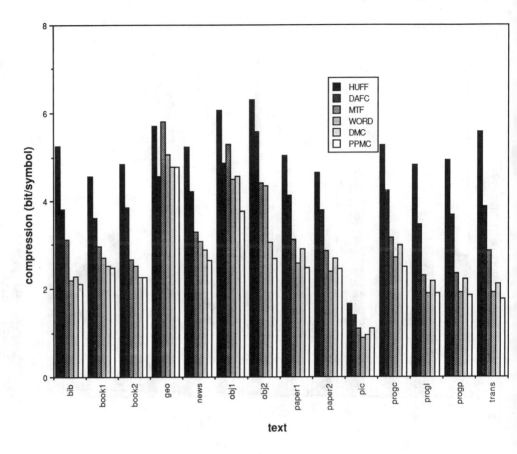

Figure 9-9 Compression performance of the statistical family.

into words, but maintains an order-1 model of the words. The MTF approach is really an ad hoc method of assigning order-0 probabilities to words, and is less efficient than the more principled approach of WORD.

The overall performance of WORD, DMC, and PPMC is very similar, with PPMC achieving the best average compression. Not surprisingly, WORD did well on the files containing language, and works satisfactorily on other files for the same reason that MTF does. The similarity of the results for PPMC and DMC confirm that they are using similar models, as discussed in Section 7-4.

An interesting feature of the "geo" file is that every fourth byte is almost always a zero. This is known as a counting event, which is discussed in Section 7-1. It can be captured by a state model, but not by a context model. Since all of the schemes here use context models, the feature is not exploited. This can be verified by generating random text from the models built for "geo", after the style of Section 9-2. Then zero bytes occur in random positions with no bias to every fourth one.

Figure 9-10 shows the "final" of our tournament with the best scheme from each of the three families. PPMC almost always achieves the best compression, and this is to

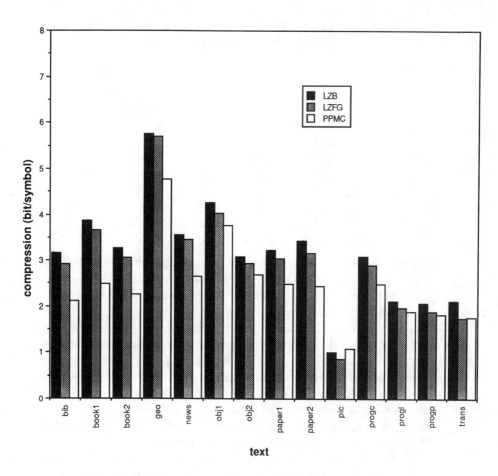

Figure 9-10 Compression performance of the best of the three families.

be expected in the light of the comparison in Section 9-1. Nevertheless, LZFG and, to a lesser extent, LZB are competitive, and consume considerably less time and memory than PPMC. Also, their performance can be improved by allowing more memory for coding. In the next section we examine the resource requirements of the different schemes, and how compression, speed, and memory are related.

9.3.5 Speed and Storage

Some methods give significantly better compression than others, but they usually require more resources to achieve this. In this section we look at the memory and time required by the better performers to illustrate the costs involved. A careful implementation may prove more economical than is indicated here, so the figures should be used only as a rough guide.

The resources required by the better compression schemes are summarized in Table 9-3. Speeds are given for coding the 769-Kbyte file "book1" on a 1-MIP

TABLE 9-3   RESOURCE REQUIREMENTS OF SOME
COMPRESSION SCHEMES FOR "book1"

Scheme	Memory (Kbytes)		Speed (characters per second)	
	Encoding	Decoding	Encoding	Decoding
PPMC	500	500	2,000	2,000
WORD	500	500	3,000	3,000
DMC	5,000	5,000	1,000	1,000
LZFG	186	130	6,000	11,000
LZB	64	8	600	16,000

machine (in fact, a VAX 11/780). Of the statistical schemes, PPMC and WORD give excellent compression for a moderate cost. In comparison, DMC appears to be particularly uneconomical. The amount of storage consumed could be reduced with little impact on compression, but the speed is harder to improve. The poor performance is caused by the use of bits as the fundamental unit of input. Although the operations on each transition in the model are quite simple, there is one transition for every input bit. The algorithm could just as well be implemented for characters rather than bits, but a more sophisticated data structure would then be required to represent nodes economically. The WORD scheme is a little faster than PPM for the opposite reason that DMC is slower—it is using words as a fundamental unit, so for English each coding step is dealing with about 5.5 characters on average. PPMC′ would be about twice as fast as PPMC, but does not give quite such good compression.

While encoding and decoding consume similar resources in the statistical methods, the Ziv–Lempel schemes offer a different balance. LZFG is a lot faster, and requires less memory, especially for decoding. For LZB, decoding is particularly cheap, but encoding is slow. The figures given here are for an implementation of LZB in which a binary tree is used to perform searching during encoding; only 8 Kbytes of memory is required to encode using a simple linear search, but the speed will decrease by an order of magnitude.

The speeds given in Table 9-3 are for English text. They will often be different for other types of input. The effect is most dramatic for files that are easy to compress, such as "pic". If PPMC is obtaining good compression, it will be using higher-order contexts more often. Since it is the high-order context that is evaluated first, compression will be faster in this situation. DMC also runs faster if the input is very predictable because fewer cloning operations occur. The LZ78 family is a little faster because fewer phrases are created during compression. In contrast, the LZ77 family can be significantly slower if the search technique is fairly simple, because many strings will have common prefixes. The binary tree searching algorithm is particularly sensitive to this, and methods to prevent poor performance are discussed in Section 8-4.

All the schemes in Table 9-2 are capable of working with different amounts of memory, and making more available will almost always improve compression. Figure 9-11 illustrates the trade-off between storage and compression for PPMC, LZB, and LZFG, again using the English text file "book1". In this case, when PPMC ran out of memory the model was cleared and rebuilt starting with the previous 2048 characters. For PPMC the storage is required for nodes of the trie; for LZB it is the size of the window. The LZB encoder is shown with more memory than the decoder because it uses a tree to search for longest matches. Because the model for PPMC grows so rapidly it is impractical for small amounts of memory. In contrast, LZB is able to work in a very small space—with only 512 bytes of memory it achieves compression as good as the HUFF scheme. After 8 Kbytes any extra memory yields little improvement, although some is always achieved until the amount of memory equals the size of the input. The performance of LZFG for a given amount of memory is very similar to that of LZB, but encoding is faster and decoding is slower. PPMC is slower than the LZ schemes, but it makes better use of the available memory and its compression continues to improve as larger models can be constructed.

In general, PPMC is appropriate when plenty of memory is available and if a coding speed of around 2000 characters per second is fast enough. Suitable situations include data transmission over slow-to-medium-speed channels, and file compression that can be performed at a low priority. If PPMC is too slow, LZFG offers more speed and almost as much compression given a similar amount of memory. LZB is suitable if

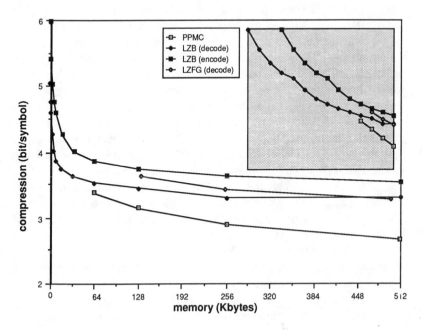

Figure 9-11   Compression performance against memory for PPMC, LZB, and LZFG (inset shows same curves plotted with a logarithmic horizontal axis).

decoding must be particularly efficient—either when the same file is to be decoded many times, or when decoding is to be performed on a small machine.

9.4 CONVERGENCE

Adaptive compression schemes improve their models as coding proceeds, so we would expect compression to be a lot better at the end of a file than at the beginning. Until now we have only measured the average compression for entire files, but it is interesting to examine how compression improves during coding. This will indicate how compression performance depends on the length of the input, and show the value of constructing larger and larger models. Also, some schemes (most notably LZ78 and LZR) are known to achieve compression converging on the entropy of an ergodic source, as the size of the input increases. This is sometimes taken to mean that the scheme is optimal, but we shall see that the convergence is far too slow to be of benefit in practice.

In this section three adaptive schemes are considered that can build large models: LZ78, DMC, and PPMA.[2] The convergence of these is plotted for two types of input —English text (the file "book1") and an artificially generated file with known entropy. The compression is measured after each 5000 characters of input, and over those 5000 characters only. The compression given in the preceding section is the average of all these "instantaneous" values; toward the beginning of encoding the instantaneous compression will usually be worse than the average, but at the end it will be better.

Figure 9-12 shows how compression varies while encoding the file "book1" with LZ78, DMC, and PPMA. All were given unlimited memory, so their models continued to grow throughout. It is clear that better compression is achieved as the models become larger, although the most dramatic improvement is at the beginning. There is considerable variation in compression for consecutive blocks of 5000 characters, reflected by the jagged lines. The peaks generally correspond to unusual language in the text, such as colloquial conversation in an otherwise formal book. The similarity in the shapes of the three curves indicates that all methods had difficulty with the same parts of the text, reinforcing the observations in Sections 7-4 and 9-1 that they are exploiting the same features of text to achieve compression. It also confirms that the ranking of schemes on one text is likely to be valid for other texts of similar type.

The slow convergence of LZ78 is strikingly illustrated in Figure 9-12. The entropy of English is certainly well under 3 bits/char, yet a sample much larger than the 770,000 characters provided would be needed to reach this figure. DMC and PPMA achieve it after just 30,000 characters.

The similarity between DMC and PPM is shown in Figure 9-12 by how closely their two curves follow each other. The main difference is that while PPM is a little better initially, it is overtaken by DMC at the end. This is most probably because DMC can represent arbitrarily large contexts in its model, suggesting that PPM will perform better if the maximum prediction context is increased during coding.

---

[2]PPMA is used here because PPMC's periodic halving of counts interferes with convergence.

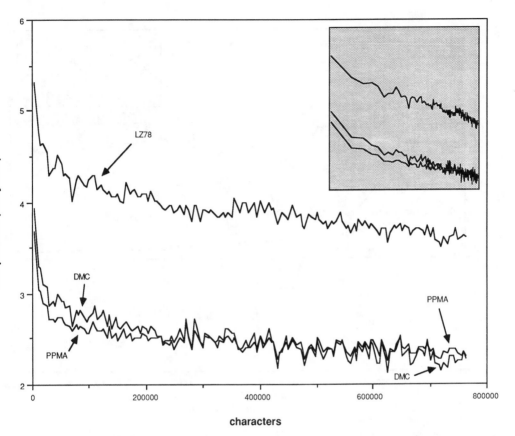

Figure 9-12   Instantaneous compression during coding of "book1" (inset shows same curves plotted with a logarithmic horizontal axis).

Unfortunately, the entropy of English text is not known, so there is no asymptote to gauge the convergence of the curves in Figure 9-12. To provide a yardstick, an artificial text has been created from a source with a known entropy. The source is very simple—it has an alphabet of 16 characters, which are equiprobable. Its entropy is 4 bits/char, and this is the best possible compression that can be achieved on its output. Figure 9-13 shows how the compression varies as 1 million characters from the source are encoded.

We know from the optimality of LZ78 that it will eventually converge on the asymptote of 4 bits/char, but this is obviously happening very slowly. (The sudden jumps in the coding rate are due to the pointer size being increased by one bit each time the number of dictionary phrases doubles). In contrast, the DMC curve does not converge at all, yet it consistently outperforms LZ78, for the first 1 million characters at least. In fact, DMC reaches its best compression almost instantly but never approaches the asymptote because its ceaseless cloning of states prevents the statistics from ever settling down. Cloning can be retarded by increasing the parameter values (t and T),

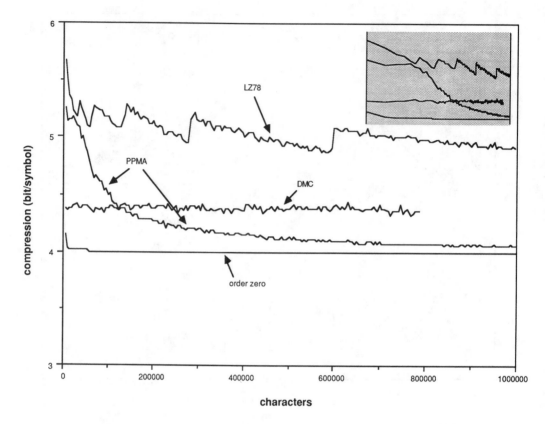

Figure 9-13   Instantaneous compression during coding of an artificial file (inset shows same curves plotted with a logarithmic horizontal axis).

although this is only beneficial because the source is so simple. The PPMA scheme converges toward the 4-bit/char asymptote considerably faster than LZ78 because convergence depends on each of the 4096 different three-character contexts being observed enough times to overcome the sampling error, and this occurs relatively quickly.

It is ironic that the initial models of PPMA and DMC both capture the structure of the source exactly, and that poor compression is caused by looking for structure where none exists. The fourth curve in Figure 9-13 is for an order-0 model that behaves as DMC and PPM would if no structural adaptation took place. The very rapid convergence shows how well the other schemes might do if they didn't try so hard!

9.5 COMPRESSION IN PRACTICE

Until now we have assumed that compression is performed under "laboratory" conditions. Unfortunately, the practitioner must confront problems such as processing arbitrarily long texts with a finite amount of memory. In this section we consider some of the problems encountered when implementing a compression scheme and show how these can be overcome.

9.5.1 Finite Memory

Many of the better adaptive schemes can consume arbitrarily large amounts of storage for coding and decoding. As the message is encoded the size of the model grows because more detail is added to the structure. If complex data structures are used to accelerate coding, even more memory is consumed. If the text is very long, or if transmission is continuous, storage will eventually be exhausted. Also, the amount of space available may be quite restricted; some of our experiments in Section 9-3 consumed several megabytes, but a personal computer may have only a few hundred kilobytes available. Fortunately, there are several avenues to follow when memory runs out.

The simplest strategy when storage is exhausted is to stop adapting the model. Compression continues with the now static model, which has been constructed from the initial part of the input. A slightly more sophisticated approach for statistical coders is obtained as follows. Recall that these models have two components: the structure and the probabilities. Memory is usually consumed only when the structure is adapted, for adapting probabilities typically involves simply incrementing a counter. When space is exhausted, adaptation need not be abandoned altogether—the probabilities can continue to change in the hope that the structure is suitable for coding the remainder of the input. There is still the possibility that a counter will eventually overflow, but this can be avoided by detecting the situation and halving all counts before overflow occurs. A serendipitous side effect of this strategy is that symbols seen in the past will receive less and less weight as coding proceeds.

Turning off (or limiting) adaptation can lead to deteriorating compression if the initial part of a text is not representative of the whole. An approach that attacks this problem is to clear the memory and begin a new model every time it becomes full. Poor compression will occur immediately after a new model is started, but this is generally offset by the better model obtained later. The effect of starting the model from scratch can be reduced by maintaining a buffer of recent input and using it to construct a new initial model. Also, the new model need not be started as soon as space is exhausted. Instead, when no more storage is available and adaptation is necessarily switched off, the amount of compression being achieved could be monitored. A declining compression ratio signals that the current model is inappropriate, so memory is cleared and a new model begun.

All of these approaches are very general, but suffer from regular "hiccups" and the fact that storage is not fully utilized while a model is being built. A more continuous approach is to use a "window" on the text, as for the LZ77 family. This involves maintaining a buffer of the last few thousand characters encoded. When a character enters the window (after being encoded) it is used to update the model, and as it leaves, its effect is removed from the model. The catch is that the representation of the model must allow it to be contracted as well as expanded. No efficient method has been proposed yet to achieve this for DMC, but it can be applied to other schemes. A slow, but general, way to achieve the effect is to use the entire window to rebuild the model from scratch every time the window changes (which happens for each character encoded!). Clearly, each model will be very similar to the preceding one, and the same result might be obtained with considerably less effort by making small changes to the model. Alternatively, the window effect might be approximated by pruning infrequently used parts of the structure, in the style of the LZJ scheme.

It is unlikely that both encoder and decoder will have access to exactly the same amount of storage, so it is important that the one with the larger memory be aware of the resources available to the other, so that both know precisely when memory is exhausted and can remain synchronized after corrective action is taken.

9.5.2 Error Control

Another practical consideration is that of reducing the impact of errors in the coded data. Changing only one bit in the input to an adaptive decoder can render the remainder of the message unintelligible; the better the compression achieved, the more serious the effect will be. Fortunately, good methods are available for detecting and correcting errors, and the redundancy that these introduce will not usually outweigh the benefits of compression. Most computer storage systems incorporate their own error-handling systems, so if the compressed data are to be stored (rather than transmitted), there is no further need to deal with errors. Many data transmission and file transfer systems also incorporate mechanisms to ensure that data are received intact. The main situation where error handling needs to be included in a compression system is when transmitting over a link where errors are normally ignored—for example, a line to a terminal, possibly via a modem. In this case a variety of techniques can be employed, such as a cyclic redundancy check (CRC) with retransmission of erroneous blocks, or a BCH error-correcting code. Chapter 10 discusses another alternative, which uses arithmetic coding itself to detect and correct errors.

9.5.3 Upward Compatibility

One final practical consideration is worth mentioning. Care should be take to ensure that compressed files can be decoded in the future, perhaps years after they were compressed. The art of compression is still evolving. Better methods are discovered each year, and others are becoming practical as storage and processing costs decrease. However, if an old compression program is discarded or upgraded, any files it has compressed become unreadable. Also, most compression algorithms must be supplied with one or two parameters, and these must be known for decompression as well. Decoding a file if the parameters have been forgotten is not straightforward! A simple way to alleviate such problems is to attach a small header to each compressed file, identifying the program (and version) and any parameters needed to perform decompression. The program identification need only be a code number (in keeping with the spirit of compression!) The decoding program should check this header and decide which version of the decompressor to use. This feature will encourage the use of compression because users can be sure of decoding any compressed file with the same command.

From time to time it may become necessary to discard a decompression program, in which case all corresponding files should first be decoded and recompressed using a new program.

NOTES

The Australian compression competition was run by the *Australian Personal Computer* magazine, with sponsorship from Microsoft (Australia). The deadline for entries was January 4, 1988, and during the period September to December 1987 the magazine ran a series of articles about compression, mainly describing ad hoc techniques. The two winners, announced in May 1988, were Chris Jones and Alistair Moffat (both have publications listed in the references).

The principle of decomposing dictionary schemes discussed in Section 9-1 was introduced by Shannon (1948). Rissanen and Langdon (1981) give an algorithm for decomposing schemes with the restriction that *no* string in the dictionary is allowed to be the prefix of any other string in the dictionary. Langdon (1983) gives a decomposition for LZ78 which is easily extended to the case where *every* string in the dictionary has a prefix in the dictionary. The general algorithm presented in Section 9-1, with no restrictions on the dictionary, is due to Bell and Witten (1987). Specific algorithms that decompose LZ77 and LZ78 are given by Bell (1987) and Langdon (1983).

The strategies discussed in Section 9-5 that deal with memory overflow have generally been proposed in conjunction with a compression scheme. Restarting the model was proposed for LZ78 (Ziv and Lempel, 1978), rebuilding it from a buffer is from DMC (Cormack and Horspool, 1987), monitoring the compression originated with LZC (Thomas et al., 1985), and a window was first used for LZ77 (Ziv and Lempel, 1977). Details of error-detecting and error-correcting codes (including CRC and BCH) can be found in texts on information theory and communications, such as Peterson and Weldon (1972).

THE WIDER VIEW

10.1 AN OVERVIEW

We have come a long way since the British Admiralty's eighteenth-century shutter telegraph with which our tale began. Had the Admiralty possessed fast microprocessors with megabyte memories at that time, they could have taken advantage of statistical or dictionary coding techniques to create an adaptive system with a performance of 2.5 to 3 bits/char on English text, or over two letters per 6-bit shutter configuration. (Probably the availability of such technology at that time would have caused a good many other changes to the course of history.) It is interesting to speculate how long it would have taken before words like "and," "the," "Portsmouth," "West"—and how many lives would have been lost before phrases like "Sentence of court martial to be put into execution"—were assimilated thoroughly enough by the adaptive scheme to be encoded in one shutter configuration.

Lest the story seem too clear-cut, we finish by branching out into the untidy world of broader applications—baked and, perhaps, half-baked—of the text compression techniques we have studied. Our unabashed bias toward statistical techniques will be apparent here, for all our work has been done with these methods rather than with dictionary ones. The systems described have been implemented, at least in prototype form, and, to varying degrees, tested.

One theme pervading the entire book is that compression is tantamount to prediction. We would all like to be able to predict which horse will win a particular race or which stock will double next week. If *we* knew how to do that, we would not be writing this book! Yet as we have seen, it is often quite possible to predict the future of a text stream—in a limited way—and to put the prediction to good use. This idea has many potential applications in interactive computer systems, some of which are examined below.

Another common thread is that well-compressed text should appear random. All its structure should be delegated to the model rather than being represented in the transmitted stream. This has its analog in signal processing. The method of compressing speech by linear prediction attempts to extract all structure from the signal and capture it in a model. The process of determining suitable parameters for the model is sometimes called "whitening," for when done successfully it transforms the original signal into pure, or white, noise. Similarly, text is whitened by compression. In the next two sections we present some ideas for adding controlled redundancy back into the output of an arithmetic coder for the purpose of error control, and consider the question of data security—to what extent does compression act as encryption?

Finally, we have resolutely avoided discussing compression techniques for anything but text. Text of various kinds is by far the main application of exact compression techniques. But of course our methods are eminently suitable for compressing many other kinds of data. The final section shows a way to apply the PPM method to (exact) picture compression.

10.1.1 The Reactive Keyboard

Figure 10-1a shows a sample menu display from the "reactive keyboard," a system that allows text to be entered without a conventional keyboard. The menu includes predicted character strings that are likely to appear in the current context. The 10 menu items represent alternative pieces of text from which you can choose the next character. If you wish to enter, say, "prompts the," you point at the end of the third menu item and 11 characters will be entered at a single selection. If, instead, the characters "pr" are correct but the remaining ones are not, you point between the second and third characters of the third menu item. If the next character is "p" but the "r" is incorrect, the first character alone of the third menu item should be selected.

The items are displayed from most to least likely, in terms of the predictive model of the text. Here, the most likely next character (according to the model) is "m", so the first menu item begins with this. The next letters, "uch slower than s," show the most likely future prediction following "m". Predictions become significantly less reliable as you go further into the future. Of course, in some cases more than one page of the menu will have to be examined because the required character is not predicted at the head of any menu item. Pointing at the hand shows the next page. Fortunately, it is not often necessary to use this mechanism.

In the event that a pointing device is not available to indicate the selection, a simpler display is shown (Figure 10-1b). This is intended for use with a hand-held keypad with (say) 10 buttons, or a limited speech recognizer capable of distinguishing (say) 10 words. In this mode the user keys the appropriate item number, and only one letter can be entered at a time. It is called a "one-dimensional" display since users

context	prediction
operating	much slower than s
	with compute
	prompts the
	of system)
	separately
	is through
	known word
	disregards
	to pronoun
	☞

(a)

context	prediction	
operating	0	m
	1	w
	2	p
	3	o
	4	s
	5	i
	6	k
	7	d
	8	t
	9	☞

(b)

Figure 10-1   (a) Menu display for the reactive keyboard; (b) menu format when a pointing device is not available.

select only in the vertical dimension (item number), and contrasts with the "two-dimensional" mode described above, which allows users to specify the horizontal position-within-item, too.

To enter text, the user makes a sequence of one- or two-dimensional menu selections. Whenever a selection is made, a new menu appears immediately. Because menu items are ordered according to their predicted probabilities, the user naturally scans the menu beginning with the most likely entry. The small number of previously entered characters that form the context for prediction are displayed to the left of the menu of predictions, as shown in Figure 10-1. This makes it natural to erase incorrectly entered characters by pointing back into this context. When one does so, the prediction mechanism backtracks and immediately displays an earlier menu.

Since we know that text can be compressed to around 2.5 bits/char, and $2^{2.5} \approx 5.7$, it may seem as though it could be entered at an average rate of one character per selection using a six-item menu with one-dimensional pointing. Unfortunately, this neglects the fact that probabilities are effectively quantized very crudely into a scale determined by the menu size. The average number of selections per character must necessarily exceed unity for one-dimensional selection, since each character requires at least one selection. For two-dimensional selection, an average rate of one character per selection can be achieved with a 10-item menu; but much depends on the nature of the text and how well the reactive keyboard's model is primed.

You may wonder why on earth anyone would want to enter text in this way, rather than having a trained typist key it in. Some people, such as those who are physically handicapped, are only able to select from a small number of keys at a time. Also, in some applications, such as accessing remote databases using only a home television set and telephone handset, only 10 or 12 keys are available for input. In both of these cases the reactive keyboard gives rapid access to the full alphabet. In essence, it substitutes the cognitive skill of selecting from a menu for the mechanical skill of typing.

Also, it's *fun*—like video games, it abandons the conventional keyboard in favor of a more reactive input mechanism. But note how dangerous it is to use the predictions as *suggestions* of what to type; for the result will lack variety, vigor, and verve. Instead, it is essential to conceive what is to be entered *first*, and use the predictions to facilitate its entry. Otherwise, the techniques will encourage stultified, unimaginative, turgid prose—just the kind that is very easy to compress!

10.1.2 An Autoprogramming Calculator

Another application of modeling is to the actual task of programming. The idea is that if a computer is shown the steps to perform a task a number of times it can build a model of the sequence of steps. The different input data provided each time will often cause the task to be executed in different ways, adding new paths to the model. Once the model is good enough, it can predict the next step at all times and be left to run its "program" all by itself! Completely automating the programming process in this way is a utopian dream, but it can be done in simple enough situations. One instance of this was described in Section 7-1, where a sorting algorithm was induced from a few key examples; the following system is a similar application.

Consider the simple, nonprogrammable pocket calculator shown in Figure 10-2. By arranging for a model-building system to "look over your shoulder" while you use it for a repetitive task, it is possible after a while for it to predict the keys that will be pressed next. Any that cannot be predicted correspond to "input." Thus the device can eventually behave exactly as though it had been explicitly programmed for the task at hand, waiting for the user to enter a number, and simulating the appropriate sequence of key presses to come up with the answer. Using a calculator (rather than a programming

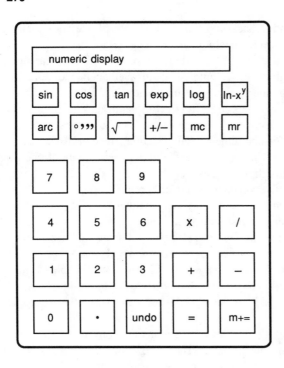

mc	clear memory
mr	retrieve from memory
m+=	add to memory

Figure 10-2   A self-programming calculator.

language) sidesteps some of the more difficult problems of automatic programming, for the calculator is suited only to simple jobs.

The calculator of Figure 10-2 constructs an adaptive model of the sequence of keys the user presses. If the task is repetitive (e.g., computing a simple function for various argument values), the modeler will soon catch on to the sequence and begin to activate the keys itself. Inevitably the prediction will sometimes be wrong, and an *undo* key allows the user to correct errors.

Figure 10-3 gives some examples of this "self-programming" calculator. The first sequence shows the evaluation of xe^{1-x} for a range of values of x. The keys pressed by the operator are in normal type; those predicted by the system are shaded. From halfway through the second iteration onwards, the device behaves as though it had been explicitly programmed for the job. It waits for the user to enter a number and displays the answer. It takes slightly longer for the constant 1 to be predicted than the preceding operators because numbers in a sequence are more likely to change than operators. Therefore, the system requires an additional confirmation before venturing to predict a number.

Figure 10-3(b) shows the evaluation of

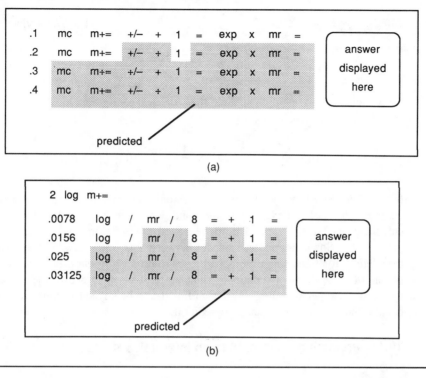

Figure 10-3 Examples of operation of the self-programming calculator: (a) evaluating xe^{1-x} for various values of x; (b) evaluating $1 + \log x/8 \log 2$ for various values of x; (c) evaluating a more complex expression.

$$1 + \frac{\log x}{8 \log 2}$$

for various values of x. The first line stores the constant $\log 2$ in memory. More complicated is the evaluation of

$$20 + 10 \log \left[1 + a^2 - 2a \, \cos \frac{180x}{4000}\right] - 10 \log \left[1 + a^2 - 2a \, \cos 45\right]$$

for $a = 0.9$. Since the calculator possesses only one memory location, it is expedient to compute the last subexpression first and jot down the result. The result of this calculation (-2.69858) only has to be keyed twice before the system picks it up as predictable. Some interference occurs between this initial task and the main repeated calculation, for three suggestions had to be "undone" by the user. The negative effect of one of these "undo's" continues right up until near the end of the interaction. This means that the penultimate "+" on each line has to be keyed by the user several times to counter the system's reluctance to predict it.

10.1.3 Predicting User Input to an Interactive System

Typical dialogues with interactive computer systems contain a great deal of redundancy. A small subset of possible commands is used very frequently, command names and incorrectly given arguments are retyped, users choose a limited set of filenames that often exhibit internal lexical structure, and so on. Measures that system designers have taken to reduce redundancy include terse commands, abbreviation processors, and command completion facilities. But these often meet with resistance—brief commands are cryptic, hard to remember, and easily mixed up; abbreviation mechanisms are complex to use and take valuable time to learn; command completion may be fine as far as it goes but lacks other things needed to make it really useful, such as filename and word completion.

Real-time text modeling can assist users in a uniform and general way by reducing the amount they have to type. The idea is to predict the entries a user is about to make. Obviously, this scheme is unlikely to predict correctly all the time—for then you could walk away and leave the computer to simulate you! It is essential to ensure that erroneous predictions are very easy for the user to ignore, while correct ones are easy to accept.

Such a system, called *predict*, has been implemented as a user interface to the UNIX operating system. Predictions appear in reverse video on the VDU terminal, and users may accept correct predictions as though they had typed them themselves. Incorrect ones can be eradicated simply by typing over them.

Because of display limitations, alternative predictions are not displayed: In effect, *predict* guesses the most likely next entry and ignores other possibilities. If the first predicted character, when accepted, would lead to others, a chain of predictions is made and displayed. Up to a full line of predictions can be shown, but they are generally shorter than this—either because the model indicates that a newline character will follow or because a point is reached where there is no prediction. No attempt is made to predict past a newline character.

When a prediction is displayed, the cursor is instantly moved back to the position preceding it. The user can accept it in its entirety, or character by character, by pressing function keys. The prediction can just be typed over if it is incorrect—it will disappear immediately (possibly being replaced by a new one). It can equally well be typed over if it is correct—perhaps the user is not looking at the screen, or does not want to interrupt keying rhythm. Hence the interface can be used in a completely transparent manner, although when typing fast one finds the screen flashing with predictions in a diverting and distracting manner.

To give some idea of performance, Figure 10-4a shows a sample input sequence recorded by *predict*. It was produced in a live terminal session and is all directed to the UNIX command interpreter. It is not necessary to understand the meanings of the commands, but it is important to note the high degree of redundancy present. For example, "*man compact*" failed the first time and had to be retried after the environment had been altered. The command "*od –c test3.c*" failed because the filename should have been "*test3.C*". Considerable redundancy is contributed by the frequent use of a small selection of commands and filenames.

The predictions made by the system are shown in Figure 10-4b. Here, "▯" represents a correctly predicted character, while "▮" flags the beginning of an incorrect prediction. The large number of good predictions is plain. Although there are also many bad ones, the user need take no action on these other than typing what would have had to be typed anyway.

In a human factors experiment designed to investigate subjects' usage of *predict* with ordinary text (rather than with command dialogues), it was discovered that most computer users could type faster than they could enter text using the adaptive system, although for some kinds of text the difference was not very large. (The odds were stacked against *predict*, however, because subjects were required to type from written copy—they had to look away from their work to see the predictions.) Interestingly enough, most subjects *thought* they worked faster using the system than without it. They liked to watch the predictions, and time passed quickly!

10.1.4 Error Control with Arithmetic Coding

The trouble with compressed data is that it is highly susceptible to transmission errors. A single corrupted bit will render the remainder of the transmission completely meaningless. Of course, we see this as an *advantage* of coding, for it indicates that little redundancy remains in the output stream. But in practice, error control techniques will have to be used to prevent transmission errors and to present the coding level with a completely noise-free communication channel. The conventional approach to error control involves blocking the input stream (usually into fixed-length blocks), adding check bits to each (usually in the form of a cyclic redundancy check), and implementing a retransmission protocol to ensure that corrupted blocks are sent again. Alternatively, forward error correction can be employed, where more check bits are used to give the

```
cd ..
ls
cd modelling
ls -l
rm *.o y.tab.c
ls -l test2
cat test2
pr test2|opr
echo test*
rm test*
ls -l
rm tty tty.out
man compact
newgrp bin
cd ..
man compact
du
cd ../bin
cd bin
ls
cat bib.make
cd ../modelling
cp ../bib.make test3
cp ../bin/bib.make test3
compact test3
ls -l
od -c test3.c
od -c test3.c
pr test3.C ../bin/bib.make|opr
pr ../bin/bib.make|opr
od -c test3.C|pr|opr
rm test3.C
ls -l ../bin
cat ../bin/bib.indiv
cp ../bin/bib.indiv test4
pr test4|opr
compact test4
od -c test4.C
od -c test4.C|pr|opr
cd ../predictor
```

(a)

```
cd ..
ls
cd█modelling
ls -l
rm *.o y.tab.c
ls███ test2
cat te███
pr te███|opr
echo te██*
rm█te███
ls████
rm██ty tt█.out
man compact
newgrp bin
cd█..
ma██████████
du
cd███/bin
cd█bi█
ls█
ca██bi█b.make
cd█.██mod██████
cp ..█b█b█████ te██3
cp██████n/bi█b███████████
com████ t████
ls███
od -c te███.c
od█████████████C
pr█████████ ..███n███b██████|op█
pr█..███n███b███████████
od████████████|pr|op█
rm█te██████
ls███ █..███n█
ca██..████/██b█.indiv
cp██████n███b██████ te██4
pr█t████|op█
co████████████
od██████████.c
od████████████|███████
cd████predictor
```

(b)

Figure 10-4   (a) Input sequence to the UNIX operating system; (b) input sequence with predictions.

receiver the chance of actually correcting errors instead of just requesting retransmission.

A particularly useful way of inserting the redundant bits is to scatter them through the transmission. In convolutional codes, for example, the extra bits depend on all of the transmission so far. The advantage is that if an error occurs it may be detected (or even corrected) when the next one or two redundant bits are seen, instead of waiting for the end of the transmission. It is also easier to locate the error, for it is likely to just precede the spot where the error was first noticed. However, these codes are difficult to discover and can be computationally demanding to compute during transmission. The first drawback is compounded by the fact that they are precisely tailored to the amount of redundancy required—different ones must be constructed for different amounts of redundancy.

It is interesting to examine whether error control can be performed within the arithmetic coding paradigm itself. It is very easy for an arithmetic coder to introduce redundancy by transmitting an extra character periodically. This character could take on two values—"good" and "bad." Only the former would ever be sent, and if the latter were ever decoded, an error must have occurred. The amount of redundancy can be controlled by varying the probability of the "good" symbol and the frequency with which the extra characters are inserted. Thus arithmetic coding provides a fast and infinitely variable way of injecting redundancy into a transmission. Like convolutional codes, the redundancy is spread evenly through the message and errors will likely be detected soon after they occur. For example, we can distribute a 5% redundancy evenly throughout a message by setting the probability of the good symbol to $2^{-0.05} \approx 0.97$ and encoding one for each bit generated by the arithmetic encoder.

The same scheme can be used for forward error correction. On detecting an occurrence of the "bad" symbol, the decoder could try inverting bits in the received bit stream, beginning at the point the error was discovered and proceeding farther back in the stream. For each bit flipped, it could check to see if that was the erroneous one by decoding the resulting bit stream. The wrong bit has been blamed for the error if the forbidden symbol is decoded in the next few symbols. Statistical arguments can quantify the sense of "few." If the forbidden symbol is not encountered soon, decoding can continue, for the offending bit has been detected and corrected.

There is a serious snag in this otherwise very attractive idea for error correction. It is possible under certain circumstances for an error to go completely undetected. The entire state of an arithmetic coder is contained in the two variables that represent the endpoints of the current interval [*low, high*) (see Figure 5-4 for a reminder of the basic coding algorithm). If a transmission error occurs, causing the decoder's [*low, high*) interval to diverge from the encoder's, sooner or later the forbidden symbol will be decoded, initiating the error-recovery procedure. But if a second transmission error, by coincidence, causes the decoder's interval to resynchronize with that of the encoder's, all opportunity for spotting the error will have been lost. Of course, this is incredibly unlikely. However, if a second error occurs that does not cause resynchronization, the decoder will try hard to correct it by searching a large space of possible bit flippings to find one that does not reveal the forbidden signal in the decoded characters. If it is possible to resynchronize the decoder and encoder without correcting the first error, it is quite likely that the search will, by mischance, happen upon the "correction" that does this. The only defense is to ensure that resynchronization is improbable except by correcting the error, and this is hard to prove.

A discussion of potential solutions to these problems would lead too far from our present path. However, it seems likely that they can be overcome, leading to a single, unified scheme where arithmetic coding can be used to achieve three goals: data compression, data integrity, and data security (discussed next).

10.1.5 Privacy and Compression

Ordinary techniques of text compression provide some degree of privacy for messages being stored or transmitted. First, by recoding messages, compression protects them from the casual observer. Second, by removing redundancy it denies a cryptanalyst the leverage of the normal statistical regularities in natural language. However, this does not offer much protection against known or chosen plaintext attacks. Intruders who can mount a "chosen plaintext" attack, which provides an opportunity to choose what text is encrypted and then intercept the coded version, can perform experiments designed to identify the model being used. Even with a less powerful "known plaintext" attack, where the intruder knows what is being encrypted (but cannot choose it at will), parts of the model can be mapped and used to decode subsequent, unknown, transmissions.

The third aspect of the text compression methods described in this book, and the most important as far as privacy is concerned, is that they use adaptive modeling in order to take advantage of the characteristics of the text being transmitted. The model acts as a very large encryption key, without which decoding is impossible. Adaptive modeling means that the key depends on the entire text which has been transmitted since the last time the encoder/decoder system was initialized.

For the sake of argument, imagine using one of the simplest adaptive compression methods—arithmetic coding based on single-character frequencies. For this to be an effective encryption device, the initial model must be conveyed through a secure communication channel. This might be done using a (relatively slow) public key method. The model need not be large; an array of single-character frequencies in the range of (say) 1 to 10, one for each character in the alphabet, would do. If necessary, these numbers could be produced by a random number generator on the basis of a single seed, securely transmitted. Compression performance would be poor initially because the model would not match the character frequencies in the messages sent. Soon, however, the frequencies would adapt close to those in the messages. The time taken for this would depend on the complexity of the initial model. For example, 26 random single-letter frequencies between 1 and 10 would correspond to a statistically misleading text of $26 \times 5^{1}/_{2} \approx 150$ characters, which would be substantially outweighed by the first 1000 characters of the actual message.

Alternatively, a constant initial model could be used and a short message, sent by a secure channel, assimilated into the model by both encoder and decoder before transmission begins. Then the key becomes a short piece of text. This has the advantage that coding is not adversely affected by an unrepresentative initial model, even at the beginning.

Adaptation poses a real problem to eavesdroppers. It means that they cannot break in partway through a transmission and expect to identify the current model, nor could an imposter easily insert or modify text. Partial knowledge of the model is likely to be of little use. As soon as a context is encountered that resides in the unknown portion of the model, the next few bits in the encoded message cannot be interpreted. Arithmetic coding ensures that once this is the case, it is very difficult to regain synchronization because the new value of the range is unknown.

The model is observable only through experiment, by causing a particular message to be sent and examining the compressed version (a chosen plaintext attack). But such experiments change the model in ways which can be very difficult to predict. If, for example, predictions are kept in frequency order—as was suggested in Section 5-3 to optimize access time—the process of updating the model to account for a single transmitted symbol may completely alter the coding of all subsequent ones. It seems likely that the structure of such a model cannot be inferred from experiments.

How can one validate an encryption device? We certainly cannot prove the security of this method. But neither can one prove the security of existing, widely used encryption techniques. It seems that adaptive compression does have something to offer in practical situations where privacy of transmission is of concern. Furthermore, not only do messages become more secure, they also get smaller!

10.1.6 Progressive Transmission of Pictures

In text, a character is most accurately predicted from the context of characters that immediately precede it. But what should be used as the context for predictions in picture coding? The easiest thing is the pixels to the left and above the one being encoded, for pictures are usually stored one line at a time, with a horizontal scan. However, there seems to be no intrinsic reason to prefer the left context to the right context, or the top context to the bottom context. It would be nice to use all eight surrounding pixels as the context, but then it is hard to see how the picture could be drawn—you've got to start somewhere!

One way to resolve this problem is to use a binary image tree. As Figure 10-5 illustrates, each level in the tree has twice as many rectangles as the level above. At the very bottom is the full picture, and each square represents a pixel with a certain numeric gray-scale value. At the top is the average gray-scale value over the whole picture. At the next level, the picture is split into halves in one direction, and the tree records the average gray level of each half. Next, each half is split again, this time in the other direction, forming four quadrants out of the original picture. This level of the tree holds the four corresponding gray-scale values. And so it proceeds, until finally the full pixel resolution is achieved at the bottom. In fact, the method works only if the picture is square and the sides are a power of 2, but any picture can be padded out to meet this requirement.

Although the tree is constructed from the bottom up, it should be transmitted from the top down, starting at the root. As the transmission is decoded, the picture can be built up gradually, over the whole screen, instead of being painted line by line. This in itself is a nice feature. The progressive transmission gives a rough representation very early on, and most of the time is spent refining it to full detail. Since it takes several minutes to send a medium-resolution picture over a 1200-bit/s telephone, the benefits can be very striking.

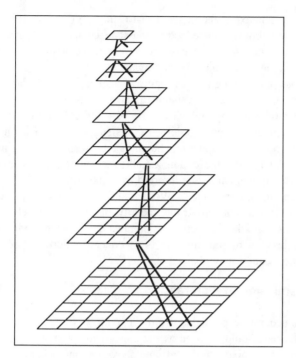

Figure 10-5   A binary image tree.

For the purpose of compression, the binary image tree makes it easy to construct contexts for the gray-scale values that are being sent. For example, the level of the tree above the current one will have been completely transmitted already. The value of a particular pixel in the current level will be strongly dependent on neighboring ones in the level above, and these can be used as context in exactly the same way that prior characters are used for text compression. Contexts constructed in this way are not sequential, so most of the modeling techniques discussed in this book are inapplicable. However, the fixed-context models of Chapter 6 can be used if they are implemented using *backward trees* as described in Section 6-5.

Figure 10-6 shows selected levels of a picture of a girl. The 256 × 256 pixels give a total of 17 levels, numbered from 0 (the top) to 16 (the final picture). The first version shown, at level 10, is 32 × 32 and has 1024 pixels—only 1.6% of the 65,500 pixels in the full picture. Although it is obviously not very good, it is clearly recognizable as a girl's face. By the time level 14 is reached the picture is very clear, even though only 25% of the information is present. It takes well over 7 minutes to transmit the complete picture at 1200 bits/s, but the almost-recognizable version at level 12 can be sent in only 27 seconds.

The catch with progressive transmission is that unless care is taken with coding, twice as many bits are needed to send the sequence of pictures at increasing resolutions than would be required for the final picture alone. This is where compression comes in. Using the PPM method with binary-tree contexts, typical pictures with 8-bit gray levels can be coded into 65% of the number of bits of the original picture (or 33% of the

Figure 10-6   Progressive transmission of a portrait.

number of bits in the full image tree). Thus level 10 would be reached in under 5 seconds, level 12 in about 18 seconds, level 14 in 1 minute 10 seconds, and the final picture in under 5 minutes. The coding is necessarily *exact*: The reconstructed picture is identical, bit for bit, with the original. Of course, any noise in the original is faithfully transmitted too, which accounts for the relatively poor compression. The low-order bit or two of each 8-bit pixel is probably effectively random, and the encoder and decoder go to great pains to reproduce these useless data correctly! Much better results are achieved with 4-bit pixels (compression to below 50%) and 1-bit, or black-and-white, pictures (compression to 18%, or 0.18 bit/pixel).

The photographs in Figure 10-7 show a picture of text, with 512 × 512 black-and-white pixels. The form and layout are visible by level 12, a 64 × 64 version, and the text is legible by level 16 (256 × 256). The full picture, transmitted normally, takes over $3^1/_2$ minutes on a 1200-bit/s line. With compression, it takes 40 seconds. Moreover, level 12, in which the layout is visible, is received in only 13 seconds. It is remarkable that the convenience of progressive transmission can be combined with significant compression!

Figure 10-7   Progressive transmission of a picture of text.

NOTES

The *reactive keyboard* is described by Witten et al. (1983). Surveys of other computer typing aids for the handicapped, which invariably incorporate some form of compression (although not usually adaptive), appear in Raitzer et al. (1976) and Staisey et al. (1982). The autoprogramming calculator was unveiled by Witten (1981). The subject of programming by example is a large one. Significant systems have been described by Andreae (1984), Halbert (1984), and Nix (1984); end-user programming is surveyed in MacDonald and Witten (1987) and Witten et al. (1987a). The *predict* system appears in Witten (1982a). The use of arithmetic coding as an encryption device is described by Witten and Cleary (1988).

The use of PPM for picture compression is described by Witten and Cleary (1983). However, while it is unique in combining compression with progressive transmission, the method has not been highly optimized for picture compression. Better performance on pictures has been obtained by Langdon and Rissanen (1981). Those interested in picture compression should also be aware of the international digital facsimile coding standards (Hunter and Robinson, 1980). The idea of progressive transmission is nicely presented by Knowlton (1980).

VARIABLE-LENGTH REPRESENTATIONS OF THE INTEGERS

A.1 CODING ARBITRARILY LARGE INTEGERS

The common binary fixed-length representation of the integers requires a prespecified number of bits for each integer, say n, and is able to represent integers in the range 1 to 2^n. Sometimes a maximum value is not known, so a variable-length representation must be used instead. Also, it is often desirable for small integers to have a shorter code than large ones. The representations here can code any integer value greater than zero, and the length of the encoding grows as the value being encoded increases.

Information theory tells us that if the representation of the integer i uses $|C(i)|$ bits, it is optimal if the probability of i is $2^{-|C(i)|}$. Thus the different representations given here imply different probability distributions, and the most appropriate for an application is the one whose probability distribution best approximates that of the integers being encoded. Figure A-1 shows the probability distributions implied by two of the codes described below, C_α and C_γ. The C_α code length increases linearly with the value being encoded, so the probability decreases exponentially. The length of the codes for C_γ (and all the other codes described here) increases logarithmically, so the implied probability decreases linearly. Consequently, C_α is suitable when almost all of the integers to be coded are very small, while the other codes are considerably more generous to larger integers. It is possible to generate an optimal set of codes (each with an

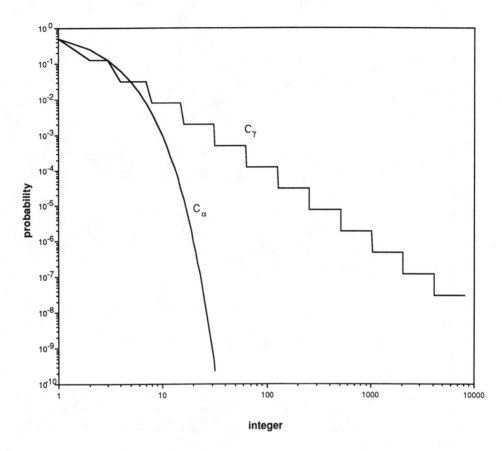

Figure A-1   Implied probabilities of the codes C_α and C_γ.

integer number of bits) using Huffman's algorithm, but this requires that a probability distribution be provided, and it is slower.

Three of these codes (C_γ, C_δ and C_ω) are *universal*, which means that assigning messages in order of decreasing probability to the codewords gives an average code-word length within a constant of the optimal average length. Unfortunately, the constant may be too large for the code to be used in preference to one based on the probabilities. The codes C_δ and C_ω have the stronger property that the average code length approaches the entropy as the entropy increases. This means that they perform best when no message is much more likely than any other, which can be seen intuitively from the fact that the code lengths increase very slowly for large integers, corresponding to a flat probability distribution.

Examples of the following codings are given in Table A-1.

C_α: C_α is unary coding; that is, $\alpha(i)$ is $(i-1)$ zeros followed by a 1; or recursively, $\alpha(1) = 1$, $\alpha(i+1) = 0.\alpha(i)$. $|\alpha(i)| = i$.

TABLE A-1 EXAMPLES OF VARIABLE-LENGTH CODINGS OF THE INTEGERS; COLONS HAVE BEEN ADDED FOR CLARITY

i	α(i)	β(i)	β̂(i)	γ'(i)	γ(i)	δ(i)	ω(i)	ω'(i)	ω''(i)
1	1	1	0	1:	1	1:	0	001:0	000:
2	01	10	1	01:0	001	001:0	10:0	010:0	001:
3	001	11		01:1	011	001:1	11:0	011:0	010:
4	0001	100	00	001:00	00001	011:00	10:100:0	100:0	011:
5	00001	101	01	001:01	00011	011:01	10:101:0	101:0	100:0
6	000001	110	10	001:10	01001	011:10	10:110:0	110:0	101:0
7	0000001	111	11	001:11	01011	011:11	10:111:0	111:0	110:0
8	00000001	1000	000	0001:000	0000001	00001:000	11:1000:0	100:1000:0	111:
9	000000001	1001	001	0001:001	0000011	00001:001	11:1001:0	100:1001:0	100:1000:0
10	0000000001	1010	010	0001:010	0001001	00001:010	11:1010:0	100:1010:0	100:1001:0
11	00000000001	1011	011	0001:011	0001011	00001:011	11:1011:0	100:1011:0	100:1010:0
12	...	1100	100	0001:100	0100001	00001:100	11:1100:0	100:1100:0	100:1011:0
13		1101	101	0001:101	0100011	00001:101	11:1101:0	100:1101:0	100:1100:0
14		1110	110	0001:110	0101001	00001:110	11:1110:0	100:1110:0	100:1101:0
15		1111	111	0001:111	0101011	00001:111	11:1111:0	100:1111:0	100:1110:0
16		10000	0000	00001:0000	000000001	0001:0000	10:100:10000:0	101:10000:0	100:1111:0
17		10001	0001	00001:0001	000000011	0001:0001	10:100:10001:0	101:10001:0	101:10000:0
18		10010	0010	00001:0010	000001001	0001:0010	10:100:10010:0	101:10010:0	101:10001:0
19		10011	0011	00001:0011	000001011	0001:0011	10:100:10011:0	101:10011:0	101:10010:0
20		10100	0100	00001:0100	000100001	0011:0100	10:100:10100:0	101:10100:0	101:10011:0
21		10101	0101	00001:0101	000100011	0011:0101	10:100:10101:0	101:10101:0	101:10100:0
22		10110	0110	00001:0110	000101001	0011:0110	10:100:10110:0	101:10110:0	101:10101:0
23		10111	0111	00001:0111	000101011	0011:0111	10:100:10111:0	101:10111:0	101:10110:0
24		11000	1000	00001:1000	010000001	0011:1000	10:100:11000:0	101:11000:0	101:10111:0
25		11001	1001	00001:1001	010000011	0011:1001	10:100:11001:0	101:11001:0	101:11000:0
26		11010	1010	00001:1010	010001001	0011:1010	10:100:11010:0	101:11010:0	101:11001:0
27		11011	1011	00001:1011	010001011	0011:1011	10:100:11011:0	101:11011:0	101:11010:0
28		11100	1100	00001:1100	010100001	0011:1100	10:100:11100:0	101:11100:0	101:11011:0
29		11101	1101	00001:1101	010100011	0011:1101	10:100:11101:0	101:11101:0	101:11100:0
30		11110	1110	00001:1110	010101001	0011:1110	10:100:11110:0	101:11110:0	101:11101:0
31		11111	1111	00001:1111	010101011	0011:1111	10:100:11111:0	101:11111:0	101:11110:0
32		100000	00000	000001:00000	00000000001	0101:00000	10:101:100000:0	110:100000:0	101:11111:0
64		1000000	000000	0000001:000000	0000000000001	0101:000000	10:110:1000000:0	111:1000000:0	110:1111111:0
128		10000000	0000000	00000001:0000000	000000000000001	000000011:0000000	10:111:10000000:0	100:1000:10000000:0	111:1111111:0
256		100000000	00000000	000000001:00000000	0000000000000000001	0000000011:00000000	11:1000:100000000:0	100:1001:100000000:0	100:1000:1111111111:0

C_β: C_β is binary coding; that is, $\beta(1) = 1$, $\beta(2i) = \beta(i).0$, $\beta(2i+1) = \beta(i).1$. This coding is not decodable unless the length of the code is known in advance. Note that the most significant bit of $\beta(i)$ is always a 1. $|\beta(i)| = \lfloor \log i \rfloor + 1$.

$C_{\hat\beta}$: $C_{\hat\beta}$ is C_β with the most significant bit removed. It is not useful on its own, but is used to build other codes. $|\hat\beta(i)| = \lfloor \log i \rfloor$.

$C_{\gamma'}$: $C_{\gamma'}$ is a unary code for the number of bits in the binary coding of the integer, followed by the the binary coding of the integer with the most significant bit removed; that is, $\gamma'(i) = \alpha(|\beta(i)|).\hat\beta(i)$. $|\gamma'(i)| = 2\lfloor \log i \rfloor + 1$.

C_γ: $C_{\gamma'}$ can be viewed as $\lfloor \log i \rfloor$ zeros followed by a 1, and then $\hat\beta(i)$. C_γ is a rearrangement of $C_{\gamma'}$, with each of the $\lfloor \log i \rfloor$ zeros followed by a bit from $\hat\beta(i)$, and ending with a 1. Thus $|\gamma'(i)| = |\gamma(i)|$, but C_γ may be easier to implement than $C_{\gamma'}$.

C_δ: C_δ is the C_γ coding of the length of the integer, followed by the integer in binary; that is, $\delta(i) = \gamma(|\beta(i)|)\hat\beta(i)$ and $|\delta(i)| = 1 + \lfloor \log i \rfloor + 2\lfloor \log(1 + \lfloor \log i \rfloor) \rfloor$.

C_ω: With $\omega(i)$, first the code $\beta(i)$ is written. To the left of this the C_β representation of $(|\beta(i)| - 1)$ is written. This process is repeated recursively, with each earlier code being the binary encoding of the length, less 1, of the following code. The process halts on the left with a coding of 2 bits. A single zero is appended on the right to mark the end of the code.

$C_{\omega'}$: $C_{\omega'}$ is very similar to C_ω, but codes begin with 3 bits rather than 2, and the integer zero can be coded.

$C_{\omega''}$: $C_{\omega''}$ is $C_{\omega'}$ altered so that the integers range from 1 instead of 0, and with a redundant bit removed from the codes for the integers 1 to 4.

A.2 PHASING IN BINARY CODES

If an upper limit can be specified for the value of an integer, it can be coded using a normal binary representation. For example, if an integer is known to be in the range 0 to 15, it can be coded as a 4 bit binary number. In general, if the integer i is known to be in the range $0 \le i < \rho$, it can be coded in $k = \lceil \log \rho \rceil$ bits. This type of coding is often used to select entries in a growing dictionary, with the limit ρ being the number of items currently in the dictionary, rather than its maximum size. The codes become longer as the dictionary grows, so the code for a full dictionary is being "phased in."

Now, if ρ is not a power of 2, codes are available that are never used—for example, the range 0 to 8 requires 4-bit codes, but in this case the codes for 9 to 15 are also available. Table A-2 shows a more efficient set of codes, most of which are only 3 bits. In general, if $i < 2^k - \rho$, it is coded in $k-1$ bits; otherwise, a k-bit coding must be employed. A $(k-1)$-bit number is coded using its normal binary representation; the k-bit coding of i is the binary representation of $i + 2^k - \rho$. Of course, this slightly improved coding will increase the encoding and decoding time.

TABLE A-2   EXAMPLE OF EFFICIENT
METHOD OF PHASING IN BINARY CODES

Integer	Code
0	000
1	001
2	010
3	011
4	100
5	101
6	110
7	1110
8	1111

A.3 START–STEP–STOP CODES

This family of codes has three parameters, *(start, step, stop)*, and each selection yields a different coding of the integers. A great variety of codes can be generated in this manner, including C_β and $C_{\gamma'}$. The parameters can also impose a maximum value on the integers being coded.

A start–step–stop code employs n simple binary codes; the first code is *start* bits, the second *start + step*, then $start + 2 \times step$, and so on, up to *start + stop* bits. Thus $n = (stop - start)/step + 1$. To show that a code belongs to set number s $(1 \le s \le n)$ it is prefixed by the unary code (C_α) for s. (If $i = n$, the final 1 of the unary code can be omitted.) The resulting codes are assigned to the integers in order of increasing size.

For example, Table A-3 shows a (1,2,5) code. Three binary codes are used: 1-bit (0 to 1), 3-bit (2 to 9), and 5-bit (10 to 41), and these are distinguished by prefixes of 1, 01, and 00, respectively. Other values for *start* and *step* will vary with the way the code length increases with the coded value, and *stop* determines the maximum value that can be encoded. The number of different codes available is

$$\frac{2^{stop + step} - 2^{start}}{2^{step} - 1}.$$

Since this increases exponentially with *stop*, very high limits can be set with relatively small parameters—a (1,1,20) code can represent over 2 million integers. Two special cases of the start–step–stop code have already been described in Section A-1: the parameters $(k,1,k)$ yield a simple k-bit binary code (C_β), while $(0,1,\infty)$ is the $C_{\gamma'}$ code.

If the upper limit on the value to be encoded is increasing, better coding is obtained by *phasing* in the start–step–stop coding, in a similar manner to the method described in Section A-2 for binary coding. For example, one could start with a (0,2,4) code capable of coding 21 different values, then change to a (1,2,5) code when more than 21 values can occur, then a (2,2,6) code when the limit is greater than 42, and so on. Even in this case there will often be unused codes; for example, a (1,2,5) code (see Table A-3) with a limit of 22 codes is wasting 20 of the codes. An economy is to apply

TABLE A-3 START–STEP–STOP
CODE FOR PARAMETERS (1,2,5)

Integer	Code
0	1:0
1	1:1
2	01:000
3	01:001
4	01:010
5	01:011
6	01:100
7	01:101
8	01:110
9	01:111
10	00:00000
11	00:00001
12	00:00010
13	00:00011
...	...
39	00:11101
40	00:11110
41	00:11111

the binary phasing-in technique of Section A-2 to the largest codes. In the example, these are 5-bit numbers intended to code the values 10 to 41. The range 22 to 41 will never be used, and the efficient phase-in can be applied to code the numbers 10 to 19 in 4 bits (plus the unary prefix), and 20 and 21 in 5 bits.

NOTES

The definitions of C_α, C_β, $C_{\hat{\beta}}$, $C_{\gamma'}$, C_γ, C_δ, and C_ω are from Elias (1975). $C_{\gamma'}$ was proposed independently by Bentley and Yao (1976). $C_{\omega'}$ is described by Rodeh et al. (1981). The efficient method of phasing in binary codes is described by Tischer (1987) and by Fiala and Greene (1989). The start–step–stop codes are due to Fiala and Greene (1989).

THE COMPRESSION CORPUS

```
45h[0j45thwGw45hqU9c
poejrg[4wky]p435q)b&
[0wejg[04jy42yj3*k!c
p0w4j5g[235-k6t0=w~n
[0ewjg04jy04jy4j;qmy
pmh][krty-jk46-[p"qb
p[jw435    h[ps0%x
[psdhkj  8w  5y9mwq
germhj-    j64k?ti
[ewjhj4  n56  0o#r0b
e[wmb[p  h65  u;g4{@
65[];.9      0.o~x6
germhj-53k=ukj64:3xf
[ewjhj4wth56430o*wm<
e[wmb[preh65,.u;aYlC
+[3fgm56rt0-"-23jsg!
[;jyt%ERghj(0;';Hd4=
lU5terEDghp=][>?kyeW
```

To evaluate the practical performance of the schemes described in this book, we have collected a corpus of texts that are likely candidates for compression. Nine different types of text are represented, and to confirm that the performance of schemes is consistent for any given type, many of the types have more than one representative.

Figure B-1 describes the texts. "Normal" English, both fiction and nonfiction, is represented by two books and papers (labeled book1, book2, paper1, paper2). More unusual styles of English writing are found in a bibliography (bib) and a batch of unedited news articles (news). Three computer programs represent artificial languages (progc, progl, progp). A transcript of a terminal session (trans) is included to indicate the increase in speed that could be achieved by applying compression to a slow line to a terminal. All of the files mentioned so far use ASCII encoding. Some non-ASCII files are also included: two files of executable code (obj1, obj2), and some geophysical data (geo)—in Figure B-1 the samples for these are shown in hexadecimal—and a "bit-map" black-and-white picture (pic). The file "geo" is particularly difficult to compress because it contains a wide range of data values, while the file "pic" is highly compressible because of large amounts of white space in the picture, represented by long runs of zeros.

Table B-1 gives the results of compression experiments on these texts. The experiments are described and their results summarized in Section 9-3, but more details are provided here for the interested reader. The best compression for each file is shown in bold type. The average compression for each scheme is *not* weighted by the size of texts, so that large files with unusual characteristics do not dominate the comparison.

Text	Type	Format	Content	Size	Sample
bib	bibliography	Unix "refer" format, ASCII	725 references for books and papers on Computer Science	111,261 characters	%A Witten, I.H. %D 1985 %T Elements of computer typography %J IJMMS %V 23
book1	fiction book	Unformatted ASCII	Thomas Hardy: "Far from the Madding Crowd"	768,771 characters	a caged canary -- all probably from the windows of the house just vacated. There was also a cat in a willow basket, from the partly-opened lid of which she gazed with half-closed eyes, and affectionately-surveyed the small birds around.
book2	non-fiction book	Unix "troff" format, ASCII	Witten: "Principles of computer speech"	610,856 characters	Figure 1.1 shows a calculator that speaks. .FC "Figure 1.1" Whenever a key is pressed, the device confirms the action by saying the key's name. The result of any computation is also spoken aloud.
geo	geophysical data	32 bit numbers	Seismic data	102,400 bytes	d3c2 0034 12c3 00c1 3742 007c 1e43 00c3 2543 0071 1543 007f 12c2 0088 eec2 0038 e5c2 00f0 4442 00b8 1b43 00a2 2143 00a2 1143 0039 84c2 0018 12c3 00c1 3fc2 00fc 1143 000a 1843 0032 e142 0050 36c2 004c 10c3 00ed 15c3 0008 10c3 00bb 3941 0040 1143 0081 ad42 0060 e2c2 001c 1fc3 0097 17c3 00d0 2642 001c 1943 00b9 1f43 003a f042 0020 a3c2 00d0 12c3 00be 69c2 00b4 cf42 0058 1843 0020 f442 0080 98c2 0084
news	electronic news	USENET batch file	A variety of topics	377,109 characters	In article <18533@amdahl.amdahl.com> tron@uts.amdahl.com (Ronald S. Karr) writes: >Some Introduction: >However, we have conflicting ideas concerning what to do with sender >addresses in headers. We do, now, support the idea that a pure !-path >coming in can be left as a !-path, with the current hostname prepended
obj1	object code	Executable file for VAX	Compilation of "progp"	21,504 bytes	0b3e 0000 efdd 2c2a 0000 8fdd 4353 0000 addd d0f0 518e a1d0 500c 50dd 03fb 51ef 0007 dd00 f0ad 8ed0 d051 0ca1 dd50 9850 7e0a bef4 0904 02fb c7ef 0014 1100 ba09 9003 b150 d604 04a1 efde 235a 0000 f0ad addd d0f0 518e a1d0 500c 50dd 01dd 0bdd 8fdd 4357 0000 04fb d5ef 0006 6e00 9def 002b 5000 5067 9def 002b 5200 5270 dd7e
obj2	object code	Executable file for Apple Macintosh	"Knowledge Support System" program	246,814 bytes	0004 019c 0572 410a 7474 6972 7562 6574 0073 0000 0000 00aa 0046 00ba 8882 5706 6e69 6f64 0077 0000 0000 00aa 0091 00ba 06ff 4c03 676f 00c0 0000 0000 01aa 0004 01ba 06ef 0000 0000 0000 00c3 0050 00d3 0687 4e03 7765 00c0 0000 0000 00c3 0091 01d3 90e0 0000 0015 0021 000a 01f0 00f6 0001 0000 0000 0400 004f 0000 e800 0c00 0000 0000 0500 9f01 1900 e501 0204 4b4f 0000 0000 1e00 9f01 3200 e501
paper1	technical paper	Unix "troff" format, ASCII	Witten, Neal and Cleary: "Arithmetic coding for data compression"	53,161 characters	Such a \fIfixed\fR model is communicated in advance to both encoder and decoder, after which it is used for many messages. .PP Alternatively, the probabilities the model assigns may change as each symbol is transmitted, based on the symbol frequencies seen \fIso far\fR in this
paper2	technical paper	Unix "troff" format, ASCII	Witten: "Computer (In)security"	82,199 characters	Programs can be written which spread bugs like an epidemic. They hide in binary code, effectively undetectable (because nobody ever examines binaries). They can remain dormant for months or years, perhaps quietly and imperceptibly infiltrating their way into the very depths of a system, then suddenly pounce,
pic	black and white facsimile picture	1728x2376 bit map 200 pixels per inch	CCITT fascimile test, picture 5 (page of textbook)	513,216 bytes	

progc	program	Source code in "C", ASCII	Unix utility "compress" version 4.0	39,611 characters	compress() {
					    register long fcode;
					    register code_int i = 0;
					    register int c;
					    register code_int ent;

progl	program	Source code in LISP, ASCII	System software	71,646 characters	(defun draw-aggregate-field (f) (draw-field-background f) ; clear background, if any (draw-field-border f) ; draw border, if any (mapc 'draw-field (aggregate-field-subfields f)) ; draw subfields (w-flush (window-w (zone-window (field-zone f)))) t) ; flush it out
progp	program	Source code in Pascal, ASCII	Program to evaluate compression performance of PPM	49,379 characters	if E > Maxexp then {overflow-set to most negative value} begin S:=MinusFiniteS; Closed:=false; end
trans	transcript of terminal session	"EMACS" editor controlling terminal with ASCII code	Mainly screen editing, browsing and using mail	93,695 characters	WFall Term\033[2`inFall Term\033[4`\033[60;1HAuto-saving...\033[28;4H\033[60;15Hdone\033[28;4H\033[60;1H\033[K\0\0\033[28;4HterFall Term\033[7` Term     \033[7`\033[12`\t CAssignment\033[18`lAssignment\033[19`aAssignment\033[ 20`sAssignment\033[21`sAssignment\033[22 `Assignmen\033[88\0t \033[23`pAssignment\033[24`reAssignment\033[26`sAssignment\033[27`eAssignment

Figure B-1 Description of the corpus of texts used in experiments.

TABLE B-1 COMPRESSION RATIOS (BITS/CHAR) OBSERVED IN EXPERIMENTS ON THE CORPUS (PLOTTED IN FIGURES 9-7 TO 9-10)

	Size	LZR	LZJ'	LZ77	LZSS	LZH	LZB	LZW	LZC	LZ78	LZT	LZMW	LZFG	HUFF	DAFC	MTF	WORD	DMC	PPMC
bib	111261	3.59	3.63	3.75	3.35	3.24	3.17	3.84	3.89	3.95	3.76	3.21	2.90	5.24	3.84	3.12	2.19	2.28	*2.11*
book1	768771	4.61	3.67	4.57	4.08	3.73	3.86	4.03	4.06	3.92	3.90	3.72	3.62	4.56	3.68	2.97	2.70	2.51	*2.48*
book2	610856	3.97	3.94	3.93	3.41	3.34	3.28	4.52	4.25	3.81	3.77	3.23	3.05	4.83	3.92	2.66	2.51	*2.25*	2.26
geo	102400	7.34	6.05	6.34	6.43	6.52	6.17	6.15	6.10	5.59	5.96	5.85	5.70	5.70	*4.64*	5.80	5.06	4.77	4.78
news	377109	4.26	4.59	4.37	3.79	3.84	3.55	4.92	4.90	4.33	4.36	3.83	3.44	5.23	4.35	3.29	3.08	2.89	*2.65*
obj1	21504	6.37	5.19	5.41	4.57	4.58	4.26	6.30	6.15	5.58	4.93	4.89	4.03	6.06	5.16	5.30	4.50	4.56	*3.76*
obj2	246814	4.21	5.95	3.81	3.30	3.19	3.14	9.81	5.19	4.68	4.08	3.20	2.96	6.30	5.77	4.40	4.34	3.06	*2.69*
paper1	53161	4.47	3.66	3.94	3.38	3.38	3.22	4.58	4.43	4.50	3.85	3.47	3.03	5.04	4.20	3.12	2.58	2.90	*2.48*
paper2	82199	4.56	3.48	4.10	3.58	3.57	3.43	4.02	3.98	4.24	3.69	3.40	3.16	4.65	3.85	2.86	*2.39*	2.68	2.45
pic	513216	1.40	2.40	2.22	1.67	1.04	1.01	1.09	0.99	1.13	0.96	0.96	*0.87*	1.66	0.90	1.09	0.89	0.94	1.09
progc	39611	4.39	3.72	3.84	3.24	3.25	3.08	4.88	4.41	4.60	3.82	3.40	2.89	5.26	4.43	3.17	2.71	2.98	*2.49*
progl	71646	3.05	3.09	2.90	2.37	2.20	2.11	3.89	3.57	3.77	3.03	2.43	1.97	4.81	3.61	2.31	*1.90*	2.17	*1.90*
progp	49379	2.97	3.14	2.93	2.36	2.17	2.08	3.73	3.72	3.84	3.09	2.43	1.90	4.92	3.85	2.34	1.92	2.22	*1.84*
trans	93695	2.50	3.52	2.98	2.44	2.12	2.12	4.24	3.94	3.92	3.46	2.45	*1.76*	5.58	4.11	2.87	1.91	2.11	1.77
Average	224402	4.12	4.00	3.94	3.43	3.30	3.18	4.71	4.26	4.13	3.76	3.32	2.95	4.99	4.02	3.24	2.76	2.74	*2.48*

GLOSSARY

A: The symbol for the input alphabet (e.g., ASCII).

adaptive coding: A class of compression schemes where the model used for coding is based on the text already encoded; also known as *dynamic* coding.

alphabet: The set of all possible characters that can occur in a text, usually denoted as *A*.

arithmetic coding: A method of assigning codes to symbols that have a known probability distribution; it achieves an average code length arbitrarily close to the entropy.

automaton: *See* finite-state machine.

bits/char: Bits per character, a measure of entropy and also an expression of the amount of compression.

bits/s: Bits per second, a measure of data transmission speed.

bits/symbol: Bits per symbol, a more general measure of entropy than bits/char.

C(m): The code for the phrase *m*.

char/s: Characters per second, a measure of data transmission speed.

character: Any member of an alphabet.

code space: The estimated probability of a symbol.

coder: The part of an encoder that transmits text using probabilities generated by a model.

compaction: Reducing the size of a file without removing any relevant information (*cf.* Compression).

compression: Compaction that is completely reversible.

context: The symbols of the message on which a model bases its prediction.

decoder: An algorithm to perform decompression.

decompression: The reverse process to compression.

dictionary coding: Compression schemes where substrings of the text are replaced by codes; a dictionary of substrings assigns the codes.

digram: A pair of letters.

digram coding: A method of dictionary coding that uses digrams.

dynamic Markov compression (DMC): A particular compression scheme based on an evolving state model.

encoder: An algorithm that performs compression.

entropy: A measure of the information content of a message with respect to a model; also the minimum number of bits per character needed, on average, to represent a message generated by that model. For a model that assigns a constant probability to each symbol of the alphabet, the entropy is calculated as $\Sigma p_i \log p_i$, where p_i is the estimated probability of symbol i.

ergodic: A model is ergodic if any sufficiently long sequence produced by it is entirely representative of the whole model.

finite-context model: A special kind of finite-state model in which predictions are based on the preceding few characters of the message.

finite-state machine (FSM): A finite set of nodes that are linked by directed transitions.

finite-state model: A model that takes the form of a finite-state machine.

hapax legomena: Words that occur only once in a body of writing.

Huffman coding: An early algorithm for assigning variable-length codes for a given probability distribution, which is optimal if the probabilities are negative powers of 2.

$L(m)$: The number of bits in the code for the phrase m.

Λ: The empty string; in other words, the message that contains no symbols.

leaf: A node in a tree with no children.

LZ: *See* Ziv–Lempel.

M: A dictionary, which is a set of phrases.

Markov model: A finite-state model (although sometimes used loosely to refer to the more restricted class of finite-*context* models).

message: Synonym for *text*.

model: An approximation to the process of generating text. A model is used to form predictions of text.

move to front (MTF): A particular compression scheme that maintains a dynamic list of words.

order: The order of a finite-context model is the number of symbols used to predict the next symbol.

p*(e)*: Probability of the event *e*.

phrase: A small string of characters.

prediction: Assigning probabilities to forthcoming characters or events.

prediction by partial match (PPM): A particular compression scheme that uses predictions based on a number of blended context models.

prefix: The string s$[1..n]$ is a prefix of the string t$[1..m]$ if $n \leq m$ and s$[1]$ = t$[1]$, s$[2]$ = t$[2]$, ..., s$[n]$ = t$[n]$.

proper prefix: The string **s** is a proper prefix of **t** if **s** is a prefix of **t** and the length of **s** is strictly less than the length of **t**.

q: The number of characters in the alphabet. For ASCII, $q = 128$.

root: The node at the base of a tree.

scheme: A compression scheme is a pair of algorithms that perform compression and decompression.

semiadaptive coding: A method of coding that creates a model based on the message to be sent, and then transmits the model explicitly, followed by the message coded with respect to that model.

source: A source generates text according to some rules; it will often be a human being.

statistical coding: Compression where the code for an input symbol is determined by the estimated probability of the symbol.

string: A finite sequence of characters.

symbol-wise: A model that predicts each symbol of the text being encoded.

text: A file that can be processed sequentially and is based on a language, natural or artificial.

transition: Link between two nodes in a graph or tree.

tree: A data structure used for searching.

trie: A multiway tree with a path for each string inserted in it, which allows rapid location of strings and substrings.

$U(\mathbf{x})$: The conditioning function, which maps a string $\mathbf{x}$ into its conditioning class on which predictions are based.

$\mathbf{x}[1..i]$: A string of i characters.

$\mathbf{x}[i]$: The ith character of $\mathbf{x}$.

$\mathbf{x}[i..j]$: The substring of $\mathbf{x}$ from character i to character j.

zero-frequency problem: The problem that there can be no rational basis for assigning probabilities to novel events about which no prior information is known.

Ziv–Lempel (LZ): A class of compression schemes based on work done by Jacob Ziv and Abraham Lempel, which builds an adaptive dictionary of substrings of the message.

REFERENCES

ABRAMOWITZ, M.O. and STEGUN, I.A. (1964) *Handbook of mathematical functions.* National Bureau of Standards, Washington, D.C.

ABRAMSON, N. (1963) *Information theory and coding.* McGraw-Hill, New York.

AHO, A.V., HOPCROFT, J.E., and ULLMAN, J.D. (1983) *Data structures and algorithms.* Addison-Wesley, Reading, MA.

ANDREAE, J.H. (1977) *Thinking with the teachable machine.* Academic Press, London.

ANDREAE, P.M. (1984) "Justified generalization: acquiring procedures from examples," Ph.D. Thesis, Department of Electrical Engineering and Computer Science, MIT.

ANGLUIN, D. and SMITH, C.H. (1983) "Inductive inference: theory and methods," *Computing Surveys, 15* (3), 237–269, September.

ATTENEAVE, F. (1953) "Psychological probability as a function of experienced frequency," *J. Experimental Psychology, 46* (2), 81–86.

AUSLANDER, M., HARRISON, W., MILLER, V., and WEGMAN, M. (1985) "PCTERM: a terminal emulator using compression," *Proc. IEEE Globcom '85*, pp. 860–862, IEEE Press, New York.

BALASUBRAHMANYAM, P. and SIROMONEY, G. (1968) "A note on entropy of Telugu prose," *Information and Control, 13*, 281–285.

BARNARD, G.A. (1955) "Statistical calculation of word entropies for four Western languages," *IEEE Trans. Information Theory, 1* (1), 49–53, March.

BELL, T.C. (1986) "Better OPM/L text compression," *IEEE Trans. Communications, COM-34* (12), 1176–1182, December.

BELL, T.C. (1987) "A unifying theory and improvements for existing approaches to text compression," Ph.D. Thesis, Department of Computer Science, University of Canterbury, Christchurch, New Zealand.

BELL, T.C. and MOFFAT, A.M. (1989) "A note on the DMC data compression scheme," *Computer J., 32* (1), 16–20, February.

BELL, T.C. and WITTEN, I.H. (1987) "Greedy macro text compression," Research Report 87/285/33, Department of Computer Science, University of Calgary, Calgary, Alberta, Canada.

BENTLEY, J.L. and YAO, A.C. (1976) "An almost optimal algorithm for unbounded searching," *Information Processing Letters, 5* (3), 82–87, August.

BENTLEY, J.L., SLEATOR, D.D., TARJAN, R.E., and WEI, V.K. (1986) "A locally adaptive data compression scheme," *Communications of the Association for Computing Machinery, 29* (4), 320–330, April.

BIERMANN, A.W. (1972) "On the inference of Turing machines from sample computations," *Artificial Intelligence, 3,* 181–198.

BIERMANN, A.W. and FELDMAN, J.A. (1972) "On the synthesis of finite-state machines from samples of their behaviour," *IEEE Trans. Computers, C-21* (6), 592–597, June.

BOOKSTEIN, A. and FOUTY, G. (1976) "A mathematical model for estimating the effectiveness of bigram coding," *Information Processing Management, 12.*

BOURNE, C.P. and FORD, D.F. (1961) "A study of methods for systematically abbreviating English words and names," *J. Association for Computing Machinery, 8,* 538–552.

BRENT, R.P. (1987) "A linear algorithm for data compression," *Australian Computer J., 19* (2), 64–68.

CAMERON, R.D. (1986) "Source encoding using syntactic information source models," LCCR Technical Report 86-7, Simon Fraser University, Burnaby, British Columbia, Canada, September.

CARROLL, J.B. (1966) "Word-frequency studies and the lognormal distribution" in *Proc. Conference on Language and Language Behavior*, edited by E.M. Zale, pp. 213–235. Appleton-Century-Crofts, New York.

CARROLL, J.B. (1967) "On sampling from a lognormal model of word-frequency distribution" in *Computational analysis of present-day American English*, edited by H. Kucera and W.N. Francis, pp. 406–424. Brown University Press, Providence, R.I.

CLEARY, J.G. (1980) "An associative and impressible computer," Ph.D. Thesis, University of Canterbury, Christchurch, New Zealand.

CLEARY, J.G. and WITTEN, I.H. (1984a) "A comparison of enumerative and adaptive codes," *IEEE Trans. Information Theory, IT-30* (2), 306–315, March.

CLEARY, J.G. and WITTEN, I.H. (1984b) "Data compression using adaptive coding and partial string matching," *IEEE Trans. Communications, COM-32* (4), 396–402, April.

CORMACK, G.V. and HORSPOOL, R.N. (1984) "Algorithms for adaptive Huffman codes," *Information Processing Letters, 18* (3), 159–166, March.

CORMACK, G.V. and HORSPOOL, R.N. (1987) "Data compression using dynamic Markov modelling," *Computer J., 30* (6), 541–550, December.

CORTESI, D. (1982) "An effective text-compression algorithm," *Byte, 7* (1), 397–403, January.

COVER, T.M. (1973) "Enumerative source encoding," *IEEE Trans. Information Theory, IT-19* (1), 73–77, January.

Cover, T.M. and King, R.C. (1978) "A convergent gambling estimate of the entropy of English," *IEEE Trans. Information Theory, IT-24* (4), 413–421, July.

Darragh, J.J., Witten, I.H., and Cleary, J.G. (1983) "Adaptive text compression to enhance a modem," Research Report 83/132/21, Computer Science Department, University of Calgary, Calgary, Alberta, Canada.

Efron, B. and Thisted, R. (1976) "Estimating the number of unseen species: how many words did Shakespeare know?" *Biometrika, 63* (3), 435–447.

Elias, P. (1975) "Universal codeword sets and representations of the integers," *IEEE Trans. Information Theory, IT-21* (2), 194–203, March.

Elias, P. (1987) "Interval and recency rank source coding: two on-line adaptive variable-length schemes," *IEEE Trans. Information Theory, 33* (1), 3–10, January.

Evans, T.G. (1971) "Grammatical inference techniques in pattern analysis" in *Software engineering*, edited by J. Tou, pp. 183–202. Academic Press, New York.

Faller, N. (1973) "An adaptive system for data compression" *Record of the 7th Asilomar Conference on Circuits, Systems and Computers*, pp. 593–597, Naval Postgraduate School, Monterey, CA.

Fang, I. (1966) "It isn't ETAOIN SHRDLU; it's ETAONI RSHDLC," *Journalism Quarterly, 43*, 761–762.

Fano, R.M (1949) "The transmission of information," Technical Report 65, Research Laboratory of Electronics, MIT, Cambridge, MA.

Fiala, E.R. and Greene, D.H. (1989) "Data compression with finite windows," *Communications of the Association for Computing Machinery, 32* (4), 490–505, April.

Fraenkel, A.S. and Mor, M. (1983) "Combinatorial compression and partitioning of large dictionaries," *Computer J., 26* (4), 336–343.

Gaines, B.R. (1976) "Behaviour/structure transformations under uncertainty," *Int. J. Man-Machine Studies, 8*, 337–365.

Gaines, B.R. (1977) "System identification, approximation and complexity," *Int. J. General Systems, 3*, 145–174.

Gallager, R.G. (1968) *Information theory and reliable communication*. Wiley, New York.

Gallager, R.G. (1978) "Variations on a theme by Huffman," *IEEE Trans. Information Theory, IT-24* (6), 668–674, November.

Gold, E.M. (1978) "On the complexity of automaton identification from given data," *Information and Control, 37*, 302–320.

Gonzalez-smith, M.E. and Storer, J.A. (1985) "Parallel algorithms for data compression," *J. Association for Computing Machinery, 32* (2), 344–373.

Good, I.J. (1969) "Statistics of language" in *Encyclopaedia of information, linguistics and control*, edited by A.R. Meetham and R.A. Hudson, pp. 567–581. Pergamon, Oxford, England.

Gottlieb, D., Hagerth, S.A., Lehot, P.G.H., and Rabinowitz, H.S. (1975) "A classification of compression methods and their usefulness for a large data processing center," *National Computer Conference, 44*, 453–458.

Guazzo, M. (1980) "A general minimum-redundancy source-coding algorithm," *IEEE Trans. Information Theory, IT-26* (1), 15–25, January.

Halbert, D.C. (1984) "Programming by example," Technical Report, Xerox PARC (Office Products Division), Palo Alto, CA, December.

Horspool, R.N. and Cormack, G.V. (1983) "Data compression based on token recognition," Unpublished manuscript, October.

HORSPOOL, R.N. and CORMACK, G.V. (1986) "Dynamic Markov modelling—a prediction technique," *Proc. International Conference on the System Sciences*, Honolulu, HA, January.

HUFFMAN, D.A. (1952) "A method for the construction of minimum-redundancy codes," *Proc. Institute of Electrical and Radio Engineers, 40* (9), 1098–1101, September.

HUNTER, R. and ROBINSON, A.H. (1980) "International digital facsimile coding standards," *Proc. Institute of Electrical and Electronic Engineers, 68* (7), 854–867, July.

JAKOBSSON, M. (1985) "Compression of character strings by an adaptive dictionary," *BIT, 25* (4), 593–603.

JAMISON, D. and JAMISON, K. (1968) "A note on the entropy of partially-known languages," *Information and Control, 12*, 164–167.

JELINEK, F. (1968) *Probabilistic information theory*. McGraw-Hill, New York.

JEWELL, G.C. (1976) "Text compaction for information retrieval systems," *IEEE Systems, Man and Cybernetics Society Newsletter, 5*, 47.

JONES, C.B. (1981) "An efficient coding system for long source sequences," *IEEE Trans. Information Theory, IT-27* (3), 280–291, May.

JONES, D.W. (1988) "Application of splay trees to data compression," *Communications of the Association for Computing Machinery, 31* (8), 996–1007, August.

KATAJAINEN, J. and RAITA, T. (1987a) "An approximation algorithm for space-optimal encoding of a text," Research Report, Department of Computer Science, University of Turku, Turku, Finland, March.

KATAJAINEN, J. and RAITA, T. (1987b) "An analysis of the longest match and the greedy heuristics for text encoding," Research Report, Department of Computer Science, University of Turku, Turku, Finland, March.

KATAJAINEN, J., PENTTONEN, M., and TEUHOLA, J. (1986) "Syntax-directed compression of program files," *Software—Practice and Experience, 16* (3), 269–276.

KNOWLTON, K. (1980) "Progressive transmission of grey-scale and binary pictures by simple, efficient, and lossless encoding schemes," *Proc. Institute of Electrical and Electronic Engineers, 68* (7), 885–896, July.

KNUTH, D.E. (1973) *The art of computer programming*, 2nd ed., Addison-Wesley, Reading, MA, 3 volumes.

KNUTH, D.E. (1985) "Dynamic Huffman coding," *J. Algorithms, 6*, 163–180.

KOLATA, G. (1986) "Shakespeare's new poem: an ode to statistics," *Science, 231*, 335–336, January 24.

LAMBERT, S. and ROPIEQUET, S. (editors) (1986) *CD ROM: the new papyrus*. Microsoft Press, Redmond, WA.

LANGDON, G.G. (1981) "Tutorial on arithmetic coding," Research Report RJ3128, IBM Research Laboratory, San Jose, CA.

LANGDON, G.G. (1983) "A note on the Ziv–Lempel model for compressing individual sequences," *IEEE Trans. Information Theory, IT-29* (2), 284–287, March.

LANGDON, G.G. (1984) "An introduction to arithmetic coding," *IBM J. Research and Development, 28* (2), 135–149, March.

LANGDON, G.G. and RISSANEN, J.J. (1981) "Compression of black-white images with arithmetic coding," *IEEE Trans. Communications, COM-29* (6), 858–867, June.

LANGDON, G.G. and RISSANEN, J.J. (1982) "A simple general binary source code," *IEEE Trans. Information Theory, IT-28*, 800–803, September.

LANGDON, G.G. and RISSANEN, J.J. (1983) "A doubly-adaptive file compression algorithm," *IEEE Trans. Communications, COM-31* (11), 1253–1255, November.

LYNCH, M.F. (1973) "Compression of bibliographic files using an adaptation of run-length coding," *Information Storage and Retrieval, 9*, 207–214.

MACDONALD, B.A. and WITTEN, I.H. (1987) "Programming computer controlled systems by non-experts," *Proc. IEEE Systems, Man and Cybernetics Annual Conference*, 432–437, Alexandria, VA, October 20–23.

MANDELBROT, B. (1952) "An informational theory of the statistical structure of language," *Proc. Symposium on Applications of Communication Theory*, pp. 486–500, Butterworth, London, September.

MANFRINO, R.L. (1970) "Printed Portugese (Brazilian) entropy statistical calculation," *IEEE Trans. Information Theory, IT-16*, 122, January (Abstract only).

MARTIN, G.N.N. (1979) "Range encoding: an algorithm for removing redundancy from a digitized message," Presented at the Video and Data Recording Conference, Southampton, Hampshire, England, July.

MAYNE, A. and JAMES, E.B. (1975) "Information compression by factorizing common strings," *Computer J., 18* (2), 157–160.

MCNAUGHTON, R. and PAPERT, S. (1971) *Counter-free automata.* MIT Press, Cambridge, MA.

MILLER, V.S. and WEGMAN, M.N. (1984) "Variations on a theme by Ziv and Lempel" in *Combinatorial algorithms on words*, edited by A. Apostolico and Z. Galil, pp. 131–140. NATO ASI Series, Vol. F12. Springer-Verlag, Berlin.

MILLER, G.A., NEWMAN, E.B., and FRIEDMAN, E.A. (1957) "Some effects of intermittent silence," *American J. Psychology, 70*, 311–313.

MOFFAT, A. (1987) "Word based text compression," Research Report, Department of Computer Science, University of Melbourne, Parkville, Victoria, Australia.

MOFFAT, A. (1988a) "A data structure for arithmetic encoding on large alphabets," *Proc. 11th Australian Computer Science Conference*, pp. 309–317, Brisbane, Australia, February.

MOFFAT, A. (1988b) "A note on the PPM data compression algorithm," Research Report 88/7, Department of Computer Science, University of Melbourne, Parkville, Victoria, Australia.

NEWMAN, E.B. and WAUGH, N.C. (1960) "The redundancy of texts in three languages," *Information and Control, 3*, 141–153.

NIX, R. (1981) "Experience with a space efficient way to store a dictionary," *Communications of the Association for Computing Machinery, 24* (5), 297–298.

NIX, R. (1984) "Editing by example," *Proc. 11th ACM Symposium on Principles of Programming Languages*, pp. 186–195, Salt Lake City, UT., January.

PASCO, R. (1976) "Source coding algorithms for fast data compression," Ph.D. Thesis, Department of Electrical Engineering, Stanford University.

PETERSON, W.W. and WELDON, E.J. (1972) *Error correcting codes*, 2nd ed. MIT Press, Cambridge, MA.

PIERCE, C.S. (1956) "The probability of induction" in *The world of mathematics*, Vol. 2, edited by J.R. Newman, pp. 1341–1354, Simon and Schuster, New York.

PIKE, J. (1981) "Text compression using a 4-bit coding system," *Computer J., 24 (4)*.

RAITA, T. and TEUHOLA, J. (1987) "Predictive text compression by hashing," *ACM Conference on Information Retrieval*, New Orleans.

RAITZER, G.A., VANDERHEIDEN, G.C., and HOLT, C.S. (1976) "Interfacing computers for the physically handicapped—a review of international approaches" *Proc. AFIPS National Computer Conference*, pp. 209–216.

RAJAGOPALAN, K.R. (1965) "A note on entropy of Kannada prose," *Information and Control, 8*, 640–644.

RISSANEN, J.J. (1976) "Generalized Kraft inequality and arithmetic coding," *IBM J. Research and Development, 20*, 198–203, May.

RISSANEN, J.J. (1979) "Arithmetic codings as number representations," *Acta Polytechnica Scandinavica, Math, 31*, 44–51, December.

RISSANEN, J.J. (1983) "A universal data compression system," *IEEE Trans. Information Theory, IT-29* (5), 656–664, September.

RISSANEN, J.J. and LANGDON, G.G. (1979) "Arithmetic coding," *IBM J. Research and Development, 23* (2), 149–162, March.

RISSANEN, J.J. and LANGDON, G.G. (1981) "Universal modeling and coding," *IEEE Trans. Information Theory, IT-27* (1), 12–23, January.

ROBERTS, M.G. (1982) "Local order estimating Markovian analysis for noiseless source coding and authorship identification," Ph.D. Thesis, Stanford University.

ROBINSON, P. and SINGER, D. (1981) "Another spelling correction program," *Communications of the Association for Computing Machinery, 24* (5), 296–297.

RODEH, M., PRATT, V.R., and EVEN, S. (1981) "Linear algorithm for data compression via string matching," *J. Association for Computing Machinery, 28* (1), 16–24, January.

RUBIN, F. (1976) "Experiments in text file compression," *Communications of the Association for Computing Machinery, 19* (11), 617–623.

RUBIN, F. (1979) "Arithmetic stream coding using fixed precision registers," *IEEE Trans. Information Theory, IT-25* (6), 672–675, November.

RYABKO, B.Y. (1980) "Data compression by means of a 'book stack,'" *Problemy Peredachi Informatsii, 16* (4).

SCHIEBER, W.D. and THOMAS, G.W. (1971) "An algorithm for compaction of alphanumeric data," *J. Library Automation, 4*, 198–206.

SCHUEGRAF, E.J. and HEAPS, H.S. (1973) "Selection of equifrequent word fragments for information retrieval," *Information Storage and Retrieval, 9*, 697–711.

SCHUEGRAF, E.J. and HEAPS, H.S. (1974) "A comparison of algorithms for data-base compression by use of fragments as language elements," *Information Storage and Retrieval, 10*, 309–319.

SHANNON, C.E. (1948) "A mathematical theory of communication," *Bell System Technical J., 27*, 398–403, July (reprinted in Shannon and Weaver, 1949).

SHANNON, C.E. (1951) "Prediction and entropy of printed English," *Bell System Technical J.*, 50–64, January.

SHANNON, C.E. and WEAVER, W. (1949) *The mathematical theory of communication.* University of Illinois Press, Urbana, IL.

SIROMONEY, G. (1963) "Entropy of Tamil prose," *Information and Control, 6*, 297–300.

SNYDERMAN, M. and HUNT, B. (1970) "The myriad virtues of text compaction," *Datamation, 1*, 36–40, December.

STAISEY, N.L., TOMBAUGH, J.W., and DILLON, R.F. (1982) "Videotext and the disabled," *Int. J. Man-Machine Studies, 17*, 35–50.

STORER, J.A. (1977) "NP-completeness results concerning data compression," Technical Report 234, Department of Electrical Engineering and Computer Science, Princeton University, Princeton, N.J.

STORER, J.A. (1988) *Data compression: methods and theory.* Computer Science Press, Rockville, MD.

STORER, J.A. and SZYMANSKI, T.G. (1982) "Data compression via textual substitution," *J. Association for Computing Machinery, 29* (4), 928–951, October.

SVANKS, M.I. (1975) "Optimizing the storage of alphanumeric data," *Canadian Datasystems,* 38–40, May.

TAN, C.P. (1981) "On the entropy of the Malay language," *IEEE Trans. Information Theory, IT-27* (3), 383–384, May.

THOMAS, S.W., MCKIE, J., DAVIES, S., TURKOWSKI, K., WOODS, J.A., and OROST, J.W. (1985) "*Compress* (version 4.0) program and documentation," available from joe@petsd.UUCP.

TISCHER, P. (1987) "A modified Lempel-Ziv-Welch data compression scheme," *Australian Computer Science Communications, 9* (1), 262–272.

TROPPER, R. (1982) "Binary-coded text, a compression method," *Byte, 7* (4), 398–413, April.

VITTER, J.S. (1987) "Design and analysis of dynamic Huffman codes," *J. Association for Computing Machinery, 34* (4), 825–845, October.

VITTER, J.S. (in press) "Dynamic Huffman coding," *ACM Trans. Mathematical Software* and *Collected Algorithms of ACM.*

WAGNER, R.A. (1973) "Common phrase and minimum-space text storage," *Communications of the Association for Computing Machinery, 16* (3), 148–152.

WANAS, M.A., ZAYED, A.I., SHAKER, M.M., and TAHA, E.H. (1976) "First- second- and third-order entropies of Arabic text," *IEEE Trans. Information Theory, IT-22* (1), 123, January.

WELCH, T.A. (1984) "A technique for high-performance data compression," *IEEE Computer, 17* (6), 8–19, June.

WHITE, H.E. (1967) "Printed English compression by dictionary encoding," *Proc. Institute of Electrical and Electronic Engineers, 55* (3), 390–396.

WHITWORTH, W.A. (1901) *Choice and chance.* Deighton and Bell, Cambridge, England.

WILLIAMS, R. (1988) "Dynamic-history predictive compression," *Information Systems, 13* (1), 129–140.

WILSON, G. (1976) *The old telegraphs.* Phillimore and Co., Chichester, West Sussex, England.

WITTEN, I.H. (1979) "Approximate, non-deterministic modelling of behaviour sequences," *Int. J. General Systems, 5,* 1–12, January.

WITTEN, I.H. (1980) "Probabilistic behaviour/structure transformations using transitive Moore models," *Int. J. General Systems, 6* (3), 129–137.

WITTEN, I.H. (1981) "Programming by example for the casual user: a case study," *Proc. Canadian Man-Computer Communication Conference,* pp. 105–113, Waterloo, Ontario, Canada, June.

WITTEN, I.H. (1982a) "An interactive computer terminal interface which predicts user entries," *Proc. IEE Conference on Man-Machine Interaction,* pp. 1–5, Manchester, Lancashire, England, July.

WITTEN, I.H. (1982b) *Principles of computer speech.* Academic Press, London.

WITTEN, I.H. and CLEARY, J.G. (1983) "Picture coding and transmission using adaptive modelling of quad trees," *Proc. International Electrical, Electronics Conference,* Vol. 1, pp. 222–225, Toronto, Ontario, Canada, September 26–28.

WITTEN, I.H. and CLEARY, J.G. (1988) "On the privacy afforded by adaptive text compression," *Computers and Security, 7* (4), 397–408, August.

WITTEN, I.H., CLEARY, J.G., and DARRAGH, J.J. (1983) "The reactive keyboard: a new technology for text entry," *Converging Technologies: Proc. Canadian Information Processing Society Conference*, pp. 151–156, Ottawa, Ontario, Canada, May.

WITTEN, I.H., MACDONALD, B.A., and GREENBERG, S. (1987a) "Specifying procedures to office systems," *Automating Systems Development (Proc. International Conference on Computer-Based Tools for Information Systems Analysis, Design, and Implementation)*, pp. 477–500, Leicester, Leicestershire, England, April 14–16.

WITTEN, I.H., NEAL, R., and CLEARY, J.G. (1987b) "Arithmetic coding for data compression," *Communications of the Association for Computing Machinery, 30* (6), 520–540, June.

WOLFF, J.G. (1978) "Recoding of natural language for economy of transmission or storage," *Computer J., 21* (1), 42–44.

WONG, K.L. and POON, R.K.L. (1976) "A comment on the entropy of the Chinese language," *IEEE Trans. Acoustics, Speech, and Signal Processing*, 583–585, December.

WRIGHT, E.V. (1939) *Gadsby*. Wetzel, Los Angeles; reprinted by Kassel Books, Los Angeles.

YOUNG, D.M. (1985) "MacWrite file formats," *Wheels for the Mind*, 34, Fall.

ZETTERSTEN, A. (1978) *A word-frequency list based on American English press reportage*. Universitetsforlaget i Kobenhavn, Akademisk Forlag, Copenhagen.

ZIPF, G.K. (1949) *Human behavior and the principle of least effort*. Addison-Wesley, Reading, MA.

ZIV, J. and LEMPEL, A. (1977) "A universal algorithm for sequential data compression," *IEEE Trans. Information Theory, IT-23* (3), 337–343, May.

ZIV, J. and LEMPEL, A. (1978) "Compression of individual sequences via variable-rate coding," *IEEE Trans. Information Theory, IT-24* (5), 530–536, September.

INDEX